Vienna and the Jews, 1867–1938

Vienna and the Jews 1867–1938

A cultural history

STEVEN BELLER

Fellow of Peterhouse, Cambridge

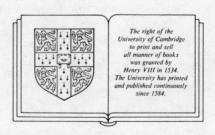

The right of the
University of Cambridge
to print and sell
all manner of books
was granted by
Henry VIII in 1534.
The University has printed
and published continuously
since 1584.

CAMBRIDGE UNIVERSITY PRESS

Cambridge
New York   Port Chester
Melbourne   Sydney

Published by the Press Syndicate of the University of Cambridge
The Pitt Building, Trumpington Street, Cambridge CB2 1RP
40 West 20th Street, New York, NY 10011, USA
10 Stamford Road, Oakleigh, Melbourne 3166, Australia

First published 1989

Printed in Great Britain by the University Press, Cambridge

British Library cataloguing in publication data
Beller, Steven
Vienna and the Jews, 1867–1938: a cultural
history.
1. Austria. Vienna. Jews, history
I. Title
943.6′13004924

Library of Congress cataloguing in publication data
Beller, Steven, 1958–
Vienna and the Jews, 1867–1938: a cultural history/Steven
Beller.
p. cm.
Bibliography.
Includes index.
ISBN 0-521-35180-4
1. Jews–Austria–Vienna–History. 2. Jews–Austria–Vienna–
Intellectual life. 3. Austria–Civilization–Jewish influences.
4. Vienna (Austria)–Civilization. 5. Vienna (Austria)–Ethnic
relations. I. Title.
DS135.A92V5213 1989
943.6′13004924–dc19   88-29971 CIP

ISBN 0 521 35180 4

Contents

Tables

Preface

Since I began researching the subject of the Jewish rôle in Viennese culture I have incurred the debt of so many people it is difficult to know where to begin (and where to end). In anticipation of their omission, I would like to thank all those not mentioned here who, nevertheless, helped me in my task.

Much of my work depends on the insights I gained from listening to the accounts of people who were part of the cultural and social phenomenon studied in the following pages. I am thus indebted to the following for their generosity in giving of their time and memories: in Vienna, Erika Czuczka, Milan Dubrovic, Marcel Faust, Ernst Federn, Bruno Frei, Ernst Fuchs, Dr Hans Goldschmidt, Iwan Hacker, Ernst Häussermann, Professor Walther Kraus, Professor Albert Lauterbach, Paul Neurath, Lily Schnitzler, Dr Michael Stern, Heinrich Sussmann, Graf Tamare, Dr Hans Thalberg and Emmy Wellesz; in England, Stella Ehrenfeld, Bettina Ehrlich, Frieda von Hofmannsthal, Rudolf Ray-Rappaport, Hilde Spiel and, in passing, Professor Frederick Wyatt; in California, Ella Heinz and Ann Unger; in New York, Professor Martha Steffy Browne; and in Venice, Manina Tischler.

For their advice and encouragement I would like to thank: in England, Sir Isaiah Berlin, Dr Tim Blanning, Richard Calvocoressi, Dr Christine Carpenter, Maurice Cowling, Dr Nicholas de Lange, Robert Evans, Professor Alexander Goehr, Martin Golding, Sir Ernst Gombrich, Dr Boyd Hilton, Dr Harold James, Daniel Johnson, Lionel Kochan, John Leslie, Dr Jan and Herta Palme, Dr Jon Parry, Laszlo Peter, Robert Pynsent, Dr Miri Rubin, Yehuda Safran, Dr Anil Seal, Dr David Sorkin, Dr Jonathan Steinberg, Professor George Steiner, Professor J. P. Stern, Trevor Thomas and Peter Vergo; in Austria, Dr Helmut Andics, Viktor Anninger, György Bence, Professor Kurt Blaukopf, Dr Wolfdieter Bihl, Dr Breicha, Dr Bernhard Denscher, Fritz Endler, Dr Peter Eppel, Professor Kurt Rudolf Fischer, Dr Hacker, Dr Hodik, Dr Hanns Jäger-Sunstenau, Dr Lothar Höbelt, Mr and Mrs Charles Kessler, Dr Eckehart Koehler, Henryk

Krzeczkowski, Dr Helmut Leitner, Dr Harald Leupold-Löwenthal, Dr Klaus
Lohrmann, Dr Lunzer, Dr Viktor Matejka, Jonny and Gwynn Moser, Dr
Werner Neudeck, Silvio Neumann, Dr Obermayer, Dr Alfred Pfabigan,
Professor Walther B. Simon, Professor Spitzy, Desider Stern, Dr Nikolaus
Vielmetti, Dr Robert Waissenberger, Professor Erika Weinzierl, Ulrich
Weinzierl and Margot Winge; in Frankfurt-on-Main, Dr Renate Heuer;
from the United States, Professor Gary Cohen and Professor Harry Zohn;
from Israel, Professor Dr Sol Lypcin and Dr Herbert Rosenkrantz; in Paris,
Professor Eugène Fleischmann and Victor Karady; and, wherever he may
be, Allan Janik.

I am indebted to Trinity College, Cambridge, the British Academy and
the Master and Fellows of Peterhouse for their financial support over the
period of my research, and here I would especially like to thank Lord Dacre
of Glanton for his encouragement. Oberrat Dr Wieser and after him Dr
Anzböck at the Stadtschulrat of Vienna kindly permitted me to view the
school records which are so central to the following study. I am therefore
especially indebted to them.

While in Vienna life was made much more enjoyable by the Institut für
die Wissenschaften von Menschen, and I would like to thank its members,
particularly Klaus Nellen, Cornelia Klinger and the Institute's director,
Krzysztof Michalski, for their great hospitality. For similar reasons I am
indebted to Christian and Renée Nebehay, Francesca Fuchs, Elisabeth de
Gelsey, Dr Mascha Hoff and Christl Fabrizii. Of all people in Vienna, I owe
most to Ingeborg Lau, whose readiness to assist me in my researches has
been virtually boundless.

There are four people who deserve particular mention. Professor Peter
Pulzer of All Souls College, Oxford, has given me much of the shrewdest
advice concerning my research. George Clare has been a constant source
of help, advice and encouragement. Professor Ivar Oxaal of Hull University
has been especially important in shaping (and reshaping) my ideas
regarding the question of how to approach the sociological aspects of the
subject, and in encouraging me in that direction. Above all, however, I
wish to thank my supervisor, Norman Stone, for his inimitable advice
(academic and otherwise), his moral support at times of crisis, and all the
effort he has expended on my behalf over the last seven years.

It remains to thank the people to whom I owe the deepest debt of
gratitude: my parents, for putting up with me for so many years, and
Esther Brimmer, for being.

While I am indebted to all the above in one way or another, none is
responsible for the views presented in this work. That responsibility is mine
alone.

Introduction
'Fin-de-siècle' Vienna and the Jewish question

In 1948 Hermann Broch produced one of the great interpretative essays on modern culture, *Hofmannsthal und seine Zeit*.[1] In this study he identified the city of Vienna as the centre of what he termed the *Wertvakuum*.[2] As such Broch was one of the first to see Vienna as the source of the problems and attitudes which have characterized the modern world. At the time he wrote Vienna was widely regarded as more or less a cultural backwater. It was only with the articles of Carl Schorske from the early 1960s on that the idea of Vienna as a major, if not the major, cultural centre in Europe around 1900 emerged.[3]

Since then interest in what has come to be known as *fin-de-siècle* Vienna has reached remarkable heights. Whereas once the art of Klimt and the music of Mahler were largely ignored, their popularity is now almost commonplace. Conferences and exhibitions on the cultural history of Vienna around 1900 abound; the literature on the same subject has increased exponentially.[4] Vienna is talked about as if everything that we do

---

[1] This essay is reproduced in Herman Broch, *Schriften zur Literatur* 1, ed. P. M. Lützeler (Frankfurt-on-Main 1975) pp.111–284. (This is vol. 9, part 1 of the annotated edition of Broch's work.) There is an English translation by Michael Steinberg, *Hugo von Hofmannsthal and his Times: the European Imagination 1860–1920* (Chicago 1984).

[2] Broch, *Hofmannsthal und seine Zeit*, pp.135ff.

[3] Schorske's first article to appear on this subject was 'Politics and the Psyche in *Fin-de-Siècle* Vienna: Schnitzler and Hofmannsthal' in *American Historical Review* vol. 66 (July 1961) pp. 930–46. Among the major works on the subject which have appeared since then are: Ilsa Barea, *Vienna* (London 1966); Frank Field, *The Last Days of Mankind* (London 1967); William M. Johnston, *The Austrian Mind: an Intellectual and Social History 1848–1938* (Berkeley 1972); Allan Janik and Stephen Toulmin, *Wittgenstein's Vienna* (New York 1973); William McGrath, *Dionysian Art and Populist Politics in Austria* (New Haven 1974); Peter Vergo, *Art in Vienna 1898–1918* (London 1975); Frederic Morton, *A Nervous Splendour: Vienna 1888–9* (London 1979); Carl E. Schorske, *Fin-de-Siècle Vienna: Politics and Culture* (London 1980); Michael Pollak, *Vienne 1900: Une identité blessée* (Paris 1984); *The Viennese Enlightenment*, ed. Mark Francis (Beckenham, Kent 1985); Kirk Varnedoe, *Vienna 1900: Art, Architecture and Design* (New York 1986); and Hilde Spiel, *Vienna's Golden Autumn* (London 1987).

[4] There have been at least five major exhibitions on the arts in Vienna in the last few years. In 1983 there was *Vienna 1900* in Edinburgh, in 1984 *Le arti a Vienna* in Venice, in 1985

1

and think somehow originated in that one city between the years 1867
and 1938.

There are many reservations to be expressed about the idea of Vienna
as the birthplace of the modern world. If one looks at what was happening
in Europe and the United States of America at the turn of the century, then
it becomes fairly clear that there was a cultural explosion in many centres,
and that, therefore, it appears a large exaggeration to claim that Vienna
was anything more than *one* of several centres which were creating the
new culture. It is, for instance, very difficult to see how Vienna was any
more important than Paris in a whole host of cultural disciplines.[5]
Similarly, the modern world is unthinkable without Darwin, Nietzsche or
Einstein. Weberian sociology, Max Planck's quantum theory, the novels of
Tolstoy and Dostoevsky, Munch's art, Marinetti's Futurism, New York's
skyscrapers – all are a part of the modern age and none of them have
much to do with Vienna. The emergence of 'the modern world' was a
Europe-wide, even world-wide phenomenon of the turn of the century, and
it would seem to require an unwarranted parochialism to put Vienna at
the centre of it all.

It might be argued that cultural movements in other cities, such as
French art and music, were not as 'modern' as the Viennese. In that case
one would have to ask, how does one define 'modern'? When Schorske,
for instance, talks of Vienna as the origin of the concept of 'psychological
man', which in turn he claims to be the denominator of 'modern', such
claims are open to doubt and refutation.[6] What about Charcot, Bourget or
Proust? And why should 'psychological man' be the ruling concept of our
world? What about the claims of a concept such as George Steiner's
'language turn', or, indeed, Broch's idea of the 'value vacuum'?[7] These

Traum und Wirklichkeit: Wien 1870–1930 in Vienna itself, in 1986 *Vienne 1880–1938:
l'apocalypse joyeuse* in Paris, and in the same year, *Vienna 1900: Art, Architecture and
Design* in New York. Two 1985 conferences have since had their proceedings published:
see Alfred Pfabigan, ed., *Ornament und Askese im Zeitgeist des Wien der Jahrhundertwende*
(Vienna 1985), and P. Berner, E. Brix and W. Mantl, eds., *Wien um 1900: Aufbruch in die
Moderne* (Vienna 1986). The latest major conference on the subject was held in the
University of London in September 1985 on *The Habsburg Monarchy in Transition
1890–1914: Decay and Innovation.*

[5] For claims of Vienna's central place in cultural innovation around 1900, see Norman
Stone, *Europe Transformed 1878–1919* (Glasgow 1983) pp.406–7; Johnston, *The
Austrian Mind*; Schorske, *Fin-de-Siècle Vienna*, p.xviii. It should be added that these authors
are more guarded in print about Vienna's pre-eminence than the current vogue for
Vienna might suggest. For the opposite view see Peter Gay, *Freud, Jews and Other Germans*
(Oxford 1978) pp.33–5.

[6] For Schorske's claim, see *Fin-de-Siècle Vienna*, pp.4–5.

[7] George Steiner, 'Le langage et l'inhumain' in *Revue d'esthétique*, new series, no. 9, 1985:
Vienne 1880–1938 (Toulouse 1985) pp.65–6. The article was originally given as a
lecture at the conference *Vienne 1880–1938: Fin de Siècle et Modernisme*, at the Georges
Pompidou Centre, Paris on 10 October 1984.

are but two of the many attempts to characterize the modern world. Indeed there are so many contradictory definitions of 'modern' that the usefulness of the word is questionable; the current popularity of the term 'post-modernism' only adds insult to injury.

On the other hand, there can be little doubt that there is something to the idea of Vienna being so significant to our culture, to the modern world. When we look at the list of major cultural figures who were in and around Vienna from roughly 1890 until 1938 it must be clear to anyone that Vienna did make an immense contribution to European intellectual and cultural history at that time.[8] What perhaps leads historians to overvalue Vienna's importance is the fact that whereas Paris has, for the last two hundred years at least, been the leading cultural centre in Europe, for a time it was rivalled for that position by Vienna, a city never before, nor since, known for its intellectual brilliance, except in the realm of music. Is it not the exceptional nature of Vienna's cultural importance at the turn of the century that is the topic which should actually be under discussion? It is not so much that Vienna was, dubiously, the source of modernity in 1900, but rather that in 1900 and until the 1930s it was a major centre of intellectual and cultural thought which should most intrigue the cultural historian.

Current explanations of why Vienna was the birthplace of the modern world do provide some sort of an answer to this rather different, alternative approach to Vienna around 1900. The leading theory is, at the moment, that of Carl Schorske. Put briefly, his explanation of Vienna's seminal rôle in modern culture hinges on the idea that Vienna was the first place in Europe where bourgeois rationalism met its demise, and that therefore the figures of that culture were in a better position to express the problems of the forthcoming age. Schorske claims that Vienna's liberal bourgeoisie found in the city an aristocratic and amoral *Gefühlskultur* which contradicted their moral–scientific liberalism (a northern Protestant approach) and was never successfully overcome by them. To an extent uncommon elsewhere in Europe, the bourgeoisie ended up imitating the aristocracy, not vice versa. When, therefore, in the 1890s this bourgeoisie was alienated from power by the success of Lueger's 'politics of the new key', its sons retreated into the aesthetic temple of art for which their parents had schooled them in their imitation of the aristocratic lifestyle. Hence 'the Austrian aesthetes were alienated not *from* their class, but *with* it, from a society that defeated its expectations and rejected its values'.[9]

---

[8] Such a list would include: Sigmund Freud, Ludwig Wittgenstein, Mahler, Schoenberg, Klimt, Schiele, Otto Wagner, Adolf Loos, Ernst Mach, Ludwig Boltzmann, Kurt Gödel, the Austrian School of Economics, the Vienna Circle of Logical Positivists, Karl Popper, Hans Kelsen, Karl Kraus, Schnitzler, Hofmannsthal, Broch, Musil, to name but a few.

[9] Schorske, *Fin-de-siècle Vienna*, p.304; for the general argument *Ibid.* pp.5–10, 302–11.

This Schorskean approach has one very attractive feature. In its use of political and social determinants of cultural attitudes, it allows, or seems to allow, for easy comparisons and integration with the general European experience of the time. The universal applicability of terms such as 'liberal' and 'bourgeois' promises a similarly universal explanation for the emergence of 'modernity' in Europe. Schorske himself suggests this universal aspect when he states that his model for Vienna 1900 is the United States of America 1950.[10]

If, however, we come down from the level of universality and look at the specific case of Vienna around 1900, we begin to see that the advantages of generality offered by terms such as 'liberal bourgeoisie' are countered by the most awkward sort of particular facts. As will be discussed in more detail later, Vienna had a rather odd 'liberal bourgeoisie'. The reason for the political collapse of liberalism in 1895, as John Boyer has shown, was that large parts of what should have been the 'liberal bourgeoisie' were actually voting for the other side, for the antisemitic Christian Socials.[11] This complication, which boils down to the fact that the applicability of the term 'liberal bourgeoisie' is limited by the specific Viennese context, is closely connected to another aspect of Vienna's cultural life around 1900 which is in many respects the most troubling of all for those seeking a universally applicable scheme of cultural development. That is the fact that a very large number, indeed most, of the best known names in Viennese *fin-de-siècle* culture, with the exception of art and architecture, are of people of Jewish descent.

Whether it be Freud, Schoenberg, Schnitzler or Wittgenstein, the number of individuals at the top level of Viennese culture – or rather that type of culture for which Vienna is today so famous – who are of at least partly Jewish descent is so large that it cannot be ignored. The answer to this problem from those who take the Schorskean approach is usually to claim that the Jewish element in Vienna, regardless of its size, was irrelevant to the general cultural history. This is so, they argue, because, though of Jewish descent, these figures were assimilated and thus just like any others in the liberal bourgeoisie in Vienna, not all of whom could have been Jewish. A further implication is that the Jewish element has been in any case exaggerated, and that, for instance, Lueger was not so important for his antisemitism, as for his rôle of harbinger of a new political style.[12] In other words, the flowering of Viennese culture at the turn of the century was the response of a class rather than primarily that of a religious or ethnic minority.

[10] *Ibid.* pp.xxiii–xv.
[11] John W. Boyer, *Political Radicalism in Late Imperial Vienna* (Chicago 1981) pp.307–57.
[12] Schorske, *Fin-de-Siècle Vienna*, pp.133–46.

Schorske has thus made the following statements: 'The failure to acquire a monopoly of power left the bourgeois always something of an outsider, seeking integration with the aristocracy. The numerous and prosperous Jewish element in Vienna, with its strong assimilationist thrust, only strengthened this trend.'[13] Then again, when discussing Herzl: 'Assimilation through culture as a second stage in Jewish assimilation was but a special case of the middle-class phaseology [sic!] of upward mobility from economic to intellectual vocations.'[14] To be fair, when it comes to Freud, Schorske does recognize some sort of effect from antisemitism and Jewish consciousness, but generally in his collection of essays he is at pains to dismiss the Jewish question in Viennese culture as a marginal one and largely irrelevant. In this he is followed by the bulk of present researchers in the field, the latest being Mark Francis with a stereotypical refutation of any Jewish aspect at all.[15]

The considerations behind such an approach are, in many respects, praiseworthy. After all, it was the dearest wish of most of the Viennese Jewish bourgeoisie themselves that they should not be treated as Jews. Is it not vaguely racist, one might ask, to insist on some kind of Jewish influence, picking the Jews out for special attention? Is this not what the Nazis did? There is also the feeling that the Jewish question is just too sensitive an issue with which to deal. And it is very awkward to deal with particular ethnic problems when what appears to be needed is a universal explanation of culture. Yet it is, as people such as William Johnston and Allan Janik have recognized, so plain that Jews played an immense rôle in the cultural life of Vienna that the subject, as Ivar Oxaal among others has insisted, is still of great relevance.[16]

The Schorskean approach to the culture of *fin-de-siècle* Vienna is not the only one. There is a long tradition, kept alive today by people such as George Steiner, that Viennese modern culture was essentially a product of

---

[13] *Ibid.* p.7.   [14] *Ibid.* p.149.

[15] On Freud, see Schorske, *Fin-de-Siècle Vienna*, pp.181–207; various works have dismissed any Jewish aspect of their subject: W. W. Bartley III attempts to do this in his biography, *Wittgenstein* (Philadelphia 1973) pp.65–6; William J. McGrath avoids the subject in discussing the background of Victor Adler and his circle in *Dionysian Art and Populist Politics*, p.6; for the same attitude in the parallel case of Germany, see Peter Gay, 'Encounter with Modernism: German Jews in German Culture 1888–1914' in *Midstream*, February 1975, vol. XXI, no.2, pp.23–65. Another version of the same essay appears as 'Encounter with Modernism: German Jews in Wilhelminian Culture' in Gay, *Freud, Jews and Other Germans*, pp.93–168. Also Francis, *The Viennese Enlightenment*, p.8.

[16] Johnston, *The Austrian Mind*, pp.23–9; Allan Janik, 'Creative Milieux: the Case of Vienna' in Janik, *How not to Interpret a Culture* (Bergen 1986) p.117; for the most sensible discussion of the methodological problems raised by this question, see Ivar Oxaal, *The Jews of Pre-1914 Vienna: Two working Papers* (Hull 1981) pp.1–53. See also I. Oxaal, M. Pollak and G. Botz, eds., *Jews, Antisemitism and Culture in Vienna* (London 1987) which contains the latest research on the subject.

the *Jewish* bourgeoisie.[17] The most humorous account of the overwhelming importance of the Jews in Vienna was Hugo Bettauer's cutting, but all too perceptive, description of what Vienna would be without the Jews, *Die Stadt ohne Juden* (1922). In this prophetic novel Bettauer envisaged what would happen if the antisemitic government of Austria were to expel all its Jews, including converts (who could not be trusted). Socially and economically everything falls apart. The banks have to be taken over by foreigners, the politicians have no ready scapegoat, the high-fashion shops cannot sell anymore for it was Jewish women who led fashion. Instead, prophesied Bettauer, the fashion shops go over to selling *Loden* clothes to suit the now peasant population of the city. The most elegant spas go out of business, as do other forms of therapy such as the prostitutes and the 'süsse Mädel' of the suburbs. The only people really happy with the situation are the socialist workers who have their Jewish leadership taken from around their necks.[18]

Culturally Bettauer made some remarkably perceptive points, considering he was writing in 1922 and not in 1988. In the cultural world, he said, the theatres were abysmal, because all the talent had gone, except that is for the opera, which maintained its high standard. The operetta world disappeared, because there were no Jews to write the music and the libretti. The central coffee-houses of Vienna were deserted, for only Jews had had the impetus to go there and get involved in the circles of the coffee-house intellectuals. The rest were quite happy to visit their local, whether it be a Heuriger or a coffee-house. The arts were not patronized. As an old antisemite says: 'Vienna is stagnant without the Jews.'[19]

Bettauer was making a polemical point rather than a serious prophecy; nevertheless, for anyone who has been to Vienna in the 1980s, there are remarkable similarities between what Bettauer foresaw and what the present city is like, even though he got it wrong economically, and exaggerated the cultural decline. Certainly his views on the cultural rôle of Jews were confirmed by a whole host of contemporary witnesses such as the novelist Jakob Wassermann, the architect Paul Engelmann, Stefan Zweig, Julius Braunthal, Käthe Leichter and Ernst Lothar; George Clare is but the latest witness of the period to stress a specifically Jewish definition of the social base of Viennese culture.[20]

[17] Steiner, *Le langage et l'inhumain*, pp.67–9.
[18] Hugo Bettauer, *Die Stadt ohne Juden* (Vienna 1922, repr. 1980) pp.37–46, 75, 113–14.
[19] 'Wein versumpert ohne Juden.' *Ibid.* pp.71–2, 81–2, 113–4.
[20] For instance, Jakob Wassermann, *My life as German and Jew* (London 1934) pp.144–5; Paul Engelmann, *Letters from Wittgenstein; with a Memoir* (Oxford 1967) p.119; Stefan Zweig, *Die Welt von Gestern* (Frankfurt-on-Main 1944, repr. 1982) pp.37–8; Julius Braunthal, *Auf der Suche nach dem Millenium* (Vienna 1964) pp.20–1; *Käthe Leichter: Leben und Werk*, ed. Herbert Steiner (Vienna 1973) p.238; Ernst Lothar, *Der Engel mit der Posaune* (Salzburg 1947) p.644; George Clare, speech at the Austrian Institute, Paris, on 27 March 1985.

Often such witnesses will state that there was no particularly Jewish character to the culture that Jews in Vienna produced, and in this respect their evidence does not contradict the Schorskean approach.[21] Yet, in their insistence on the idea of a *Jewish*, as opposed to merely liberal, bourgeoisie, these witnesses contradict Schorske's basic assumption: that the Jews can be subsumed in the bourgeoisie at large. As far as these people are concerned, there was either no other bourgeoisie, or it played no rôle in modern culture, or, to put it more judiciously, anyone who was not Jewish in the culture had to go to the Jews to find support. As Stefan Zweig put it: 'whoever wished to put through something in Vienna, or came to Vienna as a guest from abroad and sought appreciation as well as an audience, was dependent on the Jewish bourgeoisie'.[22] These witnesses seem to be saying that, despite a total assimilation, or rather because of it, Jews were the people who dominated the cultural life of Vienna, and, as a *Jewish* bourgeoisie, influenced it – though in what way they rarely say. Instead of putting the Jewish component to one side, as Schorske does, as *merely* a special case in a general Viennese phenomenon, these contemporary reports suggest that the reverse is the case, that any non-Jewish bourgeois contribution is the exception, rather than the rule, that the Jews were so dominant in this class that they merit special attention on their own. The impression given is that, while others played a part, the cultural flowering in Vienna was an essentially *Jewish* phenomenon.

The aim of this study is to clarify this question about the Jewish influence *on* Viennese culture and *in* Viennese culture. The aim is to see the Jewish question in the light of the work done over the last few years on Viennese culture as a whole, and to reach some kind of understanding about how the Jewishness of many of the main figures can be set in the context of the cultural movements. In other words it is an attempt to test the Schorskean approach against the tradition of the Jewish dominance of Viennese culture, and from the result, suggest ways in which the Jewish question and the history of the culture of the Viennese *fin de siècle* should be related.

Two main aspects of the problem are studied. The first, with which section I deals, concerns the extent to which, in personal terms, the culture of *fin-de-siècle* Vienna was 'Jewish'. Section I is thus a statistical survey of the effect of the assimilation of the Jews on the personal composition of the cultural élite of Vienna and its social base in the educated, liberal bourgeoisie: in terms of numbers, how Jewish was Schorske's *fin de siècle*?

[21] For instance, Zweig, *Die Welt von Gestern*, p.38.
[22] 'Wer in Wien etwas Neues durchsetzen wollte, wer als Gast von aussen in Wien Verständnis und ein Publikum suchte, war auf die jüdische Bourgeoisie angewiesen...' *Ibid.* p.37. English quotation taken from the translation, *The World of Yesterday*, London, 1943.

This section also attempts to suggest reasons for the fact that Jews were so prominent in Vienna's modern cultural movements.

The second aspect studied is far more complicated and much less amenable to any truly empirical approach, but it is, in the end, the central question to be faced in this area: how are we to approach the thorny topic of the 'Jewish' element in Viennese culture at the turn of the century? Section II, which attempts some sort of an answer to this, does not set out to provide a definitive statement, but tries to develop a conceptual framework for looking at the social and cultural context of Vienna at the turn of the century through the eyes of the assimilated Jews in Vienna who made up such a substantial part of the cultural élite. The section tries to develop a method of looking at the notorious 'Jewish element' in the thought and work of these individuals which avoids the usual pitfalls associated with studies of the 'Jewish mind'. By concentrating on the individual experiences of the cultural élite, and only then trying to draw these isolated histories together, it is hoped that the ramifications of the Jewish heritage, and what it meant to be Jewish, are made clearer and more understandable in the Viennese context. Having thus attempted to outline the ways in which the Jewish background might indeed have been a powerful influence in various ways on much that is most important in Viennese culture, the study concludes with a summary attempt to put what has been discussed of the Jewish influence into the context of Viennese culture as a whole, and in turn put Vienna – and the Jewish influence on its culture – in the greater context of the emergence of modernism in Europe at that time.

As will soon become apparent, this study is far from being the last word on the subject of the Jewish influence in Viennese culture, nor does it wish to be seen as such. However, it is hoped that it will effectively reopen the debate on how to approach the problem, and moreover will direct that discussion along more productive paths than has hitherto been the case. Before this can be claimed, and before disappearing into the vast jungle of Jewish aspects of the life and work of the Viennese cultural élite, we first need to study the question of numbers. Before the speculation on the 'Jewish element' can begin, we need a good base of facts. The following chapter attempts to provide this.

PART I

*Jews in Viennese culture and society:
the statistical perspective*

≫ 1 ≪

Who was a Jew in Vienna at the turn of the century?

The object of this section is to ascertain the 'Jewish' presence in modern high culture in Vienna, and then to offer some sort of context in which that presence is understandable. This might appear straightforward enough, and indeed, for the Viennese Jewish community as a whole, the number of converts was never particularly large as a proportion of the whole; but there is the awkward fact that many of the most famous 'Jewish' figures in Vienna were either baptized at birth, or later converted; even someone such as Freud was certainly not a religious Jew, and hence, by one definition, not Jewish. If such a narrow, religious definition of Jewishness were to be made, then the 'Jewish' presence in Viennese culture would be small indeed.[1]

The criterion of who is a Jew and who is not a Jew which I have chosen here is the widest, that of descent. Where it is known, I have included those figures who were of at least partially Jewish descent in the category of Jews. This criterion is not one which has been universally adopted in defining Jewish identity. Indeed it might be thought by some to have racial (and racist) connotations, harking back to the Holocaust. Objectively viewed, however, it should not be a controversial criterion: interest in someone's descent of itself need not be seen as racist. It is true that many people take offense at someone being termed 'half Jewish', yet one often hears references to someone being 'half American', 'half Austrian' or even 'a quarter Czech' without any offense being given or indeed taken. Such statements, after all, usually refer to a cultural heritage, and are the result of indulgence in a curiosity about someone's antecedents which is common to most people, and which the nobility made into a profession. Or should one regard genealogists as racists?

Surely it is only when particularly strong value judgements (usually

---

[1] Among those who were converts, the children of converts or of mixed marriages, were: Alfred Adler, Hugo Bettauer, Hermann Broch, Egon Friedell, Hans Hahn, Hans Kelsen, Karl Kraus, Gustav Mahler, Otto Neurath, Arnold Schoenberg and Ludwig Wittgenstein. Both Otto Bauer and Sigmund Freud were professed atheists.

11

negative) are involved that people take offense, justifiably. In the phrase 'half Jewish' it is not 'half' which is the problem for some people, but rather the continuing pejorative nature of the word 'Jewish'. Racism starts when one ascribes to biologically inherited characteristics certain values, and acts on those assumptions. But what I am trying to describe here is the effect of the Jewish cultural background and existential situation on the Jewish members of Vienna's cultural élite. Although this must, perforce, use the criterion of descent to define Jewish identity, the fact that it is not concerned with racial characteristics means that the criterion cannot be racist.

Is such a criterion, controversial though it might be, nevertheless historically accurate? It is one of the purposes of this book to show that it is, but here let me make some simple claims, to be affirmed later. Firstly, in Viennese society, although one had converted, or was the offspring of a mixed marriage, one was still liable to be seen by Jews and Gentiles alike as Jewish – and avoiding recognition of this fact was virtually impossible, the effort of doing so producing its own problems. Furthermore, since many of those Jews in Vienna who converted were ennobled, or married into non-Jewish noble families, it was impossible by dint of genealogy to avoid remembering the Jewish ancestor, and the fact of this Jewish ancestor was bound in such a world to make a difference to one's noble credentials. In other words, on a subjective level, public and private, Jewish descent was known and significant.

Secondly, I would argue that there is also a case on the objective level for using in this study the criterion of descent to define who was Jewish. When people talk about the 'Jewish influence' on modern culture, they are not so much talking about specific religious traditions, but rather about the social and cultural effects of one of the most important historical events in modern European history – the integration of the Jews into their host societies. This took place over a relatively brief period, considering that full emancipation came in many states only in the second half of the nineteenth century, and ceased in most of Europe less than a century later. This is a matter, in the main, of only three or four generations. Yet in this short period the group of assimilating Jews and their descendants contributed greatly to modern culture in Europe, especially Vienna. Their contribution was, as such, a product of the historical process of assimilation.

When people point out that Hofmannsthal was not 'Jewish' by religion and barely so by descent (he was only a quarter Jewish), they ignore the fact that he was nevertheless a product of the assimilation, just as Wittgenstein was.[2] Without the assimilation neither would have existed.

---

[2] On Hofmannsthal's family background see Werner Volke, *Hofmannsthal* (Hamburg 1967) pp.9–10. On Wittgenstein's descent, see W. W. Bartley III, *Wittgenstein* (Philadelphia

One might debate the significance of this, but to do so is in itself to acknowledge that we need to know about the background of assimilation. As such, both Hofmannsthal and Wittgenstein, though marginal, are nevertheless part of the historical phenomenon of the integration of the Jews into western culture and society.

It is my contention that the presence in the family past of Jewish ancestors was liable to mean that one started with a view of the world which was substantially different from that of others who were not of Jewish descent. Seen in this way, the assimilation, far from producing a complete merger with the surrounding populace, was in itself a Jewish phenomenon. Therefore anyone who was a product of this assimilation can be included as Jewish, and that must, of necessity, include converts and so on. This is not to say that everyone who came from this background fitted some stereotypical model of the 'Jewish mind', but it is saying that they are potentially relevant to our study and must therefore be included, at least initially, in our statistical analysis. Though the 'Jewish' influence on them might have been minimal, even non-existent, they were products of the process, of the historical event of the assimilation.

Our constituency is therefore all those who *could* have been affected by being part of the Jewish assimilation. What the effect of this phenomenon was on these constituents is not a matter for statistical analysis and will be dealt with in the section which follows this one. Here we are merely concerned with recording the effect, in terms of individual participation, of the assimilation on the culture and with providing some sort of explanation for it.

1973) pp.184–6, appendix. It is of note that Hermann Broch saw Hofmannsthal's background very much as that of an assimilation. See Hermann Broch, *Hofmannsthal und seine Zeit*, in Broch, *Schriften zur Literatur* 1 (Frankfurt-on-Main 1975) pp.176–81. For a contrasting view see Egon Schwarz, 'Melting Pot or Witch's Cauldron? Jews and Anti-Semites in Vienna at the Turn of the Century' in David Bronsen, ed, *Jews and Germans from 1860–1933: the Problematic Symbiosis* (Heidelberg 1979) p.265.

⤜ 2 ⤛

How Jewish was 'fin-de-siècle' Vienna?

To try to give some picture of the Jewish involvement in modern high culture in Vienna it is simplest to look at the various cultural fields in turn, and try to ascertain the proportion of Jews in the leading cultural groups. The result is remarkable.

PSYCHOLOGY

This field is dominated by Sigmund Freud and the creation of psycho-analysis. The records of the Wednesday Society, the informal group of disciples around Freud which later became the fully-fledged Psychoanalytic Society, show that all the regular members between 1902 and 1906 were Jewish.[1] Post-Freudian psychology in Vienna continued to be predomi-nantly a Jewish concern. There was the individual psychology of Alfred Adler, and, at the university after the First World War, there were the Bühlers, Karl and Charlotte, with an experimental form of Freudian psychology.[2] The memory of Otto Weininger also lived on in the ideas of people such as Gustav Grüner, the 'philosopher' of the Café Central.[3] Jews were not the only psychologists or psychiatrists in Vienna. There were doctors such as Wagner-Jauregg who were not of Jewish descent, and

---

[1] Dennis B. Klein, *The Jewish Origins of the Psychoanalytic Movement* (New York 1981) p.vii. It has been suggested that part of the reason for this was that, consciously or unconsciously, Freud barred such non-Jewish figures as Wagner-Jauregg from attending these initially informal private meetings, see Peter Drucker, *Adventures of a Bystander* (London 1979) pp.96–7.

[2] On Alfred Adler, see Manès Sperber, *Masks of Loneliness: Alfred Adler in Perspective* (New York 1974); also Kurt Adler, '*Ursprünge und Ausstrahlungen der Individualpsychologie*' in Norbert Leser, ed., *Das geistige Leben Wiens in der Zwischenkriegszeit* (Vienna 1981) pp.162–70. On the Bühlers, see Marie Jahoda's essay, 'Aus den Anfängen der sozialwissenschaftlichen Forschung in Österreich' in the same collection, *Das geistige Leben Wiens*, p.218. According to Renate Heuer at the Bibliographica Judaica in Frankfurt-on-Main, Charlotte Bühler was of Jewish descent. Her husband, Karl Bühler, appears not to have been of Jewish descent.

[3] See Hartmut Binder, 'Ernst Polak – Literat ohne Werk' in *Jahrbuch der deutschen Schiller Gesellschaft*, no.23, 1979 (Stuttgart 1979) p.384.

14

philosophers such as Brentano and his pupils.[4] The specifically Freudian hybrid and its successors in Vienna were, however, largely Jewish preserves.

PHILOSOPHY

The most important group of philosophers in Vienna in the period up to 1938 was the Vienna Circle (*Wiener Kreis*), the founding school of Logical Positivism.[5] This group saw itself as continuing the tradition of Ernst Mach, and traced its own ideas on logic back to Franz Brentano.[6] Neither Mach nor Brentano were of Jewish descent, but both had close links with Jews, Mach having as one of his closest friends Josef Popper-Lynkeus, and Brentano marrying Ida von Lieben, a relation of Josephine von Wertheimstein, whose salon he often attended.[7] Furthermore there were many Jews who were prominent figures in positivist thought in Vienna, including, apart from Popper-Lynkeus, Wilhelm Jerusalem, Rudolf Goldscheid and Theodor Gomperz (with Richard Wahle in Czernowitz also central).[8] Gomperz was chosen by Otto Neurath as exemplifying the continuation of an anti-metaphysical spirit in Vienna around 1900, when Neurath came to write the pamphlet, *Wissenschaftliche Weltauffassung*.[9]

Our main purpose here is to assess the rôle of people of Jewish descent in the Circle itself. The origins of the group lay, according to Philipp Frank, in the discussions before the First World War which he, Otto Neurath and Hans Hahn held on the problems caused in philosophy by Einstein's Theory of Relativity.[10] Of these three, Frank was Jewish by religion and the

---

[4] On the Brentanians, see William M. Johnston, *The Austrian Mind: an Intellectual and Social History 1848–1938* (Berkeley 1972) pp.290–307; also see Barry Smith, ed., *Structure and Gestalt: Philosophy and Literature in Austria-Hungary and her Successor States* (Amsterdam 1981) *passim*.

[5] For the history of this group's philosophical ideas, see Viktor Kraft, *Der Wiener Kreis* (Vienna 1950); Carl G. Hempel, 'Der Wiener Kreis und der Metamorphosen seines Empirismus' in Leser, ed., *Das geistige Leben Wiens*, pp.205–16; Friedrich Stadler, *Vom Positivismus zur 'Wissenschaftlichen Weltauffassung'* (Vienna 1982).

[6] This claim was made in the group's manifesto, *Wissenschaftliche Weltauffassung: der Wiener Kreis*, published in 1929, and reproduced in Otto Neurath, *Empiricism and Sociology* (Dordrecht 1973) p.302, cf. Kurt Rudolf Fischer, 'Philosophie 1895–1918' in Maria Marchetti, ed., *Wien um 1900: Kunst und Kultur* (Vienna 1985) pp.419–26.

[7] On Mach and Popper, see Ingrid Belke, *Die socialreformerischen Ideen von Joseph Popper-Lynkeus (1838–1921)* (Tuebingen 1978) pp.187–8; John T. Blackmore, *Ernst Mach: his Work, Life and Influence* (Berkeley 1972) pp.21–2. Also Stadler, *Vom Positivismus* pp.3ff. On Brentano, see Ilsa Barea, *Vienna* (London 1966) p.307.

[8] On Wilhelm Jerusalem, see his *Gedanken und Denker: gesammelte Aufsätze* (Vienna 1925); Stadler, *Vom Positivismus*, pp.42–4. On Rudolf Goldscheid, see Stadler, *Vom Positivismus* pp.155ff. On Theodor Gomperz, see *Theodor Gomperz: ein Gelehrtenleben im Bürgertum der Franz-Josephszeit*, eds. H. Gomperz and R. A. Kann (Vienna 1974). On Richard Wahle, see Johnston, *The Austrian Mind*, pp.201–3.

[9] Neurath, *Empiricism and Sociology*, p.301.

[10] Philipp Frank, *Between Physics and Philosophy* (Cambridge, Mass. 1941) p.7.

other two both had Jewish fathers who had converted, probably on marriage. Hahn's elder sister married Otto Neurath, and his younger sister married a Jewish painter, Walter Fraenkel. Hahn was very much a part of the world of the fully assimilated Jewish bourgeoisie.[11]

From this small group after the war came the full Vienna Circle under the title Verein Ernst Mach. The proclamation of the Circle as such was made in the pamphlet *Wissenschaftliche Weltauffassung* of 1929.[12] This pamphlet contained a list of the members of the supposed Circle, though not all the people mentioned were happy to be associated with it.[13] The list contained fourteen names. Of these eight have been identified as of Jewish descent: Gustav Bergmann, Herbert Feigl, Philipp Frank, Hans Hahn, Marcel Natkin, Otto Neurath, Olga Hahn-Neurath and Friedrich Waismann.[14] Two of the remaining six, Rudolf Carnap and Moritz Schlick, who were two of the most important members, were imports from Germany. Two others, Kurt Gödel and Karl Menger, objected to being on the list.[15] This leaves Theodor Radakovic, of whom I have been unable to trace anything, and Viktor Kraft. Kraft has always been suspected of being Jewish by descent, though this appears to be untrue.[16] That the suspicion should arise, however, is understandable, when it is considered that Jews make a majority of the group and that those who are not Jewish either are not Viennese, or did not want to be associated with the group. That Kraft was an enthusiastic supporter, and liberal as well, led people to assume that he must be Jewish.

Within the Circle, it appears, it was not Schlick, but rather Neurath and Hahn with the help of Carnap who were the main organizers and leaders. Neurath was the real driving force behind the Verein Ernst Mach, and Hahn was not only the person who first introduced Wittgenstein's *Tractatus Logico-Philosophicus* into the debate, but also the one who arranged Schlick's appointment in the first place.[17] When it is added that Wittgenstein provided the basis for the Circle's philosophical theories, it can be seen that people of Jewish descent played a very large rôle indeed

[11] The Jewish origin of Frank and Neurath is generally known. The background to Hans Hahn was provided by Paul Neurath, Otto Neurath's son, and stepson of Olga Hahn-Neurath, Hans Hahn's sister, in an interview in Vienna, 17 May 1983.

[12] On the emergence of the Vienna Circle see Stadler, *Vom Positivismus*, pp.167ff.

[13] Information from Eckehart Koehler, Vienna.

[14] On Bergmann's origin I rely on the information of Kurt Rudolf Fischer, Vienna. On Natkin I rely on the information of Eckehart Koehler, Vienna. The others are generally known, or see above note 11.

[15] Information from Eckehart Koehler.

[16] I rely here on the information of Dr Hanns Jäger-Sunstenau, Vienna.

[17] On Neurath, see Stadler, *Vom Positivismus*, pp.171ff; on Hahn, see Frank, *Between Physics and Philosophy*, p.8.

in the creation of the theories of Logical Positivism in alliance with a couple of German Protestants. That it was Karl Popper who provided the most famous critique of these ideas only confirms the point.[18]

POLITICAL THOUGHT – SOCIALISM

It is well-known that the leadership of the socialist party in Austria before and after the First World War was heavily Jewish.[19] This was also the case for the group of theorists collectively known as the Austro-Marxists, the most interesting group of political theorists to emerge from the liberal bourgeoisie of Vienna.[20] Of the major theorists in Austro-Marxism only Karl Renner was not of Jewish descent. Those who were, included Rudolf Hilferding, Otto Bauer, Max Adler, Gustav Eckstein and Friedrich Adler. The extent to which the socialist environment in Vienna was Jewish can be illustrated by a look at Ernst Glaser's book on socialist and quasi-socialist thought in Austria, *Im Umfeld des Austromarxismus.*[21] In his table of contents Glaser lists all the names of the important figures in this intellectual world. If this list of names is analysed in terms of the number of people of Jewish descent, the result is that, for people born before 1905, 81 out of the 137 names on the list (59 per cent) have been positively identified as Jewish. If half the doubtful cases are included, the number goes up to 88 (64 per cent).[22] Though this is not a particularly accurate means of assessing the Jewish presence amongst socialist intellectuals, it does appear that the Jewish element was predominant here as well.

SOCIAL THOUGHT – AROUND POPPER-LYNKEUS

Ingrid Belke, who has carried out a major study of the bourgeois social reform groups around the figure of Josef Popper-Lynkeus, has stated with regard to the various movements of social reform, such as women's rights, pacifism and popular education, that: 'In most of the Austrian reform societies mentioned here, Jews, or individuals of Jewish descent, played a leading role; it is therefore almost easier to list the exceptions: Marianne Hainisch, Rosa Mayreder, Wilhelm Börner, Edgar Herbst, R. N. Cou-

---

[18] On Popper's attitude to the Vienna Circle, see Kraft, *Der Wiener Kreis*, pp.113–36.

[19] See, for instance, Hans Mayer, *Aussenseiter* (Frankfurt-on-Main 1981) p.438.

[20] See Johnston, *The Austrian Mind*, pp.99–11.

[21] Ernst Glaser, *Im Umfeld des Austromarxismus: ein Beitrag zur Geistesgeschichte des österreichischen Sozialismus* (Vienna, 1981).

[22] The analysis was made on the information provided by Dr Renate Heuer, Dr Jäger-Sunstenau, and Sigmund Kaznelson, ed., *Juden im deutschen Kulturbereich: ein Sammelwerk.* 3rd edn (Berlin 1962).

denhove-Kalergi and a few others.'[23] She goes on to say that this was especially true of the group most closely associated with Popper-Lynkeus, the 'Verein Allgemeine Nährpflicht'.

Although Ingrid Belke does not back up her claim with any attempt at a statistical analysis, a study of the various people mentioned in her book supports it. Of the eight major reformers whom she marks out for special praise six, Rudolf Goldscheid, Julius Ofner, Max Ermers, Ludo Hartmann, Fritz Kobler and Popper himself, were of Jewish descent. (The other two, who were not Jewish, were Edgar Herbst and Wilhelm Börner.)[24] The main force behind the important movement for *Volksbildung* (popular education) was Ludo Hartmann, the son of the radical liberal and writer, Moritz Hartmann.[25] The major theorist of the peace movement, A. H. Fried, advisor to Bertha von Suttner, was also Jewish.[26] Belke lists the major figures who went to see Popper in his home out in Hietzing, on a kind of pilgrimage as she describes it. Of the twenty-five people on the list, nineteen (76 per cent) are of Jewish descent.[27] It seems from figures such as these that the cause of progressive social reform in Vienna depended for the most part on individuals of Jewish descent.

ECONOMICS – THE AUSTRIAN SCHOOL

It seems fairly certain that none of the original school of Viennese economists, Carl Menger, Friedrich von Wieser and Eugen von Böhm-Bawerk, were of Jewish descent.[28] Therefore the theory of marginal utility, with all its implications for the mathematicization of economics, was not a 'Jewish' invention. Joseph Schumpeter also appears not to have been of Jewish descent. There is some irony, given the idea that Jews are supposed

[23] 'In den meisten der genannten österreichischen Reformvereine spielten Juden, oder Bürger jüdischer Herkunft, eine führende Rolle; es ist daher fast leichter die Ausnahmen zu nennen: Marianne Hainisch, Rosa Mayreder, Wilhelm Börner, Edgar Herbst, R. N. Coudenhove-Kalergi und ein paar andere.' Belke, *Popper-Lynkeus*, p.239.

[24] *Ibid.* p.4. The origin of the individuals relies on information from Dr Renate Heuer, Frankfurt.

[25] Belke, *Popper-Lynkeus*, p.19.

[26] *Ibid.* p.29. Fried was, typically, also a prominent figure in Austrian freemasonry, see *Zirkel und Winkelmass, 200 Jahre Grosse Landesloge der Freimaurer* (Vienna 1984) pp.127–8.

[27] List appears in Belke, *Popper-Lynkeus*, pp.80–1. The Jewish origin of those on the list was checked with the help of the files of the Bibliographica Judaica, in Frankfurt-on-Main.

[28] It is often thought that Carl Menger was of Jewish descent, being born in Galicia as the son of a merchant. Ernst von Plener is reputed to have called Carl Menger's brother, Max, a Polish Jew. Among recent studies, Wolfdieter Bihl has included Menger among the prominent Jewish figures of the period: see W. Bihl, *Die Juden*, in *Die Habsburger Monarchie, 1848–1918*, eds. A. Wandruszka and P. Urbanitsch, vol.2, part 2, p.929. However, Dr Jäger-Sunstenau, who has researched Menger's genealogy, assures me that these claims are unfounded. Such claims have not been made about von Wieser or Böhm-Bawerk.

to mathematicize academic disciplines, that Schumpeter, the non-Jew, is criticized by Ludwig von Mises, who was Jewish, for introducing quantities into Viennese economic theory, instead of dealing with actual trade.[29]

If Jews were not directly part of the official academic school in the early years (and the suggestion has been made that Jews were intentionally kept out of an academic discipline regarded as the preserve of high bureaucrats and their sons), they were very prominent outside academia in the financial world and the press.[30] Schumpeter, in his *History of economic analysis*, gives especial praise to two bankers, Auspitz and Lieben, for being far in advance of their time.[31] (With regard to what has been said above, it might be remarked that, as bankers, Auspitz and Lieben were far more mathematical in their approach than the official Viennese school!) In the press world the major theorists were Josef Neuwirth and the editor of the *Neue Freie Presse*, Moritz Benedikt.[32] Also in the world of socialist economics, Karl Grünberg was a major figure before he became president of the Institut für soziale Forschung in Frankfurt, the Frankfurt School.[33]

The Jewish presence in the mainstream of economic thought in Vienna really started with the Böhm-Bawerk seminar, which included Schumpeter, but also Otto Neurath, Otto Bauer and Ludwig von Mises.[34] With the end of the First World War and the retirement of Wieser, the only heir to the tradition of the Austrian School left with any ability, at least according to himself and Hayek, was Ludwig von Mises. The holders of the three full professorships in economics at this time were Otmar Spann, a quasi-National Socialist, Ferdinand Graf Degenfeld-Schonburg, who seems to have been a nonentity, and the only serious rival, Hans Mayer. Mises was, at least partly due to his remaining Jewish it seems, only a *professor extraordinarius*. Mayer should have been Wieser's successor in the Austrian School, but seems to have been distracted by academic infighting from

---

[29] Ludwig von Mises, *Erinnerungen* (Stuttgart 1978) p.21.

[30] The claim that Jews were excluded from the official faculty positions is in Erich Streissler, 'Die Wiener Schule der Nationalökonomie' in P. Berner, E. Brix and W. Mantl, eds., *Wien um 1900: Aufbruch in die Moderne* (Vienna 1986) p.80.

[31] Joseph Schumpeter, *A History of Economic Analysis*, (London 1954) pp.844, 849.

[32] On Neuwirth, see Sigmund Mayer, *Die Wiener Juden: Kommerz, Kultur, Politik 1700–1900* (Vienna 1918) p.389. On Benedikt, see Albert Fuchs, *Geistige Strömungen in Österreich 1867–1918* (Vienna 1949) p.22; A. Wandruzcka, *Geschichte einer Zeitung: das Schicksal der 'Presse' und der 'Neuen Freien Presse' von 1848 zur Zweiten Republik* (Vienna 1958) pp.96, 98. Another economist of Jewish descent who made his name as a journalist was Gustav Stolper. See Toni Stolper, *Gustav Stolper* (Tübingen 1960).

[33] On Grünberg, see Johnston, *The Austrian Mind*, p.92; also *Käthe Leichter: Leben und Werk*, ed. Herbert Steiner (Vienna 1973) p.363–7.

[34] Mises, *Erinnerungen*, pp.23–4.

doing much serious academic work. Mises was thus left as the only competent successor to the tradition.[35]

The Mises private seminar became the new centre of the tradition of the Austrian School, and it was the proving ground of Friedrich von Hayek. A list of the members of the seminar is given in Mises' memoirs.[36] According to various sources, above all the evidence of Professor Martha Steffy Browne, a member of the seminar, twenty-three out of twenty-nine names on the list were those of people of Jewish descent, that is 79 per cent.[37] Ironically, some of the best known names on the list, Gottfried von Haberler, Hayek and Oskar Morgenstern, were among those not of Jewish descent.[38] Nevertheless, it does seem that one of the more important seminal groups for modern liberal economic theory was heavily Jewish in terms of composition.

LEGAL THEORY – THE PURE THEORY OF LAW

The history of Austrian jurisprudence is dominated by the names of people of Jewish descent, starting with Joseph von Sonnenfels, the great legal reformer of the reigns of Maria Theresa and Joseph II. The codification of the criminal and civil law in the second half of the nineteenth century was achieved by two Jewish converts, Glaser and Unger. Another convert, Emil Steinbach, introduced much social legislation at the end of the nineteenth century. In Czernowitz, Eugen Ehrlich developed the sociological approach to law. The great legal theorist in Heidelberg, Georg Jellinek, was the son of the preacher at the Viennese Temple, Adolf Jellinek.[39]

The most influential figure in the history of legal theory to come from

---

[35] *Ibid.* pp.viii–xvi (introduction by Hayek), 61. According to Professor Martha Steffy Browne, the fact that Mises was Jewish was not as large a factor in his being denied a professorship as his arrogance. Interview, New York, 12 September 1987.

[36] *Ibid.* p.65.

[37] My principal source for this is a letter of 16 November 1984, from Professor Martha Steffy Browne. Other sources, such as Dr Renate Heuer, Dr Hanns Jäger-Sunstenau and Professor Albert Lauterbach, Vienna, largely confirm Professor Browne's information. The Jewish members of the seminar were: Ludwig Bettelheim-Gabillon, Victor Bloch, Stephanie Braun-Browne, Friedrich Engel von Janosi, Walter Fröhlich, Marianne von Herzfeld, Felix Kaufmann, Rudolf Klein, Helene Lieser-Berger, Rudolf Löbl, Gertrud Lovasy, Fritz Machlup, Ilse Mintz-Schüller, Elly Offenheimer-Spiro, Adolf G. Redlich-Redley, Paul N. Rosenstein-Rodan, Karol Schlesinger, Fritz Schreier, Alfred Schütz, Emmanuel Winternitz, Herbert von Fürth, Walter Weisskopf, Erich Schiff. The non-Jews were: Gottfried von Haberler, Friedrich von Hayek, Oskar Morgenstern, Richard von Strigl, Erich Vögelin and Robert Wälder.

[38] On the history of Mises' private seminar, see the articles by Martha Steffy Browne and Gottfried Haberler in *Ludwig von Mises – seine Ideen und seine Wirkung*, special issue of *Wirtschaftspolitische Blätter* 4 (Vienna 1981) 28, pp. 110–27.

[39] See Franz Kobler, '*The Contribution of Austrian Jews to Jurisprudence*' in Josef Fraenkel, ed., *The Jews of Austria: Essays on their life, History and Destruction* (London 1967) pp.25–40.

Vienna was Hans Kelsen. His Pure Theory of Law attempted to make the study of laws into an autonomous science by making it morally neutral. Laws were not to be judged, but studied. It is worth noting that Kelsen named his theory 'Reine Rechtslehre' (Pure Theory of Law) as a conscious imitation of Hermann Cohen's *Ethik des reinen Willens*. As so often in the history of Viennese thought, there was thus a neo-Kantian background to what became a famous positivist theory. The political drawbacks of Kelsen's approach were pointed up only too obviously in the events of the 1930s, yet for theorists of international law Kelsen's ideas are still of central significance, and his was certainly the most important Austrian contribution to modern legal theory.[40]

These are only some indications of the rôle played by Jews in Austrian legal theory, but it seems clear that, at the very top, that rôle was pivotal.

LITERATURE

Literary production at the turn of the century could perhaps be regarded as the core of the culture of *fin-de-siècle* Vienna, and has certainly been so for cultural historians of the period. Attention almost always concentrates on the group of writers who came to be known collectively as Young Vienna (*Jung Wien*). This group included such central figures as Arthur Schnitzler, Hugo von Hofmannsthal, Richard Beer-Hofmann and Hermann Bahr. It was this group which articulated the ideas of Schorske's *fin-de-siècle* culture. It was in addition predominantly Jewish.

Of the five major figures, Schnitzler, Beer-Hofmann, Hofmannsthal, Salten and Bahr, only the last did not have a Jewish background of some sort. It could easily be objected that a group of five writers is not a good indication of the ethnic composition of a whole literary movement. However, a list drawn up by Schnitzler in 1891 remedies this.[41] It lists the people whom Schnitzler saw as the leading representatives in the new literature in Vienna. There are twenty-three names in all; of these sixteen appear definitely to have been of at least partly Jewish descent, that is 70 per cent.[42] If Schnitzler's list is a reliable indication of the core of the Young

---

[40] On Kelsen, see R. A. Métall, *Hans Kelsen: Leben und Werk* (Vienna 1969) esp. pp.7–8 on the connection with Hermann Cohen.

[41] The list is reproduced in Bernhard Zeller, Ludwig Greve and Werner Volke, eds., *Jugend in Wien: Literatur um 1900* (Stuttgart 1974) p.119.

[42] Most of the names were identified in the files of the *Bibliographica Judaica*, Frankfurt-on-Main. Of the others, E. M. Kafka's descent was made known to me by Professor Harry Zohn, Brandeis; Julius Kulka was identified in the *Geburtsbücher* of the *Israelitische Kultusgemeinde* in Vienna's city archive; Leo Vanjung was included on the strength of his being a witness at Richard Beer-Hofmann's Jewish wedding, and the presence of a Boris Fan-Jung in the records of the *Akademisches Gymnasium* for the eighth class of 1890. Leo Vanjung's younger brother was called Boris, and the family name was often misspelt. See

Vienna movement, then the literary experience of the Viennese *fin de siècle* was a predominantly Jewish one.

This predominance appears to have continued until 1938. Friedrich Torberg once asserted: 'if one can say that in the inter-war period three-quarters of the most prominent writers in German literature were Austrians, it is also true that of those Austrian writers a similar proportion were Jewish'.[43] While his claim about German and Austrian writers might be open to question, his claim for the Jewish presence in the Austrian literary world seems quite correct. Ernst Lothar recalls in his memoirs the group of writers who used to gather at Stefan Zweig's apartment in the Kochgasse.[44] It included the major figures of the second generation of writers, the inter-war élite: Stefan Zweig, Robert Musil, Franz Werfel, Josef Roth, Hermann Broch, Felix Braun, Grünewald, F. T. Csokor and Lothar himself. Of these nine names seven are those of Jews. Only Musil and Csokor are not. Hence 78 per cent of the group were of Jewish descent.[45] While this is not much to go on, it is in line with Torberg's claim, and indicates a very large Jewish presence indeed.

According to Stella Ehrenfeld, the reason why she and Graf Wilczek founded the Musil Society was that they felt that the only major non-Jewish writer should be given some material assistance and recognition for his almost unique achievement of being a great Viennese writer and not Jewish. For Stella Ehrenfeld all the other great writers in Vienna were Jewish.[46] While her views on the subject are not firm proof, they are another confirmation of the impression that when we are talking about the literary world of Vienna we are talking, to all intents and purposes, about a world of Jewish personalities.

Zeller, *Jugend in Wien* p.211 on Beer-Hofmann's marriage, and *Hofmannsthal – Schnitzler: Briefwechsel* (Frankfurt-on-Main 1983) p.325 on Boris Vanjung. Further confirmation is given by Norbert Abels' describing Vanjung as Schnitzler's 'Zionist friend' in Norbert Abels, *Sicherheit ist nirgends: Judentum und Aufklärung bei Arthur Schnitzler* (Königstein, 1982) p.81. Those of Jewish descent on Schnitzler's list were: Richard Beer-Hofmann, Felix Salten, Hugo von Hofmannsthal, Arthur Schnitzler, Felix Dörmann, Leo Ebermann, Karl Federn, Paul Goldmann, Jacques Joachim, Eduard M. Kafka, C. Karlweis, Julius Kulka, Rudolf Lothar, Gustav Schwarzkopf, Richard Specht and Leo Vanjung. Those seven who do not appear to have been of Jewish descent were: Hermann Bahr, Ferry Bératon, Friedrich M. Fels (Mayer), Heinrich von Korff, Friedrich Schik, Falk (Heinrich) Schupp and K. von Torresani.

[43] 'Wenn in der Zeit zwischen den beiden Weltkriegen der Ruhm der deutsch – sprachigen Literatur zu gut drei Viertel österreichisch war, so war der Ruhm der österreichischen Literatur im gleichen Ausmass jüdisch.' *B'nai B'rith 1895-1975* (Vienna 1975) p.49.

[44] Ernst Lothar, *Das Wunder des Überlebens* (Vienna 1966) p.38.

[45] The only figure in the list whose origin is perhaps not generally known is Grünewald. His Jewish descent is confirmed by the *Bibliographica Judaica* files.

[46] Interview with Stella Ehrenfeld, Surrey 25 March 1984. Also see Milan Dubrovic, *Veruntreute Geschichte* (Vienna 1985) pp.94–5.

THEATRE AND OPERETTA

There are no reliable statistics on the overall presence of Jews in these most Viennese of cultural pursuits. It is to be doubted whether there was the same predominance as in literature, especially considering the way in which the Viennese generally took to the theatre. Nevertheless, at the leading edge of drama and operetta, people of Jewish descent were very prominent.

In the theatrical world in general, one of the main salons of the liberal era was that of Friedrich Baron von Schey, who, as a close friend of Heinrich Laube, helped to establish the Stadttheater as the leading private theatre in Vienna.[47] Another theatre was built in the *palais* of the manufacturer von Wertheim on the Schwarzenbergplatz.[48] At the Burgtheater the two most famous actors before 1914, Adolph von Sonnenthal and Josef Kainz, were both Jewish.[49] After the First World War, Max Reinhardt, the master producer of the German stage, tried to establish himself in Vienna, as he had already done in Berlin. It was for him that the Jewish speculator and financier, Castiglioni, financed the restoration of the Theater in der Josefstadt, still today Vienna's most beautiful theatre.[50] Reinhardt and Hugo von Hofmannsthal, along with Leopold von Andrian, were the founders of the Salzburg Festival. All three, in their own ways, were products of the Jewish assimilation.[51]

In the world of operetta Jews were again very prominent. Of the major operetta composers Leo Fall, Edmund Eysler, Oskar Straus and Emmerich Kalman were all of Jewish descent.[52] The supreme dynasty of the world of waltz and operetta, the most Viennese of all musical families, the Strausses, also had a Jewish ancestor. The family name went back to Johann Michael Strauss, who converted to Catholicism on marriage in 1759. This was Johann Strauss the Younger's great-grandfather.[53] The most famous librettist in Viennese operetta, Viktor Leon, was also Jewish.[54] Although it cannot be more closely defined, there was thus a considerable Jewish presence in these fields.

[47] Mayer, *Die Wiener Juden*, pp.364–5; also see Robert Waissenberger, ed., *Traum und Wirklichkeit, Wien 1870–1930*, catalogue (Vienna 1985) p.225.

[48] Graf Paul Vasili (pseudonym of Princess Radziwill), *Die Wiener Gesellschaft* (Leipzig 1885) p.428.

[49] Hans Tietze, *Die Juden Wiens* (Vienna 1935) p.213.

[50] Leonhard M. Fiedler, *Max Reinhardt* (Hamburg 1975) pp.36ff; Gusti Adler, *Aber vergessen Sie nicht die chinesischen Nachtigallen* (Vienna 1980) pp.141–2.

[51] Fiedler, *Reinhardt*, pp.103ff.

[52] See Kaznelson, *Juden im deutschen Kulturbereich*; also B'nai B'rith 1895–1975, p.44.

[53] Hanns Jäger-Sunstenau, 'Die geadelten Judenfamilien im vormärzlichen Wien' (Vienna Univ. Diss. 1950) p.70.

[54] Peter Herz, 'Viktor Leon – ein jüdischer Meisterlibrettist' in *Illustrierte Neue Welt*, March 1984, p.12.

MUSIC

Vienna, as it had been at the end of the eighteenth century, was again at the end of the nineteenth the scene of a revolution in musical thought. This revolution was centred on what came to be known as the Second Viennese School. The leader of this school was Arnold Schoenberg, who was of Jewish descent. His most famous pupils, however, Berg and Webern, were not. It is thus wrong to talk, as has been done, of this new music being somehow 'Jewish', as if only Jews can write it and understand it.[55]

That said, Jews certainly did play a pivotal rôle in the life of modern music in Vienna around 1900. The great composers in Vienna in the second half of the nineteenth century were Brahms and Bruckner, neither of whom were Jewish (nor for that matter Viennese). There were, however, prominent Jewish composers as well, Karl Goldmark and Ignaz Brüll.[56] Goldmark was especially important in that he was the first composer in Vienna to adopt Wagnerian methods for his operas.[57] He was also an admirer and supporter early on of the great successor to the Viennese heritage, Gustav Mahler. Goldmark made a special point of emphasizing Mahler's great talent while Mahler was still at the Konservatorium.[58] He also employed Mahler's closer friend and advisor, Siegfried Lipiner, himself Jewish, to write the libretto of his opera *Merlin*.[59] Mahler appears, not surprisingly, to have solicited Goldmark's help in obtaining the appointment to the Vienna Court Opera in 1897.[60] There was thus some sort of Jewish presence in the musical world before Mahler arrived.

With Mahler began the transformation of music which was to result in Schoenberg's twelve-tone theory. While there were great composers in Vienna such as Hugo Wolf, it was Mahler and Schoenberg who embodied the revolutionary change. The two knew each other personally, and, from tense beginnings, came to share a great mutual respect. The original link between them, in both personal and musical terms, was Alexander von Zemlinsky, the teacher of Schoenberg and also of Alma Schindler before she married Mahler. These three – Mahler, Zemlinsky and Schoenberg – were at the centre of the shift in musical thought.[61] All three were Jewish.

[55] For instance, Ernst Ansermet's attitude to Schoenberg in *Les Fondements de la Musique dans la Conscience Humaine* discussed in Peter Gradenwitz, 'Jews in Austrian Music' in J. Fraenkel, ed., *The Jews of Austria*, p.23.

[56] Tietze, *Die Juden Wiens*, p.214.

[57] On Goldmark's Wagnerianism, see Karl Goldmark, *Erinnerungen aus meinem Leben* (Vienna 1922) p.77. Also see Caroline von Gomperz-Bettelheim, *Biographische Blätter* (Vienna 1915) pp.17–31.

[58] Kurt Blaukopf, *Mahler: a Documentary Study* (London 1976) p.162.

[59] Goldmark, *Erinnerungen*, p.153.

[60] Herta Singer, *Im Wiener Kaffeehaus* (Vienna 1959) p.243.

[61] H. H. Stuckenschmidt, *Schoenberg: his Life, World and Work* (London 1977) pp.101–14.

Zemlinsky had come from a Sephardic Jewish family and his father had written the official history of the Sephardic community in Vienna.[62] Franz Schreker, another Viennese modernist, was also partly Jewish by descent.[63]

It was then left to Schoenberg and his school to explore the possibilities of atonality, and to devise the twelve-tone method of composition. Schoenberg's circle was not uniquely Jewish, as the cases of Berg and Webern prove. However, while there are no statistical figures on which to draw, it again appears that there were many people of Jewish descent around Schoenberg in Vienna. These include such figures as David Josef Bach, Egon Wellesz, Erwin Stein, Paul A. Pisk, Heinrich Jalowetz and Hanns Eisler, and one might also mention Erich Wolfgang Korngold and Rudolf Réthi. All played a major rôle in modern music in Vienna.[64] Quite how large the Jewish contingent was in the Schoenberg circle (or the Mahler circle for that matter) is a matter for conjecture, but the impression is that it was a very major one.

In other fields of musical endeavour also in Vienna Jews were very much to the fore. The founder of the Viennese School of Musicology, Guido Adler, was Jewish.[65] The leader of the Philharmonic, Arnold Rosé, was as well, in addition to being Mahler's brother-in-law. Then there is a very long list of famous virtuosi, with names such as Eduard Steuermann, Rudolf Serkin, Alfred Grünfeld, Rudolf Kolisch (Schoenberg's second brother-in-law), the cellist David Popper, and, most famous of all, Joseph Joachim. There were also the conductors Bruno Walter and Otto Klemperer, and the singers Selma Kurz, Richard Tauber and Marya Freund among many others. Marie Pappenheim wrote the libretto for Schoenberg's *Erwartung*, and, at Universal Edition, Emil Hertzka was the main publisher of the new music. All of these people were of Jewish descent.[66] One of the major musical salons of the city and a great centre of patronage was the Wittgenstein house.[67]

Such facts give only a vague, perhaps misleading, impression of the extent of Jewish involvement in Vienna's musical revolution, and it should be borne in mind that there were others such as Richard Strauss, Hugo Wolf, and among performers Anna Bahr-Mildenburg. Until further research is undertaken, we can but conjecture; yet Jews do seem to have

---

[62] On the background of Alexander von Zemlinsky, see the *Geburtsbücher* of the *Israelitische Kultusgemeinde* (copies) for 1871. Also see Fraenkel, ed., *The Jews of Austria*, p.327 on the father, Adolf von Zemlinsky.

[63] Information from Dr Renate Heuer, Frankfurt-on-Main.

[64] For a list of Schoenberg's circle, see Stuckenschmidt, *Schoenberg*, p.80. The Jewish descent of these figures is confirmed in the files of the *Bibliographica Judaica*.

[65] See Guido Adler's autobiography, *Wollen und Wirken* (Vienna 1935).

[66] Jewish origin confirmed by Kaznelson, *Juden im deutschen Kulturbereich*, and the files of the *Bibliographica Judaica*.

[67] Allan Janik and Stephen Toulmin, *Wittgenstein's Vienna* (New York 1973) p.169.

played a leading rôle, especially in the modern movement, in Viennese musical life.[68]

The aesthetic world of *fin-de-siècle* Vienna is dominated by the *art nouveau* movement as expressed in the Secession and Wiener Werkstätte. These have an importance in Viennese cultural history which parallels that of Young Vienna. Indeed they can be viewed as equivalents, and have been.[69] A study of the membership of the Secession should tell us, therefore, what the involvement of Jews in the art world was.

It appears to have been minimal.[70] There were, it is true, several artists of Jewish descent associated with the group, such as Eugen Jettel, Max Kurzweil, Emil Orlik and Max Oppenheimer, but the number of Jews who were painters was relatively small, at least around 1900.[71]

There *were* Jewish painters, such as the traditional academicists Isidor Kaufmann and Jehudo Epstein, the society portraitist Horowitz and the impressionists Tina Blau-Lang and Broncia Koller-Pinell.[72] The most significant case of a painter of Jewish descent was probably that of Richard Gerstl, who had a Jewish father. Gerstl was Schoenberg's painting instructor, and together, as a recent exhibition has shown, they developed their style to an extreme expressionism. Some of Gerstl's last paintings, before he committed suicide over Mathilde Schoenberg in 1908, are spectacularly free in their use of colour and line, and seem stylistically to anticipate later art. It should be remembered that by 1908 neither Kokoschka nor Schiele had developed their expressionist styles, and that Kokoschka's *Die träumenden Knaben*, though anarchic in intent, is still in a very ornamental idiom. Gerstl had by that time progressed far beyond ornamentalism, and was already dead.[73]

Such cases, however, were exceptions. It is not the case that there were no Jewish painters in Vienna, but it is true that the main Viennese movement in modern art was led by Klimt, Egon Schiele and Oskar Kokoschka, none of whom were Jewish. Similarly, in the applied arts, it was Kolo Moser, Alfred Roller and Josef Hoffmann who were the leading

---

[68] Cf. Manfred Wagner's comments in Marchetti, ed., *Wien um 1900: Kunst und Kultur,* p.405.

[69] Carl E. Schorske, 'Generational Tension and Cultural Change: Reflections on the Case of Vienna' in *Daedalus* Fall 1978, pp.111–22.

[70] Interview with Dr Robert Waissenberger, Vienna, 24 February 1984.

[71] Kaznelson, *Juden im deutschen Kulturbereich*, pp.84ff; Harry Zohn, '*Fin de Siècle* Vienna: the Jewish contribution' in J. Reinharz and W. Schatzberg, eds., *The Jewish response to German Culture* (Hanover, New Hampshire, 1985) p.146

[72] *Ibid.* pp.83ff; also see *Le Arti a Vienna*, catalogue of the exhibition at Palazzo Grassi (Venice 1984).

[73] See *Richard Gerstl: Katalog*, eds. Breicha, Kassal-Mikula and W. Deutschmann (Vienna 1983); also *Vienne 1880–1938: l'apocalypse joyeuse* (Paris 1986) pp.440–75.

figures in the Wiener Werkstätte. The plastic component of Viennese culture was the creation of people not of Jewish descent. When we look at the support for these people, on the other hand, a familiar picture emerges. Whether it was the propaganda in the press, financial support, the provision of contacts with artistic groups in other countries, or even the chance, through the salon, to make contact with the rest of Viennese culture, the social support for the Secession appears to have been heavily Jewish.

Two of the major critics who propagandized for the new art were of Jewish descent: Ludwig Hevesi and Berta Zuckerkandl. Hevesi was the man who devised the motto for the new *Sezessionsgebäude*: 'To the time its art; to art its freedom.'[74] Berta Zuckerkandl, through her close contacts with the Parisian cultural élite (her sister was married to Paul Clemenceau), engineered the visit of August Rodin to Vienna in 1902.[75] It was in her salon that some of the first talk of founding the Secession occurred.[76] Her apartment in the Oppolzergasse was naturally fitted out by Josef Hoffmann.[77] She was, in many ways, the main propagandist of the movement, with Hevesi and Bahr. When Hoffmann was made a *Regierungsrat* in 1912, she wrote a letter congratulating him. In this letter she envisaged the other members of the Secession receiving similar honours, Klimt becoming 'Klimt von Frauentrieb' for example. On Hoffmann's title she wrote: 'And it is a very smart move for our revolution to obtain a lick of black-yellow paint: stupid Vienna is slowly coming round.' She thus identified very strongly with 'our revolution'.[78]

The question of patronage is a difficult one. For various reasons the Secession and the artists and architects associated with it received at one time or another substantial public patronage. This is especially true of the architect Otto Wagner, who, for instance, was commissioned to design the psychiatric institute Am Steinhof, and in turn gave much of the work for the decorations of the famous church to his friends in the Wiener Werkstätte.[79] Klimt also received a great deal of public patronage, as the notorious affair of the *Deckengemälde* makes plain.[80] Many of the artists were also employees of the state, including Hoffmann and Roller, both

---

[74] 'Der Zeit ihre Kunst; der Kunst ihre Freiheit.' Christian M. Nebehay, *Ver Sacrum: 1898–1903* (Munich 1979) p.31.

[75] Berta Zuckerkandl, *Österreich Intim: Erinnerungen 1892–1942* (Frankfurt 1970) pp.56–62.

[76] K. Blaukopf, *Mahler: a Documentary Study*, p.223, quotes Ludwig Hevesi on the central rôle played by the Zuckerkandl salon.

[77] Information from Graf Tamare, Vienna.

[78] 'Und sehr geschickt dass unsere Revolution ein bissl schwarzgelben Anstrich bekommt: blöd Wien schleicht darum.' Letter to Joseph Hofmann, February 1912, in the Manuscript Collection of the Stadtbibliothek, Vienna, no. I.N.158.767.

[79] On Otto Wagner's Am Steinhof, see *Traum und Wirklichkeit*, cat. pp.92–7, 106–13.

[80] Schorske, *Fin-de-Siècle Vienna*, pp.208–45.

professors.[81] It is as well to remember that the artists who led the new movement in art were not as alienated from the Establishment as might at first appear.[82]

When it comes to private patronage, however, it does seem that this was predominantly provided by Jews. Hence the *Sezessionsgebäude* itself is reputed to have been financed by Ludwig Wittgenstein's father Karl.[83] The Wiener Werkstätte was almost exclusively financed by the son of a Jewish textile manufacturer, Fritz Wärndorfer, who eventually had to be shipped off to the United States because he threatened to sink the whole family fortune, as well as his own, in the financial fiasco of the Werkstätte.[84] Further circumstantial evidence is provided by the names of the society ladies whom Klimt painted: these include Margarete Stonborough (Wittgenstein's sister), Adele Bloch-Bauer, Serena Lederer, Elisabeth Bachofen-Echt (the Lederers' daughter), Hermine Gallia, Frederike Maria Beer, all of whom were from Jewish backgrounds.[85] The person with by far the best collection of Klimt's work, and the man who helped Klimt out in the *Deckengemälde* affair, was August Lederer, who was also a voter in the electoral roll of the Jewish community.[86] Two of the leading members of the Secession, Josef Engelhardt and Kolo Moser, married into the wealthy Mauthner-Markhof family, which had a Jewish distiller as its dynastic ancestor.[87]

Individual cases such as these have led historians of the Secession, including James Shedel, to suggest that the great majority of the private patrons of the new art were Jewish or of Jewish descent. If this is somewhere near the truth, it is hardly surprising that the Secession came

[81] Peter Vergo, *Art in Vienna 1898–1918* (London 1975) pp.129 (on Hoffmann), 156 (on Roller).

[82] For a similar view see James Shedel, *Art and Society: the New Art Movement in Vienna 1897–1914* (Palo Alto 1981) p.60.

[83] Janik and Toulmin, *Wittgenstein's Vienna*, p.172.

[84] Lecture by Peter Vergo at the Edinburgh Festival 1983, 23 August 1983; cf. Nicholas Powell, *The Sacred Spring: the Arts in Vienna 1898–1914* (London 1974) p.92.

[85] On Adele Bloch-Bauer, information from her niece Bettina Ehrlich, London, 4 January 1984; on Hermine Gallia, information from Frieda von Hofmannsthal (Gallia), London, 31 May 1984; on the Lederers, mother and daughter, see C. M. Nebehay, *Gustav Klimt und Egon Schiele und die Familie Lederer* (Berne 1987) p.27. See also Schorske, *Fin-de-Siècle Vienna*, p.264.

[86] Lederer appears in the *Verzeichnis der im Wiener Gemeindegebiete wohnhaften Wähler für die Wahlen in den Kultusvorstand und der Vertrauensmänner im Jahre 1910* (Vienna 1910); on the relations of the Lederer family to Klimt, see Nebehay, *Klimt, Schiele und die Familie Lederer*, also C. M. Nebehay, *Gustav Klimt* (Munich 1976) pp.142–3. On his rôle in the *Deckengemälde* affair, see Alice Strobl, 'Zu den Fakultätsbildern von Gustav Klimt' in *Albertina Studien*, II (Vienna 1964), notes 88 (p.168) and 124 (p.169). On Klimt and his Jewish clients, see Powell, *Sacred Spring*, p.144.

[87] Nebehay, *Ver Sacrum*, p.90; on the history of the family, see Jäger-Sunstenau, '*Die geadelten Judenfamilien*', pp.154–5.

to be known as 'le goût juif', for, as far as the people who bought it are concerned, it was.[88]

There is an interesting epilogue to the Jewish support of the non-Jewish *Sezession*. Between the wars Jews began to assume a more important position in the art world as artists. There were people such as Georg Ehrlich, Heinrich Sussmann and Rudolph Ray-Rappaport.[89] Ironically, this process continued after the Second World War in a city almost devoid of Jews. One of the major schools of art in Vienna today is the school of Fantastic Realism, whose mentor was Albert Paris Gütersloh. According to Ernst Fuchs, of the five leading representatives of the school, four, Fuchs himself, Arik Brauer, Arnold Hausner and Hutter, are of at least partly Jewish descent. Friedrich Hundertwasser, the fifth and best known in the group, is also on record as claiming Jewish descent. Certainly there is a large irony in the fact that three of Vienna's leading artists, Fuchs, Hundertwasser and Brauer, consciously use Jewish imagery in their work.[90]

ARCHITECTURE

What can be said for art can also be said for architecture, as far as Jewish involvement is concerned. The major architects of Viennese modernity, Otto Wagner and Adolf Loos, were not Jewish.[91] Yet, especially in the case of Loos, much of his patronage came from Jews.[92] Most importantly, the famous (or infamous) Looshaus on the Michaelerplatz in Vienna was commissioned by the Jewish tailor Leopold Goldman for his firm Goldman

[88] See James Shedel, *Art and Society*, p.61; also see *Die Fackel*, no.44, mid June, 1900, p.15. For the rôle Jews played as patrons for Expressionism, see Oskar Kokoschka, *My Life* (London 1974) p.35.

[89] On Georg Enrlich, information from Bettina Ehrlich, London, 4 January 1984, also Bettina Ehrlich, *Georg Ehrlich 1897–1966: biographische Notizen*; on Heinrich Sussmann, interview with the artist, Vienna, 7 June 1983; on Rudolf Ray-Rapaport, interview with the artist, London, 4 January 1984. Also interview with Viktor Matejka, Vienna, 21 November 1983.

[90] Interview with Ernst Fuchs, 15 May 1984. Manina Tischler, herself the daughter of a Viennese Jewish painter of some repute, Viktor Tischler, expressed some scepticism about Ernst Fuchs' claims about the descent of the various artists, especially with respect to his claim that Hundertwasser was not of Jewish descent. (Indeed Hundertwasser himself has reputedly made this claim, see Avram Kampf, *The Jewish Experience in the Art of the Twentieth Century* (South Hadley, Mass. 1984) pp.119–20.) Be that as it may, the consciously Jewish element in the painting of Fuchs and Brauer is remarkable in the present Viennese context. Interview with Manina Tischler, Venice, 1 May 1985.

[91] Loos was definitely not Jewish, despite claims to the contrary, for example, Johnston, *The Austrian Mind*, p.269.

[92] Information from Yehuda Safran, London. Richard Calvacoressi also informs me that Knize, one of Loos' main business patrons, was owned by the Jewish family, Wolf, later Knize-Wolf. Also see Burkhardt Rukschcio and Roland Schachel, *Adolf Loos: Leben und Werk* (Salzburg 1982) p.295.

& Salatsch.[93] While before the First World War, as in art, not many of the major architects were Jewish, after the war several major figures did emerge, such as Paul Engelmann, Loos' assistant and a friend of Wittgenstein, Josef Frank, brother of the philosopher Philipp Frank, and Oskar Strnad, Max Reinhardt's principal stage designer between the wars.[94] However, as in the art world, the Jewish participation here was later and less spectacular than in many of the other cultural spheres.

AN EXAMPLE FROM WITHIN THE CULTURAL ÉLITE

A small episode, unearthed by Ulrich Weinzierl, illustrates the type of milieu in which the small group of the cultural élite lived. It concerns the background to Schnitzler's unfinished play, *Das Wort* (recently performed in Vienna for the first time). The plot of the play was originally written down not by Schnitzler, but by Hofmannsthal.[95] In Schnitzler's version, a young artist, Willi Langer, starts an affair with a married woman, which continues until the point is reached where he forces the woman to ask her husband for her freedom. The husband laughs her down and refuses. The artist, in despair, asks his friend, Anastasius Treuenhof, what he should do next. Treuenhof says what he *should* do is kill himself, but what he *will* do is get over it and carry on living. Langer, not seeing the sardonic humour of the remark, goes off and shoots himself. The play becomes a moral lesson about the responsibility of language:

TREUENHOF Words are nothing.
WINKLER Words are everything. We do not have anything else.[96]

This makes an interesting background to the concept of Wittgenstein's Vienna, but in this context the events of Schnitzler's play have a further significance for they were based on fact. The characters portray real people and there was a young man who committed suicide in similar circumstances. This was the 'plot' which Hofmannsthal had sketched out and which Schnitzler recast. The real people represented in the play are:

---

[93] See Helmut Weihsmann, *Wiener Moderne 1910–38* (Vienna 1983); also see the article by Friedrich Achleitner on Austria's inter-war architecture in Norbert Leser, ed., *Das geistige Leben Wiens* pp.277–92. The Jewish origin of Oskar Strnad is given in Kaznelson, and confirmed in the *Hauptkatalog* of his school, the Realschule im I. Bezirk.

[94] In Alfred Polgar, *Sperrsitz*, ed. U. Weinzierl, with an essay by Weinzierl, *Wien, Jahrhundertwende, der junge Alfred Polgar* (Vienna 1980) p.236–43.

[95] *Ibid.* p.236.

[96] 'Treuenhof – Worte sind nichts. Winkler – Worte sind alles. Wir haben ja nichts anderes.' *Ibid.* p.243.

ANASTASIUS TREUENHOF – Peter Altenberg
LINA VAN ZACK (the married woman) – Lina Loos
THE HUSBAND – Adolf Loos
GLEISSNER – Alfred Polgar
RAPP – Stefan Grossmann
WILLI LANGER – Heinz Lang
WINKLER – Schnitzler

Heinz Lang committed suicide in 1904 after being spurned by Lina Loos in the manner which Schnitzler's play describes. He came from one of the families at the centre of Viennese culture. His mother was Marie Lang, the women's rights campaigner. His father was the lawyer, Edmund Lang. They were great friends of Rosa Mayreder and had been close to the composer, Hugo Wolf.[97] Marie Lang was the centre of the 'colony' that used to gather in Schloss Bellevue above Grinzing in the summer months.[98] Marie Lang came from an old Viennese family and was part of what there was of a native liberal bourgeoisie. Her husband, however, had been born into a Jewish family in 1860, the son of a factory owner, Leopold Lang. Edmund had converted to Protestantism, probably at marriage. Perhaps even more revealing, however, is the fact that his mother had been Ernestine von Hofmannsthal.[99] When Hofmannsthal wrote down the plot, he was, consciously or unconsciously, describing the fate of a cousin, however distant. This was the extent of assimilation.

Of the main protagonists in the play, Loos and his wife are alone in not being of at least partially Jewish descent. All the others in the list above were, to some extent, products of the Jewish assimilation.

THE GENERAL IMPRESSION

The background to a play by Schnitzler is no guarantee of the ethnic composition of the cultural élite as a whole. It is, after all, an élite seen from Schnitzler's perspective. Yet it is, I think, a pointer; it shows that the élite

---

[97] On Rosa Mayreder, see her autobiography, *Das Haus in der Landskrongasse* (Vienna 1948).

[98] Friedrich Eckstein, *Alte unnennbare Tage!* (Vienna 1936) p.183; on Marie Lang, see entry in *Österreichisches Biographisches Lexikon (ÖBL).*

[99] Edmund Lang's Jewish origin is mentioned in Stefan Grossmann, *Ich war begeistert: eine Lebensgechichte* (Berlin 1931) p.160. Confirmation of this was found by finding the rough date of Lang's death in the *ÖBL* entry for Marie Lang. The exact date of death, 6 April 1918, was then found by searching through the *Todesbeschauprotokolle* in the Stadtarchiv. This gave the date of birth of the deceased, which was then traced in the *Geburtsbücher* (copies) of the *Israelitische Kultusgemeinde*, stored in the 7th District, in the Kandlgasse. Here the entry for Edmund Lang was found. He was born on 12 November 1860.

was not all Jewish, and it would be most odd if it were. On the other hand, this example, taken together with our analyses of the other fields, does indicate an enormous Jewish presence in the élite and, in many of the most important groups, a predominant one. It is true that this presence is patchy, with a far smaller creative involvement in the graphic arts than the other fields (something predictable given the Jewish religion's hostile attitude to the graven image). Yet, even in those fields where they were not creative, Jews played a very large rôle in supporting the new culture. Given the kind of proportions we have come across in the preceding pages, we can see very clearly why there has been a long tradition of describing Viennese modern high culture as 'Jewish'. I would also suggest that such a presence makes any attempt at a comprehensive picture of Viennese culture which were to ignore the Jewish aspect look rather foolhardy.

It appears that, while Vienna's cultural élite was not uniquely Jewish, and the proportions varied between cultural fields and groups, Jews did provide a substantial majority of the élite in general and an overwhelming one in many individual groups. This raises several questions of context, cause and effect. Most immediately, was the Jewish presence in the small groups of the élite reflected in the social context of the culture? Was, in other words, the liberal educated class, the audience of this culture, similarly largely Jewish? At a more fundamental level, how was it possible for people of Jewish descent to be so predominant in the cultural élite? Can this be explained in readily acceptable sociological and cultural terms, or must we adopt some sort of quasi-metaphysical explanation on the lines of a special, innate propensity of Jews for intellectual innovation (otherwise termed decadent, materialist abstraction)?

The third and by far the most complicated question is that, given this large Jewish presence, however it came about, was it a significant aspect of these individuals that they were of Jewish descent? Can we talk of a 'Jewish element' in Viennese culture at the turn of the century and, if so, in what way? Before we tackle that, it would be as well to answer the first two questions which we have set ourselves.

3

The social context

The social reservoir of the cultural élite of *fin-de-siècle* Vienna, and its audience, was the liberal educated class. How one would define such a class is open to debate; my own attempt at a definition, as a subset of the liberal bourgeoisie, is given below. Most would accept, however, that the backbone of such a class, and its leading sector, would include the members of the university and of the liberal professions: law, medicine and journalism. The Jewish presence in these areas will be looked at in turn. In addition, the cultural world of the liberal bourgeoisie in Vienna had as its two central, but informal, institutions the salon and the coffee-house – these are always taken to have been the milieu of the *fin de siècle*. We will also look at these to see what rôle the Jewish part of Viennese society played in the social context of the culture.

JEWS IN VIENNA UNIVERSITY

Students

Vienna University was the most prestigious centre of learning in the Monarchy, and, as a national centre, attracted students from a large catchment area of which Vienna was only a part. Hence the student body was more a national élite than a Viennese one. That said, the Jewish presence, by religion, was very considerable. Table 1 shows that at one point in the late 1880s Jews made up one third of all students at the University, though this was a peak which declined by 1904 to just under 24 per cent, a decline which one commentator partly blamed on the antisemitism of a large part of Vienna's student body.[1] The strength of the Jewish presence varied between the faculties, as Table 2 shows. Until after the First World war the medical faculty had by far the highest proportion of Jews, a situation partly due to the influx of poor Jewish students from

---

[1] Jakob Thon, ed., *Die Juden in Österreich* (Berlin 1908) p.101.

Table 1. *The proportion of Jews in the student body of Vienna University*
1881–1904

Year	Total	Jews	Percentage
1881–6	3,456	1,706	33·00
1886–91	3,875	1,905	33·00
1891–6	3,939	1,621	29·20
1896–1901	4,660	1,527	24·80
1901–04	5,027	1,561	23·70

Source: Die Juden in Österreich: Veröffentlichung des Bureaus für Statistik der Juden,
ed. Jakob Thon (Berlin 1908) p. 104.

Table 2. *The proportion of Jews in the separate faculties 1880–1926*
(percentage)

Year	Law	Medicine	Philosophy
1880[a]	22·30	38·60	15·50
1890[b]	22·00	48·00	15·00
1914[c]	25·81	40·56	16·43
1926[c]	24·20	33·84	34·26

Sources: [a] Berthold Windt, 'Die Juden an den Mittel- und Hochschulen Österreichs
seit 1850' in *Statistische Monatschrift,* 7 (1881) pp. 452–5.
[b] Hans Tietze, *Die Juden Wiens* (Vienna 1935) p. 232.
[c] Leo Goldhammer, *Die Juden Wiens: eine statistische Studie* (Vienna 1927) p. 40.

the eastern part of the Monarchy, which gave rise to one of the first events
in the growth of antisemitism in Vienna, Billroth's speech of 1875.[2]

That up to a third of all students in the University were Jewish is a fact
which gains in significance once the context of the University is taken
into account. The main practical purpose of a university education in
Austria had always been to provide the state with enough teachers and
civil servants to fill the ranks. The University was thus for what might
be termed the 'official intelligentsia' and not really for the 'liberal
intelligentsia'. Moreover, as we shall see, this 'official intelligentsia' was by
no means an automatic ally of its liberal counterpart. When it is further
considered that the prospect of a career as a teacher or official at the higher
levels, the traditional course for a graduate, was not open to Jews unless
they converted, then the Jewish presence becomes quite remarkable. Add

[2] Klaus Lohrmann, ed., *1,000 Jahre österreichisches Judentum* (Eisenstadt 1982) pp.161ff.

to this the fact that from the 1880s onwards racial antisemitism was fashionable in a wide swathe of the student body, then it does begin to look as if most of the students who would have retained a liberal outlook and gone on to be part of a liberal educated class would have been Jewish.[3]

University teachers

While, generally speaking, the student body ceased being part of the liberal educated class, the professorate remained liberal. There is a major difficulty in assessing the Jewish presence in the teaching body of the University, which is that, as is well known, many of the best minds in Austria had to convert to get on in the academic world. The result was a spate of conversions. Rabbi Dr Bloch recalled in his memoirs how he refuted a charge that Jews were taking over the medical and legal faculties by showing that, of the fifty-five professors in the two faculties whom the antisemitic deputy Türk claimed to be of Jewish descent, only one in each faculty was a full professor and Jewish by religion. The twenty-two other teaching members of the two faculties who were Jewish by religion were either *Privatdozenten* or *ausserordentliche Professoren*, that is to say, according to Bloch, unpaid.[4] This was in 1885. Hans Tietze saw the same phenomenon in the figures for the medical faculty of 1894. Then there were two *ordinarii*, fourteen *extraordinarii* and thirty-seven *Privatdozenten* of the Jewish faith. For Tietze this illustrated the fact that the full professorships, being high government posts, came under the same rules as the rest of the bureaucracy: no Jews without conversion.[5] To find the underlying Jewish presence therefore requires looking at the question of descent rather than religion.

There are no statistics which take this into account (apart from those of Türk!). Therefore the required data has to be reconstructed. If the list of lecturers given in the lecture list (*Vorlesungsverzeichnis*) of the University for the year 1910 is taken as our base, then, by using various sources, we can arrive at the figures given in Table 3.[6] These figures are a very

[3] For a thorough study of the social composition of the student body of Vienna University which tends to this conclusion, see Gary B. Cohen, 'Die Studenten der Wiener Universität von 1860 bis 1900: ein soziales und geographisches Profil' in R. G. Plaschka and K. Mack, eds., Wegenetz europäischen Geistes II: Universitäten und Studenten (Vienna 1987), pp.290–316.

[4] Dr Joseph S. Bloch, *Erinnerungen aus meinem Leben* (Vienna 1922) p.261.

[5] Hans Tietze, *Die Juden Wiens* (Vienna 1935) p.232.

[6] The list of lecturers in the *Vorlesungsverzeichnis* for the summer semester 1910 was taken as representative of the teaching body of the university. The names on the list were then traced in the Viennese address book, *Lehmann*. The address list was then compared with four main sources: a) Helmut Leitner, *Alphabetisches Register wissenschaftlich bedeutender Mediziner jüdischer Abstammung in Österreich (mit Einschluss der Emigranten).* (A copy

Table 3. *The Jewish presence, by descent, in the teaching faculties of Vienna University in the summer semester 1910*

Faculty	Jews	Total	Percentage
Law	24 (26)	64	37·5 (40·6)
Medicine	131 (152)	256	51·2 (59·4)
Philosophy	36	167	21·6
Total	191 (214)	487	39·2 (43·9)

Source: Öffentliche Vorlesungen an d. KK. Universität Wien, Sommer 1910 (Vienna 1910); see also note 6, p. 35.

conservative estimate of the Jewish presence in the faculties, as it is in the nature of the process that we can but ascertain the core of the Jewish presence, not its full extent. The figures given in brackets are a calculation of the proven figures plus a half of those names which look as if they might have been Jewish, but which cannot as yet be proven (e.g. Samuel Jellinek, Bertold Spitzer), and which have been marked out by the two experts in the field, Dr Heuer and Dr Jaeger-Sunstenau. These figures are probably a better reflection of the true situation. Thus it looks very much as if half of the medical faculty was of Jewish descent, well over a third in the legal faculty, over a fifth in the philosophical faculty, and over 40 per cent in the three faculties taken together. Considering that there was the problem over conversion for the higher posts (especially in the philosophical faculty), and that even converts could face problems with promotion, these figures show a very high Jewish presence in the official academic intelligentsia of the capital.[7] It is also notable that the faculty with the largest Jewish presence, the medical faculty, was by far the most renowned of the three.[8]

of this was kindly allowed me by Dr Leitner at the Institut für die Geschichte der Medizin, Vienna.) b) *Verzeichnis der im Weiner Gemeindegebiete wohnhaften Wähler für die Wahlen in den Kultusvorstand und der Vertrauensmänner im Jahre* 1910 (Vienna 1910). (A copy of this was kindly provided by Professor Ivar Oxaal, Hull.) c) The archives and file index of the office of the *Bibliographica Judaica*, directed by Dr Renate Heuer, Frankfurt-on-Main. d) The genealogical archives of Dr Hanns Jäger-Sunstenau, Vienna. With these and other sources the results of Table 3 were obtained.

[7] *Theodor Gomperz: ein Gelehrtenleben im Bürgertum der Franz-Josephszeit*, eds. H. Gomperz and R. A. Kann (Vienna 1974) pp.67–8, on awareness of this problem. Also, on converts, R. A. Métall, *Hans Kelsen: Leben und Werk* (Vienna 1969) pp.10–11.

[8] William M. Johnston, *The Austrian Mind: an Intellectual and Social History 1848–1938* (Berkeley 1972, 1983) pp.221–38.

Table 4. *The Jewish presence, by religion, in the groups of lawyers and doctors*

	Lawyers			Doctors		
Year	Jews	Total	Percentage	Jews	Total	Percentage
1880[a]	—	—	—	1,015	2,140	47·43
1881[b]	—	—	—	—	—	61·00
1890[c]	394	681	57·92	—	—	—
	(310)	(360)	(86·11)	—	—	—
1930[a]	—	—	—	—	4,110	50·00
1936[d]	1,341	2,163	62·00	1,531	3,268	47·18

Note: 1880 figures for Austria; others for Vienna. Figures in brackets show number of *Advokatur* candidates.
Sources: [a] K. Lohrmann, ed., *1,000 Jahre österreichisches Judentum* (Eisenstadt 1982) p. 166.
[b] W. Bihl, 'Die Juden', in *Die Habsburgermonarchie 1848–1918*, eds. A. Wandruszka and P. Urbanitsch, vol. 2, part 2, p. 911.
[c] Hans Tietze, *Die Juden Wiens* (Vienna 1935) p. 232.
[d] Sylvia Maderegger, *Die Juden im österreichischen Ständestaat 1934–8* (Vienna 1973) p. 220. Quoted from Leo Goldhammer's article in *Der Jude* 14 January 1938.

LIBERAL PROFESSIONS – LAW AND MEDICINE

The liberal professions of law and medicine can be regarded as providing a large part of any liberal educated class. To be a lawyer (*Advokat*) in liberal bourgeois society in Vienna meant being an intellectual.[9] Amongst the doctors in Viennese society, one might mention Freud, Schnitzler and Victor Adler as evidence that the medical profession made a sizeable contribution to Viennese cultural life.

In the legal profession in Vienna there was a special circumstance in that there was a virtual bar on people of Jewish faith obtaining a state-paid post in the judicial hierarchy. Therefore the only road open to a Jew who refused to convert was a career as a lawyer. This explains to some extent the large majority which Jews had in the group of Viennese lawyers, as shown in Table 4. These figures are by religion alone. Quite how many lawyers were of Jewish descent is an open question. According to at least one contemporary, Dr Michael Stern, now the senior lawyer in Vienna, the proportion of Jews by descent was approaching three-quarters by the 1920s. The Jewish presence in the judiciary itself can only be guessed at present, and one can only point at the list of great Jewish converts in the

[9] *Käthe Leichter: Leben und Werk*, ed. Herbert Steiner (Vienna 1973) p.242–3.

legal world given in an earlier section. Dr Stern has suggested that roughly half of the higher judiciary in inter-war Vienna was of Jewish descent.[10]

In the medical profession also it did not pay to be Jewish. There is at least one reported case where a Jewish doctor was refused a job because of his religion, and this was probably a common occurrence.[11] Here again conversion could be a great help in getting the well-paid positions in the hospital hierarchy. There is thus a need to revise the figures for the medical profession upwards to account for conversions. Hence Table 4 shows a situation where Jews make up well over half of Vienna's doctors and lawyers from as early as the 1880s right up until 1938.

LIBERAL PROFESSIONS – JOURNALISM

It is almost a cliché to say that the Viennese liberal press was very Jewish. The problem with antisemitic attacks on the 'Jewish press' was that, in Vienna at least, they were based on hard fact.[12] All the major daily newspapers of the liberal press were either owned or edited by people of Jewish descent. There were Bacher and Benedikt at the *Neue Freie Presse*, regarded by many as *The Times* of central Europe. This paper had a circulation rival in the *Neue Wiener Tagblatt*, whose founder and chief editor was Moritz Szeps. When Szeps left to start the rival *Wiener Tagblatt* in 1886, after a dispute with the board, the Singer brothers took it over. Then there was the evening *Wiener Allgemeine Zeitung*, edited by Theodor Hertzka, and later by Szeps' son, Julius. The socialist newspaper, the *Arbeiter Zeitung*, was edited by Friedrich Austerlitz. All these figures, the central actors in the history of the Viennese liberal press, were of Jewish descent.[13] This by no means exhausts the list of newspapers run by Jews. Even newspapers which were conservative in profile, clerical or anti-semitic, could be staffed by Jews. Tietze gives the example of the *Neue Wiener Journal*, but this was not the only case.[14] The history of Jewish journalism and of the Viennese press in general, it has been said, almost amount to the same thing.[15] Especially noteworthy is the fact that the

[10] Interview with Dr. Michael Stern, 23 January 1984.

[11] For the problems of acquiring medical posts as a Jew, see the *Neue Freie Presse* 18 August 1895, morning edition *(NFPm)* pp. 3–4.

[12] See John M. Boyer, *Political Radicalism in Late Imperial Vienna* (Chicago 1981) p.82. For the antisemitic viewpoint, see *Statistisches zur modernen Judenfrage*, by K. H. (pamphlet c.1905) pp. 5–29.

[13] On the Jewish presence in the press: Richard Grunberger, 'Jews in Austrian Journalism' in Joseph Fraenkel, ed., *The Jews of Austria* (London 1967) pp.83–94; Gerda Barth, 'Der Beitrag der Juden zur Entfaltung des Pressewesens in Wien zwischen 1848 und dem ersten Weltkrieg' in Lohrmann, ed., *1,000 Jahre*, pp.152–60; Tietze, *Juden Wiens*, pp.257–8.   [14] Tietze, *Juden Wiens*, p.258.

[15] In her article 'Der Beitrag der Juden', pp.152–3, Gerda Barth states: 'Die Geschichte der jüdischen Journalistik ist daher faktisch auch der Geschichte der Wiener Presse gleichzusetzen.'

three main cultural journals of the turn of the century were run primarily by Jews: *Die Zeit* by Heinrich Kanner and Isidor Singer, along with Hermann Bahr (not of Jewish descent), *Die Wage*, edited by Rudolf Lothar, and *Die Fackel*, by Karl Kraus.[16] At the editorial level of the liberal press the Jewish presence was dominant.

This leaves the question of the Jewish presence in the lower ranks, in the main body of journalists. The *Festschrift* of the journalists' and writers' society in Vienna, *Concordia*, contains a list of all the members of the society from its inception in 1859 to the year 1909 – the year of the *Festschrift's* publication.[17] This list also shows which of the members were still alive in that year. Using a similar procedure to that taken with the University faculties, we can compile a list of those members alive in 1909 who were of Jewish descent, and hence ascertain a figure for the Jewish presence in the group. Since the society was in effect the journalists' trade union, complete with pension scheme, it attracted journalists not only from the liberal press, but also from the more conservative papers.[18] Therefore the results of the survey show the Jewish presence not only in the liberal press, but also in much of the conservative press as well. At present the proven figure for the Jewish presence, out of a total membership of 359, is 185, 51·5 per cent. If we then, as with the professors, count in half of those names regarded by Dr Heuer and Dr Jäger-Sunstenau as probably Jewish, then the total goes up to 227, 63·2 per cent.

Such a figure has large implications for the cultural élite in Vienna, for the links between the press and such key groups as Young Vienna were very strong. This was an age when journalists were still regarded in liberal circles as 'knights of the intellect'.[19] In Vienna especially the *feuilleton* review was one of the great arbiters of taste. When Arthur Schnitzler wanted to prove the worth of his play *Liebelei* so that Burckhard would perform it (against the advice of Hermann Bahr), he persuaded Theodor Gomperz to ask Ludwig Speidel, the Burgtheater *feuilletoniste* for the *Neue Freie Presse*, to give his opinion. Speidel's praise meant that the performance went ahead.[20] Hanslick, Speidel's colleague for the music review, is well known to have ruled the musical taste of the whole city.[21] His successor was Julius Korngold. After 1918, the *feuilleton* staff of the

---

[16] The Jewish origin of Kanner, Singer and Lothar was confirmed in the file index of the *Bibliographica Judaica*.

[17] See Julius Stern, *Werden und Walten der Concordia* (Vienna 1909) pp.239–58.

[18] Information from Dr Peter Eppel, Vienna.

[19] 'Ritter vom Geiste', see Richard Kola, *Rückblick ins Gestrige: Erlebtes und Empfundenes* (Vienna 1922) p.56. On the influence of the press, see Edward Timms, *Karl Kraus: Apocalyptic Satirist: Culture and Catastrophe in Habsburg Vienna* (London 1986) pp.30–1.

[20] *Gomperz: ein Gelehrtenleben*, pp.252–4; D. G. Daviau, ed., *The Letters of Arthur Schnitzler to Hermann Bahr* (Chapel Hill 1978) p.19, on Bahr's criticism of Liebelei.

[21] Johnston, *The Austrian Mind*, pp.132–4; Allan Janik and Stephen Toulmin, *Wittgenstein's Vienna* (New York 1973) pp.35, 103–8.

Neue Freie Presse consisted of five of Vienna's best critics: Raoul
Auernheimer, Felix Salten, Ernst Lothar, Korngold and A. F. Seligmann.
All five were of at least partly Jewish descent.[22]

It should be pointed out that the Viennese press was not totally Jewish;
some of the most famous of the journalists, such as Bahr (and probably
Hanslick), were not of Jewish descent.[23] Nevertheless, the Jewish presence
was predominant. The reason for this is fairly obvious. Journalism was the
only career where you could get to the top without having to concern
yourself with the question of religion, something from which, as we have
seen, not even law and medicine were exempt.[24] The reason, however, is
not as important as the result: in an age when the press was the only mass
medium, cultural or otherwise, the liberal press was largely a Jewish
press.

CENTRES OF CULTURE – SALON AND COFFEE-HOUSE

The two institutions which provided the main milieu for liberal cultural life
in Vienna were the salon and the coffee-house. Neither lends itself to any
well-based statistical analysis, unlike the groups in the preceding sections.
The only evidence we have is that of contemporaries. This suggests,
however, a very high Jewish presence.

The salon as a centre of intellectual and cultural life was imported
to Vienna from Berlin by Fanny von Arnstein in the late eighteenth
century.[25] Salon life continued, according to Hilde Spiel and Sigmund
Mayer, to be dominated by Jewish hostesses throughout the nineteenth
century.[26] Fanny von Arnstein's daughter, Henriette Pereira, carried on
her mother's tradition. After her the greatest liberal salon in Vienna was
that of Josephine von Wertheimstein. She, in turn, was followed by Berta
Zuckerkandl, the daughter of Moritz Szeps. Her salon was intimately
connected with the creation of the *Sezession*, and it was there that Mahler
met Alma Schindler. While the Zuckerkandl salon courted *Jugendstil*
culture, the salon of Eugenia Schwarzwald was the meeting place for
Schoenberg, Loos, Kokoschka and others in the more radical set. All these
hostesses were Jewish.[27] There were also many salons on a much smaller

---

[22] List in Ernst Lothar, *Das Wunder des Überlebens: Erinnerungen und Ergebnisse* (Vienna
1966) p.45. Jewish descent was confirmed by the file index of the *Bibliographica
Judaica*.

[23] On Hanslick's non-Jewish descent, see Wolfdieter Bihl, 'Die Juden' in *Die Habsburger
Monarchie 1848–1918*, eds. A. Wandruszka and P. Urbanitsch, vol.2, part 2, p.931.

[24] Boyer, *Political Radicalism*, p.82.

[25] Hilde Spiel, 'Jewish Women in Austrian Culture' in Fraenkel, ed., *The Jews of Austria*,
pp.97–110, esp. pp.97–101; Sigmund Kaznelson, ed., *Juden im deutschen Kulturbereich:
ein Sammelwerk*, 3rd edn (Berlin 1962) pp.891ff.

[26] Spiel, 'Jewish Women', pp.99–109; Sigmund Mayer, *Die Wiener Juden: Kommerz,
Kultur, Politik 1700–1900* (Vienna 1918) pp.296–8, 364–5, 459–61.

[27] Spiel, 'Jewish Women', pp.97–109.

and more modest scale and it is impossible to tell how many of these were run by Jewish hostesses. It should be said that there were non-Jewish hostesses, such as Karoline Pichler or later Alma Mahler-Werfel.[28] Yet the evidence suggests that there was a tradition of the salon in Döbling run by a 'kulturbeflissene' Jewish lady where there was no such tradition in the non-Jewish world, where the salon is regarded as a *cultural*, and not mainly social institution.[29]

The impression given of the salon is the same for the coffee-house. It is a proverbial saying in Vienna that: 'The Jew belongs in the coffee-house.'[30] We can begin to understand this if we look at the major literary coffee-houses in the centre of Vienna. Café Griensteidl was the coffee-house most frequented by Young Vienna and immortalized by Karl Kraus in *Die demolierte Literatur*. We have seen that that group was largely Jewish. The next famous centre was Café Central, followed by Café Herrenhof after the First World War.[31] The impression given of the clientèle in both by contemporary reports is that it was predominantly Jewish. Milan Dubrovic, a young reporter at the time, himself not Jewish, claims that 80 per cent of the regulars around the intellectuals' *Stammtische* in the Café Herrenhof between the wars were Jewish.[32] This figure is perhaps a little generous, but the impression that the life of the coffee-house as a centre of modern culture was peopled mainly by Jews is confirmed by the characters who appear in Friedrich Torberg's set of anecdotes about coffee-house culture, *Die Tante Jolesch*, most of whom are Jewish. When Hugo Bettauer described the desertion of the coffee-houses in the centre of Vienna due to the Jewish expulsion, he was only pointing out a commonplace, that most of the significant figures in the coffee-houses important to cultural life were Jewish.[33]

A JEWISH LIBERAL EDUCATED CLASS?

People of Jewish descent appear to have been a substantial minority in the 'official intelligentsia' of academia and a substantial majority in the 'liberal intelligentsia' of the liberal professions. This seems also to have been reflected in the life of the salon and coffee-house. This strongly suggests that the liberal educated class was largely Jewish, and thus that the

[28] This point was made to me by Hilde Spiel, 15 March 1985, Vienna.
[29] The tradition of the Döbling villas was brought to my attention by Bruno and Gerda Frei, 12 October 1982, Klosterneuburg.   [30] 'Der Jud' gehört im Kaffeehaus.'
[31] *Das Wiener Kaffeehaus*, introduced by Hans Weigel (Vienna 1978) pp.56–80; Herta Singer, *Im Wiener Kaffeehaus* (Vienna 1959) pp.197–227, 256–59.
[32] Interview with Milan Dubrovic, 29 September 1983, Vienna.
[33] Friedrich Torberg, *Die Tante Jolesch, oder der Untergang des Abendlandes in Anekdoten* (Munich 1977); Torberg, *Die Erben der Tante Jolesch* (Munich 1981); Hugo Bettauer, *Die Stadt ohne Juden* (Vienna 1980 repr.); also Hartmut Binder, 'Ernst Polak – Literat ohne Werk' in *Jahrbuch der deutschen Schiller Gesellschaft*, 23 1979 (Stuttgart 1979) pp.366–415.

figures for the cultural groups taken singly are part of a larger phenomenon and not mere accident. It also implies that not only were the cultural producers Jewish, but also the consumers, the audience.[34]

It is, however, difficult to confirm this, and, even if we were to have, for example, lists of audiences at various performances, there would still be the problem of the reasons for the visit, as attending a cultural event is often a social action, nothing more. What we can do is look at the readership of one of the leading liberal newspapers, the *Neue Freie Presse*. Lists of readers no longer exist, if they ever did. What do exist are the death notices at the back of the newspaper. These are not a foolproof guide to who read the newspaper; the *Neue Freie Presse*, as a prestigious *Weltblatt*, would have carried the death notices of the figures of the Establishment and of people who would not have been regular readers.[35] Given these qualifications, the number of death notices in a given period which were for Jewish individuals would be some guide to the extent to which the readership of the *Neue Freie Presse* was Jewish. Between September 1900 and August 1901, on a rough calculation, 60 per cent of the death notices were for Jews (or people of Jewish descent). If half the doubtful cases are included, the figure becomes 64 per cent. This is a considerable figure; if it is an accurate reflection of the newspaper's readership, it is a revealing one.[36]

Such a figure would suggest that the oft-repeated claim that the liberal educated class of Vienna was mostly Jewish is based more on fact than fiction. This makes the predominance of Jews in specific cultural groups understandable, and indeed something to be expected. However, we are still left with the question of how it was that a tiny minority, such as the Jews represented in the Habsburg Monarchy, could come to play such a central rôle in the capital's liberal educated class, and from this in the circles of modern high culture. The next section offers some sort of explanation.

---

[34] Cf. Jakob Katz, 'German culture and the Jews' in Jehuda Reinharz and Walter Schatzberg, eds., *The Jewish Response to German Culture: from the Enlightenment to the Second World War* (Hanover, New Hampshire 1985) pp.85–99.

[35] Adam Wandruszka, *Geschichte einer Zeitung: das Schicksal der 'Presse' und der 'Neuen Freie Presse' von 1848 zur Zweiten Republik* (Vienna 1958) pp.99–101.

[36] These figures are really only an impression of the number of death notices, not the number of deceased mentioned. It is possible, therefore, that differing approaches to arranging burials between the Catholic and Jewish religious communities may account for some of the apparent Jewish predominance, although this is only conjecture.

4

Education and class – the position of the Jews in Viennese society

THE GENERAL PICTURE

Much work has been done recently on the social and economic position of the Jews in Vienna, especially by Ivar Oxaal and Marsha Rozenblit.[1] We therefore have a fairly clear picture of the basic facts. These do not augur well for a sociological explanation of Jewish predominance in liberal culture.

Figures for the Jewish proportion of the population of Vienna as a whole are given in Table 5. It can be seen from this that the Jewish presence in Vienna rose rapidly until 1890, and then remained fairly stable at about 9 per cent. The inclusion of the outlying districts from 1890 resulted in the Jewish presence in the city proper being underestimated. It probably remained at something like 12 per cent from 1890 onwards. This is relatively high for a capital city in Europe, but still meant that the Jews were a small minority.

The Jewish population was not spread evenly across the city, but was concentrated in certain districts. Table 6 gives the figures for the districts with the highest percentage of Jewish population. The concentration in the three districts I, II and IX is significant, because they were the only three districts in which the Second Curia remained Liberal in the electoral collapse of 1895.[2] Nevertheless, Jews in these districts were still only a minority, even on the 'Mazzesinsel'.[3]

Such figures provide a setting, but do not start to explain a cultural

---

[1] Marsha Rozenblit, *The Jews of Vienna 1867–1914: Assimilation and Identity* (Albany 1983); Ivar Oxaal, *The Jews of Pre-1914 Vienna: Two Working Papers* (Hull 1981); see also Ivar Oxaal and Walter R. Weizman, 'The Jews of Pre-1914 Vienna: an Exploration of Basic Sociological Dimensions' in Leo Baeck Institute Yearbook (LBIY) no. xxx (1985) pp. 395–432.

[2] *Neue Freie Presse*, morning edition (*NFPm*), 24 September 1985, p. 6: results of the elections to the Second Curia. For an explanation of the electoral franchise system, see below, p. 45.

[3] This is the Viennese slang term for the Second District, Leopoldstadt.

43

Table 5. *The Jewish population of Vienna*

Year	Total	Jews	Percentage
1869	607,510	40,227	6·6
1890	827,567	99,441	12·0
1890[a]	1,364,548	118,495	8·7
1910[a]	2,031,498	175,318	8·6

[a] This includes the new districts XI–XX.
Source: Ivar Oxaal, *The Jews of pre-1914 Vienna: Two Working Papers* (Hull 1981) p. 60.

Table 6. *Highest density of the Jewish population in Vienna in 1910 by district*

District	Jews	Percentage
I	10,807	20·35
II	56,779	33·95
IX	21,615	20·50

Source: Leo Goldhammer, *Die Juden Wiens: eine statistische Studie* (Vienna 1927) p. 10.

predominance. To do this we must look at the social history of Vienna and the social base of the cultural élite.

AN ALIENATED LIBERAL BOURGEOISIE

When looking for the social roots of modern cultural movements, the group usually at the centre of attention is the liberal bourgeoisie, however defined. Current explanations for the cultural flowering at the turn of the century in Vienna tend to concentrate on the idea of a liberal bourgeoisie, alienated by their political defeats at the hands of the Christian Socials, turning to art as a refuge from the realities of political impotence. This is a line taken most notably by Carl Schorske.[4] Looking at the background of the central and secondary figures of the culture, this seems a fairly convincing theory; but it does have its weaknesses. One of these is its vague definition of a 'liberal bourgeoisie'. If it is assumed, as seems likely, that this class is supposed to have consisted of those groups which were

[4] Carl E. Schorske, *Fin-de-Siècle Vienna: Politics and Culture* (London 1980) pp. 5–10, 302–11.

defeated by the Christian Socials and cast in the political wilderness, then John Boyer has shown that much of what might be assumed to be a 'liberal bourgeoisie' was in fact the reverse, in that it voted against the Liberals in the traumatic elections of 1895.[5] Moreover, if we look at the nature of Austrian liberalism's constituency, much of it appears incompatible with the kind of modernity of which Schorske is talking.

Boyer makes plain that the franchise for the Viennese municipal elections was so structured that it would have been impossible for Lueger and his party to beat the Liberals in 1895 unless they had captured key sectors of what, in theory, should have been a Liberal constituency. This stems from the fact that the franchise was divided into three curiae, each with a third of the council seats. The Third Curia was given over to those who paid a minimum five *Gulden* in tax, in other words to the rather large lower middle class of artisans and the like. This curia was voting heavily for the antisemites from the 1880s on.[6] The First Curia was that of the richest voters, though, as Boyer points out, it also included a large number of middling landlords (*Hausbesitzer*), due to the idiosyncrasies of the electoral law. This curia continued to vote mainly for the Liberals in the years after 1895, especially in the inner districts, but even here, according to Boyer, the votes of the landlords for the Christian Socials severely eroded the Liberals' position.[7] The Second Curia was the crucial battleplace in the Christian Socials' victory. It should have been a safe bet for the Liberals, because it was specially designed to be the curia of the intelligentsia, 'Wahlkörper der Intelligenz'.[8] Its main constituents were the officials and teachers, the official educated classes of the Monarchy. In the 1860s and 1870s they had been loyal members of the Liberal coalition of interests. Things began to change with the Liberal disappearance from central power in 1879, which naturally upset the patron–client relationship set up between the Liberals and these two state-employed classes. By 1895, due it seems to economic disenchantment with the performance of the Liberals in the coalition government of the time, these two groups voted in large numbers for the antisemitic and anti-Liberal party of Lueger.[9]

This switch in allegiance was common knowledge at the time, and a source of great vexation for the reporters of the *Neue Freie Presse*, who reported with horror the way in which officials came straight from the

---

[5] John W. Boyer, *Political Radicalism in Late Imperial Vienna* (Chicago 1981).
[6] *Ibid.* pp. 90–109.
[7] *Ibid.* pp. 298–300, 396–403.
[8] *Ibid.* pp. 285–6; *NFPm* 24 September 1895 p. 1; *Wiener Tagblatt* 1 April 1895 p. 1.
[9] Boyer, *Political Radicalism*, pp. 258–68, 281–5, 349–57; see also *NFPm* 29 September 1895 p. 3, *Brief von einem alten liberalen Beamten*; and E.W., 'Das Martyrium der Lehrer' in *Die Wage*, 26 February 1899, no. 9, p. 134.

office, still in uniform, to vote ostentatiously for Lueger's men.[10] The supposed liberalism of the Austrian official Establishment thus had rather narrow limits: instead of being the alienated victims of Lueger's victory, the officials and teachers were actually the cause of that victory.

This does not mean that all officials and teachers of all ranks deserted the Liberals.[11] It has been suggested that the bulk of the higher bureaucracy remained in the Liberal camp, and should therefore be included in the 'liberal bourgeoisie'. There are, however, many problems with this. Firstly, there is no clear evidence that the higher bureaucracy was, in fact, politically Liberal, and, considering the long period under Taaffe, any initial liberalism must have been well-tempered.[12] Secondly, the type of liberalism prevalent among bureaucrats was Josephinism. Though this insisted on rational solutions to administrative problems, and perhaps preferred liberalism's politics to other forms, it did not specify the goals of government, and functioned as readily under an autocrat as under a constitution. This leads to a third point: the status of the bureaucracy in the Monarchy meant that it was, or was supposed to be, above politics, its first loyalty to the emperor and the State. In other words it shared the same type of étatist attitudes found in most other bureaucracies in western and central European countries, and, like them, its relationship to political liberalism was ambiguous at best. This did not prevent Austria's top bureaucrats being in a sense 'liberal', but this was a different liberalism from that in the liberal professions or among merchants.[13] The fourth point to bear in mind is that this higher bureaucracy, far from being alienated from power in the 1890s, was actually put in more or less full control in the succession of *Beamtenministerien*, starting with Koerber in 1900. They therefore can hardly be classed as 'alienated' politically.[14] The bureaucracy continued to be, as it always had been, the Establishment, while it was liberalism and its supporters, who were not so fortunate as to be within the Monarchy's official hierarchy, which were 'dis-established' in the triumph of mass politics in the 1890s.

[10] *NFPm* 2 April 1895 p. 1; *NFPm* 8 May 1895 p. 4; *NFP*, evening edition (*NFPe*) 23 September 1895 p. 1, 4–5. Teachers in the elections of March 1896 were reported as wearing white flowers, the sign of the Christian Socials, *NFPe* 2 March 1896 p. 2. Further, *NFPm* 3 March 1896 p. 2. Also see *Wiener Tagblatt*, 2 April 1895 p. 3; 24 September 1895 p. 1. On teachers' antisemitism, see Joseph S. Bloch, *Erinnerungen aus meinem Leben* (Vienna 1922) p. 24.

[11] This point was made to me by Professor P. G. J. Pulzer, All Souls College, Oxford.

[12] Cf. E. W. 'Gewaltpolitik' in *Die Wage*, 6 August 1899, no. 32, p. 547.

[13] William M. Johnston makes some comment on the nature of Josephinism and the bureaucracy in his *The Austrian Mind: an Intellectual and Social History 1848–1938* (Berkeley 1972) pp. 17–19, 45–50. See also Arthur J. May, *The Habsburg Monarchy 1867–1914* (London 1965) pp. 488–9.

[14] For comments along these lines, see James Shedel, *Art and Society: the New Art Movement in Vienna 1897–1914* (Palo Alto 1981) p. 60.

It looks, therefore, as though even those high bureaucrats who continued to vote for the Liberals at elections were not affected in the way in which Schorske's liberal bourgeoisie is supposed to have been, nor held the requisite attitudes. While it is necessary to remember that there were other groups which retained liberal values, it does not seem to me that the high bureaucracy can be regarded as liberal bourgeois. There are signs that other groups which might be expected to be part of a liberal bourgeoisie were, in the Viennese context, part of an anti-Liberal, antisemitic coalition. Boyer talks of support for the antisemites among non-Jewish *Privatbeamten* and small shopkeepers.[15] This means that if we want a working definition of the 'liberal bourgeoisie', of the core group which was alienated by the rise of anti-Liberal politics (on Schorskean lines), then we are reduced to a fairly small number of categories. It does not seem too wide of the mark to say that the great bulk of Vienna's liberal bourgeoisie was concentrated in the following socio-economic sectors: commercial independents and semi-independents, finance, industry, lawyers, doctors, journalists and private income. We are talking, in other words, of an almost purely capitalist base for the liberal part of Vienna's educated class, if Boyer and Schorske are both correct.

We have already seen that Jews made up a large part of the 'superstructural' element of the liberal bourgeoisie, as defined here (that is to say the liberal professions). If we were to believe antisemitic reports of the time (but also some philosemitic ones), we might suppose that Jews were also predominant in the other 'capitalistic' groups mentioned here, especially in banking and commerce. Present evidence, from the census of 1910 especially, does not support this view. It is certainly true that the social structure of the Jewish population of Vienna was quite different from that of the rest of the Viennese with a much larger proportion of independents and far fewer labourers; in other words it was largely middle class, compared to a mainly working-class, non-Jewish population.[16] This naturally meant that Jews were 'over-represented' in such groups as commercial independents. Yet, as Ivar Oxaal has pointed out, even where the figures show the highest Jewish over-representation, Jews are still by no means predominant in the group, even in commerce. As he puts it: 'For every one Jew in Austria in 1900 it appears that four Catholics were engaged in a trade which was fundamental to the perpetuation of the Jewish stereotype.'[17] The claim is that the idea of a Jewish bourgeoisie is an invention of the antisemites.

[15] Boyer, *Political Radicalism* pp. 306–11.
[16] Oxaal and Weizman, *The Jews of Pre-1914 Vienna* p. 427; Rozenblit, *The Jews of Vienna* pp. 66–7.
[17] Oxaal and Weizman, *The Jews of Pre-1914 Vienna* p. 111.

Table 7. *The proportion of Jews among independents in the economic sectors in Vienna according to the census of 1910*

Occupational class	Jews	Total	Percentage
Agriculture	68	2,328	2·92
Industry	7,919	75,605	10·47
Commerce and transport	15,806	93,269	16·95
Liberal professions, officials and military	20,953	147,636	14·19

Source: Berufsstatistik, 3. vol. 1. vol. (new series) *Österreichische Statistik* (Vienna 1916), cited in Oxaal, *The Jews of pre-1914 Vienna*, p. 113.

Table 8. *The proportion of Jews among male independents in the economic sectors in Vienna according to the census of 1910*

Occupational class	Jews	Total	Percentage
Industry	5,445	49,535	11·00
Commerce and transport	12,905	42,024	30·71
Liberal professions, officials and military	9,797	66,909	14·64

Source: Calculation from source of Table 7.

The census figures of 1910 would certainly seem to bear out Oxaal's view. As Table 7 shows, Jews made up only 17 per cent of the independents in the sector Commerce and Transport in Vienna in 1910. Even when only male independents in this sector are assessed, where Jews are far more prominent, their percentage is still only 31 per cent, as can be seen in Table 8. This is not enough to give a sociological explanation of the Jewish cultural predominance, on the lines of Schorske and Boyer. Part of this, it could be argued, is due to the breadth of the definitions of the census' categories. For instance, the low proportion of Jews in the sector Industry can largely be explained by the inclusion of both large-scale industry and the artisan trades. Nevertheless the 1910 census figures do not encourage the idea of a Jewish predominance in the liberal bourgeois economic sectors, and certainly nothing approaching the proportions required to explain the Jewish predominance in the liberal educated class and its cultural élite.

If we consider this problem, however, it becomes plain that, instead of simply looking at the socio-economic base, the liberal bourgeoisie as defined here, we should be looking at the way in which various social groups entered the liberal educated class. It is fairly self-evident that what we really need to look at is the educated élite of the liberal bourgeoisie, for it was the intermediary stage of education which produced from the liberal bourgeoisie its educated class, and from the latter its cultural élite. If the Schorskean interpretation of the *fin de siècle* is correct, then it must have been the *educated* part of the liberal bourgeoisie which articulated the supposed alienation. Assessing the Jewish presence among the group of liberal bourgeois parents who sent their children to higher secondary schools would thus be one way of putting the 'Jewish' cultural élite in its social and cultural context. What we need to do is look at the educational base of Vienna's cultural élite, the Gymnasien.

The rôle of the Gymnasium in Viennese society

If we want to find out about the composition of the educated élite in Vienna, the best place to go to is the institution of classical education in Austria, the Gymnasium. Until 1904 the Gymnasium was the only form of secondary education in the Monarchy which enabled entry into the university, the goal of all with cultural pretensions and of those who wanted to become either a doctor or a lawyer.[18] Although the Realschulen also offered a good education, they only qualified their graduates for entry into the technical or trade school equivalents of the university. Whereas the Gymnasium taught both Latin and Greek, prerequisites of proper education in the nineteenth century, the Realschule provided a much more practical education, teaching modern languages instead of classics.[19] This was a marked dividing line in Vienna's educated society. Those who went to Realschule are exceptions in the cultural élite. Wittgenstein went to a technical school in Linz (typically different).[20] Schoenberg was a pupil in the Realschule in the Leopoldstadt.[21] Alban Berg went to the Realschule in the First District, as did Hermann Broch. Broch's case, however, is the exception which proves the rule. Throughout his life he held a grudge against his father for refusing to send him to the Gymnasium, precisely because going to the Realschule effectively barred his way to the university, and hence to the world of the intellect. His subsequent life story reads very much like an attempt to overcome this setback.[22]

Most of the cultural élite thus went to a Gymnasium. For some this

---

[18] Gustav Strakosch-Grassmann, *Geschichte des Unterrichtswesens in Österreich* (Vienna 1905) p. 321.   [19] Ibid. pp. 249, 276.

[20] Allan Janik and Stephen Toulmin, *Wittgenstein's Vienna* (New York 1973) p. 174.

[21] H. H. Stuckenschmidt, *Schoenberg, His Life, World and Work* (London 1977) p. 21.

[22] Manfred Durzak, *Hermann Broch* (Hamburg 1966) p. 23; Paul Michael Lützeler, *Hermann Broch: a Biography* (London 1987) p. 12.

meant a Gymnasium outside Vienna. Yet the central Gymnasien account for most of the major figures of Vienna's cultural life. Sigmund Freud went to the Sperlgymnasium in the Leopoldstadt.[23] Arthur Schnitzler, Hugo von Hofmannsthal, Richard Beer-Hofmann, Peter Altenberg, Hans Kelsen, Ludwig von Mises, as well as the nuclear physicist Erwin Schrödinger and Thomas Masaryk, all went to the Akademisches Gymnasium.[24] Stefan Zweig, Felix Braun and the philosopher Philipp Frank attended the Wasagymnasium.[25] Karl Kraus was at the Franz-Josephsgymnasium, Otto Weininger at the Piaristengymnasium and Victor Adler at the Schotten-gymnasium.[26] It is true that not all of the cultural élite attended a Gymnasium, due to their involvement in specialist fields. The artists Klimt, Kokoschka and Schiele never received a full humanist education, but a much more skills-oriented one.[27] As such, however, they represented an anomaly in the intellectual élite of Vienna, though a well-established one. The usual educational base of a member of Vienna's educated élite was the Gymnasium. A study of the social and ethnic composition of the group of graduates from the central Gymnasien of Vienna would therefore be a fairly representative picture of the social and ethnic composition of the base of the educated élite as a whole.

Constructing a sample

During the period 1870 to 1910 there were eleven schools in Vienna's central districts producing Gymnasium graduates (*Maturanten*).This included the two Realgymnasien: the Sperlgymnasium and the Mariahilfer-gymnasium.[28] Of the eleven, nine have at least some sort of records

[23] R. W. Clark, *Freud: the Man and the Cause* (London 1980) p. 17.

[24] *Vierhundertjahre Akademisches Gymnasium: 1553–1953: Festschrift* (Vienna 1953) pp. 14, 67–9.

[25] *Maturaprotokolle* of the Real-und-Ober-Gymnasium im IX. Bezirk (the Wasagymnasium), 1900, 1902, 1904.

[26] Paul Schick, *Karl Kraus* (Hamburg 1965) pp. 17ff; *Maturaprotokoll* of the Gymnasium im VIII. Bezirk (the Piaristengymnasium) 1898 (Weininger spent his first four years at the Franz-Josephsgymnasium); William McGrath, *Dionysian Art and Populist Politics in Austria* (New Haven 1974) pp. 17ff.

[27] Klimt went to the Kunstgewerbeschule des Österreichischen Museums für Kunst und Industrie (see *Traum und Wirklichkeit: Wien 1870–1930*, catalogue (Vienna 1985) p. 472). So did Kokoschka (see Peter Vergo, *Art in Vienna 1898–1918* (London 1975) p. 189). Schiele attended the Academy of Fine Arts (see Frank Whitford, *Egon Schiele* (London 1981) p. 32).

[28] These schools were peculiar in having a syllabus which offered a choice of Realschule or Gymnasium after the fourth year. In the upper school, however, a normal Gymnasium education was given, leading to a standard *Matura* examination. Freud attended one of these schools, the Sperlgymnasium. They are not to be confused with later forms of secondary schools which were also given the name Realgymnasien, but had a quite different structure and purpose.

intact. The loss of records at two schools, as is explained below, is not as damaging as might at first appear. The records of the schools, in the form of *Maturaprotokolle* (examination records) and *Hauptkataloge* (class reports), offer us the following information: the religion of the student; his father's occupation; his place of birth; and often his choice of career or university subject. The material is there, in other words, for a major survey of the religious, social, geographical and career patterns of a key sector of society. For the moment we are only interested in the first two categories: religion and father's occupation.

The constraints of space and time and the partial lack of records in many schools meant that the most sensible way of approaching the records was to take a sample of every fifth graduating year, from the arbitrarily chosen year of 1870 to that of 1910 (hence the graduating classes of 1870, 1875, 1880 and so on). Sampling always produces distortions, especially when the grouping in question is small. In its larger terms, however, the sample which was constructed here seems to have retained a fair degree of accuracy: the proportion of Jews by denomination in the sample is 39·1 per cent, against an expected figure, calculated from the schools' *Jahresberichte* (annual reports), of 38·8 per cent, a difference of 0·3 per cent. In addition, calculations on a chronological plan also show variations of only a per cent here and there.[29] In its larger results, therefore, the sample's accuracy can be assumed, and since, as we shall see, the results are fairly obvious, the need for a more sophisticated statistical approach seems to be obviated.

That the records of two of the schools in the centre of Vienna are missing might raise doubts as to the objectivity or balance of the sample. It is a great pity that the schools in question, the Theresianum and the Elisabethsgymnasium, do not figure in the statistics.[30] Yet the nature of both schools means that, in a study of the liberal bourgeois cultural élite, their loss is not particularly significant. The Theresianum had been set up in the eighteenth century as the Ritterakademie for the Austrian aristocracy, and this remained its primary purpose throughout the nineteenth century as well, with most of the students coming from the families of the Monarchy's landed aristocracy.[31] This naturally meant that it was never really considered a part of Vienna's educational structure.

[29] The percentage of Jews in the 1870–80 sample is 34 per cent against an expected 32 per cent. In the 1885–95 sample the figures are 41 per cent against an expected 40 per cent, and in the 1900–1910 sample they are 45 per cent against an expected 45 per cent. These are figures which include known converts as Jews.

[30] According to the two directors of the schools concerned, the relevant records were lost during the Second World War.

[31] Strakosch-Grassmann, *Geschichte des Unterrichtswesens* p. 107; Eugen Guglia, *Das Theresianum in Wien* (Vienna 1912) pp. 156–7.

While, in 1870, it was only one of four Gymnasien in Vienna, and was taking in pupils from the Fourth District, at least one contemporary reported its special situation, clearly separate from the other schools.[32] Its special status and aristocratic nature mean that its loss from a study of the liberal bourgeois cultural élite should not affect the findings unduly. In the case of the Elisabethsgymnasium, also in the Fourth District, it is the fact that the school was the youngest Gymnasium in the group which is significant. This meant that it had produced a mere 4 per cent of all graduates of the eleven schools by 1910.[33] Hence its loss is also not too serious.

A third school, the Landstrassergymnasium, has records for only three consecutive years, 1905–7. Since this school is the nearest as regards its catchment area to the Elisabethsgymnasium, these figures are of increased significance, and have been included in the total sample, despite the injury to the chronological grid. Fortunately for our findings, they show a very similar picture to the general one. This will be discussed a little later. Here the point to note is that the sample we have looks as if it is a fairly accurate picture of the Gymnasien, and that we can proceed with some confidence in assessing the Jewish rôle in these schools.

Jews in the Gymnasien

Existing statistics already show that Jews, roughly ten per cent of the general population in Vienna, made up about 30 per cent of Gymnasiasten.[34] This degree of over-representation was typical of the Habsburg Monarchy as a whole.[35] In the eighth class of the Gymnasien in the central districts (I–IX) the proportion was even higher and increasing. For the period 1870–83 the average was 26·8 per cent, for 1884–97, 32·5 per cent, and for 1898–1910, 35·3 per cent. If the figures for the anomalous Theresianum are subtracted the proportions are 31·8 per cent, 37·1 per cent and 39·2 per cent respectively. The general proportion for 1870–1910 is 32·2 per cent (36·7 per cent).[36]

This very large Jewish presence was, in addition, not spread evenly over the city's eleven Gymnasien. In three schools Jews were in the majority

---

[32] In 1865 the director of the Leopoldstädter Communal-Realgymnasium commented: 'da man das theresianische [Gymnasium] als ein der freien Aufnahme zugängliches [Gymnasium] nicht füglich mitzählen kann'. *Jahresbericht des Leopoldstädter Communal-Realgymnasiums* 1865 (Vienna 1865) p. 3.

[33] Calculation from the records of the *Jahresberichte* of the eleven schools.

[34] See *Statistisches Jahrbuch der Stadt Wien* 1886–, section on Mittelschulen for the official statistics. Also see Rozenblit, *The Jews of Vienna*, pp. 102–5.

[35] Berthold Windt, 'Die Juden an den Mittel- und Hochschulen Österreichs seit 1850' in *Statistiches Monatschrift*, 7 (1881) pp. 442–3.

[36] Calculation from the records of the *Jahresberichte* of the eleven schools.

and in two others comprised over 40 per cent, while in the two socially prestigious schools, the Theresianum and the Schottengymnasium, they were a very small minority indeed.[37] The Jewish pupils were concentrated in schools in the 'liberal' districts, the First, Second and Ninth; 79·8 per cent of all Jewish pupils went to schools in those districts, compared to a general percentage of 55·7 per cent and a non-Jewish percentage of 44·3 per cent. The result was that, in these 'politically liberal' districts, Jews made up 46·1 per cent of Gymnasiasten. If the figures for the clerical and rather aristocratic Schottengymnasium are discounted this goes up to 57·4 per cent.[38] Even before we look at the occupational structure, therefore, we can see that the correlation between Jews and the liberal educated class, at least geographically, must have been very large.

If we now look at our sample distribution of pupil's religion (descent) against father's occupation, as given in Table 9, we can see confirmation of this general impression. Whereas Jews make up just under 40 per cent of the sample as a whole, they comprise over 80 per cent of the commercial sector, almost 60 per cent of the financial and industrial sectors, a majority in Private Income and almost half the doctors, and are slightly over-represented among lawyers and journalists. The groups mentioned here are, as discussed earlier, the 'liberal bourgeoisie', if we are to accept the argument of both Boyer and Schorske. These groups together: commerce, finance, industry, lawyers, doctors, journalists and private income, form what has been called Group A in Table 9. According to our sample, 65·3 per cent of the pupils in Group A were Jewish. If this figure is anything near accurate, it would suggest that the reason for the Jewish predominance in both the cultural élite and the liberal educated class was due to the fact that the educated part of the liberal bourgeoisie was heavily Jewish in any case. The 'Jewishness' of cultural life was a function of the place of Jews in the educational system and liberal bourgeois society.[39]

---

[37] The three schools with a Jewish majority were the Sperl-, Sophien- and Wasagymnasien. The two over 40 per cent were the Akademisches and Franz-Josephsgymnasien.

[38] These figures are based on the records for the eighth class in the *Jahresberichte* of the eleven schools. With regard to the Schottengymnasium's aristocratic character, see *Vierhundertjahre Akademisches Gymnasium* p. 14, where the Schottengymnasium is grouped with the Theresianum and the Jesuit school at Kalksburg. Also see Rozenblit, *The Jews of Vienna*, p. 103; McGrath, *Dionysian Art*, pp. 27ff.

[39] This conclusion depends on the correctness of my analysis of Vienna's 'liberal bourgeoisie', based on the claims of Schorske and Boyer. There are very good arguments for producing a different and much more detailed analysis of the occupational structure, which would include high-level bureaucrats perhaps, the university professors definitely, in the 'liberal bourgeoisie' to give only two salient examples. Against this, it might be argued that, firstly, if this was to be done, *all* Jews, regardless of occupation, would have to be included in the 'liberal bourgeois' sector, and secondly, as it is, the dominant presence of Jews in the 'capitalist' sectors is obvious, and the most significant factor in terms of the *new* element in the educated élite. In other words, although the Jewish

Table 9. *Distribution of father's occupation against son's religion (and/or ethnic descent) among the Maturanten of Vienna's central Gymnasien 1870–1910 (sample)*

Occupation	Jewish	Catholic	Protestant	Other	Total	Percentage	Jewish	Catholic	Protestant	Other
1. Commerce	318	53	16	4	391	21·6	81·3	13·6	4·1	1·0
2. Finance	34	17	6	—	57	3·1	59·6	29·8	10·5	—
3. Industry	68	37	11	1	117	6·5	58·1	31·6	9·4	0·9
4. Handicrafts	19	96	2	—	117	6·5	16·2	82·7	1·7	—
5. Public employee	23	297	12	3	335	18·5	6·9	88·7	3·6	0·9
6. Private employee	62	112	12	2	188	10·4	33·0	59·6	6·4	1·1
7. Railway employee	14	52	2	—	68	3·8	20·6	76·5	2·9	—
8. Lawyer	37	49	3	1	90	5·0	41·1	54·4	3·3	1·1
9. Doctor	44	38	7	1	90	5·0	48·9	42·2	7·8	1·1
10. Journalist	7	10	—	—	17	0·9	41·2	58·8	—	—
11. Teacher	34	87	13	—	134	7·4	25·4	64·9	9·7	—
12. Miscellaneous professions	16	29	12	2	59	3·3	27·1	49·2	20·3	3·4
13. Landlord	6	14	1	—	21	1·2	28·6	66·7	4·8	—
14. Agriculture	2	47	1	—	50	2·8	4·0	94·0	2·0	—
15. Private income	39	33	2	2	76	4·2	51·3	43·4	2·6	2·6
Total	723	971	100	16	1,810	100	39·9	53·6	5·5	0·9
(+/– converts)	(707)	(982)	(101)	(20)	—	—	39·1	54·3	5·5	1·1
Group A	547	237	45	9	838	46·3	65·3	28·3	5·4	1·1
Group B	176	734	55	7	972	53·7	18·1	75·5	5·7	0·7
Group A*	88	97	10	2	197	10·9	44·7	49·2	5·1	1·0

Group A = 1–3, 8–10, and 15; Group B = 4–7, 11–14; Group A* = 8–10.
Source: see p. 50–2, above.

It might be argued that the lack of information from the other two schools may make this an exaggerated figure. Yet the evidence from the Landstrassergymnasium, the school in the district nearest in character to that of the missing schools, Wieden, tends to defuse this argument. There, although Jews make up only 22·7 per cent, they still manage to comprise 65·5 per cent of Group A, that is above the general average. This is due to the fact that Group A makes up a mere 26·4 per cent in the Landstrasser sample, compared to a general average of 46·3 per cent. This suggests that we can be pretty sure that our figure of roughly 60 to 65 per cent of the liberal bourgeois sector in the Gymnasien being Jewish is dependable. There are even arguments to suggest that it might be a conservative estimate: although a few fairly well-known or obvious converts could be traced, there are, it can be assumed, quite a few cases in the data of unremarked converts. If these were included in the Jewish sector they would, perhaps, more than compensate in Group A for the missing schools. That roughly two-thirds of the cultural élite in Vienna were Jewish is not much of a surprise, for, it would seem, the same can be said for the educated social base of that élite.

The dynamics of the Jewish situation

The figures in Table 9 can be broken down further, chronologically, as in Tables 10, 11 and 12. These show that, as perhaps should be expected, there was an internal dynamic to the figures. For the first three sample years, 1870, 1875 and 1880 (Table 10), the Jewish presence in Group A is under 60 per cent. By the last three sample years, 1900, 1905 and 1910 (Table 12), it is over 70 per cent. The liberal bourgeois sector was becoming increasingly Jewish. The reason for this, from the figures, appears to have been a very steep rise in the proportion of Jewish doctors, lawyers and journalists, the liberal professions (Group A* in the tables). This was a result both of a rise in the number of Jewish liberal professionals, but also of an absolute fall in the numbers of Catholic equivalents. The proportion of Jews whose fathers are in the liberal professions goes up steadily from 9 per cent in the first sample to 14 per cent in the last, whereas the Catholic proportion falls from over 15 per cent to under 7 per cent. Thus the Gymnasium data seem to suggest that the cultural élite's 'Jewishness' was a result of the intellectualizing of the Jewish liberal bourgeoisie at a time when the Catholic populace was turning to other career options away from the liberal professions.

predominance in Group A is only a rough indication of the state of affairs, other analyses would only confirm the general impression which it gives of the educated part of the liberal bourgeoisie.

Table 10. *Distribution of father's occupation against son's religion (and/or ethnic descent) among the Maturanten of Vienna's central Gymnasien 1870–80 (sample)*

Occupation	Jewish	Catholic	Protestant	Other	Total	Percentage	Jewish	Catholic	Protestant	Other
1. Commerce	62	13	2	—	77	19·7	80·5	16·9	2·6	—
2. Finance	13	3	1	—	17	4·4	76·5	17·6	5·9	—
3. Industry	10	7	2	—	19	4·9	52·6	36·8	10·5	—
4. Handicrafts	3	24	—	—	27	6·9	11·1	88·9	—	—
5. Public employee	1	89	—	—	90	23·1	1·1	98·9	—	—
6. Private employee	6	11	—	—	17	4·4	35·3	64·7	—	—
7. Railway employee	2	5	—	—	7	1·8	28·6	71·4	—	—
8. Lawyer	3	20	1	—	24	6·2	12·5	83·3	4·2	—
9. Doctor	7	15	1	1	24	6·2	29·2	62·5	4·2	4·2
10. Journalist	2	2	—	—	4	1·0	50·0	50·0	—	—
11. Teacher	7	15	2	—	24	6·2	29·2	62·5	8·3	—
12. Miscellaneous professions	6	7	2	—	15	3·8	40·0	46·7	13·3	—
13. Landlord	2	4	—	—	6	1·5	33·3	66·7	—	—
14. Agriculture	—	19	1	—	20	5·1	—	95·0	5·0	—
15. Private income	10	9	—	—	19	4·9	52·6	47·4	—	—
Total	134	243	12	1	390	100	34·4	62·3	3·1	0·3
Group A	107	69	7	1	184	47·2	58·2	37·5	3·8	0·5
Group B	27	174	5	—	206	52·8	13·1	84·5	2·4	0·5
Group A*	12	37	2	1	52	13·3	23·1	71·2	3·8	1·9

Group A = 1–3, 8–10, and 15; Group B = 4–7, 11–14; Group A* = 8–10.
Source: see p. 50–2, above.

Table 11. *Distribution of father's occupation against son's religion (and/or ethnic descent) among the Maturanten of Vienna's central Gymnasien 1885–95 (sample)*

Occupation	Jewish	Catholic	Protestant	Other	Total	Percentage	Jewish	Catholic	Protestant	Other
1. Commerce	111	18	2	4	135	21·7	82·7	13·3	1·5	3·0
2. Finance	11	11	4	—	26	4·2	42·3	42·3	15·4	—
3. Industry	24	10	9	—	43	6·9	55·8	23·2	20·9	—
4. Handicrafts	10	28	—	—	38	6·1	26·3	73·7	—	—
5. Public employee	8	82	3	—	93	15·0	9·7	88·2	3·2	—
6. Private employee	10	32	2	1	45	7·2	22·2	71·1	4·4	2·2
7. Railway employee	7	28	1	—	36	5·8	19·4	77·8	2·8	—
8. Lawyer	8	16	1	1	26	4·1	30·8	61·5	3·8	3·8
9. Doctor	18	14	2	—	34	5·5	52·9	41·2	5·9	—
10. Journalist	2	5	—	—	7	1·1	28·6	71·4	—	—
11. Teacher	19	30	9	—	58	9·3	32·8	51·7	15·5	—
12. Miscellaneous professions	4	12	5	2	23	3·7	17·4	52·2	21·7	8·7
13. Landlord	2	5	—	—	7	1·1	28·6	71·4	—	—
14. Agriculture	1	19	—	—	20	3·2	5·0	95·0	—	—
15. Private income	17	12	1	1	31	5·0	54·8	38·7	3·2	3·2
Total	252	322	39	9	622	100	40·5	51·8	6·3	1·4
Group A	191	86	19	6	302	48·6	63·2	28·5	6·3	2·0
Group B	61	236	20	3	320	51·4	19·1	73·8	6·3	0·9
Group A*	28	35	3	1	67	10·8	41·8	52·2	4·5	1·5

Group A = 1–3, 8–10, and 15; Group B = 4–7, 11–14; Group A* = 8–10.
Source: see p. 50–2, above.

Table 12. Distribution of father's occupation against son's religion (and/or ethnic descent) among the Maturanten of Vienna's central Gymnasien 1900–10 (sample)[a]

Occupation	Jewish	Catholic	Protestant	Other	Total	Percentage	Jewish	Catholic	Protestant	Other
1. Commerce	133	22	11	—	166	24·1	80·1	13·3	6·6	—
2. Finance	10	3	1	—	14	2·0	71·4	21·4	7·1	—
3. Industry	33	17	—	—	50	7·3	66·0	34·0	—	—
4. Handicrafts	5	31	2	1	39	5·7	12·8	79·5	5·1	2·6
5. Public employee	14	112	5	2	133	19·3	10·5	84·2	3·8	1·5
6. Private employee	41	48	9	1	99	14·4	41·4	48·5	9·1	1·0
7. Railway employee	5	15	—	—	20	2·9	25·0	75·0	—	—
8. Lawyer	23	12	1	—	36	5·2	63·9	33·3	2·8	—
9. Doctor	16	8	3	—	27	3·9	59·3	29·6	11·1	—
10. Journalist	3	1	—	—	4	0·6	75·0	25·0	—	—
11. Teacher	8	32	2	—	42	6·1	19·0	76·2	4·8	—
12. Miscellaneous professions	6	6	3	—	15	2·2	40·0	40·0	20·0	—
13. Landlord	2	5	1	—	8	1·2	25·0	62·5	12·5	—
14. Agriculture	1	9	—	—	10	1·5	10·0	90·0	—	—
15. Private income	12	11	1	1	25	3·6	48·0	44·0	4·0	4·0
Total	312	332	39	5	688	100	45·3	48·3	5·7	0·7
Group A	230	74	17	1	322	46·8	71·4	23·0	5·3	0·3
Group B	82	258	22	4	366	53·2	22·4	70·5	6·0	1·1
Group A*	42	21	4	—	67	9·7	62·7	31·3	6·0	—

Group A = 1–3, 8–10, and 15; Group B = 4–7, 11–14; Group A* = 8–10.
[a]This excludes, for the sake of continuity with Tables 10–11, data from the Landstrassergymnasium.
Source: see p. 50–2, above.

It might be objected that this conclusion cannot be sustained on the limited data available. Certainly there is much less accuracy in a discussion of tendencies within the liberal professions in the sample, due to the small numbers involved. Nevertheless, this is not the only evidence available from the records of the Gymnasien about the dynamics of Jewish (and non-Jewish) career choice (social mobility). The career (faculty) choices of about two-thirds of the general sample have been recorded, and for two schools we have lists of the careers achieved by former pupils from a number of graduating years. These additional sources support the idea that the predominance of Jews among those coming from a liberal bourgeois background was compounded by differences in career choice and achievement between Jews and non-Jews once they had left the Gymnasium.

The accuracy of these additional sources of data is not as great as for the general sample. However, for the career choice distribution Jews compose 40 per cent of the sample, against the general sample's 39·9 per cent when converts are included – thus fairly similar. This suggests that the other large-scale trends will be roughly representative. With achieved career, however, based on an almost completely different sample, the lists of ex-pupils provided by the *Jahresberichte* of two schools, the Mariahilfer-gymnasium and the Wasagymnasium, claims to any degree of accuracy must be slight. This is due both to the small size of the sample – taken together the schools' lists only provide 676 cases – and to the more complex analysis required by our study. Nevertheless, the two schools' samples display certain striking similarities, and their results are crude enough to suggest definite trends.

In all these figures it is best to look at the percentages, for it is there that we can see the divergence between Jewish and non-Jewish career distributions within a specific social class. Tables 13 and 14 show us the relative percentage distributions of career choice for Jews and non-Jews. These show that, although Jews and non-Jews in the sample opted for law and medicine, the two major faculties at the university, to a degree of something over 60 per cent, the distribution between the two faculties was quite different, and this was even more so within equivalent social classes. In Commerce slightly more Jews opted for medicine than for law, whereas their non-Jewish equivalents chose law almost fivefold over medicine. When all Group A classes are combined, the percentage lead of law over medicine is still only 8 per cent for Jews, but 41 per cent for non-Jews. Tables 13 and 14 show further that in Group B (all those not in Group A) the difference was just as great as in Group A. This suggests that there was a definite Jewish propensity to choose medicine, however it is to be explained.

Table 13. *Percentage distribution of the career (subject) choice of Viennese Maturanten by father's occupation 1870–1910 (sample): Jews*

Father's occupation	Law	Medicine	Philosophy	Theology	Art	Music	Chemical/Technical	Agriculture	Military/Official	Commerce	Miscellaneous	Percentage total	Sum total
1. Commerce	33	33	8	0**	0**	2	8	1	2	12	1	46	232
2. Finance	42	16	11	—	—	—	21	5	—	15	5	4	19
3. Industry	38	17	13	—	—	2	15	2	—	11	—	9	48
4. Handicrafts	67	22	20	—	—	—	13	—	—	—	—	2	9
5. Public employee	47	13	20	—	—	7	13	—	—	—	—	3	15
6. Private employee	42	40	9	—	—	—	2	—	2	4	—	9	45
7. Railway employee	46	23	8	—	—	—	8	—	8	8	—	3	13
8. Lawyer	75	7	7	—	—	3	7	—	—	4	—	5	28
9. Doctor	28	50	3	—	—	3	9	3	—	3	—	6	32
10. Journalist	75	25	—	—	—	—	—	—	—	—	—	1	4
11. Teacher	12	40	20	—	—	4	16	—	4	4	—	5	25
12. Miscellaneous professions	27	—	27	9	9	9	9	—	—	9	—	2	11
13. Landlord	40	40	—	—	—	—	—	20	—	—	—	1	5
14. Agriculture	—	—	—	—	—	—	—	100	—	—	—	0**	1
15. Private income	35	22	22	—	—	2	17	—	—	4	—	5	23
Percentage total	37	29	10	0**	0**	2	9	1	1	8	1	100	—
Sum total	189	148	52	2	2	9	48	7	7	43	3	—	510
Group A	37	29	9	0**	0**	2	10	1	1	10	1	76	386
Group B	37	30	13	1	1	2	7	2	2	2	5	24	124
Group A*	52	28	6	—	—	2	8	2	—	3	—	13	64

Group A = 1–3, 8–10, and 15; Group B = 4–7, 11–14; Group A* = 8–10.
Source: see p. 50–2, 59 above.   0** = less than 0.5%

Table 14. *Percentage distribution of the career (subject) choice of Viennese Maturanten by father's occupation 1870–1910 (sample): non-Jews*

Father's occupation	Law	Medicine	Philosophy	Theology	Art	Music	Chemical/ Technical	Agriculture	Military/ Official	Commerce	Miscellaneous	Percentage total	Sum total
1. Commerce	53	11	11	—	—	2	6	2	4	13	—	7	55
2. Finance	61	22	6	—	—	—	—	—	6	6	—	2	18
3. Industry	54	13	3	3	—	1	8	3	3	15	—	5	39
4. Handicrafts	57	13	10	10	—	—	3	—	7	—	—	8	60
5. Public employee	56	9	13	4	1	—	5	2	10	—	—	25	195
6. Private employee	39	8	16	5	2	2	8	4	13	4	—	13	101
7. Railway employee	47	20	7	2	2	—	—	4	18	—	—	6	45
8. Lawyer	70	3	15	3	—	—	3	—	8	—	—	5	40
9. Doctor	39	36	19	—	—	—	3	—	3	—	—	4	31
10. Journalist	44	33	22	—	1	—	—	—	—	—	—	1	9
11. Teacher	34	19	26	1	1	—	11	1	4	1	—	9	70
12. Miscellaneous professions	47	3	16	11	—	—	16	9	9	—	—	4	32
13. Landlord	42	25	—	—	8	—	25	—	—	—	—	2	12
14. Agriculture	68	6	6	3	—	—	—	6	10	—	—	4	31
15. Private income	56	4	19	11	—	—	4	—	4	4	—	4	27
Percentage total	51	12	13	4	1	0**	6	2	8	3	—	100	—
Sum total	388	93	103	27	6	3	44	18	63	20	—	—	765
Group A	55	14	12	2	—	0**	4	1	4	7	—	29	219
Group B	49	11	14	4	1	0**	6	3	10	1	—	71	546
Group A*	55	19	18	1	—	—	3	—	5	—	—	10	80

Group A = 1–3, 8–10, and 15; Group B = 4–7, 11–14; Group A* = 8–10.
Source: see p. 50–2, 59, above. 0** = less than 0·5%.
(Percentage of Jews in sample is 510/1,275 = 40 per cent)

Table 15. *Percentage distribution of son's achieved career against father's occupation for Maturanten of the Mariahilfergymnasium 1872–3, 1875–85, 1892–1907: Jews*

Father's occupation	Son's achieved career 1	2	3	4	5	6	7	8	9	10	11	12	13	14	15	Percentage total	Sum total
1. Commerce	11	—	—	—	11	7	7	40	20	2	2	—	—	—	—	38	45
2. Finance	20	20	—	—	—	—	—	20	40	—	—	—	—	—	—	4	5
3. Industry	13	—	6	—	6	3	3	38	19	—	13	—	—	—	—	27	32
4. Handicrafts	—	—	—	—	—	—	13	38	25	—	13	—	—	—	—	7	8
5. Public employee	—	—	—	50	—	—	—	50	—	—	—	—	—	—	—	2	2
6. Private employee	—	—	—	—	15	15	8	15	46	—	—	—	—	—	—	11	13
7. Railway employee	—	—	—	—	—	—	50	50	—	—	—	—	—	—	—	2	2
8. Lawyer	—	—	—	—	—	—	—	100	—	—	—	—	—	—	—	1	1
9. Doctor	—	—	—	—	—	20	—	—	40	20	—	20	—	—	—	4	5
10. Journalist	—	—	—	—	—	—	—	—	—	—	—	—	—	—	—	—	—
11. Teacher	—	—	—	—	—	—	—	—	—	—	—	—	—	—	—	—	—
12. Miscellaneous professions	—	—	—	—	—	33	—	33	—	—	—	33	—	—	—	3	3
13. Landlord	—	—	—	—	—	—	—	100	—	—	—	—	—	—	—	1	1
14. Agriculture	—	—	—	—	—	—	—	100	—	—	—	—	—	—	—	1	1
15. Private income	—	—	—	—	—	—	—	—	—	—	—	100	—	—	—	2	2
Percentage total	8	1	2	1	8	8	6	35	23	2	5	3	—	—	—	100	—
Sum total	10	1	2	1	9	9	7	42	27	2	6	4	—	—	—	—	120
A	11	1	2	—	8	6	4	36	21	2	6	3	—	—	—	75	90
B	—	—	—	3	7	13	10	33	27	—	3	3	—	—	—	25	30
A*	—	—	—	—	—	17	—	17	33	17	—	17	—	—	—	5	6

The categories 1–15, A, B and A* for father's occupation and son's achieved career correspond to those in Tables 9–12.
Source: see p. 50–2, 59, above.

Table 16. Percentage distribution of son's achieved career against father's occupation for Maturanten of the Mariahilfergymnasium 1872–3, 1875–85, 1892–1907: non-Jews

Father's occupation	Son's achieved career															Percentage total	Sum total
	1	2	3	4	5	6	7	8	9	10	11	12	13	14	15		
1. Commerce	4	—	4	—	33	—	4	30	4	—	19	4	—	—	—	8	27
2. Finance	—	100	—	—	—	—	—	—	—	—	—	—	—	—	—	0**	1
3. Industry	—	—	5	—	40	5	5	14	12	—	12	7	—	—	—	13	42
4. Handicrafts	—	—	—	—	34	—	—	17	15	—	32	2	—	—	—	13	41
5. Public employee	1	—	—	—	62	4	4	8	7	—	11	4	—	—	—	26	84
6. Private employee	—	—	—	—	39	3	3	9	12	—	27	6	—	—	—	10	33
7. Railway employee	—	—	—	—	43	—	43	14	—	—	—	—	—	—	—	2	7
8. Lawyer	—	—	—	—	33	—	17	50	—	—	—	—	—	—	—	2	6
9. Doctor	—	—	—	—	25	—	8	8	50	—	8	—	—	—	—	4	12
10. Journalist	—	—	—	—	—	—	—	—	50	—	50	—	—	—	—	1	2
11. Teacher	—	—	—	—	45	—	14	—	10	—	31	—	—	—	—	9	29
12. Miscellaneous professions	—	—	—	—	57	3	—	5	5	—	10	10	—	—	—	7	21
13. Landlord	—	—	25	—	25	—	25	—	—	—	—	25	—	—	—	1	4
14. Agriculture	—	—	—	—	75	—	—	—	25	—	—	—	—	—	—	1	4
15. Private income	—	—	—	—	20	—	10	20	—	—	50	—	—	—	—	3	10
Percentage total	1	0**	1	—	45	2	5	12	11	—	18	5	—	—	—	100	—
Sum total	2	1	4	—	144	7	17	39	34	—	59	16	—	—	—	—	323
A	1	1	3	—	33	2	6	20	13	—	17	4	—	—	—	31	100
B	0**	—	0**	—	50	2	5	9	9	—	19	5	—	—	—	69	223
A*	—	—	—	0**	25	—	10	20	35	0**	10	—	—	—	—	6	20
Jews + non-Jews Total	3	0**	1	0**	35	4	5	18	14	0**	15	5	—	—	—	100	443

Percentage of Jews in sample is 120/443 = 27·1 per cent.
The above categories 1–15, A, B and A* for father's occupation and son's achieved career correspond to those in Tables 9–12.
Source: see p. 50–2, 59, above.   0** = less than 0.5 per cent.

Table 17. *Percentage distribution of son's achieved career against father's occupation for Maturanten of the Wasagymnasium 1876–88: Jews*

Father's occupation	Son's achieved career															Percentage total	Sum total
	1	2	3	4	5	6	7	8	9	10	11	12	13	14	15		
1. Commerce	3	—	—	—	5	13	—	21	44	—	10	5	—	—	—	46	39
2. Finance	38	—	—	—	—	—	—	38	25	—	—	—	—	—	—	9	8
3. Industry	—	—	20	—	—	—	—	40	20	—	—	20	—	—	—	6	5
4. Handicrafts	—	—	—	—	—	—	—	—	—	—	—	—	—	—	—	—	—
5. Public employee	—	—	—	—	—	14	14	29	43	—	—	—	—	—	—	8	7
6. Private employee	—	—	—	—	33	—	—	33	33	—	—	—	—	—	—	4	3
7. Railway employee	—	—	—	—	—	—	—	—	—	—	—	—	—	—	—	—	—
8. Lawyer	17	—	—	—	17	—	—	33	—	17	17	—	—	—	—	7	6
9. Doctor	—	—	—	—	—	—	—	—	100	—	—	—	—	—	—	1	1
10. Journalist	—	—	—	—	25	—	—	—	—	25	50	—	—	—	—	5	4
11. Teacher	—	—	—	—	—	—	—	—	50	—	50	—	—	—	—	5	4
12. Miscellaneous professions	—	—	—	—	—	50	—	50	—	—	—	—	—	—	—	2	2
13. Landlord	—	—	—	—	—	—	—	—	—	—	—	—	—	—	—	—	—
14. Agriculture	—	—	—	—	—	—	—	—	—	—	—	—	—	—	—	—	—
15. Private income	—	—	—	—	17	33	—	17	33	—	—	—	—	—	—	7	6
Percentage total	6	—	1	—	7	11	1	24	34	2	11	4	—	—	—	100	—
Sum total	5	—	1	—	6	9	1	20	29	2	9	3	—	—	—	—	85
A	7	—	1	—	7	10	—	23	33	3	10	4	—	—	—	81	69
B	—	—	—	—	6	13	6	25	38	—	13	—	—	—	—	19	16
A*	9	—	—	—	18	—	—	18	18	—	27	—	—	—	—	13	11

The above categories 1–15, A, B and A* for father's occupation and son's achieved career correspond to those in Tables 9–12.
Source: see p. 50–2, 59, above.

Table 18. *Percentage distribution of son's achieved career against father's occupation for Maturanten of the Wasagymnasium 1876–88: non-Jews*

Father's occupation	_ Son's achieved career _															Percentage total	Sum total
	1	2	3	4	5	6	7	8	9	10	11	12	13	14	15		
1. Commerce	9	—	—	—	27	—	9	9	18	—	18	9	—	—	—	7	11
2. Finance	—	—	—	—	—	—	100	—	—	—	—	—	—	—	—	1	1
3. Industry	—	—	—	—	75	—	—	25	—	—	—	—	—	—	—	3	4
4. Handicrafts	—	—	—	—	60	—	—	—	40	—	—	—	—	—	—	3	5
5. Public employee	—	—	—	—	66	—	8	11	8	—	5	2	—	—	—	42	62
6. Private employee	—	—	—	—	63	—	—	—	25	—	—	13	—	—	—	5	8
7. Railway employee	—	—	—	—	25	—	—	—	50	25	—	—	—	—	—	3	4
8. Lawyer	—	—	—	—	40	—	—	40	—	—	—	10	—	—	10	7	10
9. Doctor	—	—	—	—	—	—	—	33	67	—	—	—	—	—	—	4	6
10. Journalist	—	—	—	—	50	—	—	50	—	—	—	—	—	—	—	1	2
11. Teacher	—	—	5	—	24	—	—	5	24	—	33	10	—	—	—	14	21
12. Miscellaneous professions	—	—	—	—	33	—	17	—	50	—	—	—	—	—	—	4	6
13. Landlord	—	—	—	—	100	—	—	—	—	—	—	—	—	—	—	1	1
14. Agriculture	—	—	—	—	25	—	—	25	—	—	25	25	—	—	—	3	4
15. Private income	—	—	—	—	67	—	—	—	—	—	33	—	—	—	—	2	3
Percentage total	1	—	1	—	49	—	5	12	17	1	9	5	—	—	1	100	—
Sum total	1	—	1	—	72	—	8	18	25	1	14	7	—	—	1		148
A	3	—	1	—	35	—	5	24	16	1	8	5	—	—	3	25	37
B	—	—	1	—	53	—	5	8	17	1	10	5	—	—	—	75	111
A*	—	—	—	—	28	—	—	39	22	—	—	6	—	—	6	12	18
Jews + non-Jews																	
Total	3	—	1	—	34	4	4	16	23	1	10	4	—	—	0**	100	233
Percentage of Jews in sample is 85/233 = 36.5 per cent.																	

The above categories 1–15, A, B and A* for father's occupation and son's achieved career correspond to those in Tables 9–12.
0** = less than 0.5 per cent.
Source: see p. 50–2, 59, above.

The reason for the great emphasis in the non-Jewish sector on law is no doubt because a legal training was a prerequisite not only for a legal career, but primarily for a career in the higher civil service. As we have seen, an unofficial official antisemitism meant that the official career was never really open to a Jew who wished to remain a Jew. While the career of lawyer, *Advokat*, was an attractive one to Jews, it was much easier to get a reasonable living in the medical profession, though even here there could be difficulties. If it is further considered that the practice of medicine had a strong tradition among Jews, then the difference in distribution might be expected.

If this explanation is correct, what we would expect from the distribution of achieved careers is a high proportion of civil servants among non-Jews, against a low proportion of civil servants and a high proportion of doctors and lawyers among Jews. If we now look at Tables 15–18 we can see that this is precisely what happens, with a little variation between the schools (surprisingly small, given the size of the samples). In Group A, the key group for liberal bourgeois trends, the percentage differences are marked. In the Mariahilfergymnasium, 8 per cent of the Jews become officials, whereas 33 per cent of non-Jews do; 36 per cent and 21 per cent of Jews become lawyers and doctors respectively, compared to 20 per cent and 13 per cent for non-Jews. Ironically, perhaps, the differences in Group B are even more marked. At the Wasagymnasium the situation is more or less the same, though with different proportions of doctors and lawyers among the Jewish group. There is still a large disparity between the proportion of Jews and non-Jews entering the bureaucracy, 7 per cent compared to 35 per cent in Group A. The proportions for lawyers here are almost the same at 23 per cent for Jews and 24 per cent for non-Jews. Yet this is more than compensated for by a large difference in the proportions for doctors, a third of all Jews in Group A, but only 16 per cent of non-Jews in the group.

If we take the categories of lawyers, doctors and journalists together, Jewish proportions in Group A are far above the non-Jewish ones. In the Mariahilfergymnasium these three careers account for 59 per cent of Jews, and only 33 per cent of non-Jews. In the Wasagymnasium the equivalent figures are 59 per cent and 41 per cent respectively. In equivalent groups Jews are heavily over-represented in the liberal professions. What is more, a substantial part of non-Jewish representation in these careers is due to the sons of doctors and lawyers following their fathers' careers, something which appears to have been much rarer among Jews, though the numbers are too small to give this much weight. (The figures and percentages are given in Group A* in Tables 15–18.) If the movements from the sectors commerce, finance and industry are taken on their own, the disparity between the Jewish and non-Jewish entry into the liberal professions is even greater. The figure in the relevant sector for the Mariahilfergymnasium is 60 per cent of Jews, 29 per cent of non-Jews. For the Wasagymnasium the figure is more varied, at 64 per cent of Jews, and 25 per cent of non-Jews. In terms of the social mobility from the capitalist to the intellectual wing of the liberal bourgeoisie, Jews seem to have chosen this route with far greater frequency than non-Jews, who chose other career opportunities, notably in the bureaucracy.

The results of these differences in achieved careers were fairly dramatic for the liberal educated class of Vienna, as is made evident even in the limited sample from our two Gymnasien. Jews comprise only 30 per cent of the sample when the two schools' figures are combined. Yet they comprise half of all doctors and lawyers in the area of achieved careers. This compares with a base in the area of father's occupation of only 28 per cent. The figures for Group A are even more plain. Jews comprise 53 per cent of Group A in the sample, compared to 65·3 per cent in the general sample of occupations. From this group Jews comprise 65 per cent of doctors and lawyers. Thus, even when under-represented, Jews comprise about two-thirds of the sons of liberal bourgeois parents who went on to become lawyers and doctors. It is hence understandable that people referred to Vienna's liberal educated class as more or less a Jewish group. As described here, the Jewish predominance in this group appears to have been a product of the special position of the Jews within the educational system, and the special form of social mobility – keeping within the liberal bourgeoisie – which Jews adopted to a far greater degree than their non-Jewish counterparts *within the same social classes.*

It is probable that a large degree of divergence was due to the fact that an official career was out of consideration for most without conversion. There may also have been 'internal' Jewish reasons for the difference. The main point for us is that there was this divergence, and that it explains how Jews could have constituted such a large presence in the liberal wing of the educated classes.

TOWARDS AN EXPLANATION OF JEWISH PREDOMINANCE IN THE CULTURAL ÉLITE IN VIENNA

The evidence from the Gymnasien strongly suggests that there were several factors at work in creating the situation of Jewish predominance described earlier in this chapter. What is plain is that, once the stage of superior secondary education was reached, the formation of a liberal bourgeois sector dominated by Jews, and due to the patterns of social mobility increasingly so, had been achieved. There still remains the question of how it was that Jews could assume this position within the educational system.

Even given their over-representation in the sector of commercial independents, it seems very unlikely that Jews could have constituted the 80 per cent of merchants and salesmen that they do in the school figures. Unfortunately we cannot confirm or deny this, for the detailed statistics are not available.[40] The story in Hungary is different, and there Victor Karady has conducted a thorough evaluation of the actual, as opposed to class-biased, over-representation of Jews in the Hungarian system of secondary education before 1914. According to him, the Jewish over-representation can be reduced to a ratio of 3:2.[41] This still means that, before the First World War, if you were Jewish you were one and a half times as likely to go to school as a non-Jew, regardless of your social class. What is more, Karady's figures, in generalizing the case, miss what I take to be a central element of any explanation of the Jewish predominance in the liberal educated class, that it was the sons of capitalists (merchants) who were the new part of that educated class and that this sector saw the largest Jewish presence.

Table 9 shows something besides a Jewish over-representation in the capitalist sectors. It shows also that they are not over-represented, or only marginally so, in groups such as liberal professions or public employment. This is a reflection of the fact that in German (Austrian) society there was a tradition of learning similar to that of the Jews. This was especially so amongst the bureaucracy with its Josephinist legacy and the need to keep up status as a family in the governing élite.[42] There were social considerations involved with education, and hence there was a large number of officials' sons in the Gymnasien, which is to be expected. What is unexpected is the even larger number of Jewish merchants' sons, if we were working with a purely sociological, class-based explanatory framework. Here, at the core of the liberal bourgeois sector, we have a

[40] Rozenblit, *The Jews of Vienna*, pp. 65–8 discusses Jewish occupational structure, but does not provide any comprehensive statistics about the place of Jews in the general occupational structure. Statistics on the Jewish position in the occupational structure of Vienna are available, but only for the period after the First World War. See Sylvia Maderegger, *Die Juden im österreichischen Ständestaat 1934–8* (Vienna 1973) pp. 219–20; Herbert Rosenkranz, 'The Anschluss and the Tragedy of Austrian Jewry 1938–1945' in Josef Fraenkel, ed., *The Jews of Austria, Essays on their Life, History and Destruction* (London 1967) p. 480.

[41] Victor Karady, Jewish Enrolment Patterns in Classical Secondary Education in Old Régime and Inter-War Hungary' in *Studies in Contemporary Jewry I* ed. J. Frankel (Bloomington 1984) pp. 225–52, esp. pp. 240–1.

[42] See Paul R. Mendes-Flohr, 'The Study of the Jewish Intellectual: Some Methodological Proposals' in Frances Malino and Phyllis Albert, eds., *Essays in Modern Jewish History* (London 1982) pp. 158–9.

Jewish over-representation, which, I suggest, can only be explained by the different cultural backgrounds and goals of a Jewish and Catholic trader in the Monarchy.[43] It was this flood of sons of the Jewish commercial classes which was the truly dynamic factor in Vienna's cultural world at the end of the nineteenth century. It looks very much, therefore, as if some recourse to the old idea of the Jewish emphasis on education is necessary as a supplement to the social explanation of Jewish predominance in the liberal educated class and cultural élite.

VIENNA 1900 – A JEWISH EXPERIENCE?

The various statistics gathered in the preceding pages indicate that Jewish individuals occupied a predominant place in both the cultural élite and in its supposed social and educational base. What our evidence from the Gymnasien especially shows is that, if Schorske is right about the 'liberal bourgeoisie' and if Boyer is right about the social history of politics in the late nineteenth century in Vienna, then it was inevitable that Viennese modern culture would be largely Jewish, for the cultural élite tended to be made up of Jews among other Jews.

It might be objected that this is an irrelevancy, that though this élite was largely composed of Jews those Jews were no different from the non-Jews; in their basic attitudes and background they were all merely 'liberal bourgeois'. The problem with this is that it begs the question of whether there was a difference in background, and how important the Jewish background and being Jewish was to these individuals. Whether it was due to 'internal' or 'external' reasons, it is quite clear from my figures that there were definite differences *within* the liberal bourgeois sector between Jews and non-Jews when it came to important decisions such as university subject or career. Furthermore, these variances in career choice and achievement exacerbated the already large difference in social background between the bulk of Jews and non-Jews (Jewish merchant, Catholic official). When all the large Jewish preponderances in the various liberal bourgeois groups are taken together, we can see that many 'liberal bourgeois' backgrounds in Vienna amounted in reality to Jewish backgrounds, and hence an almost monopolized Jewish experience.

One of the most clear-cut cases is that of the most famous Viennese Jew, Sigmund Freud. Freud was born in Moravia, the son of a merchant, came to Vienna and attended the *Sperlgymnasium* in the Leopoldstadt. This in

---

[43] On this point see Julius Carlebach, 'The Forgotten Connection – Women and Jews in the Conflict between Enlightenment and Romanticism' in *LBIY* 1979 pp. 113–18. Carlebach describes how the Jews are 'bourgeois' from the religious and cultural tradition, before their rôle in the economy is taken into account. This applies to the attitude to education as well. Catholic traditions are different. See below, p. 88 ff.

itself was a background almost exclusively Jewish.[44] He chose to study medicine. My figures on career choice show that Jews constituted 78 per cent of those sons from the liberal bourgeois sector who chose medicine, and 93 per cent of merchants' sons who did so. He went on to be a doctor. As we have seen, when under-represented, Jews constituted 65 per cent of those from the liberal bourgeois sector who became doctors or lawyers. In other words, it appears that Freud and those like him could hardly help being Jewish, for their career plan in the Viennese context was a Jewish one. It was no accident, on this reckoning, that the circle around Freud in the early days was almost exclusively Jewish.

There were non-Jews who followed similar career patterns and who came from backgrounds much the same. It must be stated that Vienna 1900 was not an exclusively Jewish phenomenon. Especially in the graphic arts where, it might be added, Jews were not well-represented in the educational system, there were non-Jews who mirrored and reflected the same modern culture as the Jews. It might be considered that this shows the 'Jewish element' to be irrelevant, as there were non-Jews with the same ideas, the same attitudes. Yet the point to remember is that the majority of these figures were the products of a specific background, that of the assimilation. While ideas and movements in art and culture are, or can be, socially objective, and hence available to all who care to look for them, there is nevertheless room for studying the effects of social, religious, cultural or ethnic affinities and shared experiences to delineate influences on a larger scale. Individuals will always appear in the history of cultural movements from the most diverse backgrounds, but when a great many individuals appear from the same group, then the natural thing is to see if that group's history or experience provides traditions and ways of looking at the world which make individuals from that group more receptive to types of already existing thought, and inspire them to new ideas and insights.

The Jews were not alone in Vienna 1900, but they constituted by far the largest part of it, and their situation made them in many ways the core of the modern culture. While there are other traditions and backgrounds which added to Vienna 1900, it was the Jewish experience which was the most prevalent among its central figures and its audience, even when that experience is defined in social and not even ethnic terms, as Freud's case illustrates. The sheer preponderance of Jews at strategic points in Viennese cultural history means that the Jewish background of these people cannot be dismissed as irrelevant. It now remains for us to see whether it was significant for these individuals and the culture they generated that they were Jewish, from a Jewish background.

[44] The ten examples from my sample at the Sperlgymnasium, which fit Freud's background, were all Jewish.

PART II

The Jewish background to Viennese culture

5

Jewish consciousness; Jewish mind?

There are two ways in which the Jewish background to Vienna's cultural élite might be researched. They vary greatly in their complexity and empirical verifiability. The first approach is to look at what various members of the élite themselves say about their Jewishness and its consequences. If the assimilation had been entirely successful, this self-consciousness would not have survived. The degree to which it did still exist is thus some sort of empirical pointer to the persistence of a separate Jewish identity, even if this is a negative one as far as the individuals themselves were concerned.

The second way of studying the significance of the Jewish background is far more complex and speculative; it involves looking beneath the empirical surface and attempting to make connections on the lines of some sort of 'Jewish element' surviving in Vienna's modern culture. There are various difficulties in such an approach which need some elaboration. It would therefore be as well to establish that there is a problem to study, at least on a conscious level, before getting embroiled in fraught discussions of the 'Jewish mind'.

THE SURVIVAL OF CONSCIOUSNESS

Before the assimilation Jews had some idea of what being Jewish entailed. Full assimilation would have meant that this sense of a Jewish identity would have disappeared. It has been claimed that Jews, having assimilated, became the same as everyone else with the same liberal bourgeois background, that they ceased being Jews in any meaningful sense, and were merely liberal bourgeois, sharing the same self-image as their social counterparts. For this to have occurred, the Jewish question would have had to have left the consciousness of Jews and non-Jews. This is not what happened in Vienna at the turn of the century.

It is perhaps true that for many people of Jewish descent a positive approach to their religious and cultural heritage was lacking. Many 'Jews' did not know the first thing about the religion, nor did they wish to. Many made a point of claiming that their Jewishness was irrelevant or overcome. All this implies, however, that at a deeper and wider level there was a considerable consciousness of the problem of being Jewish.

How great the survival was depends on how the word 'consciousness' is defined. On the one hand one can be a 'conscious Jew' in the affirmative sense which the German phrase '*bewusster Jude*' conveys. Few of the central figures in Viennese culture were 'conscious Jews' in that sense. On the other hand, most were self-conscious about the fact of their being Jews, and, as such, we can conclude that any position taken on the Jewish question, either positive or negative, is evidence that it was still a conscious factor in the minds of these people.

Given the widest definition of 'consciousness', it is plain that the Jewish question was still very prominent in Vienna around 1900. This was true for Jews and non-Jews. Vienna was governed by an antisemitic party after 1895 and was also the birthplace of modern Zionism. Vienna was the city where Hitler learnt to see Jews.[1] Two of the major published works of the period, Schnitzler's *Der Weg ins Freie* and Weininger's *Geschlecht und Charakter* discussed the Jewish question at length, and, as we shall see, the same was true about private correspondence. The ways in which this survival of consciousness affected the ways these individuals saw themselves and the world is the subject of a later section. Here we merely wish to map out the limits of consciousness, and show how even a negative attitude, or the denial of being Jewish, might be held to be a sign of residual recognition of the Jewish problem.

Many figures in Vienna's cultural élite denied that they were Jewish. This did not mean that the Jewish problem went away. Max Adler, the socialist thinker, treated his Jewishness as an irrelevancy, as did the legal theorist, Hans Kelsen, and the psychologist, Alfred Adler. All three, however, experienced the fact that others still regarded them as Jewish, especially when it came to academic promotion.[2] I would argue that not wanting to be regarded as Jewish, but still being treated as such, is not the same thing as being unaffected in any way by the Jewish problem, that is to say, being totally unconscious that there is a problem. A wish not to address the question is also consciousness that there is a question in the first place. It is just that the consciousness involved is a negative one.

Many witnesses claim that they were never conscious of being Jewish to the extent of not even denying it. Their sincerity need not necessarily be

---

[1] Ivar Oxaal, *The Jews of Pre-1914 Vienna: Two Working Papers* (Hull 1981) pp. 1–4.
[2] On Alfred Adler, see Manès Sperber, *Masks of Loneliness, Alfred Adler in Perspective* (New York 1974) p. 31; on Hans Kelsen and Max Adler, see R. A. Métall, *Hans Kelsen: Leben und Werk* (Vienna 1969) pp. 10–12, 43.

questioned. It was, no doubt, possible for some to avoid any sense of the Jewish predicament, either through sheltered lives or blithe ignorance. However, when many of the claims to a lack of Jewish consciousness are put under closer inspection, it often turns out that these statements have been misunderstood, or that, within context, they actually reveal some sort of implicit Jewish self-consciousness. Sigmund Mayer states in his memoirs that he was not conscious of being a Jew until the 1880s.[3] This has been quoted as evidence that it was possible to forget the Jewish problem in the heyday of liberalism.[4] Elsewhere, however, Mayer claims that there was indeed antisemitism during this era in that the Liberal government did not recruit Jews to its bureaucracy, because they feared the response from their electorate to too many Jews being in the administration.[5] Mayer's statement about not thinking himself Jewish appears a rhetorical device to emphasize the huge impact on him and his kind of the emergence of racial antisemitism as a strong political force in the 1880s. Mayer, it turns out, was very consciously Jewish after the 1880s.[6]

A similar example is afforded by the memoirs of Käthe Leichter, the daughter of a typically Jewish, liberal bourgeois family, who later became a left-wing sociologist. She seems to have been so sheltered from antisemitic prejudice that she could claim until 1938 that no one regarded her as Jewish among her colleagues.[7] This begs the question of how she knew this was so. In fact, it was not so. Many of her colleagues, perhaps behind her back, saw her very much as Jewish.[8] With regard to her knowledge that no one saw her as Jewish, this can only have been the result of a consciousness which she had that she herself was not like her Jewish friends. It all seems to have been the result, on her own evidence, of a semi-conscious assimilation into the lifestyle of the non-Jewish girls at her school. She is quite open about the fact that she saw herself as mediating between what she identified as a definite Jewish group and the others.[9]

In other words, the statement about not being regarded as Jewish is actually an admission of pride in not being taken for a Jew. This is a classic case of 'negative consciousness', the wish, or the belief, that you had escaped your Jewishness. The irony of this is that it is a uniquely Jewish

[3] Sigmund Mayer, *Ein jüdischer Kaufmann 1831–1911: Lebenserinnerungen* (Leipzig 1911) p. 289.
[4] For instance, Wolfgang Häusler, 'Toleranz, Emanzipation und Antisemitismus' in N. Vielmetti, Drabek, Häusler, Stuhlpfarrer, *Das österreichische Judentum* (Vienna 1974) p. 109.
[5] Sigmund Mayer, *Die Wiener Juden: Kommerz, Kultur, Politik 1700–1900* (Vienna 1918) pp. 478–9.
[6] Mayer, *Ein jüdischer Kaufmann*, p. 289.
[7] *Käthe Leichter: Leben und Werk*, ed. Herbert Steiner (Vienna 1973) p. 309.
[8] *Ibid.* p. 24. [9] *Ibid.* p. 309.

experience, for it makes no sense to talk about the pride of a person not of Jewish descent in not being regarded as Jewish, while in the case of someone such as Käthe Leichter, the fact that she was proud to appear Aryan is just one more sign of Jewish consciousness of a rather odd kind.

The cases of both Mayer and Leichter illustrate the ambiguities in any denial of consciousness of being Jewish. Indeed any contemporary denial will in itself be evidence of at least a negative consciousness, of which there was much in Vienna in the first years of the century. The background to this is the fact that Vienna was the major centre of antisemitism in Europe before the First World War, and the only capital city at that time to have an elected antisemitic government.[10] In other words, it was next to impossible to *ignore* the Jewish problem – affirmation and denial were just two sides of the same coin.[11] This is true at the limits of our study as well as at its centre, as is shown in the cases of totally assimilated figures of only partial Jewish descent such as Hugo von Hofmannsthal and Ludwig Wittgenstein.

It has often been claimed that such individuals, because of their marginality in the Jewish question, cannot be included as part of that question.[12] Yet neither Hofmannsthal nor Wittgenstein were totally free in their minds from their Jewish heritage. In the case of Hofmannsthal there is little firm evidence for a consciousness of his heritage except, perhaps, the often quoted lines:

> Weariness of long forgotten races,
> I cannot brush off my eyelids.[13]

The question of what Hofmannsthal's actual attitudes to the Jewish part of his heritage were is a vexed one. Broch, for instance, saw him very much as the product of an assimilation, repeating in his poetry the attempt to realize the assimilationist dream of his great-grandfather, Isaak Löw-Hofmann.[14] There is circumstantial evidence, however, that Hofmanns-

---

[10] On the general history of the antisemitic triumph in Vienna see P. G. J. Pulzer, *The Rise of Political Antisemitism in Germany and Austria* (New York 1964) pp. 128–85; John W. Boyer, *Political Radicalism in Late Imperial Vienna* (Chicago 1981).

[11] Cf. Ludwig Hirschfeld, *Was nicht im Baedeker steht: Wien und Budapest* (Munich 1927) p. 56, where Hirschfeld lists as one of Vienna's specialities the way in which the first question asked about anyone is: 'Ist er ein Jud?'

[12] For instance, Klaus Lohrmann, ed., *1,000 Jahre österreichisches Judentum* (Eisenstadt 1982) p. 200.

[13] Quoted in Ilsa Barea, *Vienna* (London 1966) p. 300.

[14] Hermann Broch, *Hofmannsthal und seine Zeit*, in Broch, *Schriften zur Literatur 1* (Frankfurt-on-Main 1975) pp. 178–9, 207; see also, Lohrmann, ed., *1,000 Jahre*, p. 339, on Hofmannsthal's Jewish descent.

thal was, to say the least, very edgy about his Jewish descent, as his relationship to Willy Haas suggests.[15] Felix Salten certainly saw him as acting on the fact of his Jewishness in not attempting to gain admittance to the high aristocracy.[16] The effect of this will be discussed later, but what is important here is that there was a remainder, however slight, of apparent consciousness.

With Wittgenstein the story is similar. For many years it was quite unclear how Jewish the Wittgenstein family actually was. It now appears that Ludwig Wittgenstein was three-quarters Jewish by descent.[17] It is also now apparent that, at least at one stage in his life in the 1930s, Wittgenstein was far more conscious of his Jewishness than was once thought. This has been revealed by the publication of some of his notes in the volume *Culture and Value* (*Vermischte Bemerkungen*). It includes the following confession: 'Amongst Jews "genius" is found only in the holy man. Even the greatest of Jewish thinkers is no more than talented. (Myself for instance.)'[18] This is an extremely thin shaft of light, but it does illuminate Wittgenstein's way of thinking, as a 'Jew'.

A cryptic comment such as this is only the most obvious of a number which Wittgenstein makes in this volume about Jews. Rush Rhees has examined these and pointed out that though they show some resemblance to the thought of Otto Weininger, they do not (unlike Weininger) show a particular wish to deny his own Jewishness; they are, rather, an attempt to come to terms with being Jewish, an acceptance of this.[19] If this is so, then comments such as the suggestion that Jewish and non-Jewish thinkers should not be measured by the same standards are clear signs that, in the 1930s at least, Wittgenstein seriously considered himself (from the above quotation) to be somehow Jewish, part of the Jewish intellectual heritage and separate.[20] The tantalizing question is whether this view was preceded by another attitude to being Jewish, and if so, in what form? It is often supposed that Wittgenstein came to his Jewishness only in the 1930s and was not aware of it before then. We shall see that this was rather unlikely in the context of the Viennese élite. It is enough here to

---

[15] Willy Haas, *Hugo von Hofmannsthal* (Berlin 1964) p. 10; also Willy Haas, *Die literarische Welt: Erinnerungen* (Munich 1960) pp. 46–9.

[16] Felix Salten, 'Der junge Hofmannsthal: das Bild eines Dichters' in the *Neue Volkszeitung*. Date unknown. The article is part of the Steininger Bequest, in the archives of the *Bibliographica Judaica*, Frankfurt-on-Main.

[17] See the appendix in W. W. Bartley, *Wittgenstein* (Philadelphia 1973) pp. 184–6.

[18] Ludwig Wittgenstein, *Culture and Value* (Oxford 1980) p. 18. The original reads: 'Das jüdische "Genie" ist nur ein Heiliger. Der grösste jüdische Denker ist nur ein Talent. (Ich z.B.)' in Wittgenstein, *Vermischte Bemerkungen* (Frankfurt-on-Main 1977) p. 43.

[19] Rush Rhees, ed., *Recollections of Wittgenstein* (Oxford 1984) pp. 177–80.

[20] *Culture and Value*, p. 16, 19.

show that one of the great philosophers of this century, at a critical time in his life, felt he had to come to terms with his Jewish heritage, though he was at the very limit of the assimilation.

THE MYTH OF THE JEWISH MIND

Jews were predominant numerically in much of Viennese modern culture, and, when it is carefully considered, it seems plain that there was a much greater awareness of Jewishness among the cultural élite than might at first appear. The question remains, therefore, how to assess the 'Jewish influence' in Viennese culture.

It is not as if this were a novel question. The rôle of Jews in modern European culture has been much discussed, although the debate on the 'Jewish intellectual' appears far from closed.[21] Our statistical survey allows us to avoid much of this debate in that it suggests that we do not need to provide any special Jewish characteristic, such as greater intelligence, as a given factor. If we accept some sort of cultural explanation for the over-representation in the educational system (which a later section will show to be a reasonable assumption), then the apparent Jewish predominance in the cultural élite is explicable in terms of what we know of the socio-political history of Vienna and its repercussions on the culture. Hence Peter Gay's seemingly valid remark that we should study stupid Jews becomes an irrelevancy.[22]

We can see why Jews would be predominant in the cultural élite, on one level at least; what we now want to find out is whether the Jewishness of these people was a distinct influence on the way they viewed the world and on what they did. The point at issue is whether being Jewish meant, in the Viennese context, being more open to certain ideas in a way that would not have been so pronounced had there not been this Jewish element. We are interested not so much in the causes of Jewish predominance as in the effects on the culture of this remarkable phenomenon.

Having decided this, we are still faced with the thorny methodological problem of how to construct a conceptual framework to deal with the question of a specific, Jewish influence. This depends on how we regard the words 'Jewish influence'. They could be taken to mean merely the teachings of a religion, Judaism. This is the narrowest definition, but, given the fact that there was a Jewish awareness even among converts and non-

---

[21] See Paul R. Mendes-Flohr, 'The Study of the Jewish Intellectual: Some Methodological Proposals' in F. Malino and P. Albert, eds., *Essays in Modern Jewish History* (London 1982) pp. 142–66.

[22] Peter Gay, 'Encounter with Modernism: German Jews in German Culture 1888–1914' in *Midstream*, Feb. 1975, vol. XXI, no. 2, p. 25.

believers (such as Freud), too narrow for our purposes. The alternative extreme would be to regard the Jewish element as a matter of race. There is a middle option, some kind of socio-cultural influence. This looks unattractive because so hard to define and leaving little room for detailed theorizing; it is vague and often presented as a hotch-potch of various theories about the Jewish mind, from which one is expected to select at random.[23] None of these options looks particularly promising.

The traditional approach has seen the Jewish mind usually in what amounts to racial or at least metaphysical terms. Although more recent attempts to define it have been more circumspect, it is more or less innate in the idea of the Jewish mind that it deals in large generalities. The results of this can be seen most clearly in the older, classic attempts to describe the Jewish mind, which reveal the shortcomings of the idea when studying a concrete historical phenomenon such as the Jewish influence in Vienna.

The main source of difficulty is the way in which the concept of the Jewish mind encourages universal claims, based on the idea of racial characteristics or some common spiritual quality, which amounts to the same thing. This is true both of those who are for the Jews and those against, and can be illustrated by a few examples. Houston Stewart Chamberlain's *Die Grundlagen des 19. Jahrhunderts*, one of the most notorious works of cultural antisemitism, developed the concept of the Jew as the idea of abstract materialism and thus the destroyer of western values.[24] The book was, ironically, dedicated to Julius von Wiesner, who was of Jewish descent. This kind of problem was easily solved by Chamberlain for Judaism, being an idea, could though inherent be overcome by the individual.[25] That is to say, whenever evidence was brought against the theory in the form of a non-Jewish Jew, then this was evidence of a metaphysical overcoming of the idea. There was thus no empirical way of proving or disproving the theory.

In another case, that of the Zionist Theodor Lessing's *Der jüdische Selbsthass*, the claim was just as metaphysical and even more absolute. For Lessing, Jewishness was a matter of the blood and no Jew, however much he had assimilated into German society, could really put down roots in the 'blood and soil of the homeland'. Lessing talked of how the German-Jewish writers had abused their blood by devoting themselves to a racially foreign culture.[26] Again, there was no real way of arguing with the main thesis, just as there was no way of arguing with the Nuremberg Laws, because,

---

[23] For instance, William M. Johnston, *The Austrian Mind: an Intellectual and Social History 1848–1938* (Berkeley 1972, 1983) pp. 23–9.
[24] Houston Stewart Chamberlain, *Die Grundlagen des 19. Jahrhunderts* (Munich 1899) pp. 230–1.   [25] *Ibid.* pp. 453–5.
[26] Theodor Lessing, *Der jüdische Selbsthass* (Berlin 1930) pp. 68ff.

a priori, Jewish contributions to German culture were decadent and artificial. The only hope for Jews was their own land.

The problem with such large-scale assertions is that it is impossible to refute them. There is no way to get past the system's defences. Yet this means that there is no way of testing the theories empirically, for in the one case the theory cannot be contradicted, and in the other the theory states that any contradiction is necessarily an illusion. On the other hand, this means that there is no way to prove that the theories are correct either. There is simply no criterion for empirical study, and thus, as far as historical understanding is concerned, such concepts can be ignored.

Although they are impervious to argument, such unitary explanations show some very bizarre tendencies when they attempt to deal with concrete instances of Jewish influence. This stems from the fact that, despite their universalist claims on it, the Jewish mind has manifested itself in a tremendous multiplicity in the empirical world. Chamberlain's theory, in principle, could accommodate this, as we have seen, by allowing for the individual to overcome his metaphysical inheritance. This drove him to some rather odd conclusions. Thus, when he attacked revolutionary atheists for showing typically Jewish traits, he contrasted these Messianic zealots with the peace-loving, honest rabbi, who cared for his community. That type of person, said Chamberlain, is *not* Jewish.[27] How a rabbi, in the thrall of the evil religion of Judaism, could not be Jewish, he did not explain.

In the case of Lessing, as soon as he starts to make claims on the real world, the evidence, at least as far as the particular case of Vienna is concerned, begins to pile up against him. One of the major claims of his book is that the Jews, somehow, because they were alienated from their environment, were the people who made mathematics with its tendency to destroy limits into the ruler of the sciences.[28] This, in itself, is an echo of the traditional theory represented in Chamberlain of the Jew as an abstract thinker, and still survives in the diluted version which claims that Jews naturally make better mathematicians than others. This may appear the case elsewhere, but as far as Vienna at the turn of the century is concerned, Jews were remarkably under-represented in the 'mathematicizing of culture'. In physics Ernst Mach and Ludwig Boltzmann were the figures who put mathematics into a dominant position. Mach championed the positivistic approach of disregarding real factors and making physics a series of formulae.[29] Boltzmann founded statistical mechanics.[30]

[27] Chamberlain, *Die Grundlagen*, pp. 450–1.   [28] Lessing, *Selbsthass*, pp. 84–5.
[29] On Mach, see John T. Blackmore, *Ernst Mach: his Work, Life and Influence* (Berkeley 1972) pp. 165–79; also Johnston, *The Austrian Mind* pp. 181–6.
[30] On Boltzmann, see Johnston, *The Austrian Mind*, pp. 186ff; also Allan Janik and Stephen Toulmin, *Wittgenstein's Vienna* (New York 1973) pp. 143–5.

In economics the Austrian School of Menger, Wieser and Böhm-Bawerk developed the theory of marginal utility. Architectural functionalism, where the mathematics of construction costs came before decoration, was the product of the thought of Otto Wagner and Adolf Loos in Vienna.[31] The greatest mathematical achievement in Vienna was that of Kurt Gödel, who proved that mathematics itself is only relative.[32] None of these people was from a Jewish background.

Some Jews, conversely, showed a marked aversion to putting too much emphasis on a rationalizing of the world. Theodor Gomperz, despite his positivism, attacked Wilhelm Ostwald for suggesting that the historical languages should be replaced by some rational, new language. Gomperz's argument was, interestingly, that the disappearance of the old languages would mean the loss of their ability to express the beauty of the world in their own special way.[33] The classics were defended as a school subject because of the way they taught the spiritual values of Greece and Rome.[34] There is even a famous example where someone of a Jewish background was completely misinterpreted by a non-Jew as having developed a mathematical system, when he had really contributed to the defence of the very values that Chamberlain and Lessing thought the assimilated Jew attacked. I am thinking here of Russell's introduction to Wittgenstein's *Tractatus Logico-Philosophicus*.[35] These examples do not prove that Jews did not excel at mathematics in some cases. They do mean, however, that for Vienna this idea that the Jews were the mathematicizers of western culture simply does not stand up.

The problem with any idea of a Jewish mind is that there is clearly more than one type of Jew. One need only think of the huge differences between the western Jew and the traditional *Ostjude*, and that is only the most extreme case. The great multiplicity of the Jewish mind has led to some rather embarrassing disagreements within the various camps. Thus it was Theodor Lessing who pointed out that, whereas most people viewed the Jews as too abstract and too materialistic, Eugen Dühring, the arch-antisemite of the early 1880s, regarded the Jews as oriental mystics, whose superstition meant that they could not understand or appreciate the finer points of the great German tradition of rational thought and positivist science. The Jew of one was the German of the other.[36]

It is not difficult to see the root of these confusions. Apart from the

---

[31] On Otto Wagner, see Carl E. Schorske, *Fin-de-Siècle Vienna: Politics and Culture* (London 1980) pp. 72–110. On Adolf Loos, see Janik and Toulmin, *Wittgenstein's Vienna* pp. 98–102.

[32] Johnston, *The Austrian Mind*, p. 189.

[33] *Theodor Gomperz: ein Gelehrtenleben im Bürgertum der Franz-Josephszeit*, eds. H. Gomperz and R. A. Kann (Vienna 1974) pp. 419–25.

[34] Theodor Gomperz, *Essays und Erinnerungen* (Stuttgart 1905) p. 214.

[35] Janik and Toulmin, *Wittgenstein's Vienna* pp. 213–4.

[36] Lessing, *Selbsthass*, pp. 83–4.

multiplicity of Jewish types, there was also, as George Mosse has pointed out, the fact that the antisemites' view of what was Jewish depended on what they feared.[37] Thus, if you were part of the *völkisch* movement, the Jew became the symbol of the attack on German values as the harbinger of an abstract rationality, and if you were a positivist such as Dühring, then the Jew became a magician. Whatever the case, the huge over-conceptualization to which Germans of the time were prone meant that personal prejudices became inflated into pseudo-metaphysical systems, with the result that any sensible approach to the question of the Jewish influence was swamped in a flood of rhetoric and quite lost.

Any racial approach, whether it comes from the antisemitic or the philosemitic side, will be useless as an historical tool and open to all kinds of contradictions. Indeed *any* system which starts with the premiss that there is *one* Jewish mind, which can explain all manifestations of the Jews in western culture, will fall down in face of the huge variety of the Jewish experience. If put in this way, it could be said that *the* Jewish mind does not exist, that it is a myth.

THE HISTORICAL PERSPECTIVE

Yet, as we have seen, there *was* a phenomenon in Vienna, which demands some sort of recognition. Nor is it unreasonable to suggest that there was indeed a specific, Jewish influence on the élite's attitudes and hence the culture. In the case of the leading figures of the Viennese cultural élite, we are, at most, talking of a distance from traditional Judaism of three generations, with Hofmannsthal and Wittgenstein being the limiting cases. It would be very surprising if something from the past had not been transferred to these people, and there is, in addition, the point that merely being Jewish by descent, in a period of quite strong antisemitism, created its own responses. It is not the idea that there was a Jewish influence on the culture which is wrong, but rather the idea that this can be expressed in the comprehensive terms of a unitary Jewish mind. What is needed is a new conceptual framework which gets away from this simplistic approach.

The answer proposed here and hinted at earlier is to treat the particular case of Vienna on its own terms, as a historical phenomenon in its own right, regardless of higher philosophizing. What is needed is to put the particular experiences of the members of the cultural élite in the context of what happened in Vienna during the age of assimilation. This involves tracing the background of tradition from which these people originated

---

[37] George L. Mosse, *Germans and Jews: The Right, the Left and the Search for a 'Third Force' in Pre-Nazi Germany* (London 1971) p. 37.

and the degree to which these traditions were transmitted, albeit in secularized forms, to the attitudes of the assimilated community. Following on from this, the special experience of the Jews as assimilants in an antisemitic environment will have to be described, and then, through the experiences of the individuals themselves, an attempt made to show how this complex process culminated in certain common attitudes, which came in turn to be reflected in their work.

Such an approach, looking at the phenomenon for what it was, a dynamic historical process, has many advantages, not least of which is that it is naturally built to allow for variations and contrasts *within* the framework. At each stage in the process, which the following pages will describe, there were several possible responses, resulting in a rich panoply of varying attitudes. Yet these attitudes can still, according to the framework, be related because of their common origin. The result may therefore be seen in terms of a network of *family resemblances*, association by common historical origin rather than by being part of some impossible metaphysical construction.[38]

The following chapters will attempt to describe the historical process of the Jewish influence on Viennese culture in terms of the empirical evidence of how the members of the cultural élite were affected by the various moments of the process. As this is a description, with no attempt to verify the unverifiable, any conclusions offered must necessarily be tentative. I do not think that this type of cultural history allows for definitive answers on such questions as Jewish influence, or any other influence for that matter. Yet we can describe the context of the culture and of the Jewish assimilation. The very act of description should clear away some of the mystification which attempts to build a model of the Jewish mind have tended to produce.

If it is true that the Jewish mind is a myth as far as Vienna is concerned, we might nevertheless claim that what we are dealing with are many different *Jewish minds* and how they came to their cultural achievement. In showing the ways in which the Jewish background could affect the ideas of individuals, we can perhaps add a significant perspective to our understanding of Viennese culture.

[38] The phrase 'family resemblances' is borrowed from Wittgenstein himself, see his *Philosophical Investigations* (Oxford 1958) para. 67, (p. 32).

⨾ 6 ⨽

The distance from tradition

Very few of the cultural élite came from a background which had much to do with a traditional, religious Jewish upbringing. Their success in becoming central figures in European culture would, after all, have been very unlikely if that had been the case. It was the assimilation, the giving up of specifically Jewish forms of life and thinking, which had made possible this great participation in the surrounding culture. These people were brought up as German-Austrians and they dealt with Viennese themes.

The attitude to Judaism among the assimilated bourgeoisie was generally one of indifference. Conversion to Christianity was felt by many to be some sort of betrayal, not so much of the religion as of the family's history, Judaism being reduced, in the words of Theodor Gomperz, to 'un pieux souvenir de famille'.[1] Whether it was regarded as cowardly to betray the past and convert, or to submit to the past and not convert, the religious issue was a merely formal, if delicate, matter.[2] In the case of Hermann Broch's family it was such a formality that one child was Jewish, the other Catholic.[3]

A sizeable number of individuals did take the step 'out', usually on marriage. As a result some of the foremost 'Jewish' figures of Viennese culture, such as Hofmannsthal and Wittgenstein, were brought up as Christians. For such people it is very difficult to speak of any direct influence from the religious tradition at all.

The same can be said for those brought up as Jews. The Bar Mitzvah was regarded by many as another occasion for presents.[4] Compulsory religious instruction at school was treated by Schnitzler as a joke, and Karl Kraus claimed the poor quality of teaching had a negative effect on the pupils'

---

[1] Theodor Gomperz, *Essays und Erinnerungen* (Stuttgart 1905) p. 197.
[2] For these conflicting attitudes, see Stella Klein-Löw, *Erinnerungen: Erlebtes und Gedachtes* (Vienna 1980) p. 13; Felix Braun, *Das Licht der Welt* (Vienna 1962) p. 36.
[3] Manfred Durzak, *Hermann Broch* (Hamburg 1966) p. 17.
[4] Braun, *Das Licht der Welt*, p. 95.

attitude to Judaism.[5] The impression given by the accounts of Fritz
Mauthner and Hans Kohn in Prague is that religious instruction was a
sham.[6] Sigmund Mayer could claim in Vienna that none of the Jewish
children understood Hebrew, and there were complaints to this effect at
the time.[7] Given this context it is hard to understand how it can still be
claimed that Karl Kraus displayed Talmudic qualities in his work.[8] It is
very doubtful whether Kraus had ever seen a copy of the Talmud, let alone
been able to read it. Thus claims that most of the Viennese élite displayed
forms of the Jewish tradition can fairly safely be said to be pure rhetoric
with no basis of fact.

There are, however, some cases where this is not so clear. Even the most
assimilated sometimes reveal in their memoirs that they had once been
much nearer to the religious tradition than one might have thought. Fritz
Mauthner, from a totally anti-religious house, for a time became a strictly
Orthodox Jew to save his soul and that of his godless family.[9] The positivist
Theodor Gomperz was, until his thirteenth year, a strict follower of the
Jewish ritual laws.[10] Käthe Leichter, under the influence of her Orthodox
grandfather and a *good* religious instructor, became for a while a fairly
strict Jew fasting on the Day of Atonement, to the horror of her liberal
parents.[11] Manès Sperber, the writer, grew up in a Galician shtetl, as did
Joseph Roth.[12] In such cases it is not so easy to reject the idea of some sort
of direct Jewish influence, though it remains problematic.

There are some other cases which show evidence of a clear Jewish
religious consciousness. Max Reinhardt described himself as a 'frommer
Jude', though this was a marginal consideration for his work.[13] Richard
Beer-Hofmann was brought up in an Orthodox home. His *Schlaflied für
Mirjam*, which Rilke lauded as one of the most perfect poems in German
literature, was actually an affirmation of the Jewish heritage.[14] Käthe

[5] Renate Wagner, *Arthur Schnitzler* (Vienna 1981) p. 20; Karl Kraus, *Die Fackel* Nr. 13 (August 1899) p. 30. Cf. Paul Schick, *Karl Kraus* (Hamburg 1965) p. 23.
[6] Fritz Mauthner, *Erinnerungen* (Munich 1918) pp. 116–20; Hans Kohn, *Bürger vielen Welten* (Vienna 1965) p. 62.
[7] Sigmund Mayer, *Die Wiener Juden: Kommerz, Kultur, Politik 1700–1900* (Vienna 1918 pp. 304–5; J. S. Bloch, 'Wie gebieten wir Einhalt dem rapiden Verfall des religiösen Geistes?' in *Österreichische Wochenschrift. Centralorgan für die gesammten Interessen des Judenthums* 15 October 1884 nr. 1 pp. 3–5.
[8] Nike Wagner, *Geist und Geschlecht* (Frankfurt-on-Main 1982) p. 194.
[9] Mauthner, *Erinnerungen*, p. 110.   [10] Gomperz, *Essays*, p. 15.
[11] *Käthe Leichter: Leben und Werk*, ed. Herbert Steiner (Vienna 1973) pp. 239–40.
[12] See Manès Sperber, *Die Wasserträger Gottes* (Munich 1983) for the account of his early life. On Joseph Roth, see David Bronsen, *Joseph Roth: eine Biographie* (Munich 1981) pp. 43ff.
[13] Gottfried Reinhardt, *Der Liebhaber* (Munich 1975) p. 207.
[14] Sol Liptzin, *Germany's Stepchildren* (Philadelphia 1944) p. 240. On Rilke's admiration, see B. Zeller, L. Greve and W. Volke, eds., *Jugend in Wien: Literatur um 1900* (Stuttgart 1974) p. 213.

Leichter's fleeting religiosity was echoed by other survivals of the Jewish past in an otherwise totally assimilated family. Her father, whom she described as a 'universalist', counted one of his abilities the reading of Hebrew. When he taught his daughter about the great freedom fighters of old he would mention the heroic struggle of the Maccabees, something it is very difficult to imagine a Catholic father doing. With an Orthodox grandfather in the background some contact with the Jewish traditions was inevitably maintained.[15]

The most famous but very difficult case in this respect is that of Freud. There has been much disagreement on the degree to which Freud was brought up in Jewish religious traditions. On one side it is claimed that his parents, especially his mother, retained Orthodox practices in the home.[16] Paul Roazen, however, points to a lax Jewish tradition in the home.[17] The truth seems to have lain somewhere in between. Jacob Freud was a typical liberal with the accompanying secular attitudes. Yet he had been brought up with a Talmudic education and continued to be a diligent student of the Talmud. It seems likely that Freud was brought up at home by his father until the age of ten.[18] There is thus ground for thinking that Freud could have been influenced by Talmudic ways of thought or even the Cabbalah. Freud himself hinted as much when he wrote to Jung that he (Jung) would probably see signs of Jewish mysticism in Freud's work.[19]

Yet the case is far from proven. The method of free association and the idea of discerning many levels of meaning in one symbol, for instance, need not have come from Freud's training in the Talmud. It is true that the Talmudic method, with its emphasis on multi-level interpretation of a small text, looks very similar.[20] Yet there are other potential sources. Freud read Börne's essay, *How to Write a Book in Three Days*, and he also heard Theodor Gomperz's lecture on *Traumdeutung und Zauberei*.[21] Gomperz used the empiricists' idea of association to show how the connections which the *interpreters* of dreams used were the result of false causal associations in the real world. Gomperz then set the researcher the task of searching out

[15] *Käthe Leichter*, pp. 252, 262.
[16] R. W. Clark, *Freud: the Man and the Cause* (London 1980) p. 8.
[17] Paul Roazen, *Freud and his Followers* (London 1976) p. 71.
[18] Dennis B. Klein, *The Jewish Origins of the Psychoanalytic Movement* (New York 1981) p. 42.   [19] Clark, *Freud*, p. 220.
[20] This idea is elaborated in Ernst Simon, 'Sigmund Freud, the Jew' in *Leo Baeck Institute Yearbook (LBIY)* 1957, p. 290.
[21] On Börne's influence, see Clark, *Freud*, pp. 18, 120. On Gomperz's lecture, see *Theodor Gomperz: ein Gelehrtenleben im Bürgertum der Franz-Josephszeit*, ed. H. Gomperz and R. A. Kann (Vienna 1974) p. 17. The letter which Freud wrote to Elise Gomperz where he mentions Gomperz's influence on him, of the 12 November 1913, is reproduced in translation in *Sigmund Freud: his Life in Pictures and Words*, eds. Ernst Freud, Lucie Freud and Ilse Grubrich-Simitis (London 1985) p. 85.

the original mistaken association from which all subsequent mystifications had stemmed. Gomperz thus predicted the later method of psychoanalysis only for the interpreter and not the patient.[22] The idea of tracing the associations was already there based on the tradition of Locke.

The case of Freud shows the problems faced when trying to establish a definite influence from any specific Jewish tradition. This is before we even contemplate the fact that what was held to be the Jewish tradition of the mid nineteenth century had in many ways changed considerably from that of a century before.[23] Nevertheless, as recent research has shown, Freud's case provides evidence that a vague, indefinite influence from just such a 'tradition' was more than likely to be present.[24] Just because this tradition had a *vague* influence does not mean that the influence was any weaker than a more definite one. It is often the indistinct influences, the ones which cannot easily be defined, which are the most powerful. As far as Jewish influence on the secularized community is concerned there seem to be two traditions which are especially worthy of attention in the context of Viennese culture. These are the emphasis on education and learning – on the Word – and the special character of Judaism as a religion of ethics and individualism. The following chapters will show how strong these traditions were in the non-assimilated community, and to what extent they survived in Vienna's assimilated cultural élite.

[22] The lecture is reproduced in Gomperz, *Essays*, pp. 72–86.

[23] Jakob Katz's book on the emancipation and assimilation of German Jewry, *Out of the Ghetto* (Cambridge, Mass. 1973), ends in 1870 when mine officially begins, and David Sorkin, in *The Transformation of German Jewry, 1780–1840* (Oxford 1987) shows that the new Jewish identity was already in place in Germany by 1840. While the Jews of the Habsburg Monarchy were rather later in adopting this new identity, the fact of its presence had a profound effect on their debate on what was or was not 'Jewish' around mid century. The following discussion of tradition therefore must be recognized to rest on shifting sands, at least to a degree.

[24] For a subtle and revealing view of the influence of Jewish tradition on Freud, see William J. McGrath, *Freud's Discovery of Psychoanalysis: the Politics of Hysteria* (Ithaca, New York, 1986).

⇒ 7 ⇐

Education

A RELIGIOUS TRADITION

The fact that Jews place a greater emphasis on learning than most other religious groups in western Europe is a common theme in the literature on Jewish culture. The low degree of illiteracy among Jews has been remarked, and the emphasis on education has been used to explain why Jews in central Europe played such a large rôle in cultural life.[1] George Steiner is in this tradition when he sees the Jewish rôle in the 'language turn' as stemming from the reverence for the Word.[2] This kind of idea was also used by contemporaries such as Popper-Lynkeus to explain the greater frequency of middling talents among Jews. Indeed it was so often reiterated by contemporaries that, even if it were seen to have had no historical basis, the claim would still be valid, ideologically.[3] Yet it is fairly clear that there is such an historical base.

The tradition of learning can be traced back in Jewish history at the latest to the teaching of Johanan ben Zacchai of Yabneh after the destruction of the Temple. Since the Jews could no longer worship God in the Temple, Johanan taught that they must do so in other ways, notably through the study of the Holy Word of Scripture by each individual Jew. Israel would thus become a 'kingdom of priests', for each through study

---

[1] For instance, Walter B. Simon, 'The Jewish Vote in Austria' in *Leo Baeck Institute Yearbook* (*LBIY*) 1971, p. 97; W. E. Mosse, 'Judaism, Jews and Capitalism – Weber, Sombart and Beyond' in *LBIY* 1979, p. 6; Claudio Magris, *Weit von wo?* (Vienna 1974) p. 114.

[2] Lecture given by George Steiner, at the Centre Georges Pompidou, Paris 10 October 1984, published as 'Le langage et l'inhumain' in *Revue d'esthétique*, new series no. 9, 1985, *Vienne 1880–1938* (Toulouse 1985) pp. 67–8.

[3] Ingrid Belke, *Die sozialreformerischen Ideen von Josef Popper-Lynkeus 1838–1921* (Tübingen 1978) p. 117. On other contemporary attitudes, see for an early account, Solomon Maimon, *The Autobiography of Solomon Maimon* (London 1954) pp. 12–13, 39. For a mid century Viennese account, Gershon Wolf, *Statistik der Schuljugend in Wien im Jahre 1862*, in *Die Neuzeit*, eds. L. Kompert and S. Szanto, 12 August 1864, no. 33. Also G. Wolf, *Geschichte der Juden in Wien 1156–1876* (Vienna 1876) p. 178.

would worship God.[4] The Jewish place of worship became not a temple but a synagogue, or, as it was called in Yiddish, a *Shul*, where the rabbi was a teacher, not a priest.[5] Judaism thus became dominated by the Book, and its homeland in the Diaspora was the 'land of the Bible'.[6] In the Middle Ages the Jewish ideal of manhood was the *talmid hakham*, the Talmud scholar versed in the Law.[7] The only crown the Jews of the Diaspora recognized was the crown on the Torah, the books of the Law.[8]

This religious tradition quite plainly survived into the nineteenth century, as is clearest from those with an Orthodox background. Manès Sperber reports how in his Galician shtetl regardless of the wretched poverty of many in the village, they all saved money to pay the teacher at the Cheder. Every child was sent off at the age of three to learn how to read and write Hebrew.[9] This is a typical account, echoed in the experience of such people as Heinrich Sussmann and from a much earlier date Sigmund Mayer, who stated that Jewish children were sent to school as soon as they could talk.[10] In Galicia, at least, this approach was worlds away from that of the surrounding peasants:

A Jewish child had to learn to read aged three, had to sit under the strict supervision of the teachers in the Cheder and learn to spell, then to translate difficult texts of Hebrew. The Christian children, on the other hand, only went to school at age six or seven, and they were only gradually taught to read – and only in the language which they already knew.[11]

This different attitude to education seems to have been more or less the same in German Austria, at least among the lower classes. Josephinist efforts to create an educated populace achieved only modest and limited

---

[4] Abraham Leon Sachar, *A History of the Jews* (New York 1965) pp. 120, 145; *Encyclopaedia Judaica* (Jerusalem 1972) vol. 10, pp. 148–54.

[5] Nicholas de Lange, *Judaism* (Oxford 1986) p. 38.

[6] Friedrich Heer, *God's First Love* (London 1970) p. 52; Sol Liptzin, *Germany's Stepchildren* (Philadelphia 1944) p. 147.

[7] David Sorkin, *The Transformation of German Jewry, 1780–1840* (Oxford 1987) pp. 45ff; de Lange, *Judaism*, p. 59.

[8] Heer, *God's First Love*, p. 52; on the status of education in the traditional Jewish community, see Jakob Katz, *Out of the Ghetto* (Cambridge, Mass. 1973) pp. 20ff. For contemporary recognition of the status of scholarship in Judaism, see J. S. Bloch, 'Jüdischer Idealismus' in *Österreichische Wochenschrift. Centralorgan für die gesammten Interessen des Judenthums* (ÖW) 13 February 1885 (no. II.7) p. 1.

[9] Manès Sperber, *Die Wasserträger Gottes* (Munich 1983) pp. 15, 42, 153.

[10] Interview with Heinrich Sussmann, Vienna 7 June 1983; Sigmund Mayer, *Ein jüdischer Kaufmann 1831–1911: Lebenserinnerungen* (Leipzig 1911) pp. 39, 61.

[11] 'Ein jüdisches Kind musste schon mit drei Jahren lesen lernen, viele Stunden des Tages unter der Fuchtel der strengen Cheder-Lehrer mit Buchstabieren und bald auch mit Übersetzen schwerer hebräischer Texte zubringen. Die christlichen Kinder aber kamen erst mit sechs oder gar sieben Jahren in die Schule, man lernte sie allmählich lesen – und nur in der Sprache, die sie schon kannten.' Sperber, *Wasserträger*, p. 42.

success, faced as they were with the weight of tradition. Wittgenstein had to fight against the hostility of parents to too much school for their children, and the political expression of popular Catholicism, the Christian Social party, was well-known for its rejection of the supremacy of education.[12]

Much of this discrepancy between the Jewish and Catholic attitude to education depended on the differing economic bases of the Jewish and Catholic populations (Catholics making up the great bulk of the population). Peasants' children were needed in the fields, while the usual Jewish occupations needed more mental than physical work. Behind this, however, did lie basic religious attitudes, and it is worth sketching these, even though we run the risk of being over-simplistic. The religious Jew had to study as the central tenet of his religion; the Catholic did not have to study, unless he was to be a priest. In fact there was a long tradition in the Catholic hierarchy against too much learning for the masses. While there were teaching orders and so forth, the basic structure of Catholicism, and especially the Counter-Reformation type found in the Monarchy, was of a small qualified élite, the clergy, who preached the doctrine, and the rest of the populace, who merely had to accept their lot and their religion. This was almost the exact reverse of the tradition of the Jewish Diaspora, which had much more in common with the Protestant view.[13]

Jewish children were thus, in the main, taught much more at an early age than the average non-Jew.[14] On the other hand, the education they received was traditionally a purely religious one, the study of the Bible and of the Talmud. While the tradition of education at first offered the advantage of literacy, that literacy was often channelled into fields which would never have provided contact with the mainstream of western secular culture. The point has been made that, though it may well be true that the Jewish religious tradition put more emphasis on education, this was purely religious and not involved with the secular world. Ivar Oxaal has pointed to the example of India, where a religious tradition of

---

[12] Gustav Strakosch-Grassmann, *Geschichte des österreichischen Unterrichtswesens* (Vienna 1905) pp. 298–315, especially the comparison of Austrian with Prussian rates of literacy, pp. 310–15; W. W. Bartley, *Wittgenstein* (Philadelphia 1973) pp. 93–135. The most notorious statement of the Christian Social attitude to culture is that of the Reichsrat deputy, Bielohlawek, in 1907: 'Kultur ist was ein Jud' vom anderen abschreibt.' Quoted in Friedrich Heer, *Land in Strom der Zeit* (Vienna 1958) p. 295.

[13] E.g. the article, 'Das jüdische Übergewicht' in ÖW 1 June 1888 (no. v.22) p. 345, where the Jewish respect for education is contrasted to the negative attitude of the 'Ultramontanen'. Also see Katz, *Out of the Ghetto*, p. 21; Sorkin, *German Jewry*, pp. 45–6; de Lange, *Judaism*, p. 39.

[14] Heinrich Sussmann was translating passages of the Pentateuch from Hebrew by the age of five (interview 7 June 1983); also see Sperber, *Wasserträger*, pp. 153–4 on the relative advancement of Jewish children over Polish.

education has remained divorced from secular thought.[15] If it does sound plausible to refer to a Jewish tradition of education and the Word, as George Steiner and others have done, it still remains to show how this was transferred from the religious to the secular spheres.[16]

Oxaal's observation gains in credibility when we look at reports of traditional Jewish life. Joseph Ehrlich was brought up in the Hasidic community of Brody to be a *Gelehrter* (religious scholar). This meant parrot-learning and terribly cruel teaching, unrelated to the real world. Ehrlich's guardian was completely opposed to the new secular school set up by the *Maskilim* of the town, seeing it as a danger to the Hasidic faith.[17] Karl Goldmark, the composer, similarly described the total rejection in his Hungarian Jewish family of the idea of culture; his mother did read German books, but in secret, for it was regarded as a sin.[18] The Jews might have their tradition of education, and they might have the idea of the subsidization of scholars ('im Kost genommen'), but this was all based on religious precepts, which were, or could be, hostile to secular learning.

The examples of Ehrlich and Goldmark indicate, however, that the transition to secular education was indeed possible, for both became figures, if minor, in the cultural élite. The reason that people from the religious tradition were able to secularize is twofold. Firstly, the hostile attitude to worldly study, although prevalent in traditional communities in Germany and Poland, had never gained a total monopoly in the Jewish world; most significantly for us here, neither in Bohemia nor in Hungary had there been such a complete ban on secular study.[19] Secondly, from the late eighteenth century, the exclusion of secular study had been opposed within Judaism by the Haskalah, the Jewish Enlightenment. The followers of the Haskalah, the *Maskilim*, had taken the rationalist trends which existed in Judaism and stressed them at the expense of the ritualistic and pietistic trends which the Hasidim, at around the same time, adapted and developed.[20] Moses Mendelssohn, the inspirer of the Haskalah, had looked

---

[15] Ivar Oxaal, *The Jews of Pre-1914 Vienna: Two Working Papers* (Hull 1981) p. 26.

[16] Cf. George Steiner, 'Some "Meta-Rabbis"' in Douglas Villiers, ed., *Next Year in Jerusalem: Jews in the 20th Century* (London 1976) pp. 64ff.

[17] Josef R. Ehrlich, *Der Weg meines Lebens* (Vienna 1874) pp. 7–16, 22.

[18] Karl Goldmark, *Erinnerungen aus meinem Leben* (Vienna 1922) p. 15.

[19] On the attitude to secular learning among traditional Jews in Austria, see Michael Silber, 'The Historical Experience of German Jewry and its Impact on Haskalah and Reform in Hungary' in *Toward Modernity*, ed. J. Katz (Oxford 1987) pp. 113–15. On the presence of secular learning in other Jewish communities, see Katz, *Out of the Ghetto*, pp. 34, 126; Sorkin, *German Jewry*, pp. 50ff.

[20] Sachar, *History of the Jews*, pp. 267–72; Katz, *Out of the Ghetto*, pp. 47–66, 131–2, 208–9; Raphael Mahler, *A History of Modern Jewry 1780–1815* (London 1971) pp. 154–63. One prominent example of rationalist thought within the Jewish tradition, much

forward to a time when the religions of dogma would be replaced by a natural religion of faith.[21] Judaism for him was not revealed truth but revealed law, and faith could only be gained through experience of the natural world.[22] The study of the world would thus bind men together in a common faith, while the Jews could continue their own form of observance.

It was this interpretation of the Jewish tradition which allowed the prestige of study to transfer so readily from religious learning to its secular counterpart. The Mendelssohnian revolution was helped in that task by the very nature of traditional Judaism itself. The lack of a clear set of dogmas – only traditions, and a tradition of disputation on those traditions – allowed Judaism to be seen by the *Maskilim* as a religion without any dogmas, a view which itself had become a dogma of the reform-minded by the mid nineteenth century.[23] Once this view was accepted it had the far-reaching consequence that profession of the Jewish religion could not be affected by knowledge of the real world; in fact the reverse happened: worldly knowledge came to be seen as a necessary aid to religious knowledge. While Christian churches came to fear the discoveries of science, the new interpretation of Judaism could welcome them as further evidence of God's ways. It was this form of Judaism which Fritz Mauthner was taught at school, and which he described as natural religion and learning the Bible; this he contrasted with the great amount which Catholics had to learn in terms of doctrine.[24]

The outcome of all this was that by the mid nineteenth century although there still existed a strong body of opinion within the traditional Jewish community against secular study, this was opposed by an increasingly successful movement within Judaism which argued the opposite from within the religious tradition, albeit with a radical

---

used by the Haskalah, was Maimonides, see Solomon Maimon, *Solomon Maimon's Lebensgeschichte*, ed. K. P. Moritz, in S. Maimon, *Gesammelte Werke* (Hildesheim 1965) vol. 1, pp. 306ff.   [21] Heer, *God's First Love*, pp. 175–7.

[22] Sorkin, *German Jewry*, p. 70; Selma Stern-Täubler, 'The First Generation of Emancipated Jews' in *LBIY* 1970, pp. 24–5; Jacob Allerhand, *Das Judentum in der Aufklärung* (Stuttgart 1980) pp. 121–7.

[23] On the dogma issue, see Katz, *Out of the Ghetto*, pp. 23–4; Sorkin, *German Jewry*, pp. 70, 162–4; de Lange, *Judaism*, pp. 4–5, 107. A mid nineteenth-century example of the no-dogma view in Vienna is provided by the Kompert trial of 1863–4, reported in detail in *Die Neuzeit*, 1 January 1864, no. 1, pp. 6–11, where Vienna's chief rabbi, I. N. Mannheimer, had claimed that the exact nature of the truths of Judaism was always open to differing interpretations. Two decades later, Josef S. Bloch, in *ÖW*, 30 October 1884 (no. I.2) pp. 4–5, insisted that the idea of clerical authority was foreign to Judaism. He also claimed that Judaism had no dogmas, *ÖW*, 30 January 1885 (no. II.5) p. 4. One of the most famous examples of the claim that Judaism is not dogmatic is that of Walther Rathenau, see Liptzin, *Germany's Stepchildren*, p. 147.

[24] Fritz Mauthner, *Erinnerungen* (Munich 1918) p. 117.

interpretation thereof. Secular learning had come in some ways to be a substitute for religious learning among Jews, and the former had inherited the latter's prestige as well.

Given what had gone before and the example of the Haskalah, it is not surprising that Austrian Jews at the beginning of our period approached secular learning with the same reverence in which they had held religious study. Besides, whatever the attitude to the nature of one's own education, there was a great bias in traditional communities against the *uneducated*. Sigmund Mayer described this well in an episode from his own childhood. His father had interrupted a discussion between Michael Kittsee, a rentier living in their house in the Pressburg ghetto, and a rabbi. Kittsee told the intruder to leave, calling him a vulgar person, whereupon Mayer's mother in a fury demanded to know what he meant by that. Kittsee replied:

Madam Toni, I shall tell you why your husband is common. Reb Naftali is a poor man, he lives from *Reschach* (communal subsidy); but he is a *Lamden* (scholar), and cannot be called common. And our *Schochem* (neighbour), Dr Weissweiller, also has nothing, but he is a *Roife* (physician) and has studied, if not Gemara, and also, therefore, cannot be classed as common. He, however, who has studied neither Talmud nor anything else, is, as far as I am concerned, common, even though he be the best of men.[25]

Even in a traditional religious community such as the Pressburg ghetto what mattered was not so much a religious education, but *any* education, otherwise you really were a nobody.

When, therefore, the Haskalah proclaimed that Jews should adopt the culture of the Enlightenment and study nature as well as the Holy Law, there were many Jews who were prepared to listen. While plainly the secularization of learning did constitute a break with traditional Judaism in many ways, the emphasis on learning which certain individuals brought to the newly found western culture obviously sprang from their Jewish background. Their whole attitude to the world amounted to Jewish religious ideas wrapped up in different, western clothes.

The case of Wilhelm Neurath amounts to a stereotype of this process of

---

[25] 'Madam Toni, ich werde Ihnen sagen, wer ein gemainer Mann ist. Herr Reb Naftali ist ein armer Mann, er lebt von *Reschach* (Gemeindegehalt); aber er ist ein *Lamden* (Gelehrter), kann kein gemainer Mann sein. Und unser *Schochem* (Nachbar), Dr Weissweiller, hat auch nichts, aber er ist ein *Roife* (Arzt) und hat studiert, wenn auch ka Gemorrhe, gehört also gewiss nicht zu den gemainen Leuten. Wer aber nix "gelernt" und auch nicht studiert hat, das is bei mir ein gemainer Mann, und wenn er auch der bravste Mensch ist.' in Mayer, *Ein jüdischer Kaufmann*, p. 39. Even in traditional communities, physicians, members of a secular branch of learning, had always had high status, see: Klaus Lohrmann, ed., *1,000 Jahre österreichisches Judentum* (Eisenstadt 1982) p. 161; Moshe Atlas, 'Jüdische Ärzte' in Josef Fraenkel, ed., *The Jews of Austria: Essays on their Life, History and Destruction* (London 1967) p. 41; Mahler, *History of Modern Jewry*, p. 148.

direct transferral. Neurath was born in St. Miklos near Pressburg in June 1840, the son of very religious parents, who were extremely wary of the effects of secular education. He left home and earned his keep as a tutor, learning as he taught. The questions he sought to answer stemmed from his father:

From early youth I had heard my father discuss questions of the cause of human suffering, and of the miraculously purposeful organization of nature; my father was inclined toward theological contemplation and fanatical condemnation.

The result was that the young boy took long walks in the surrounding woods, leading the life of a loner even in towns:

In my shyness I…continued to dream about God's ways. This gave me strength to bear hunger, cold and sickness. I turned to science for insight; what was taught at schools was not enough; I wanted to read the great books about physics and astronomy. My mathematics, however, was insufficient; I then studied mathematics with such intensity that I tried to read Euler and Lagrange at the age of seventeen. When I was nineteen, Lagrange's *Mécanique analytique* was my favourite book. At the same time I studied ethnology. Anything unclear was unbearable, even in language; I wanted to clarify the origins of Latin, Greek and German words, and I turned to linguistics and the comparative study of languages. Problems of the infinitesimally small, of evidence in mathematics and mechanics, etc. made me think about the foundations of knowledge in general, but I did not know how to go about this.

He went on to Kantian philosophy and ended up as a professor of economics at the Hochschule für Bodenkultur.[26]

The start of this long intellectual odyssey had been wondering about the ways of God which his father had discussed when he was a small child. This had sparked off a process which had taken Neurath out of a merely Jewish tradition of Bible and Talmud into the world of Nature, and then into the world of western culture, so that at one point he decided that God no longer existed. Perhaps it was inevitable, however, that this son of a strictly Orthodox Jew should end up professing a faith in the mysticism of Jakob Böhme.[27] It was all very much of a piece. The transformation, though dramatic, took place in several logical stages and with no great breaks. Neurath was impelled by the same concept of which his father had talked, the miraculous order of the universe, and it was always this idea of order, as Sigmund Mayer pointed out, which lay behind Neurath's endeavour.[28] Science, in Neurath's case was secularized Judaism. His son Otto inherited this.

[26] Otto Neurath, *Empiricism and Sociology* (Dordrecht 1973) pp. 1–2. Sigmund Mayer, who apparently knew Neurath quite well, gives a similar account of Neurath's background and history, in *Ein jüdischer Kaufmann*, p. 253.

[27] Neurath, *Empiricism and Sociology*, p. 3.

[28] Mayer wrote of Neurath's intellectual odyssey: 'Die Gesetzmässigkeit der physischen Welt suchte er dann – einen Weg den schon viele vor ihm gegangen – im Leben der menschlichen Gesellschaft.' *Ein jüdischer Kaufmann*, p. 253.

Neurath's case is mirrored in others. Behind Popper-Lynkeus was the figure of his uncle, Selig Kohn, a Jewish scholar who later became interested in western thought and ended up as the Catholic F. Korn.[29] For Joseph Ehrlich, the poet, the process was almost as spectacular as for Neurath. By a trick he went to the secular German school set up by the local *Maskilim*, which his guardian hated, and became a great admirer of German culture and the beauties of the natural world.[30] Yet this remained within a Jewish context, that of the Haskalah, and he could always justify his new-found attitudes from within Judaism, reacting as a religious Jew to the new knowledge. When he was taught natural history the reaction was that: 'New presentiments of God sprang forth in my soul.'[31] Though he revolted against his Hasidic upbringing, he retained a naïve, mystical faith in God. He concluded that the meaning of life was to remember God through thought, word and deed. Ehrlich, too, became a great admirer of Jakob Böhme.[32]

The way in which religious learning could so easily change into secular learning is also well illustrated by the history of the Gomperz family. Theodor Gomperz wrote of the 'bridge which leads from religious to secular study', and then proceeded to list the members of his family who embodied the principle, such as the German, A. S. Gumperz, secretary to Maupertuis.[33] The greatest example on which Gomperz could call was that of his maternal grandfather, Lazar Auspitz. Auspitz was totally committed to Enlightenment thought and rejected the ritual of Judaism. It is worth noting the way in which he expressed this rejection: 'On the rare occasions when he appeared in the synagogue, instead of a prayer book he always had a book of science in front of him.'[34] It seems from this that God could be worshipped through a book of science just as well as a prayer book. The example of Lazar Auspitz is almost a direct echo of what Moses Mendelssohn had stated in *Jerusalem*: that faith was taught 'at all times through nature and things, never through words or written signs'.[35] The Jews who followed the Haskalah therefore came to see science as a new form of faith. In a way, education was never really secularized, for behind the pursuit of knowledge lay the pursuit of faith. Lazar Auspitz was making a gesture of revolt against the principles of religion, but he was also using a book of science as a book of prayer. The goal remained the same.

[29] Belke, *Popper-Lynkeus*, p. 58.

[30] Ehrlich, *Der Weg meines Lebens*, pp. 36–57.

[31] 'Neue Ahnungen von Gott stiegen in meinem Geiste auf.' *Ibid.* pp. 58–70. Quotation on p. 64.

[32] *Ibid.* pp. v (introduction by Josef Weilen), 78–125.

[33] Theodor Gomperz, *Essays und Erinnerungen* (Stuttgart 1905) pp. 1–2.

[34] 'Wenn er, was selten genug geschah, in der Synagoge erschien, so lag statt eines Gebetbuches eine Naturlehre vor ihm aufgeschlagen.' *ibid.* p. 5.

[35] Stern-Täubler, 'The First Generation' in *LBIY* 1970, p. 25.

'BILDUNG' AND CULTURE IN VIENNA'S CULTURAL ÉLITE: THE GOMPERZ FAMILY

The people who abandoned the traditional forms of faith through the tenets of the Haskalah, entered a world of learning whose forms were quite different from that of the *Yeshivot*. The greatest change came with the realization that there existed an aesthetic world. Fritz Mauthner claimed that, despite living in one of the most beautiful cities in Europe, Prague, he had no sense of figurative beauty for 'art' was frowned upon in his home.[36] Similarly, though there was no hostility, Otto Neurath grew up in a house with no tradition of discussing visual beauty. His lessons in perspective are a sign of the changes wrought by the assimilation.[37]

Yet, despite the new fields of culture which now opened up for Jews, their attitude to learning about these new ideas remained the same. Just as Selig Kohn and Wilhelm Neurath started off on the Talmud and progressed to science and philosophy, so now Jewish patrician families such as the Gomperzes applied the same emphasis on learning to cultural pursuits such as music and art. It was still knowledge of sorts and still study of God's ways in a very vague sense.

The power behind the Gomperz family was Lazar Auspitz, for it was he who supervised the upbringing of his daughter's children and his tradition which Henriette Gomperz continued after his death. Theodor Gomperz described the education he received as a 'worldly Puritanism'. It was a combination of a simple way of life and a tremendous stress on education: 'Our education was provided for in most lavish measure – remarkably lavish measure. Absolutely no available means of education was left unused... Our father bore the cost without any complaint, but the initiative usually came from our mother.'[38] Although the children were taught the aristocratic pursuits of drawing and art appreciation, it was all in an atmosphere of study, not of hedonism. Gomperz described it as a 'Bildungsluxus', which was combined with a physical and emotional modesty. Aesthetics here was an intellectual pursuit.

This is important to remember for one of Gomperz's sisters later became Josephine von Wertheimstein, one of the most famous salon hostesses of nineteenth-century Vienna. Carl Schorske has seen the *haute bourgeoisie* as assimilating into Austrian aristocratic culture, and the sponsorship of classical theatre and music as a sign of this, a sign of the adoption of an

---

[36] Mauthner, *Erinnerungen*, p. 29. [37] Neurath, *Empiricism and Sociology*, p. 5.
[38] 'Für unseren Unterricht aber war in ausgiebigstem Masse gesorgt. In erstaunlich ausgiebigem Masse. Denn schlechterdings kein verfügbares Bildungsmittel ist ungenutzt geblieben... Den Aufwand trug der Vater ohne Murren; aber der Anstoss ist zumeist von der Mutter ausgegangen.' Gomperz, *Essays*, p. 9.

aesthetic culture as a replacement for the moral culture of North German Protestantism or of Judaism.[39] Yet the salon culture which provided the backbone for much of Vienna's culture actually had little or nothing to do with the *Austrian* aristocracy and did not substitute an aesthetic approach for a moral one, but rather, as in the case of the Gomperzes, approached the former in the spirit of the latter.

As was mentioned earlier, the tradition of the cultural, as opposed to the merely social and aristocratic, salon was introduced to Vienna in the late eighteenth century from Berlin by Fanny von Arnstein, the daughter of the Jewish banker, Itzig. Until her arrival the salons of the high aristocracy had not been places for the cultural élite to meet, so much as occasions at which the nobly born could affirm their membership of the élite of the blood. They were social, not cultural occasions. The attitude to culture among the Austrian aristocracy was generally not an intellectual one – 'ungeistig' – and their aesthetic interest was largely confined to music.[40]

The type of *Salonkultur* which was to become famous in Vienna was actually imported wholesale from Berlin. What Fanny did when she reached Vienna in 1776 was to reproduce the same atmosphere as had been cultivated by the famous Jewish hostesses of Berlin, such as Rahel Varnhagen and Henriette Herz. As such she was an exception in Viennese society. she acted as a mediator between Berlin and Vienna, bringing all the latest ideas. Hers was a new element in Viennese society, and one which became very powerful, playing its own role during the Vienna Congress.[41] As Sigmund Mayer explained, the salons of the Bohemian high aristocracy were too exclusive and not interested in intellect, while the native middle class was simply not interested in the life of high culture, 'without any other sense than for profit and vulgar pleasures'. According to Mayer, at least, the salons of the Jewish ladies, Eskeles, Pereira and Arnstein, were therefore the only refuge for the cultured.[42]

From the start the intellectual salon culture of Vienna had been Jewish. It continued to be so. Fanny's tradition was carried on by her daughter, Henriette Pereira and other Jewish ladies from such families as the Wertheimers, the Leidesdorfs, the Biedermanns and the Hofmanns joined in. So did, in much smaller numbers, the native bourgeoisie, such as the

[39] Carl E. Schorske, *Fin-de-Siècle Vienna: Politics and Culture* (London 1980) p. 8.

[40] See Paul Lindau, 'Gesellschafts-Kultur' in S. Kaznelson, ed., *Juden im deutschen Kulturbereich* (Berlin 1962) p. 891. Also see Mme de Stael, *De l'Allemagne* (Paris 1958, repr.), vol. 1, pp. 129–35. This point was also made to me by Hans Thalberg, interview, Vienna, 22 March 1987.

[41] Hilde Spiel, 'Jewish Women in Austrian Culture' in Fraenkel, *The Jews of Austria*, p. 100.

[42] Sigmund Mayer, *Die Wiener Juden: Kommerz, Kultur, Politik 1700–1900* (Vienna 1918) pp. 297–8.

Schwinds and the Kupelweisers, otherwise the cultural scene would have been exclusively Jewish.[43] The greatest salon of mid century was that of Josephine von Wertheimstein. If Schorske's argument were accepted, then her salon would have to be seen as an attempt to achieve assimilation through the adoption of aristocratic culture. (For Schorske, it seems, all aesthetic culture is necessarily aristocratic.) The assimilation of this culture was to be used as a badge of affirmation, an ornament of triumphal arrival, and Schorske cites the fact that the Wertheimstein children were brought up as artists.[44] Yet this view, I think, is a misrepresentation.

We have seen that Josephine was brought up in a puritan household dedicated to learning of all types. Her brother became a professor of Classics at the University of Vienna. Already in that generation education, the world of *Bildung*, meaning education as well as culture, held priority over career prospects, at least for some members of the family who did not have to take over the business. So it would be wrong to think that education, or culture, was at first a mere ornament to crown the arrival of the bourgeoisie, as Schorske thinks. Instead it should be stressed that the Gomperz family had *always* had a tradition of education, even if, now, it was in an aesthetic form. It would be futile to deny that the cultural salon was a useful instrument of social integration, and one of Josephine's achievements was her acceptance in non-Jewish society from an early age.[45] Yet the Jewish salon hostess was a figure which was not a complete innovation, but rather the utilization of something which was already there, the Jewish emphasis on education now combined with the German ideal of *Bildung*. Josephine was thus a cultured person, who conducted a salon peopled by liberals and the cultured, the *Gebildeten*.[46] She had exceptionally fine feelings, but more in a German Romantic tradition than anything Austrian, and, as with all good liberals, she took a very dim view of the aristocracy in general.[47] This was, incidentally, the old lady of whom Hofmannsthal wrote in his *Terzinen über die Vergänglichkeit* of 1894.[48]

The tradition of the cultural salon lived on in the salons of Berta Zuckerkandl and others, and these people continued to emphasize intellect and achievement rather than hereditary exclusivity.[49] The salon remained

[43] Spiel, 'Jewish Women', p. 102.   [44] Schorske, *Fin-de-Siècle Vienna*, pp. 298–9.
[45] Julius von Gomperz, *Jugend-Erinnerungen* (Bruenn 1903) pp. 21, 35–6.
[46] Spiel, 'Jewish Women', p. 103' among the guests at the Villa Wertheimstein were:
    Bauernfeld, von Saar, Schwind, Lenbach, Adolf Wilbrandt, Fleischl von Marxow, Theodor
    Meynert, Josef Unger and von Plener, see H. Gomperz and R. A. Kann, eds., *Briefe an, von
    und um Josephine von Wertheimstein* (Vienna 1981) *passim*. Also Ilsa Barea, *Vienna*
    (London 1966) pp. 306ff.
[47] See Felice Ewart (Marie Exner), *Zwei Frauenbildnisse* (Vienna 1907) pp. 38–9.
[48] Spiel, 'Jewish Women', p. 104.
[49] *Ibid.* pp. 107–10; also Berta Zuckerkandl, *Österreich Intim: Erinnerungen, 1892–1942*
    (Frankfurt 1970) *passim*.

a refuge for the artists, a place to meet and discuss. It continued to be in opposition to, or at least separate from, the social culture of the aristocracy. It continued to be what it had started as, a place where the Jewish ladies could use their education to carve their own niche in society, by latching onto the wish of the intellectual élite for a cultural setting where they could be understood and encouraged. What these ladies meant by culture was not what the aristocrats meant; for them culture was primarily a continuation of the Jewish heritage of learning; it was what Hilde Spiel has called 'spiritual achievement' not some form of hedonism.[50]

Schorske's concept of a bourgeoisie supinely adopting the aesthetic culture of the aristocracy describes only a part of the story. Another more significant part was that the culture associated with the salons was the continuation of a Jewish return to the world of the mind, of learning and of thought. This return was so easily accomplished in Vienna because the Jews had never really had much experience of any other way of looking at the world. It was simply that what was learnt now was not the Bible, but German culture.

JEWISH ATTITUDES TO CULTURE AROUND 1900

All that changed between the traditional Jewish attitude to education and the secularized forms was the subject matter. The spirit remained the same, as did the main tenet: 'Learn, learn, learn!'[51] It was just that now all types of learning, all fields of *Geist* (intellect) were to be explored. Totally assimilated Jews still started their children's education as soon as possible, even though it might take a completely different form from the Cheder. Käthe Leichter, for instance, was allowed free range in her father's study, so that she was reading the German classics while at primary school, and began to read the great European novelists at the age of ten.[52] This was not particularly unusual among the Jewish bourgeoisie of Vienna, and they certainly seem to have had a greater interest in getting their children a good education. Indeed such a view was a commonplace of the time.[53]

---

[50] Spiel, 'Jewish Women', p. 104; cf. E. Bondi, *Geld und Gut oder Erziehung und Bildung: Jüdisches Familien- und Culturbild aus dem ersten Drittel des vorigen Jahrhunderts* (Brünn 1902), esp. pp. 89–91.

[51] Leopold Hichler, *Der Sohn des Moses Mautner: ein Wiener Roman* (Vienna 1927) p. 258; also see Stefan Zweig, *Die Welt von Gestern* (Frankfurt-on-Main 1982) p. 25–6. The phrase 'lernen, nichts als lernen' and variants thereof were frequently used in the contemporary Jewish press, see, e.g. 'Die Geister werden wach!' by Fr. in *Die Neuzeit*, 31 May 1895, no. 22, p. 233.

[52] *Käthe Leichter: Leben und Werk*, ed. Herbert Steiner (Vienna 1973) pp. 260–5.

[53] 'Das jüdische Übergewicht' in *ÖW* 1 June 1888 (no. v.22) p. 345. Also Hans Kohn, *Bürger vielen Welten* (Vienna 1965) p. 63; Hannah Arendt, *Die verborgene Tradition* (Frankfurt-on-Main 1976) pp. 78–9.

As we have seen, such a view is borne out by the statistics for the Gymnasien. The reasons for the over-representation in the schools are made clearer if we look at evidence from the early life of members of the cultural élite. In most cases there was a heavy emphasis on education, a secondary stage of the Jewish reading of scripture. Wilhelm Neurath had surrounded himself with books by the time Otto was a young child roving around the bookshelves, and, quite naturally, he was reading Kant at the same time as he was playing with his toy soldiers.[54] Karl Popper also recalls how his father would sit in his study surrounded by books translating Horace – even though he was a lawyer by profession – or working on the history of the Hellenistic period.[55]

In the case of Gustav Mahler we know that his father, Bernhard, while trading his wares, would sit on his waggon reading the works of French philosophers.[56] Victor Adler's father, Salomon, started out as the son of an Orthodox Jew, who nevertheless had a great respect for the French Enlightenment. Salomon was sent to the Öffentliche hebräische Lehranstalt in Prague, in order for Salomon to become a *Gelehrter*, the only respectable status for a Jew. Salomon, however, ended up studying French at the university and became a revolutionary. When the revolution failed, he had to gain freedom another way, by making money, all, however, in the cause of gaining for his children what he had been deprived of, an intellectual career. One of his sons, Heinrich, said: 'As a father he was self-sacrificing. His children ought to partake in the intellectual delights which were to be found in all forms of study; in short, they should have all those things, the denial of which in his day had caused him such pain.'[57] His children were thus to become secularized *Gelehrten*.

In the case of the Adler family the Jewish element is quite obvious. Even in assimilated and converted families, however, it still makes sense to talk of a Jewish tradition of education. The Wittgenstein family, though Protestant for two generations, preserved what they felt to be a *Jewish* tradition of 'aesthetic idealism'.[58] In the case of Hofmannsthal, Broch suggested that the intensive education of Hugo at an early age was due to a need to restore the validity of assimilation lost by the financial collapse of the Hofmannsthal interest in 1873.[59] Would it not be worth asking, however, why *education* was chosen to achieve assimilation?

[54] Neurath, *Empiricism and Sociology*, pp. 4–5.
[55] Karl Popper, *Unended Quest: an Intellectual Biography* (Glasgow 1976) pp. 10–11.
[56] Kurt Blaukopf, *Mahler: a Documentary Study* (London 1976) p. 147.
[57] 'Er war ein aufopfernder Vater. Seine Kinder sollten an allen geistigen Freuden teilhaben können, sich in allen Studien bilden, kurz alles erreichen, was ihm verwehrt geblieben war, unter dem er litt.' In Rudolf G. Ardelt, *Friedrich Adler: Probleme einer Persönlichkeitsentwicklung um die Jahrhundertwende* (Vienna 1984) pp. 16–18.
[58] Allan Janik and Stephen Toulmin, *Wittgenstein's Vienna* (New York 1973) pp. 172–3.
[59] Hermann Broch, *Hofmannsthal und seine Zeit*, in *Schriften zur Literatur 1* (Frankfurt-on-Main 1975) p. 184.

The exact source of the tradition varied within the family structure, but there was usually someone in the lives of the cultural élite who came more or less directly from the Jewish tradition of learning.[60] Furthermore, the opposition to a career in culture was, when present, weak. Stella Klein-Löw's father was enthusiastic about her meeting Peter Altenberg, despite the latter's reputation. Although many fathers had initial misgivings about their sons taking up writing as a career (in which they were more than likely justified), they had usually encouraged their original talent. In the case of someone such as Zweig or Werfel, the father eventually accepted the situation, persuaded often by an enthusiastic mother.[61] Someone who had been unable to become a 'Ritter des Geistes' (journalist), Richard Kola, but became a wealthy financier instead, nevertheless loved to dabble in writing as theatre correspondent for one of the papers he owned.[62] Both Karl Goldmark and Gustav Mahler were allowed, despite many misgivings, religious and economic, to study music.[63] In this respect it is worth mentioning that Arthur Schnitzler's father, Johann, born a carpenter's son, was enabled to study in Vienna by subsidies from the Jewish owner of the local estate in Nagykanizsa, Gutmann-Gelsey.[64]

Much of what has been said above will come as no surprise. It is generally acknowledged that Jewish families have been keener than others on giving their children a good education. The reasons for this are not so unanimously agreed. On the one hand there is the idea that it was merely an extreme case of the need to assimilate, to get on in the society by succeeding in the culture, education as an instrument of social strategy. This is Schorske's view.[65] The other view is that the Jews held a special regard for culture quite separate from any advantage which culture might bring with it.[66] We have seen that in the salon Jews, though they might reap social benefits, were largely continuing an old tradition of respect for learning and indeed introducing this into Austrian society. It is difficult to

---

[60] In the case of Freud the mother was the main source of educational ambition: R. W. Clark, *Freud: the Man and the Cause* (London 1980) pp. 19ff. The same was true of Guido Adler: Guido Adler, *Wollen und Wirken* (Vienna 1935) p. 3. For Schoenberg, it was his uncle, Hans Nachod: H. H. Stuckenschmidt, *Schoenberg: his Life, World and Work* (London 1977) p. 19. For Felix Braun, his grandfather: F. Braun, *Das Licht der Welt* (Vienna 1962) p. 26.

[61] Stella Klein-Löw, *Erinnerungen: Erlebtes und Gedachtes* (Vienna 1980) p. 25; for the negative attitude of fathers, see Siegfried Trebitsch, *Chronik eines Lebens* (Zurich 1951) pp. 47–8 (on Werfel), 84–6 (on Zweig). For the positive attitude of fathers, see Braun, *Licht der Welt*, p. 129; Moritz Benedikt, *Aus meinem Leben: Erinnerungen und Erörterungen* (Vienna 1906) p. 4; D. A. Prater, *European of Yesterday: a Biography of Stefan Zweig* (Oxford 1972) p. 4. (Prater gives the opposite view to Trebitsch.)

[62] Richard Kola, *Rückblick ins Gestrige: Erlebtes und Empfundenes* (Vienna 1922) pp. 56, 269.

[63] Goldmark, *Erinnerungen*, pp. 16–18; Blaukopf, *Mahler*, pp. 149–51.

[64] Interview with Erika Czuczka (née Gutmann-Gelsey), Vienna 7 June 1983.

[65] Schorske, *Fin-de-siècle Vienna*, p. 149.   [66] Arendt, *Die verborgene Tradition*, p. 78.

see how they could have assimilated into a type of high culture which they to a large degree first instigated. Schorske's view is rather weak here. Yet one might still question the accuracy of the assimilationist argument for the Jewish 'invasion' of culture and the intellectual professions as a whole.

In many cases it was true that Jews were trying to use culture to enter society, or at least to paper over their origins, the grandfather who was a pelt merchant, as Karl Kraus put it.[67] A smattering of German culture, Schiller, history and French were what was needed for a Jewish girl from a moderately well-off family to find a good match in the assimilated (but still Jewish) world.[68] Education was seen by Jews as the one way to overcome the dilemmas of their situation. The great flood of Jews into intellectual professions such as journalism could easily be explained by barriers to Jews in the bureaucracy, and the lack of a proper Jewish peasantry to act as a dead-weight on Jewish educational ambitions. There was not much option, unless they wanted to remain merchants or the equivalent.[69]

Schorske does have a point when he says that Jews used education to escape the ignominy of commerce. Gustav Mahler's father seems to have had a typical 'will to get on'. Alma Mahler said of his attitude: 'His children were to achieve what had been denied him.'[70] Hans Kelsen was sent to a humanist Gymnasium despite his great ability at mathematics, because only a Gymnasium offered the chance of becoming a lawyer or a doctor, escaping the 'straitened lower middle-class circumstances' in which he had grown up.[71] Similar things happened in the *haute bourgeoisie*: according to Hannah Arendt, Stefan Zweig used his fame as a writer as a means of entering the upper circles of society, to overcome antisemitic prejudice, as a tactic of assimilation.[72]

All this has an air of half-truth about it. It is true that Jews used culture as a means of creating an assimilation which did not exist in society. Yet it is not at all clear why there was such an emphasis on *cultural* assimilation in the first place. Again, the salons were obviously a tactic of entering society. At the same time, in the Viennese environment, they were a Jewish phenomenon in a sea of cultural indifference. The Jewish interest in the culture around them when, it would seem, the natives largely ignored it, cannot merely be passed off as the pressure to assimilate. Rather it stemmed from the Jewish heritage, which made them look at

---

[67] Karl Kraus, *Eine Krone für Zion* (Vienna 1898) p. 27.
[68] Ehrlich, *Der Weg meines Lebens*, p. 46.
[69] Mayer, *Die Wiener Juden*, p. 398.
[70] Alma Mahler, *Gustav Mahler: Erinnerungen und Briefe* (Amsterdam 1940) p. 10.
[71] R. A. Métall, *Hans Kelsen: Leben und Werk* (Vienna 1969) p. 3.
[72] Prater, *European of Yesterday*, pp. 6–8; Arendt, *Die verborgene Tradition*, p. 79.

things in a special way. Apart from those Jews who were just interested in social climbing were others who continued a purer tradition of learning.

An example, already mentioned, is Theodor Gomperz. He started a career as an academic, but after the Concordat of 1855 had no prospect of gaining a post. Yet he continued as a private scholar unperturbed.[73] He eventually became an *ordinarius* in Classics and was offered a title. As a good Liberal he refused, as did Ernst Mach.[74] Leo Strisower, a brilliant legal theorist, also had to remain a *Privatdozent* because he was Jewish, but continued to study and write, despite his lack of official recognition.[75] There were cases such as Karl Kraus' father who subsidized and encouraged his son's satirical writing even though it attacked his own kind.[76] Or there was Otto Neurath's deep faith in the beneficial effects of mass education, a belief shared by the leadership of the Austrian socialists and especially Otto Bauer.[77] It is a distortion to think that Jews were simply using culture or education as a way to advance socially; there were other aspects.

The conflicting approaches to culture could often occur within one family, depending on the background of the parents. In Käthe Leichter's family there was a dramatic split between her mother, who followed the model of a social climber, and her father, who belonged completely to that group which pursued learning for its own rewards. Her mother came from a *parvenu* family in Galatz, Rumania, and she used her education to overcome this background. She typified the attempt to use culture to impress and gain status in Austrian society.[78] Leichter's father, on the other hand, was not concerned with the outer niceties of society, and would often appear at a function in a shabby office suit instead of the mandatory tails. He called the ostentations of bourgeois, *nouveau riche* society 'Flausen' (humbug). Instead he submerged himself in the world of culture and learning. As a young man he was a frequent attender of the Stehplätze in the old Burgtheater, and he also enjoyed the opera, his favourite being notably *Fidelio*. He had spent his whole life collecting experiences and learning. Leichter calls him 'a universalist'; she remembers him reading Humboldt one day and Michelet the next. When it came to his daughters' education he was prepared to spend any amount on their *intellectual* (*geistig*) education, but hated spending anything on the

---

[73] Gomperz, *Essays*, p. 24.
[74] *Theodor Gomperz: ein Gelehrtenleben im Bürgertum der Franz-Josephszeit*, eds. H. Gomperz and R. A. Kann (Vienna 1974) pp. 14–15.
[75] Métall, *Hans Kelsen*, p. 6.
[76] Paul Schick, *Karl Kraus* (Hamburg 1965) p. 43.
[77] Ed. Friedrich Stadler, *Arbeiterbildung in der Zwischenkriegszeit, Otto Neurath*, catalogue (Vienna 1982) p. 127; Otto Leichter, *Otto Bauer: Tragödie oder Triumph?* (Vienna 1970) p. 320.   [78] *Käthe Leichter*, pp. 276–78.

balls and other devices on which their mother insisted for their *social* education.[79] Dr Josef Pick, the son of a rich textile manufacturer in Nachod in Bohemia, had been brought up to believe that social finery was unnecessary, and saw no reason why he should not travel third class on the train.[80] His wife, however, coming from a very newly rich Rumanian Jewish banker's family, needed the social confirmation of having arrived.[81] These were two attitudes to culture. Both existed in Vienna at the turn of the century.[82]

The goal of entering the cultural élite often conflicted with other demands. Arthur Schnitzler, when he announced that he wanted to become a full-time writer, did so in revolt against his father, who wanted him to continue to be a doctor.[83] Hermann Broch studied and wrote in spite of his father's will that he head the firm.[84] In certain families the status of the scholar was not all that high, but these cases were relatively rare.[85] Jews *did* generally have a great respect for education and culture.

Sigmund Freud once described the title of professor as his ticket to salvation in Austrian society.[86] Henry Wickham Steed saw it another way: 'Scientists, University professors, writers, or artists had no standing in their own right, nor did members of the aristocracy mingle with them freely as they had done in Rome.'[87] This apparent total contradiction is only a result of seeing the society from different angles. For someone such as Freud, brought up to respect intellect in a Jewish environment, the title of professor was the ultimate social goal. Yet, as Freud himself was at times acutely aware, there were other Viennas in which cleverness was looked down upon as unworthy. There was the military and the bureaucracy in which the highest virtue was not brilliance but solidity. There was the exclusive aristocracy, the target of Freud's 'Graf Thun' dream, in which culture was to be enjoyed but not taken seriously. If Jews adopted culture as an instrument of assimilation, they were choosing a most ineffective means of real integration. Alternatively, one can see them as following the old Jewish idea of a people who had survived on their wits for centuries, that 'thought is power'.[88]

[79] *Ibid.* pp. 251–5, 284.   [80] *Ibid.* p. 257–8.   [81] *Ibid.* pp. 274–8.
[82] For a didactic example of this dialectic in an earlier period, see Bondi, *Geld und Gut, passim.*
[83] Schorske, *Fin-de-Siècle Vienna*, p. 10.
[84] Manfred Durzak, *Hermann Broch* (Hamburg 1966) pp. 23ff.
[85] In Käthe Leichter's family, her father, the 'intellectual', was looked down upon by the richer members of the family, but primarily because he kept losing on the stock exchange and had to beg money off them. As an intellectual, however, he was respected. *Käthe Leichter*, pp. 242–3.   [86] Schorske, *Fin-de-Siècle Vienna*, p. 203.
[87] Henry Wickham Steed, *Through Thirty Years* (London 1924) p. 195.
[88] Kola, *Rückblick ins Gestrige*, p. 296. On Freud's attitude to the aristocracy, see Schorske's discussion of the Graf Thun dream, in Schorske, *Fin-de-Siècle Vienna*, pp. 193–6.

That the Jews assimilated into the culture rather than into the society may have been partly due to the barriers against any other form; but it was also a natural thing for them to do anyway. They had been for centuries the 'allies of the spirit', and prided themselves on it.[89] They simply transferred these ideas into another field of endeavour, western art and culture. That Vienna became a city devoted to *all* areas of high culture (and not only to the hedonism of *Gemütlichkeit*) had more to do with its Jewish heritage than with that of the Baroque. The culture that arose in Vienna at the end of the nineteenth century was not that of the nobility of the blood, but of the mind. It was much more devotion to *Bildung* than to aristocratic *Kultur*. The great achievements in culture could not have come about if there had not been from the start a group of people prepared to devote their time and money to the world of *Geist*, to the world of ideas and creativity. In Vienna this meant to a great extent people from the Jewish background described here.

[89] See Olga Schnitzler, *Spiegelbild der Freundschaft* (Vienna 1962) p. 81.

⋙ 8 ⋘

Ethics and the individual

AUSTRIA'S NON-CONFORMISTS: ETHICS AND RESPONSIBILITY

Behind the great emphasis placed on education lay another, even more powerful aspect of the Jewish tradition: its stress on the ethical side of life, and, as a consequence, on the responsibility of the individual for his actions. By the mid nineteenth century this aspect was not unique to Jews. The common origin of Judaism and Christianity ensured that many forms of Christianity shared such an emphasis on the ethical responsibility of the individual, and this was especially so in Protestant countries. There were, however, very few Protestants in the Habsburg Monarchy. Instead their scourge, the Counter-Reformation, had ensured a Catholic supremacy which had achieved its triumphant apotheosis in the lavish baroque culture of the late seventeenth and eighteenth centuries.[1] Placed in the context of Austrian baroque Catholicism, the Jewish emphasis on the ethical responsibility of the individual stands out much more than it would in other contexts.

There were two areas in which the approach of traditional Jewish communities in the Monarchy particularly stood out: the ethical nature of their lifestyle at the cost of almost all aesthetic pursuits; and the legal and political structure of their religious community, which, at least in theory, provided a great deal more room for the individual to shape his religious life with a concomitantly larger responsibility for his actions.

Austrian Catholicism revelled in its power. Its style from the Counter-Reformation on was triumphalism, celebrating the political and religious status quo, and stressing the fact of salvation through Christ and his Church. Some of its most potent symbols were the monasteries which dominated the surrounding countryside politically, but also aesthetically. The message to the ordinary Catholic which such baroque edifices were

---

[1] For the history of the Counter-Reformation in Austria, see R. J. W. Evans, *The Making of the Habsburg Monarchy, 1550–1700* (Oxford 1979); Ilsa Barea, *Vienna* (London 1966) pp. 44–57.

intended to convey was the need to submit to authority, but also the glory
of that authority, expressed in aesthetic grandeur.[2] Indeed the latter came
to seem as important as the former, even a justification of it. The beauty
of the forms chosen to convey the revealed truths of the religion came to
overshadow those truths; from being a means of propaganda aesthetic
form came to be valued on its own terms. By the mid nineteenth century
this had led to Austria possessing a culture of aesthetic celebration of
authority which had a large element of aesthetic enjoyment for its own
sake.[3]

The Jewish tradition was quite different. Centuries of being in the
Diaspora, as the archetypal non-conformists of European society, left Jews
without the status of establishment on which Catholicism in Austria
thrived. There was thus little to celebrate, and instead Jews looked forward
to the coming of a Messiah, who, unlike Christ, had not yet brought
salvation.[4] Instead the most prominent literary movement in traditional
communities was the *Musar* tradition, that is a tradition of ethical
admonition.[5] Jews, just as Catholics, were brought up to submit to
authority, but that authority, instead of being conveyed through the
aesthetic splendour of stone and paint, was based squarely on the tradition
of the Word and transmitted through the book – the Book of the Law,
which demanded not simply recognition of the revelation, but also
action.[6] There was little aesthetic celebration here. Indeed this was a
religion in which the use of aesthetic images to embody the deity was
explicitly banned, as leading to idolatry.[7] Thus in the traditional Jewish

[2] See the comments of Evans, *Habsburg Monarchy*, pp. 443ff; Julius Bab and Willi Handl, *Wien und Berlin: Vergleichendes zur Kulturgeschichte der beiden Hauptstädte Mitteleuropas* (Berlin 1918) pp. 73–119.

[3] Hermann Bahr, *Wien* (Munich 1906) pp. 45–64; Carl E. Schorske, *Fin-de-Siècle Vienna: Politics and Culture* (London 1980) p. 7; William Johnston, *The Austrian Mind: an Intellectual and Social History, 1848–1938* (Berkley 1972) p. 14–15; Allan Janik, 'Creative Milieux: the Case of Vienna' in Janik, *How not to Interpret a Culture* (Bergen 1986) pp. 113–14; also see Hermann Broch, *Hofmannsthal und seine Zeit*, in Broch, *Schriften zur Literatur 1* (Frankfurt-on-Main 1975) pp. 169ff.

[4] This point is made by George Steiner in his 'Some "Meta-Rabbis"' in D. Villiers, ed., *Next Year in Jerusalem: Jews in the 20th Century* (London 1976) pp. 66ff; for a contemporary view, see the speech by M. Lazarus, reported in *Die Neuzeit* (Nz.), 16 April 1897, no. 16, p. 165. Also see Theodor Lessing, *Der jüdische Selbsthass* (Berlin 1930) p. 36, on the role of the prophet in Judaism.

[5] David Sorkin, *The Transformation of German Jewry, 1780–1840* (Oxford 1987) pp. 45ff; Joseph Dan, 'Jewish Ethical Literature' in M. Eliade, ed., *The Encyclopaedia of Religion* (New York 1987) vol. 8, pp. 82–7.

[6] Friedrich Heer, *God's First Love* (London 1970) p. 53; Manes Sperber, *Die Wasserträger Gottes* (Munich 1983) p. 42; for a more contemporary view see *Die Gegensätze in Judenthum*, in Nz. 5 August 1864, no. 32, pp. 363–4.

[7] This point was made to me by Dr Lionel Kochan, University of Warwick. It was a commonplace of the late nineteenth century, see Rabbi Dr Leopold Goldschmidt, *Die Stellung der Juden zur modernen Kunst*, in Nz. 26 April 1895, no. 17, pp. 177–9.

view there was no central role for aesthetics as there was in Catholicism. Instead the emphasis in the religion was almost exclusively ethical, following God's laws.[8] Sigmund Mayer expressed this when he discussed the question of why Jews lacked a choir to pray for them, but all prayed at the same time in what approached total cacophony. His comment sums up the difference between the Jewish and Austrian Catholic approach to religion: 'That is, to be sure, not aesthetically pleasing according to our present European standards, but then prayer can only ever be ethical.'[9]

The difference in attitude to the structure of the religious world sprang from the same source as this divergence over the question of the relation between ethics and aesthetics: the nature of authority. In Catholicism authority devolved from the Pope downwards through a huge hierarchical structure, which was so characteristic of the Church that 'hierarchy' has come to be shorthand for its leadership. The individual Catholic was an integrated member of the system linked to the deity, but in such a way that he was dependent on a long chain of intermediaries. In this chain his superiors had powers over his spiritual standing which could act as limits on his independence, but which could also absolve him from responsibility for his actions; thus the confessional acted to ensure that good Catholics remained the children of mother Church, especially in the Austrian context.[10]

The situation was quite different in the traditional Jewish community of early nineteenth-century Austria. There was little questioning of the authority of tradition, but that tradition consisted of the Book of the Law and its time-honoured interpretation.[11] Since ideally all Jews were supposed to study the laws, this had the effect that in theory at least the Jewish religion had what might be described as a democratic base, as authority was dependent not on a divinely created religious hierarchy, but rather on a divinely revealed set of laws which all could, or should, know and understand.[12]

[8] M. Lazarus, *Die Ethik des Judenthums* (Frankfurt-on-Main 1898) pp. 23–9, 75–7; also see Jakob Katz, *Out of the Ghetto* (Cambridge, Mass. 1973) p. 132; Nicholas de Lange, *Judaism* (Oxford 1988) pp. 69ff.

[9] 'Das ist allerdings nach unseren heutigen, europäischen Begriffen nicht ästhetisch, aber Beten ist ja überhaupt nur ethisch.' Sigmund Mayer, *Die Wiener Juden: Kommerz, Kultur, Politik 1700–1900* (Vienna 1918) p. 368.

[10] See Richard P. McBrien, 'Roman Catholicism' in *Encyclopaedia of Religion*, vol. 12, pp. 429–45, esp. 442–3; on the Austrian context, see Evans, *Habsburg Monarchy*, pp. 117ff; Bab and Handl, *Wien und Berlin*, p. 119; Johnston, *The Austrian Mind*, p. 14; for a mid nineteenth-century Jewish view of papal government, see the letter from Rabbi Oppenheim, in *Nz.* 15 April 1864, no. 16, p. 188. Also see Hermann Bahr, *Selbstbildnis* (Berlin 1923) p. 82.

[11] Katz, *Out of the Ghetto*, pp. 5–6; Lazarus' speech, in *Nz.* 16 April 1897, no. 16, p. 164.

[12] See Sorkin, *German Jewry*, p. 46; for a mid nineteenth-century view, see 'Wiener Briefe' in *Nz.* 20 September 1861, no. 3, pp. 26–7.

In practice the rabbi tended to accrue authority because of his being, as it were, an 'authority' on the text of the laws – 'the living Torah'.[13] It should also be said that in traditional Jewish society the rabbi was not without political clout, still possessing the power of excommunication, at least in theory.[14] Nevertheless he had nothing like the powerful hierarchy supporting him which the Catholic priest had, nor did he have the latter's priestly status. His authority rested squarely on his learning, something on which he was liable to be challenged, albeit only formally.[15]

By the mid nineteenth century, with the lay communal leadership becoming increasingly independent of his guidance, the rabbi was coming to be seen as only a teacher, to be listened to with respect, but who was nevertheless a paid employee of the community, and thus its servant.[16] In this setting the more democratic interpretation of authority, whereby each head of household held the status of priest through his knowledge of the laws, could have the upper hand. This idea had always been there potentially in the traditional community and much was made of it by liberal and reform-minded Jews in the nineteenth century.[17] If this idea of the responsibility of the head of household for the moral and religious life of his family is then seen in combination with the idea mentioned earlier of the freedom of Judaism from the kind of dogmatic truths which Catholicism proclaimed, then it is clear that there was great scope for individualistic ideas in interpretation of the Jewish tradition. And in this the Jewish tradition was quite different from Austrian Catholicism.

A COMMUNITY OF INDIVIDUALS

There were also good sociological reasons why Jews should have a more individualistic attitude to life. The Pressburg ghetto, as Sigmund Mayer

[13] Sorkin, *German Jewry*, p. 45; Eugene B. Borowitz, 'Judaism: an Overview' in *Encyclopaedia of Religion*, vol. 8, pp. 127–49, esp. p. 137; also see *Nz*. 24 March 1865, no. 12, p. 133, where the phrase 'das lebendige Religionsgesetzbuch' is used to describe the rabbi's status.

[14] Raphael Mahler, *A History of Modern Jewry, 1780–1815* (London 1971) pp. 140–7; Katz, *Out of the Ghetto*, pp. 20–5; also 'Wiener Briefe' in *Nz*. 20 September 1861, no. 3, p. 27.

[15] See Rabbi Dr Löwy, 'Jugenderinnerungen eines Greises aus dem Ghetto' in *Nz*. 20 August 1897, no. 34, p. 348; also see J. S. Bloch's comments in *Österreichische Wochenschrift für die gesammten Interessen des Judenthums* (*ÖW*), 30 October 1884, no. 2, pp. 4–5: 'Es ist geradezu eine Tollheit, dem Judenthume, dessen Organization so durch und durch antihierarchisch ist, dass einer Vereinigung von zehn Laien möglich ist – den Rabbiner zu excommuniciren [sic!], den blöden Aberglauben rabbinischer oder geistlicher Unfehlbarkeit anzulügen.'

[16] Heer, *God's First Love*, pp. 9, 52; Sigmund Mayer, *Ein jüdischer Kaufmann 1831–1911; Lebenserinnerungen* (Leipzig 1911) p. 47; also, 'Wiener Briefe', in *Nz*. 20 September 1861, no. 3, p. 27.

[17] A good example from literature is Leopold Kompert, *Zwischen Ruinen* (Leipzig 1887) pp. 155–6, 164; also see Sol Liptzin, *Germany's Stepchildren* (Philadelphia 1944) p. 147.

describes it, was a breeding ground for liberal ideas: 'The Jews of the ghetto were almost all in commerce.'[18] This was due to the restrictions on Jews having any other profession, but the result was strange enough for all that. The ghetto lacked the upper estates of nobility and clergy; with regard to the rabbi the president of the *Gemeinde* would say: 'He who is paid by us should not meddle in our deliberations.' There was also no proletariat. Everyone was in trade, whether rich or poor. Mayer speaks of a certain equality in status, if not in wealth, a 'Gleichartigkeit' (homogeneity): 'The whole ghetto was, as it were, "Third Estate".'[19] Other witnesses testify to a wide gulf, indeed class struggles, between the rich and the poor in traditional communities, but even this evidence does not contradict Mayer's description. The difference was in terms of wealth, not legally recognized castes, and the fact that the poor could appeal to tradition, and their rabbi, for support shows that, though the rich might try to change their status, the traditional community continued to subscribe to ideals which were bourgeois and even in a sense egalitarian.[20]

The ghetto was obviously a centre of urban, Third Estate ideas, and this is generally accepted. In opposition to the idea that the Jews were only city men and merchants, the shtetl is often used as an example of Jewish life which was rural. However, though the shtetl was set in the countryside, its rôle was exactly that of a shtetl, *Städtchen*, a little city.[21] Compared to the big city it might appear rural, but for the Jews who lived in it the shtetl was a *civitas dei*, an outpost of (Jewish) civilization in the savage hinterland of the Polish and Ruthenian peasants.[22] The Jews here too were merchants and craftsmen. Each head of family was a full member of the community, even though he was desperately poor. In a sense the extreme poverty of the shtetl saw the Jews trying desperately to preserve their essentially bourgeois way of life; hence the way in which all saved, regardless of dire need, to send their sons to the Cheder.[23]

Manès Sperber tells the following story: his home town of Zablotow was proud of the fact that no one ever died of starvation. It was law that, if a starving man ask for bread, he be given some; one day, however, the *Gemeinde* members woke the rabbi to report, in horror, that someone had died of hunger. The rabbi replied:

---

[18] Mayer, *Ein jüdischer Kaufmann*, p. 9.
[19] *Ibid.* p. 47.
[20] See, for instance, Dr Frankl-Grün, 'Der Classenkampf im Ghetto' in *Nz.* 4 May 1900, no. 18, pp. 181–2, 11 May 1900. no. 19, pp. 192–3.
[21] Claudio Magris, *Weit von wo?* (Vienna 1974) p. 124.
[22] Sperber, *Die Wasserträger*, p. 18.
[23] *Ibid.* p. 15. Julius Carlebach makes a similar point about the bourgeois aspirations of Jewish communities in his article, 'The Forgotten Connection: Women and Jews in the Conflict between Enlightenment and Romanticism' in *LBIY* xxiv 1979, p. 118.

'That is not true. Indeed it is impossible. Would you, or you, have refused him a piece of bread, if he had asked for one?' 'No', they said, 'but Elieser was too proud to ask for anything.' 'So, do not say that one amongst us has died of hunger, for Elieser was killed by his pride.'[24]

It was up to the individual to decide his own fate in this society, even if it was also the duty of other individuals to help him – if he could bring himself to demean himself in this way. The *Schnorrer* (beggar) also has his place in the Jewish tradition, as the foil to the self-made man. They are two sides of the same coin.

An individualistic approach to society was a noticeable feature amongst the reform movements in Vienna at the turn of the century. Ingrid Belke has talked of 'die soziale Technik' (social technology) which these groups applied to social problems with the individual at base. For the Jewish members of these movements, who were very prominent, the background of the ghetto and the shtetl with its emphasis on an ahierarchical approach to the community, combined with a great concern for the community as a collection of individuals, had a large influence.[25] The spirit that characterized these movements was not some pseudo-medieval holism as elsewhere (and among Christian Socials), but rather the concept of justice, *Gerechtigkeit*, which was closely associated with Judaism. Joseph Popper-Lynkeus for one attributed his sense of social justice to the Talmudic saying: 'If you kill a man, you have killed the world; when you support a man, you support the world.'[26] The law that the starving man who begs for food must be fed was taken over directly in the Viennese bourgeois progressive class in the form of the Popperian society, 'Verein Allgemeiner Nährpflicht'. Popper was the centre of a group of middle-class individuals who showed a social conscience which ignored class lines and allegiance, but saw society as it had been in the ghetto, a collection of individuals, some richer, some poorer. Out of this kind of background could emerge the bourgeois social reformer or the fully-fledged Marxist, both tracing their commitment back to the teachings of Jewish law.

Joseph Popper-Lynkeus and Wilhelm Neurath were very much in the same mould, and had known each other from early on, when they had sat in the coffeehouse together discussing social theory.[27] Neurath's social

---

[24] '"Das ist nicht wahr. Ja, es ist unmöglich. Hättest du oder du ihm ein Stück Brot verweigert, wenn er es verlangt hätte?" "Nein", antworteten sie, "aber Elieser war zu stolz, um etwas zu bitten." "Also, sagt nicht, dass mitten unter uns einer Hungers gestorben ist, denn Elieser ist an seinem Stolze zugrunde gegangen."' Sperber, *Die Wasserträger*, p. 16.

[25] Belke, *Popper-Lynkeus*, pp. 102–6. On the Jewish presence, *ibid.* p. 239.

[26] 'Wenn du einen Mensch tötest, hast du die Welt getötet, wenn du einen Mensch erhältst, erhältst du die Welt. *ibid.* p. 79. Also see Wassermann, *My Life*, p. 24, on Judaism and justice.   [27] Belke, *Popper-Lynkeus*, p. 90.

theory shows similar individualistic traits to Popper's. He thought that society should be run on the lines of a comprehensive business corporation with each individual, as it were, being a shareholder in the enterprise. This fits quite nicely into the Jewish tradition, although there is a large irony in that Neurath's ideas were to be the indirect basis of Lueger's municipalization of services in Vienna.[28] Otto Neurath continued very much in the same vein as his father when he proclaimed the need for 'planning for freedom'. Behind his apparent Marxism lay the same sort of concern for the individual which marked his father and Popper.[29] It is significant that, when he was in charge of the Zentralwirtschaftsamt in Munich's revolutionary republic of 1919, he sent a telegram to Popper telling him that his (Popper's) ideas were finally being put into practice.[30] Otto Neurath's ideas could thus be seen to be a mediated form of the sense of social justice present in the Jewish community, whether it be a Slovakian shtetl or a Bohemian *Gasse*.

Otto Neurath is one of those people who visited Popper in Hietzing. Another name on the list is Carl Colbert.[31] Colbert represents another form of the essentially bourgeois reformer. His mother was one of the more legendary figures in Vienna's financial world, creator of the Merkur bank, though she started in the Pressburg ghetto.[32] The son enjoyed a fittingly high bourgeois lifestyle and ran the fairly successful journal, *Wiener Mode*. He was also famed as a great enemy of capitalist exploitation of the workers, and the *feuilletons* of his newspapers condemned the businesses which his mother financed.[33] Colbert thus exemplified a double-life which many other Viennese Jews led in their approach to society and their place in it.[34] It is hard to say how much it was due to the social structure of the Jewish community left behind, but it does seem that a social conscience about the working classes was particularly strong in the Jewish bourgeoisie, which was mirrored in the fact that most of Austria's socialist leadership came from the homes of the Jewish *haute bourgeoisie*.[35] It is also

[28] Mayer, *Die Wiener Juden*, p. 254.

[29] Friedrich Stadler, ed., *Arbeiterbildung in der Zwischenkriegszeit, Otto Neurath*, (Vienna 1982) p. 10; Otto Neurath, *Empiricism and Sociology* (Dordrecht 1973) p. 41.

[30] Belke, *Popper-Lynkeus*, pp. 214–5.   [31] *Ibid.* p. 80.

[32] Mayer, *Ein jüdischer Kaufmann*, p. 52; Richard Kola, *Rückblick ins Gestrige: Erlebtes und Empfundenes* (Vienna 1922) p. 191.

[33] Kola, *Rückblick*, p. 191; also, interview with Bruno Frei, Klosterneuburg, 13 October 1982.

[34] A similar example is Theodor Hertzka, editor of the *Wiener Allgemeine Zeitung*, but also founder of the *Freiland* movement. See Johnston, *The Austrian Mind*, pp. 361–2. Hertzka made an explicit identification between his utopian social theory and what he identified as the Jewish ethical tradition, see his speech 'Arischer und semitischer Geist' publ. in *ÖW* 20 January 1893 (x.3) pp. 37–40.

[35] The classic case is Otto Bauer who came from one of the richest textile families in Bohemia, see Otto Leichter, *Otto Bauer: Triumph oder Tragödie?* (Vienna 1970) p. 22.

worthy of note that a Marxist theorist such as Max Adler recognized the large influence which Popper, a Jewish bourgeois social reformer, exerted on him, which might help explain Adler's great emphasis on the individual within the Marxist schema.[36]

The relationship between Carl Colbert and Bruno Frei, later editor of the Communist *Volksstimme*, illustrates the way in which the Jewish sense of social justice could reach across boundaries of class and acculturation. Colbert employed Frei, then a young radical journalist, on his newspaper *Der Abend*.[37] It was extraordinary that the retirement-aged son of one of the richest houses in Vienna should now found a radical newspaper. More extraordinary in many ways, however, was that he should employ Frei, who, from a strictly Orthodox house, regarded his socialism as based on the biblical idea of justice.[38] Here then were two Jews from opposite ends of the social and cultural spectrum, sharing a sense of social justice which came, it seems, from their Jewish background.

JEWISH STOICISM

If the ethics of individualism could express itself in some search for social justice, it could also lead to a retreat from the social sphere; this internalization in turn led to the individual adopting a markedly stoic attitude to the world, whether it be in traditional Jewish society or the assimilated bourgeoisie.

Käthe Leichter's father created for himself a strict ethic of simplicity and rectitude, while at the same time refusing to betray the values of his high bourgeois capitalist family. As described by his daughter, Josef Pick became the stereotype of a liberal caught between the values of justice and individualism and the facts of the new economy. He could admire Lincoln for freeing the slaves and even the Communards of 1871, but he could not accept the conclusions of Marx. He enthused over the fight of liberalism for the individual's freedom from tyranny, but he could not countenance social revolution. His position was highly ambiguous: 'Despite his personal admiration for Victor Adler and Pernerstorfer, which he shared with so many in the liberal bourgeoisie, he would never have gone the way of socialism.' It became a question of what was meant by justice and freedom; he supported the Dreyfusards' battle for justice, but he was thankful to the police for quelling the protests of starving workers. Despite being an intellectual, he was a member of his family's class, and he

[36] Belke, *Popper-Lynkeus*, pp. 211–2.
[37] Karl Kraus quipped, untranslatably, on this new venture: 'Der Sohn der Merkur-Kohn setzt sich bolschewistisch zu Ruhe'.
[38] Interview with Bruno Frei, 12 October 1982.

identified with it: 'Though he was not wealthy, there was always culture to be protected from the levellers.'[39]

Yet he was deeply disturbed by the ethical shortcomings of the *parvenu* class at the top of the economy and showed this by internalizing the ethical imperative, by travelling third class on the train and by denying as much as possible his wife's desire for 'Flausen'; his aim in life was 'to be straightforward in all things', regardless of the social consequences. What sustained him was an unshakeable belief in the goodness of man.[40]

In this he was following a trend amongst assimilated Jews. From the early nineteenth century, if not earlier, Jews were concluding that 'God is conscience', an idea which received much encouragement from the Jewish concept of man as made in God's image.[41] Faith in God as conscience could further be secularized into a simple faith in 'the Good in Man, in every person, also in oneself'.[42] The stress on individual conscience can be seen in the work of many Enlightenment thinkers, and above all Kant; it was a common feature among liberals all over Europe. Yet, from the perspective of the Viennese Jewish bourgeoisie, it should be emphasized that in the realm of individualist ethics the idea of God as conscience can also be seen as the development of an already existing tradition within Judaism, the individual's personal relationship, often struggle, with God – outside the social arena. The attitude which Josef Pick adopted, the refusal to kow-tow to social convention and the preservation of ethical commitment within the private if not the social sphere, had direct parallels in the ghetto and the shtetl with a tradition which Claudio Magris has named Jewish Stoicism.[43]

Magris defines Jewish stoicism as the belief in an indestructible individual ethos which cannot be affected by an external and relative system of values. This idea comes from a quotation from Salomon Maimon that Jewish morality is 'the true stoicism', and it is summed up for Magris by the saying of the rabbi Shloime Mayer in a novel by I. B. Singer: 'You should not fear the countenance of man'. Magris sees this as connected to the patriarchal structure of the Jewish family. Be that as it may, his main point is very important: 'Jewish stoicism' recognizes itself in the individualistic culture of the nineteenth century, and in antiquated

---

[39] 'Den Weg zur Sozialdemokratie wäre er bei aller persönlichen Hochachtung, die er wie so viele aus dem freiheitlichen Bürgertum für Victor Adler und Pernerstorfer hatte, nie gegangen.' 'Hatte er keine Reichtümer, so hatte er eben die Kultur vor der Gleichmacherei zu schützen.' *Käthe Leichter: Leben und Werk*, ed. Herbert Steiner (Vienna 1973) pp. 255–6.

[40] *Ibid.* pp. 257–8.

[41] See Heer, *God's First Love*, p. 216. On the significance of the idea of man as made in God's image, see Erich Kahler, *Die Philosophie von Hermann Broch* (Tübingen 1962) p. 80.

[42] Stella Klein-Löw, *Erinnerungen: Erlebtes und Gedachtes* (Vienna 1980) p. 24.

[43] Magris, *Weit von wo?* pp. 159–62; cf. de Lange, *Judaism*, pp. 87ff.

classical humanism.' That is to say, the Jews made their own contribution
to the individualistic culture of central European humanism, to the world
of Grillparzer as well as Schnitzler and Werfel: 'In this type, largely a result
of the coming together of the autumnal bureaucratic ideal – with its
pathos of self-denial – and Jewish introversion – with its knowledge of
suffering – what is perhaps the noblest part of central European humanism
took shape.'[44]

The basis of this Jewish component of the humanism of *Mitteleuropa* was
the idea of man as created in God's image, as the individual struggling to
make sense of, to articulate the creation, as unity giving unity to the world,
as Erich Kahler put it.[45] Yet the individual was at base independent of the
world around him, could look all in the face for he was in God's
company.[46] It was the knowledge that God was there which could sustain
the Jew through all adversity, reconcile him to his harsh fate. A poignant
description of this attitude is Joseph Roth's reworking of the story of Job,
Hiob.

It is the same story, the man of faith who is persecuted by fate until he
rejects God as unjust. Yet Roth's book is about a man, Mendel Singer, who
even in the godless environment of New York retains his faith that there
is a God, even if he is unjust. He is angry with God who has killed his sons,
made his wife mad and uprooted him from his home in Poland. His
revenge is to go to the Italian quarter and eat pork to anger God. He even
refuses to pray to God, but behind the rebellion lies a deep belief, a need to
have God once again as a friend: '"I shall not pray," thought Mendel. Yet
he suffered because he did not pray. His rage hurt him, and the impotence
of his rage. Although he was angry with God, God still ruled the world.
Hate could move him no more than piety.'[47]

Mendel's relationship to God, whether it be antagonistic or, as at the

---

[44] 'Der "jüdische Stoizismus" erkennt sich in der vergangenen individualistischen Kultur
des 19. Jahrhunderts und in antiquierten klassischen Humanismus wieder.' 'In diesem
Typus, der wesentlich aus der Begegnung zwischen dem herbstlichen bürokratischen
Ideal mit seinem Pathos des Verzichts und der jüdischen Introversion mit ihrer
Leidenserfahrung entstanden war, hat das vielleicht Edelste des mitteleuropäischen
Humanismus Gestalt genommen.' Magris, *Weit von wo?* p. 161. Maimon's spirited
defence of traditional Jewish morality is given in *Solomon Maimon's Lebensgeschichte*, ed.
K. P. Moritz (Berlin 1792), repr. in Solomon Maimon, *Gesammelte Werke* (Hildesheim
1965) vol. 1, p. 176. The chapter in which the quotation appears has been elided from
the English translation.   [45] Kahler, *Broch*, pp. 80ff.

[46] See, e.g. J. B. Strasser, 'Blätter der Erinnerung' in *Nz*. 18 March 1898, no. 11, p. 112;
also see Maimon's discussion of Maimonides's philosophy, in Maimon, *Lebensgeschichte*,
pp. 446–7.

[47] '"Ich bete nicht!" sagte sich Mendel. Aber es tat ihm weh, dass er nicht betete. Sein Zorn
schmerzte ihn und die Machtlosigkeit dieses Zorns. Obwohl Mendel mit Gott böse war,
herrschte Gott noch über die Welt. Der Hass konnte ihn ebensowenig fassen wie die
Frömmigkeit.' Joseph Roth, *Hiob* (Cologne 1982) p. 172. Translation in Roth, *Job: the
Story of a Simple Man*, tr. D. Thompson (London, 1983) p. 189.

end, one of grateful affirmation, is that of two old friends, completely personal and immediate.[48] *Hiob* thus illustrates the huge ambiguity in the Jewish stoic's relation to God. On the one hand there is the idea that God must be held to account for his side of the covenant, that to wrestle with the unjust fate which God may have decreed is in itself a duty of man; the image of Jacob wrestling with the angel comes to mind here. On the other is the fact of belief that there is a higher order of things despite the present chaos in the world; that one day the Messiah will come, that God is ultimately good and a friend. In this sense, then, the wrestling with God is but a moment in the condition of being chosen, of having direct contact with God. It was the effect of this knowledge which Sigmund Mayer identified in the attitude of the pious Jew in the Pressburg ghetto: 'there in the *Schul* he stood immediately under, and closely under, God, and looked down from a great height on those who persecuted and insulted him.'[49] The Jew might have nothing but his relation to God and it might be a bad relation, but its mere existence made everything else in the world trivial.

The explanation for this stoical approach in the traditional Jewish community would at first sight appear self-evident: centuries of persecution had to find compensation in some form, and there is no greater compensation than a direct relation to the deity. Yet in a longer perspective this appears to be putting the cart before the horse – for it can be equally well argued that the survival of Jewish communities, despite all the persecution, was itself based on the strength of the Jewish stoic tradition. However one explains it, the stoic approach seems to have been a major force in the traditional communities of Austrian Jewry. The great-grandfather of Manès Sperber, Rabbi Boruch, provides a good example of this view of the world. What was important for him was not the daily story of human relations, but the search for the true understanding of God's creation and his laws, which could only be discovered through reading the holy books:

He spent his whole life 'learning', studying the holy scriptures and their commentaries... in the very early morning he would run out of the house to take his cold bath. He ran because he had no time to waste. When the doctor advised the old man to moderate his zeal, he explained to him: 'I cannot afford to lose one minute, for only now am I *really* beginning to understand. Only now is it becoming clear to me what the only true reality is.[50]

---

[48] For instance Roth, *Hiob*, p. 209.

[49] 'Da in der "Schul" stand er unmittelbar unter und dicht unter dem Herrgott und sah auf jene, die ihn verfolgten und beschimpften, tief herab.' Mayer, *Ein jüdischer Kaufmann*, p. 59.

[50] 'Er verbrauchte sein Leben mit "Lernen", dem Studium der heiligen Bücher und ihrer Kommentare... In frühester Morgenstunde lief er aus dem Haus, um sein kaltes

It was the search for the *real* truth which took him away from the
banalities of the world around him; he despised the pretentiousness of
wealth and social status.

Sperber saw him as the loneliest man he ever knew in the middle of the
densely packed shtetl, because he could not forgive his fellow men for their
inability to follow God's ways in their entirety: 'He refused to forgive them
for not being true (gerecht) to the commandments, whose fulfilment was
the only thing he recognized as justification for existence.'[51] It was the
need to be 'gerecht', righteous, which was the leading principle, to be
worthy of God's choice of him and his fellow Jews. Sperber talks of the Song
of Songs as the story of the chosen people, the guilty lover seeking the
beloved, God. It was this relation which gave meaning to the life of his
great-grandfather:

Great-grandfather could also sometimes argue with his God, just as the Tsaddik of
Bardshev had dared to do in his Yiddish prayers. Had he found out that his great-
grandson threw stones at the sky to challenge God and to look in his angry
countenance, he would probably not have regarded it as blasphemy. The Almighty
was everywhere; even a child must come across him, and depending on the
circumstances, push against him and feel his palpable presence. It was as if I was
taking dictation from Rabbi Boruch when I wrote the words which I gave to a
figure in one of my novels, the adolescent Rabbi Bynie. As he lies dying he takes
his leave from his comrade-in-arms, an atheistic Viennese Jew, with the following
words: 'Poor man, you are totally alone. How can you live without God?'[52]

Figures such as Rabbi Boruch could remain on the fringes of the
community, even demand a kind of respect, but there were other 'Jewish
stoics' who, in serving their God, ended up breaking with the community.
Joseph Ehrlich, raised in a Hasidic community, came through experience
of the Haskalah to adopt a stoic approach, rejecting social action for an
immediate experience of God. He studied nature with a passion, but as
God's creation, not his replacement. He felt himself 'integrated into the

Tauchbad zu nehmen. Er lief denn er hatte keine Zeit. Dem Arzt, der dem Greis nahelegte,
seinem Eifer zu mässigen, erklärte er: "Ich habe keine Minute zu verlieren, denn erst
jetzt beginne ich *wirklich* zu verstehen. Jetzt erst offenbart mir, was allein das Wesentliche
ist."' Sperber, *Die Wasserträger*, p. 30.

[51] 'Er verzieh es ihnen nicht, dass sie den Anforderungen nicht gerecht wurden, deren
Erfüllung allein er als Rechtfertigung des Daseins ansah.' *Ibid.* p. 31.

[52] 'Auch der Urgrossvater konnte manchmal mit seinem Gott rechten, wie der Zaddik von
Bardtschew in seinen jiddischen Gebeten es gewagt hatte. Hätte er erfahren dass sein
Urenkel Steine gegen den Himmel warf, um Gott herauszufordern und in sein böses
Gesicht zu blicken, er hätte es wahrscheinlich nicht als Gotteslästerung empfunden. Der
Allmächtige war überall; selbst ein Kind musste auf ihn stossen, unter Umständen ihn
anstossen und mit ihm handgreiflich werden. Ich schrieb fast unter Rabbi Boruchs Diktat
die Worte, die ich einem Romanhelden, dem halbwüchsigen Rabbi Bynie in den Mund
legte, mit denen er sterbend von seinem Kampfgefährten, einem ungläubigen Wiener
Juden, Abschied nahm: "Armer Mensch, Ihr bleibt ganz allein. Wie werdet Ihr ohne Gott
leben können?"' *Ibid.* pp. 33–4.

ordered universe...part of a higher world'.[53] In Moses Mendelssohn's *Phaedon* he discovered the principle of *Tugend* (virtue) and the idea of the immortality of the soul, but behind this lay no rational explanation of the world, as perhaps might be expected from a pupil of the Enlightenment, but rather a deep faith in God: 'I felt that God loved me and so I swore him eternal loyalty'. He shouted to God: 'God, I wish I had a whole world to defy, as long as there were justice and truth to defend!'[54] What drove Ehrlich on was a 'desire for the metaphysical' and the need always to remember God.[55] Far from being a break with the high religiosity of the Hasidim, Ehrlich's adoption of the Haskalah was a means for him to get closer to the meaning of life, God as mystical experience – as conscience.

The break with organized religion could thus be a natural consequence of Judaism itself. It is true that there were many aspects of the tradition which could act in the opposite direction – the pull of the community and of tradition itself was very strong, and for many continued to be the dominant factor.[56] Yet it took only a small, if critical, shift in the balance of the religion for the outer shell of the ritual laws and customs to be regarded as secondary, and hence trivial, in contrast to the personal relation with God, which was open to the Jew as one of the chosen. The extremely pious Rabbi Boruch could, for instance, prefer to worship God in his study than go through the unpleasant task of praying with his fellows, the imperfect and despised.[57] Ehrlich could decide that the worship of God in the synagogue did not provide the edification of praying to God alone in the forest. Judaism could therefore be reduced to a faith of the individual in God, with nothing else being *necessary*.[58]

The stoic aspect of the Jewish tradition thus survived easily into the assimilated community; indeed, because it stressed the individual's inter-subjective autonomy, it became an aspect on which the ideologues of emancipation and assimilation put much emphasis, providing as it did a strong argument against the claims of the traditional community.[59] On the other hand, the adoption of a radically stoical definition of religion, as outlined above, meant that a denial of a rôle for religion in the inter-subjective world no longer meant a denial of religion itself. Thus, when

[53] Ehrlich, *Der Weg meines Lebens*, pp. 91–7.
[54] *Ibid.* p. 78.   [55] *Ibid.* p. 124.
[56] Katz, *Out of the Ghetto*, pp. 5–6, 142ff; Strasser, 'Blätter' in *Nz.* 21 January 1898, no. 3, p. 26. Also see Lazarus, *Ethik des Judenthums*, pp. 56–7, where he identifies two dominant strands in Judaism, rationalism and traditionalism.
[57] Sperber, *Die Wasserträger*, p. 30.   [58] Ehrlich, *Der Weg meines Lebens*, p. 64.
[59] For instance, Maimon, *Lebensgeschichte*, pp. 306, 448; *Nz.* 22 November 1861, no. 12, p. 133; Adolf Jellinek, 'Der jüdische Stamm' in *Nz.* 6 December 1861, no. 14, pp. 165–6; J. J. Hamburger, 'Denk-, Glaubens-, Lehr-, und Redefreiheit im Judenthume' in *Nz.* 31 January 1896, no. 5, pp. 42–3; Lazarus, *Ethik des Judentums*, pp. 94–119, 273.

a leader of enlightened thought in Vienna such as Wilhelm Neurath professed faith in the mysticism of a Jakob Böhme, he was simply reflecting the even more direct attraction of Böhme's approach to an Ehrlich, who would have seen the same ideas in Böhme as he had arrived at himself in the meeting of Hasidic and Haskalah ideas.[60] It is in keeping with this strange mixture of the religious and secular that Wilhelm Neurath himself was likened to a founder of religion in his ideas about society.[61] What emerged as the secularized form of Jewish stoicism was a great emphasis on the ethical mission of the individual, which based itself on what can only be called an areligious faith – whether it be in God or conscience, within Judaism or outside it.[62]

Behind the cultural élite of Vienna lay a heritage of individual defiance in a stoic manner of the world of appearances. An example is afforded by Lazar Auspitz, Theodor Gomperz's grandfather:

His whole being was grand: the strength of his will, his independent-mindedness, the autonomous nature of his judgement. He approached as near as possible the ideal of the cynics and stoics of 'freedom from delusion'. He hated all prejudice, all conventionality, all vanity (in a letter he called this 'the false wish to impress'). His mind was only concerned with what was true, which he pursued with a heavy, often curt seriousness, and with an impatient disdain for the devotees of any type of deluding superficiality...He was merciless in excising from within himself anything he had decided was unhealthy, and he fought such things with unrelenting vigour among those nearest him. This was true for moral crimes at one pole to small lapses in behaviour, posture and dress at the other...To bow before no man, to seek no man's favour, were principles deeply set in his nature.[63]

This description of a 'true son of the Enlightenment' could equally well serve as a description of Sperber's Rabbi Boruch. The type of the Jewish

[60] Neurath, *Empiricism and Sociology*, p. 4.

[61] Mayer, *Ein jüdischer Kaufmann*, p. 254.

[62] The ideas of Wilhelm Jerusalem are of interest here. He accepted Judaism on the grounds that the 'ethische Monotheismus des Judentums' did not contradict science and was hence fully compatible with it. See Jerusalem, *Gedanken und Denker: gesammelte Aufsätze*, new series (Vienna 1925) p. 10.

[63] 'Wuchtig...war sein ganzes Wesen: die Kraft seines Willens, seine Unabhängigkeitssinn, die Selbstständigkeit seines Urteils. Dem kynisch-stoischen Ideal der "Wahnfreiheit" stand er so nahe als möglich. Allem Vorurteil, allem Konventionalismus, aller Eitelkeit ("falsche Glanzsucht" nennt er sie in einem Briefe) war er fremd und feindlich. Nur auf das Wesentliche war sein Sinn gerichtet mit schwerem, oft mit schroffem Ernst und mit heftiger, auch unduldsamer Abneigung gegen die Vertreter jedes Scheinwesens...Was er als unheilsam erkannt hatte, rottete er mitleidlos in sich aus und bekämpfte es unablässig und mit unnachsichtiger Strenge bei seinen Nächsten: von moralischen Gebrechen angefangen bis zu den kleinen Mangeln des Gehabens, der Haltung, der Kleidung herab (...) Sich vor niemandem zu beugen, um niemandes Gunst zu werben, war tief in seiner Natur begründet.' Theodor Gomperz, *Essays und Erinnerungen* (Stuttgart 1905) pp. 2–5. Mahler's grandmother appears to have been a similar type, see Alma Mahler, *Gustav Mahler: Erinnerungen und Briefe* (Amsterdam 1940) p. 13. Also see Stefan Zweig, *Die Welt von Gestern* (Frankfurt-on-Main 1982) pp. 22–3, on his father; note especially the phrase 'das Gefühl der inneren Freiheit'.

stoic seems to have transferred with no difficulty at all into the assimilated world of capitalism. As noted above, all that had changed was that the prayer book had been replaced by a book of natural science.

The stoic approach thus bridged the traditional and assimilated community. Both Rabbi Boruch and Lazar Auspitz were only concerned with 'das Wesentliche'. For one it meant a conscious contact with God, for the other a more or less unconscious contact with God as conscience. The form which this same search for the real took in Viennese culture at the turn of the century was what might be termed an ethical search for truth. Magris has picked up this point in the work of Freud and Schnitzler, and this appears fair for Freud at least.[64] In addressing a patient he would say the following: 'Finally, never forget that you have promised absolute honesty, and never leave anything unsaid because for any reason it is unpleasant to say it.'[65] This was the same idea as Lazar Auspitz's, only radicalized. It rested on the same stoic foundations, as epitomized by Freud's comment in *Civilization and its Discontents*: 'Fate can do little against one.'[66] By telling the truth, finding out what the truth was, the intellect for Freud could regain its rightful place in the world – the place of primacy.

The 'Wahrheitsliebe' (love of truth) of which Guido Adler talks as being the guiding principle in his family was a cliché of Enlightenment thought, but it received especial emphasis among Jewish families as a result of the inheritance of what has here been called Jewish stoicism.[67] The search for truth as an ethical goal, originating in Jewish culture in the form of the religious scholar, came to be transferred straighforwardly enough into the realm of science, as in the case of Freud. It came to be mirrored in the philosophies of assimilated Jewish thinkers such as Broch and Weininger. The former saw the spread of logic as the ethical goal of mankind.[68] The latter came to see consciousness and logic as the ends of man and the achievement of them as the performance of God's will, the will to value.[69] Yet the thought processes traced here did not stop at the barriers of religion and science, nor of philosophy, but entered the realm of aesthetics as well, something which Judaism, the religion without happiness as Mayer described it, had not tackled in any comprehensive way.[70] The

---

[64] Magris, *Weit von wo?* p. 163; it is of note that the conclusion that the final ethical purpose of man was the 'search for truth' was shared explicitly by Maimonides, see Maimon, *Lebensgeschichte*, pp. 453–4.

[65] Quoted in R. W. Clark, *Freud: the Man and the Cause* (London 1980) p. 123.

[66] Quoted in Paul Roazen, *Freud and his Followers* (London 1976) p. 131.

[67] Guido Adler, *Wollen und Wirken* (Vienna 1935) p. 4.

[68] Kahler, *Broch*, pp. 41ff.

[69] Otto Weininger, *Geschlecht und Charakter* (Vienna 1903, 1919) p. 198 (for instance).

[70] Mayer, *Ein jüdischer Kaufmann*, p. 60.

result, from what has been described here, was predictable: 'Music should not decorate, it should be true.'[71] This slogan of the Schoenberg circle simply used the criteria of the ethical stoic in a field where it had no place traditionally, in aesthetics.

The idea that aesthetics derived from and was secondary to ethics was not completely new in western culture, but it was an especially prominent feature of turn of the century Vienna. Weininger had been among the first in that city to try and make the connection by making aesthetics an imperfect mirror of the inner ethical self.[72] He had a long list of colleagues in this pursuit. Among them were Schoenberg, Karl Kraus, Hermann Broch, and most intriguingly, Ludwig Wittgenstein. Janik and Toulmin have written a book on what Wittgenstein meant by the phrase: 'Ethics and aesthetics are one and the same.' They have drawn attention to connections with Kraus' ethicization of the writer's rôle. They have also shown how Wittgenstein's social behaviour reflected a deeply ethical individualism, which made itself manifest in the *Tractatus*, despite appearing only a side issue.[73] Wittgenstein's attitude to the world appears one of pure stoicism, setting the ethical self in a higher world of true values divorced from the bonds of causation. Such ideas have already been seen in the figures described in this chapter. If we then note that, apart from Adolf Loos, all the main contemporaries who affected Wittgenstein's ethical approach came from Jewish backgrounds, the question arises as to how far we can attribute to this Jewish background, to the phenomenon of Jewish stoicism, the type of ideas which appeared in Viennese culture around 1900 and which underlay Schoenberg's music and the young Wittgenstein's philosophy. Was there in any serious way a connection between the stoics of the shtetl and the 'expressionists' of Viennese culture? Before this can be answered, however, we must look at the history of how the Jews got from the shtetl to the garden of high culture: we must look at one of the more remarkable phenomena of Austrian cultural history, the Jewish assimilation.

[71] 'Musik soll nicht schmücken, sie soll wahr sein.' Quoted in Peter Gorsen, 'Das Pathos der einsamen Seele' in *Frankfurter Allgemeine Zeitung*, 18 February 1984 p. 25.
[72] Weininger, *Geschlecht und Charakter*, pp. 307–34.
[73] For instance, Allan Janik and Stephen Toulmin, *Wittgenstein's Vienna* (New York 1973) pp. 190–9.

≫ 9 ≪

The Enlightenment

LIBERALISM AND THE JEW

The entry of the Jews into the mainstream of European society and culture was a result of the acceptance of enlightened thought during the course of the nineteenth century. The fortunes of the Jewish emancipation were intimately bound up with those of the political expression of the Enlightenment: liberalism. The status of the Jews in Germany and Austria depended almost exclusively on the general success of liberal ideas and shared their ups and downs. The year 1848 thus brought full emancipation, only for it to be snatched away. Only with the German Liberal triumph by default in 1867 were the Jews finally given fully equal rights in Cisleithania, the Austrian half of the Dual Monarchy.[1]

This large dependence on the success of liberalism had predictable results amongst Austrian Jews:

To the Jew liberalism was more than just a political doctrine, a comfortable principle and a popular opinion of the day – it was his spiritual asylum, his port of shelter after a thousand years of homelessness, the final fulfilment of the vain wishes of his ancestors, his patent of liberty after a slavery of indescribable severity and shame. It was his divine protectress, the queen of his heart, whom he served with the whole ardour of his soul, for whom he fought on the barricades and in the people's assemblies, in the parliament, in literature and the press. For her he gladly bore the wrath of the powerful.[2]

---

[1] Abraham Leon Sachar, *A History of the Jews* (New York 1965) pp. 273–98; Wolfgang Häusler, 'Toleranz, Emanzipation und Antisemitismus' in eds. N. Vielmetti, Drabek, Häusler, Stuhlpfarrer, *Das österreichische Judentum* (Vienna 1974) pp. 89–123; Klaus Lohrmann, W. Wadl and M. Wenninger, 'Die Entwicklung des Judenrechtes in Österreich und seinen Nachbarländern' in K. Lohrmann, ed., *1,000 Jahre österreichisches Judentum* (Eisenstadt 1982) pp. 42–53.

[2] 'Dem Juden war der Liberalismus mehr als eine politische Doctrin [sic], ein bequemes Prinzip und eine populäre Tagesmeinung – er war sein geistiges Asyl, sein schützender Port nach tausend-jähriger Heimatslosigkeit, die endliche Erfüllung der vergeblichen Sehnsucht seiner Ahnen, sein Freiheitsbrief nach einer Knechtschaft namenloser Härte und Schmach, seine Schutzgöttin, seine Herzenskönigin, welcher er diente mit der ganzen Glut seiner Seele, für die er stritt auf den Barrikaden und in den Volksversammlungen,

This description of the total dedication to liberalism given by Joseph Bloch reflects fairly accurately the attitudes of Jews in Vienna at the time. The *Neue Freie Presse*, regardless of its actual dealings, continually used the rhetoric of the most primitive liberalism, identifying at one point liberalism with civilization.[3] As Jonny Moser has said, liberalism had freed the Jews from centuries of repression, and its *laissez faire* economic policies also suited the Jewish economic forms (excluded from the protected guild economy). Jews thus became the 'Kerntruppe' (crack troops) of liberalism in Austria.[4]

The Jewish dedication to the tenets of liberalism was not without sacrifices, however. If the Jews had been given the rights of the citizen, as it were, they were also forced to acknowledge their duties, and, according to enlightened, liberal thought, this meant becoming fully human individuals or, to put it another way, sloughing off their Jewishness, as liberals understood it.[5] George L. Mosse has graphically described how the most popular German liberal authors of the mid nineteenth century carried with them the worst kinds of prejudice against 'the Jew'.[6] He illustrates this through Gustav Freytag's *Soll und Haben* and Felix Dahn's *Ein Kampf um Rom*. Hans Mayer has complemented this with his own study of the same prejudices in Wilhelm Raabe's *Der Hungerpastor*. In these works the essence of evil is represented by a Jewish figure. In Freytag's book there is Veitel Itzig – ugly, dishonest, slovenly and rootless, a symbol of the new, 'unreliable' capitalist middle class, which threatens the equanimity of the old, 'honest' German middle classes. Dahn has the Goths (thinly disguised Germans) betrayed by the Jew, Jochem.[7] Raabe's pastor, Hans Unwirrsch, comes to the rescue of the weak Jew, Moses Freudenstein, only for Freudenstein, now alias Dr Theophile Stein, to go off to Berlin, deserting the cause of the Enlightenment to become a lackey of the government.[8] Being liberals, these authors also included 'good' Jews in their books, but what they meant by the 'good' Jew was the Jew who had become as German as possible, civilized because not Jewish any more.

---

in dem Parlament, in der Literatur und in der Tagespresse; ihretwegen ertrug er willig den Zorn der Mächtigen.' Joseph S. Bloch, 'Das Problem des Antisemitismus' in *Österreichische Wochenschrift. Centralorgan für die gesammten Interessen des Judentums* (ÖW) 2 January 1885 (II.1) p. 3. This is also reproduced in J. S. Bloch, *Der nationale Zwist und die Juden in Österreich* (Vienna 1886); cf. Häusler, 'Toleranz, Emanzipation', p. 109.

[3] *Neue Freie Presse*, morning edition (*NFPm*) 23 March 1895 p. 1.

[4] Jonny Moser, 'Von der antisemitischen Bewegung zum Holocaust' in Lohrmann, *1,000 Jahre*, p. 250.

[5] Hans Mayer, *Aussenseiter* (Frankfurt-on-Main 1981) pp. 326–79 for a discussion of this point.

[6] George L. Mosse, *Germans and Jews: the Right, the Left and the Search for a 'Third Force'* in *Pre-Nazi Germany* (London 1971) pp. 38–9.

[7] *Ibid*. pp. 63–72.   [8] Mayer, *Aussenseiter*, pp. 385ff.

In Freytag there is Bernhard Ehrenthal (whose Germanicized name is a sign of progress in itself), and in Dahn there is the patriarch Isaak, whose virtue is shown by supporting the Goths and really wanting to leave his Judaism behind him.[9] The good Jew defined himself for such authors, the spokesmen for the emerging Germany, as the Jew who wanted to cease being Jewish for to be Jewish was to embody all that was hated by the German liberal spirit.

As Mosse points out, the animosity shown to the Veitel Itzig caricature was a common response in the literature of the Enlightenment. The idea of such emancipators as C. W. Dohm was not to emancipate Judaism so much as Jews, that is to say, Jewish individuals. In his seminal work for the emancipation *Über die bürgerliche Verbesserung der Juden* (1781) he had stated that the only proper solution to the problem of the Jews was: 'Let them cease to be Jews.'[10] With such statements it is necessary to understand that for people such as Dohm this did not seem to be a biased or bigoted approach, forcing the Jews to do something they did not want to do. Rather they felt they were freeing the Jews, emancipating them from Judaism. When the circumstances of the Jewish community of the time are considered this becomes credible.

The Jews in the ghetto, while cut off from the rest of society by the laws of the host state, had also, by their special laws and customs, consciously cut themselves off from others. Theodor Gomperz saw the very survival of the Jews as a separate religious group as largely due to this 'Hecke' (hedge) which they had built around themselves.[11] The ghetto gate was in this sense a double barrier, locking Jews in and the rest of the world out.[12] The Jewish individual was thus forced to remain a Jew cut off from the world whether he liked it or not, unless he made a great effort to escape what he, as an individual, might regard as the chains of his Jewish heritage.

This is how the Enlightenment, with its faith in the rationality of the individual, and its mission to free man from the bonds of superstition (as they called organized religion) necessarily saw the Judaism of the ghetto of eighteenth-century Europe. The whole tendency of the Enlightenment was to free the rational actor from the bonds of historical, social and intellectual hierarchies, especially the Catholic Church, but the same applied to Judaism. As Gershom Scholem put it, the policy was: 'For the Jews as individuals everything; for the Jews as a people nothing.'[13] Such attitudes

[9] *Ibid.* pp. 391–2; Mosse, *Germans and Jews*, pp. 64–5.

[10] Quoted in Mosse, *Germans and Jews*, p. 39. Also see Jakob Katz, *Out of the Ghetto* (Cambridge, Mass. 1973) pp. 58ff. For a positive view of Dohm, see J. Carlebach, 'The Forgotten Connection: Women and Jews between Enlightenment and Romanticism' in *Leo Baeck Institute Yearbook* (*LBIY*) 1979, pp. 118ff.

[11] Theodor Gomperz, *Essays und Erinnerungen* (Stuttgart 1905) p. 198.

[12] Desmond Stewart, *Theodor Herzl* (London 1974) p. 17.

[13] Gershom Scholem, *Jews and Judaism in Crisis* (New York 1976) p. 63.

clearly marked the strategy which Joseph II employed in his famous *Toleranzpatent* of 1782. The actual formula used by the *Hofkanzlei* was 'to make the totality of Jewry harmless, but the individual useful'.[14] This reflected the general tenor of Joseph's Enlightenment: all particularist bodies in his state had to be integrated into a rational structure. The Jews were only one of many cases where the idea of a society as the sphere of rational man, of common humanity, necessitated the destruction of old structures in favour of new.

Hannah Arendt has described how the Jew offered the humanists of the Enlightenment, such as Herder, the chance to prove that, beyond the confines of religious traditions, there could exist a pure form of human existence, which relied on its humanity and nothing else. The sheer radical nature of the transformation needed to create a human being from an oriental such as the Jew would be proof of education's power in creating a purer human, the 'new types of humanity' which would form the rational society of the future.[15] In the philosophy of someone such as Lessing, man, the rational actor, is placed above revealed truth. The possibility of attaining truth becomes more important than the belief that it had already been revealed; tolerance should replace dogma as the object of faith.[16] The Jews were, for Europeans, the obvious group on which to practice these theories, for they were the only non-Christian group in the midst of the Enlightenment. Lessing's great expression of the faith in man thus came to have a Jew as its central character.

Nathan der Weise is the plea for a pure humanism, regardless of the differences among men. Its message is summed up in the lines: 'Are Christian and Jew more Christian and Jew than human being?'[17] This is elaborated in the famous parable of the rings, whose message is that none of the three religions can claim the certainty to truth, but all, in order to prove themselves, must do so through their empirical actions, by the practical effect of their belief. As none of the religions could claim to have always produced the best in man, this ensured the continual toleration of all religions in respect for the individual.[18] The lesson of Lessing's parable

---

[14] Quoted in Nikolaus Vielmetti, 'Zur Geschichte der Wiener Juden im Vormärz' in Lohrmann, *1,000 Jahre*, p. 95. It should be added that, while the final patent was highly ambiguous towards the Jews, it fell far short of Joseph's original intention of liberating the Jews as individuals. The compromises were actually described in 1790 as 'Schonung des philosophischen Kaysers für die Vorurtheile seines Volckes'. Many of the less attractive aspects of the patent can thus be attributed to force of circumstance. Lohrmann, *1,000 Jahre*, pp. 94–5, 334.

[15] Hannah Arendt, 'Privileged Jews' in *Jewish Social Studies* (*JSS*) VIII 1946 pp. 14–16. It is worth noting that an antisemite such as Houston Stewart Chamberlain could quote Herder approvingly. See his *Die Grundlagen des 19. Jahrhunderts* (Munich 1899) p. 458.

[16] Hannah Arendt, *Die verborgene Tradition* (Frankfurt-on-Main 1976) pp. 108–24.

[17] 'Sind Christ und Jude eher Christ und Jude, Als Mensch?' G. E. Lessing, *Nathan der Weise* (Stuttgart 1925, 1982) p. 50. [18] *Ibid.* pp. 71–5.

was still being stated almost two hundred years later by the ageing Otto Neurath: 'no one can use logical empiricism to ground a totalitarian argument'.[19]

When *Nathan der Weise* was performed in a special charity performance in Vienna in 1895 with Adolf von Sonnenthal in the title rôle for the first time, the theatre critic of the *Neue Freie Presse*, Ludwig Speidel, summed up the message of the play. He saw its power as stemming from the twin bases of joy in a morality of reason independent of religion and the cosmopolitan preference of personality over the divisiveness of nationality. He continued: 'On these two pillars rests the whole classical literature of the German people...a German stage on which *Nathan the Wise* does not live is only half a German stage. It lacks the spiritual patent of nobility.'[20] In other words, Lessing's play was the hallmark of a higher humanity, of a nobility of the mind which lay above mere religious form and was open to all.

The language made this look as if it related to the nobility, to an aristocratic way of life. Yet this nobility of the mind was in direct opposition to the older forms of nobility, as well as the forms of religion, as absolute, exclusive systems. This nobility was open to all who were prepared to be educated. An article a few months later, also in the *Neue Freie Presse*, put forth the prospect of the 'Veredlung' of the masses through the medium of art, to create what it called a 'Menschensadel', which was a denial of aristocratic privilege. This would be a society in which barriers of ignorance would be swept away by the recognition of man's nobility, by the acceptance of humanity as the only religion, as the obituary in the *Neue Freie Presse* for Georges Clemenceau's father put it. It was the nobility of humanity which counted.[21]

The noble savage was a favourite device of western writers of the time for proving the potential goodness of man. The Austrians did not have to go too far afield; for them the noble savage was the Jew. A letter appeared in the *Neue Freie Presse* in April 1896 from a teacher convinced that his fellow teachers should continue to vote for the Liberals, not the Christian Socials. He explained: 'we cannot afford the luxury of flirting a little with the reaction. Our holiest mission resides in the ideal goal of striving for the spiritual welfare of mankind, and thus in the defense of the free school.' He had nothing against most Jewish pupils, apart from the 'Auswüchse des Ghettos', and saw that the Jews had only been forced into the commercial world by the Aryan host peoples. He concluded: 'A truly progressive party

[19] Friedrich Stadler, ed., *Arbeiterbildung in der Zwischenkriegszeit, Otto Neurath*, catalogue (Vienna 1982) pp. 10–11.

[20] Auf diesen beiden Grundsäulen ruht die ganze classische [sic] Literatur des deutschen Volkes...Eine deutsche Bühne, auf der "Nathan der Werse" nicht lebt, ist nur halb eine deutsche Bühne. Ihr fehlt der geistige Adelsbrief.' *NFPm* 20 January 1895 p. 1.

[21] NFPm 7 July 1895 p. 1; on Clemenceau, NFPm 24 July 1897 p. 4.

would automatically seek the ennobling of such a people.'[22] This was saying what liberals and enlightened thinkers had always said, that through education the Jews could once again become part of the new enlightened society of the West (*Abendland*); they would, in Herder's words, become 'more purely humanized'.[23]

The Jewish emancipation was thus made possible by the idea that a man was more than a prince if he was a human being, 'ein Mensch'.[24] The history of the Jews in German culture in the nineteenth century was thus summed up by the attempt 'als Juden Menschen zu sein'.[25] The emancipation, the assimilation, was to be achieved through education by the individual. This was the task which the Enlightenment set the Jews at the beginning of the assimilation.

LEAVING THE GHETTO

The man on whom Lessing modelled *Nathan* was Moses Mendelssohn, one of the most important figures in the history of modern Jewry.[26] Ludwig Speidel, ironically writing a review of Herzl's play *Das neue Ghetto* in 1898, spoke of Mendelssohn single-handedly taking the Jews out of the ghetto.[27] As 'merchant and philosopher', Mendelssohn came to personify the possibility of the Jew becoming an acceptable human being, part of the *Menschensadel*. As *Nathan* he was the symbol of the ability of *Bildung und Besitz*, wealth and education, to overcome the handicap of being Jewish.[28]

Mendelssohn, and his followers in the Haskalah, the *Maskilim*, tried to bring Jews, as Jews, into the modern world. Outmoded tradition was rejected in favour of the study of the real scientific world, and, while the study of biblical Hebrew was encouraged to purify the religion, the study of German took on a central significance in enabling the Jew to enter German society.[29] Mendelssohn thought that Jews could be Jews within

---

22 'Wir können uns nicht den Luxus bieten, ein wenig mit der Reaktion zu kokettieren. Unsere heiligste Aufgabe besteht in dem idealen Ziele, die geistige Wohlfahrt der Menschheit anzustreben und daher in der Vertheidigung der freien Schule.' 'Eine wahrhaft fortschrittliche Partei würde unwillkürlich die Veredlung eines solchen Volkes anstreben.' *NFPm* 9 April 1896 p. 3. 23 Arendt, 'Privileged Jews', *JSS* 1946 p. 16.

24 Cf. Schikaneder's slogan from *Die Zauberflöte*.

25 Arendt, *Die verborgene Tradition*, p. 47.

26 On Mendelssohn, see Heer, *God's First Love*, pp. 175–7; Selma Stern-Täubler, 'The First Generation of Emancipated Jews' in *LBIY* 1970 pp. 24ff; Sachar, *A History of the Jews*, pp. 267–73; Scholem, *Jews and Judaism in Crisis*, pp. 74–5; Katz, *Out of the Ghetto*, pp. 59ff; Jacob Allerhand, *Das Judentum in der Aufklärung* (Stuttgart 1980) pp. 51–142.

27 *NFPm* 16 January 1898 p. 1. 28 Mayer, *Aussenseiter*, p. 335.

29 In Austria the main *Maskil* protagonists were Hartwig Wessely and Herz Homberg. On their careers and attitudes, see Lohrmann, *1,000 Jahre*, pp. 141, 335; Katz, *Out of the Ghetto*, pp. 66ff; Sachar, *A History of the Jews*, p. 271.

society and did not have to be cut off by traditional forms and the idea of the promised land.[30] It was more important to spread God's message in society and to join forces with the Enlightenment of mankind. The antagonism to the bonds of tradition was something on which enlightened parties on both sides of the ghetto gate could agree. Education was to break these bonds.

The initial efforts of the *Maskilim* at reform, such as Homberg's new schools in Galicia, were dismal failures, and the reformers met large-scale opposition from both flanks, from traditionalist Jews and conservative elements such as the Polish aristocracy or, in the 1850s, clerical-minded Habsburg ministers.[31] From an early date, however, the Jewish community in Vienna, especially its richer element, was a firm supporter of the Haskalah and its implication of complete assimilation. Far from being some idyllic object of nostalgic contemplation, the ghettos and shtetls from which these people came were hated by them, and the life they had led there was remembered with shame and horror, the religious and cultural traditions along with it.[32] As Leon Kellner put it, the assimilated community regarded the ghetto as a black spot on the horizon.[33]

Joseph II, whose *Toleranzpatent* can be seen as a direct attack on the traditional Jewish way of life, was regarded as a hero by the Viennese Jewish community, as the deliverer of the Jews from the ghetto, the good Habsburg.[34] When the ghettos were finally opened up from without, the external obstacles to Jews removed, many Jews responded by relaxing the other, self-imposed set of restrictions on contact with the outside world. This was understandable. Since there was no longer any threat from the outside world, the Jews saw no need to protect themselves from it. In Pressburg, for instance, this meant that visiting the theatre was no longer regarded as a sin.[35] This, however, brought all kinds of problems for the Jews as a community. If theatre visits were now acceptable, it was difficult to decide what was unacceptable. Where was the line to be drawn between accepting the new freedoms and retaining the traditional restraints? In

[30] Heer, *God's First Love*, pp. 176–7.

[31] Lohrmann, *1,000 Jahre*, p. 335; Raphael Mahler, *A History of Modern Jewry* (London 1971) pp. 260–1.

[32] Thus the attempt by the Orthodox Ignaz Deutsch to interest the Minister of Culture, Graf Leo Thun, in the 1850s in a Jewish Concordat to parallel the Catholic one of 1855 in opposition to the Jewish *Kultusgemeinde*. See Hans Tietze, *Die Juden Wiens* (Vienna 1935) p. 218; Sigmund Mayer, *Die Wiener Juden: Kommerz, Kultur, Politik 1700–1900* (Vienna 1918) pp. 366–70.   [33] *NFPm* 1 September 1896 p. 1.

[34] Sigmund Mayer, *Ein jüdischer Kaufmann 1831–1911: Lebenserinnerungen* (Vienna 1911) p. 82; *Käthe Leichter: Leben und Werk*, ed. Herbert Steiner (Vienna 1973) p. 240; Lohrmann, *1,000 Jahre*, p. 210; Israel Jeiteles, *Die Kultusgemeinde in Wien mit Benützung des statistischen Volkszahlungsoperates vom Jahr 1869* (Vienna 1873) pp. 9, 22; G. Wolf, *Geschichte der Juden in Wien, 1156–1876* (Vienna 1876) pp. 78–86.

[35] Mayer, *Die Wiener Juden*, p. 192.

many cases what the enlightened thinkers had hoped for happened: by destroying the outer shackles on the Jews as a group, the internal restraints of the Jews against western culture were also relaxed with no measure as to how much; the decision could in the confusion only be taken by the individual. Many decided to break with the hated life of the ghetto altogether and to adopt the new culture of reason and progress. These individuals were the people who provided the dominant tone in the Viennese Jewish community, who were proud to have left the world of prejudice behind and to have entered the history of progress.

It was natural that Jews should accomplish their entry into western society through the book, through the acquiring of *Bildung*. Many escaped their ghetto existence by the simple expedient of swapping their prayer books for books of science. Moshe Atlas has described how Jewish boys devoted themselves to the new culture by learning in secret.[36] Joseph Ehrlich, who went through the same experience, reported how his teacher, Barat, a follower of the Haskalah, described this experience: 'I had to go in secret up to the attic to learn German and study science, to avoid the tyranny of my overzealous father.'[37] With such language was created a mystique of the struggle through education for freedom from the reactionary traditions of Judaism itself. Behind many assimilated families of Vienna lay the figure of the student who, through experience of enlightened thought, had escaped from ghetto culture.[38] The polarity between ghetto and education continued until the end of the assimilation. In 1938 Käthe Leichter could still say that her friend Hedi Planner had not been able to study, 'because her family–ghetto would not allow it'.[39]

One figure who came from this kind of background was Leopold Kompert, who, as a student at the Jeschivah in Pressburg, broke away under the influence of the German Enlightenment to become a leading writer of his day, especially as a popularizer of the ghetto tale.[40] Kompert's ghetto stories exemplify the fact that the argument between the Enlightenment and the defenders of Jewish tradition was as much an internal as an external debate. The struggle such as Kompert described between reason (assimilation) and superstition (the ghetto) was one for the Jewish heritage. Both sides saw themselves as retaining the *essence* of

---

[36] Moshe Atlas, 'Jüdische Ärzte' in Fränkel, Josef ed., *The Jews of Austria: Essays on their Life, History and Destruction* (London 1967) p. 41.

[37] 'Im Geheimen musste ich, auf dem Dachboden, deutsch lernen und die Wissenschaften pflegen, um der Tyrannei meines überfrommen Vaters zu entgehen.' Josef R. Ehrlich, *Der Weg meines Lebens* (Vienna 1874) p. 63.

[38] An example is afforded by the Adler family, see Rudolf G. Ardelt, *Friedrich Adler: Probleme einer Persönlichkeitsentwicklung um die Jahrhundertwende* (Vienna 1984) pp. 16–17.

[39] *Käthe Leichter*, p. 320.

[40] See Sigmund Mayer's description of the eminent figures who started as students at the Pressburger Jeschivah, Mayer, *Ein jüdischer Kaufmann*, pp. 65–6.

Judaism. It was just that one side saw this in terms of externalities and the other in terms of some sort of basic mission of enlightenment.

Kompert's tales, of which *Zwischen Ruinen* of 1874 is perhaps the most representative, revolve around the need for Jews and Germans to co-operate to form a new society of tolerance. He wrote his tales of the ghetto, he said, as an expression of his thanks to the German people for releasing the Jews from their oppression, so that after the long night of despair the light of morning had broken.[41] Kompert, a professing Jew all his life and closely involved with the Viennese *Gemeinde*, saw assimilation with the Germans as the only way to ensure progress and freedom, even if this meant intermarriage. The enemies in *Zwischen Ruinen* are on the one hand a Czech Catholic priest, with all the old prejudices against the Jews, and on the other a fanatical Hasid. Between them they represent the ruins of prejudice, which are overcome by love between the peoples in the shape of a Jewish youth and a Christian girl.[42] The forces of reaction inside, as well as outside, were thus targets for the Jewish writers of the time. They too were intent on destroying the shackles which held them to the prejudiced world of the ghetto.

Karl Emil Franzos' life and work show even more clearly the basic themes of the Haskalah tradition in the Habsburg Monarchy. The son of a liberal doctor stationed in the border town of Czortkow in Eastern Galicia, Franzos was brought up in the spirit of his grandfather, an admirer of Lessing, who told him as a young boy:

There is one God over us all, all religions are equally good, for all oblige one to be truly human. Ceremonies are superfluous. Born a Jew, you must remain a Jew, for this is God's apparent will, and because your co-religionists, who are still – for good and bad reasons – looked at askance, need good educated men, who can purify and defend them.[43]

Franzos' writings are all in pursuit of this goal: to protect the Jews, but at the same time to purify them, to bring them out of the world of dark prejudice into the mainstream of progress. Brought up in a spirit of tolerance and humanity, Franzos regarded the world of the Hasidim as 'Halbasien', half-Asian, barbaric. Remaining Jewish, Franzos tried to take

---

[41] Bernhard Denscher, 'Vergessene jüdische Literatur' in Lohrmann, *1,000 Jahre*, p. 213.

[42] Leopold Kompert, *Zwischen Ruinen*, (Leipzig 1887) *passim*. cf. Denscher, 'Vergessene Literatur', p. 214. On Kompert's views, see also Stefan Hock, 'Komperts Leben und Schaffen' in Leopold Kompert, *Sämtliche Werke in zehn Bänden*, (Leipzig 1906) vol. 1, pp. v–lviii, esp. p. lviii.

[43] 'Es ist ein Gott über uns allen, alle Religionen sind gleich gut, weil alle zur Menschlichkeit verpflichten, Zeremonien sind überflüssig. Als Jude geboren, hast du Jude zu bleiben, weil dies offenbar Gottes Wille ist, und weil deine Glaubensbrüder, die noch – mit Recht und Unrecht – scheel angesehen werden, guter und gebildeter Männer bedürfen, die sie läutern und verteidigen.' Denscher, 'Vergessene Literatur', p. 217.

Jews out of the fanatic world of Hasidism, to help them to the true, pure version of Judaism which was the family's tradition. The Hasidim thus became his arch-enemies. He saw in them all that threatened the humanist understanding between Jew and Christian. He was especially proud when his *Die Juden von Barnow*, a strong attack on the Hasidim, was translated into Yiddish, for now he could regard it as a 'weapon for the Enlightenment in his fight against darkness'.[44]

Kompert and Franzos were the narrators of a battle between the *Maskilim* and the Hasidim for the allegiance of the Jewish masses which took place in the Monarchy throughout the nineteenth century. Joseph Ehrlich was the product of this battle in Galicia and has described quite graphically the types of strategies employed by the enlightened and much wealthier minority against the obstinate fanaticism of the Hasidim. The question which the progressive element put was plain: 'how do we lure the confused Hasidim out of their swamp into our beneficent net?'[45] The answer was, inevitably, to set up a school. This would be modern, but would nevertheless respect the forms of Jewish tradition such as the Sabbath, and it would provide free clothes and shoes to its poorest pupils. The contracts for these items would be used as bait: the Hasidim, such as Ehrlich's stepfather, would only get the contracts on condition that they sent their children to the school. In the case of Ehrlich the scheme succeeded, as it did with many other former Cheder pupils. Once lured into the school these children had to be totally re-educated, on the lines of 'enlightenment and liberty' until they were quite 'purified' of their Hasidic upbringing.[46] The education offered was still a Jewish one, and Ehrlich first learnt of the ideas of the Enlightenment from Mendelssohn's book, *Phaedon*.[47] But a completely new world, the 'real world', was revealed to the pupils, a world their fathers refused to recognize. Ehrlich's final great act of rebellion consisted in putting a map of the world in the synagogue, an act of sacrilege for the Hasidim, but a statement by Ehrlich that a real world existed outside the 'voluntary ghetto' of Hasidism.[48]

In the spring of 1849 Lazar Auspitz hoped that in fifteen or twenty years the 'forms of Judaism' would have been destroyed, and Judaism itself transformed into 'moral education with of course less priestly nonsense'. The Jewish way of life as it existed would thus disappear, be overcome by a natural religion of morality, which would however preserve 'Judentum' in its moral teachings.[49] Lazar Auspitz's great-grandson, Heinrich Gomperz, expressed a similar idea when he described the career of the Joseph Ehrlich who has featured above: 'Ehrlich...a wild-looking eastern

[44] *Ibid.* p. 218.
[46] *Ibid.* pp. 32–4.
[48] *Ibid.* pp. 67–9.
[45] Ehrlich, *Der Weg meines Lebens*, p. 32.
[47] *Ibid.* pp. 101–2.
[49] Gomperz, *Essays*, p. 5.

Jew, had, with self-overcoming and stamina, accommodated himself to western ways, and now worked as a poet and writer, not without success.'[50] The idea of self-overcoming, so prominent in thought around the turn of the century under Nietzsche's influence, thus had a very strong, practical parallel in the need for the Jew from the eastern ghetto or shtetl to master his past and his heritage so that he could take part in the cultural life of the west.

Through the transformation of the self provided by a western education the past could be overcome. Käthe Leichter's mother, for instance, coming from an uneducated Rumanian Jewish family, launched herself into western culture in order 'to overcome Galatz'.[51] The same cultural battle against the Jewish past lay behind Victor Adler's letter to his son Friedrich about the latter's Russian Jewish fiancée: 'She has...absolutely no resistance to Jewishness, which – namely the resistance – has become a fundamental part of our whole being.'[52] Behind the leader of the Austrian socialists, therefore, can be seen the continuation of the struggle against tradition which Mendelssohn had begun. Only, in the case of Adler, it had become a struggle to free himself entirely from 'das Jüdische', however defined.

There remained a fear in the assimilated community that the old, reactionary tendencies within Judaism would yet revive and spoil the progress of humanity, or at least their part in it. Friedrich Adler was not alone in detesting the prospect of a traditional Jewish wedding; Sigmund Freud had exactly the same problem and was only prevented from converting to Protestantism to avoid it by what must have been a stiff talking to from his friend Breuer.[53] It was all too much of a reminder of the world from which these people had escaped. Victor Adler was extremely reluctant to visit the home of his friend Heinrich Braun (also Freud's friend) to pay court to Braun's sister Emma. This was partly due to the fact that, as Emma put it, Adler at this time was an 'antisemite of the strictest observance'; in addition, however, as Rudolf Ardelt points out, the house in which the Brauns lived had been one in which the Adlers had lived, before getting rich and moving out of the very Jewish environment of the

---

[50] 'Ehrlich...ein verwildert aussehender Ostjude, hatte sich mit Selbstüberwindung und Ausdauer in die westlichen Verhältnisse gefunden und betätigte sich nun nicht ohne jeden Erfolg in Wien als Dichter und Schriftsteller.' H. Gomperz and R. A. Kann, eds., *Briefe an, von und um Josephine von Wertheimstein* (Vienna 1981) p. 397.

[51] *Käthe Leichter*, p. 276.

[52] 'Sie hat...gar keinen Widerwillen gegen das Jüdische, was – nämlich der Widerwille – eine der Grundlagen unseres ganzen Wesens geworden ist...' Ardelt, *Friedrich Adler*, p. 116.

[53] Dennis B. Klein, *The Jewish Origins of the Psychoanalytic Movement* (New York 1981) pp. 59–60.

Second District. It was all too much linked with the painful process which had led the family from the *Gasse* of Lipnik to a mansion in the Alsergrund.[54]

The fight between assimilation and tradition came to be symbolized by the contrast between the *Westjude*, enlightened and progressive, and the *Ostjude*, who, as Sigmund Mayer put it, was with the rise of Hasidism actually going backwards, refusing to participate in the 'integration into the full cultural life of the whole population'. A separate Jewish nationality had no place in the progressive outlook. Revealingly, when the Jewish Nationalists proposed that the Jews be given their own electoral curia, Mayer called this 'a political ghetto'.[55] It was the ghetto, left behind, which still had to be avoided at all costs for it threatened civilization.

THE SECOND EMANCIPATION

The hero of Herzl's play, *Das neue Ghetto*, dies with an impassioned plea for the Jews to leave the new ghetto which antisemitic prejudice has created. Herzl's point was that the cry was in vain, that it was impossible for the Jew in present society to do this; no matter how complete the assimilation, the Jew remained in a social ghetto.[56] This was not the interpretation of the play when it was reviewed in the paper for which Herzl was *feuilleton* editor, the *Neue Freie Presse*, in January 1898. Ludwig Speidel, the Burgtheater critic of the paper, gave the play a glowing report, but instead of concentrating on the end, which proves in the death of the hero the failure of assimilation, he ended his review with the story in the play about the Jewish child who had been butchered after being lured out of the ghetto by a false cry for help. Speidel latched onto the hero's comment on this story: 'The cry for help can also be real for once.' In other words, a message of hope was conveyed, rather than the pessimistic conclusion which Herzl had written the play to illustrate.

The rationale behind Speidel's insistence on the opportunity, or duty, to assimilate, was that for him the Jew was not fully free until part of the greater society around him. Speidel therefore faced the challenge of Herzl's play by making its hero, Dr Joseph Samuel, into an ideal hero doing the only thing possible for a Jew in civilized society: 'rather he is trying to cast off the external Jew and to assume the attitudes of his fellow citizens'. Only by following the ways of the assimilation could the Jew really be free: 'It is his most pressing task to cast aside everything that estranges him from his fellow man. That is the second, real emancipation of the Jew, without

---

[54] Ardelt, *Friedrich Adler*, p. 29.
[55] Mayer, *Die Wiener Juden*, pp. 466ff.
[56] Alex Bein, *Theodore Herzl* (London 1957) pp. 102–7.

which the first emancipation remains a formality.'[57] Speidel's 'second emancipation' was a handy formula for describing what store the Viennese Jews, and this included the powers of the *Gemeinde*, set by the achievement of a complete assimilation in all forms so that they could be freed from being different.

In Vienna there was a considerable effort at total 'Gleichstellung' with the Christians, involving, for instance, the training of Jewish boys to be artisans in 'Christian' trades.[58] Israel Jeiteles, in his statistical study of the Viennese Jews in 1873, exemplified this wish not to appear different. He made a great attempt to present the statistics so that Jews would appear socially the same as everyone else; moreover he was intent on denying Jews a special place in 'cultural life': 'We in Vienna neither wish, nor would we be able, to lay claim to the role the Greeks played among the Romans as teachers.'[59] It seems prophetic of Jeiteles that even in 1873 he refused to list the cultural achievements of Jews in Vienna, arguing that this was not to do with these people being Jewish.[60] Behind this excuse lay a major irony, for the omission of such a list was an implicit admission that Jews were somehow different. The major vehicle of assimilation had been education, with the result that the assimilated Jews were more educated than most of the members of the society which they had entered. The very strategy of assimilation through *Bildung* was jeopardizing the acceptance of Jews in general, by making them something special again: no longer Jewish, but not really Gentile either.

Most people ignored the problem at which Jeiteles had hinted. Karl Kraus in his attack on Herzl's Zionism was still insisting twenty-five years after Jeiteles that the assimilation was achievable. The worst Zionist could be 'civilized' into a European in a few years. The answer was still *Bildung* and a dedication to assimilation: 'The irrefutable faith in the assimilability of the Jewish character is the best orthodoxy. One should simply let it become...the faith of the fathers.' Even if some sort of internal difference remained, Kraus was quite clear that Jews could become acceptable if they would sacrifice the externalities which separated them from others.[61]

---

[57] 'Er ist vielmehr bestrebt, den äusseren Juden auszuziehen und die Gesinnung seiner Mitbürger in sich aufzunehmen.' 'Es ist seine angelegentlichste Arbeit, jede Fremdheit zwischen sich und seinen Nebenmenschen aufzuheben. Das ist ja die zweite und echte Emancipation [sic] des Juden, ohne welche die erste Emancipation nur eine Formalität bleibt.' *NFPm* 16 January 1898 p. 1.

[58] Mayer, *Die Wiener Juden*, pp. 301–2; also Katz, *Out of the Ghetto*, pp. 176ff.

[59] 'Wir in Wien wollen und können uns die Aufgabe der Griechen unter den Römern nicht vindiziren, die deren Erzieher gewesen.' Jeiteles, *Die Kultusgemeinde*, pp. 77–9.

[60] *Ibid.* p. 111.

[61] 'Der unumstössliche Glaube an die Anpassungsfähigkeit des jüdischen Charakters ist die beste Orthodoxie, man lasse ihn nur erst einmal den...Glauben der Väter werden.' Karl Kraus, *Eine Krone für Zion* (Vienna 1898) pp. 23–5.

Kraus did not see, or chose not to see, Jeiteles' problem that the Jews were becoming different again. This was partly due to the logic of the assimilation. Jews had been unacceptable because not versed in German culture and morals. Once Jews had achieved these they could, as Mosse says, become avid readers of Dahn and Freytag, for they could view the Jewish stereotypes there with equanimity, as something overcome.[62] That, as *Gebildeten*, they were becoming exceptional, was something most could regard as irrelevant. The reasoning behind this becomes evident if we look at another emancipatory text, written earlier than Jeiteles' study.

Heinrich Jaques was an influential lawyer, a staunch liberal and a friend of Theodor Gomperz. His *Denkschrift über die Stellung der Juden in Österreich* of 1859 was one of the major discussions of the rationale of emancipation in Austria. It illustrates well the Jewish identification of emancipation with the release from what the Jews considered the bondage of their former existence. Addressing the Austrian government Jaques couched his argument in the same language of utility which had been used to justify the *Toleranzpatent* of 1782. The restrictions on Jews imposed after 1848 should be lifted not so much for the Jews themselves but to prevent valuable intellectual and financial capital going to waste. The traditional life of the ghetto was for Jaques a complete waste of time, a condemnation to intellectual stagnation.[63]

Jaques insisted that all arguments against the Jews as a people were misguided, not because they did not describe the present situation, but because the Jews were capable of changing. They could be made better, and he quoted Dohm in support.[64] His tactic was clear in his approach to the question of the Jews and money. He pointed out that Jews were not alone in sharp financial practices, comparing the record of Polish Jews with that of the Austrian National Bank. In making the point he could not resist quoting Lessing's Nathan: 'Who is here the Jew?'[65] Jews were dominant in the capitalist world, but only because they had no choice. Wealth was the only means of gaining respect and freedom in a world of prejudice. Excluded from the administration, Jewish students had no alternative but to make money, with devastating results for the stability of the state: 'that imposing and dangerous plutocratic power', which the Jews represented in Europe, would swallow up small capital and set in train an uncontrolled movement of capital which would lead to ever more severe economic crises.[66] The worst fears of the opponents of emancipation were thus played upon to convince them to free the Jews, so that they could be changed for the better.

---

[62] Mosse, *Germans and Jews*, p. 74.
[63] Heinrich Jaques, *Denkschrift über die Stellung der Juden in Österreich* (Vienna 1859) pp. viii–xi.   [64] *Ibid.* p. 4.   [65] *Ibid.* p. 21.   [66] *Ibid.* pp. 37–9.

There were several ways in which this could be done. If Jews were allowed to buy property their supposed tendency to revolution would be tempered by the landowner's natural conservatism.[67] Above all *Bildung* would solve all problems. Jaques thought that attempts to convert Jews to Catholicism by the carrot and stick method of only allowing converts careers in the bureaucracy would not be a long-term solution, for the Jewish allegiance to their religion was marked by a great obstinacy, which could not be overcome by a mere religion. It was 'a tenacity which can only be overcome by an education in philosophy, which however is indifferent to any positive religious precept'.[68] The Jew would only convert to the religion of humanity.

Jaques argued from the same faith in the progress of European civilization which informed all the other arguments for assimilation so far discussed. This is plainest in his discussion of the *Ostjuden*. He accepted all complaints about their backwardness. Yet he could not see why the 'gebildeten civilisirten [sic] Juden' of Vienna and Bohemia should be lumped together with them.[69] He made the point that the Galician Jews lived among people at an equally low level of civilization, including 'the often no less uneducated Polish noble, whose inner crudity is frequently only weakly disguised by a gloss of French social manners'. The *Ostjude* was thus not alone in requiring the attention of the civilized world: 'they all need a good bit of European civilization before they can really be regarded as human [um erst recht Menschen zu werden]... Here for now is the true terrain for the much-discussed Austrian mission of imparting culture to the East.'[70]

The humanization of the Jew had thus become firmly set as part of the humanization of all men through western civilization. Here Jaques was echoing the central idea of the German Enlightenment, the *Menschenadel* of intellect and education. Jaques concluded that in order for Austria to compete in the modern world it had to use all its resources: 'Everyone with ability and every material resource in the whole state must be sought in the lowly hut of the Polish Jew as well as the state palaces of the high nobility, and everyone must be made to contribute to the whole and its great goals. All must work together to build the new Austria.'[71] An argument for the emancipation of the Jews thus ended in a heartfelt plea for the man of talent, for the freeing of the clever Jew from the prejudices

---

[67] *Ibid.* pp. 26–7.   [68] *Ibid.* pp. 39–40.   [69] *Ibid.* p. 46.

[70] 'Sie Alle bedürfen eben noch ein gutes Stück europäischer Civilization [sic] um erst recht Menschen zu werden...hier ist für jetzt das wahre Terrain jener vielerwähnten Mission Österreichs die Cultur [sic] nach dem Osten zu tragen.' *Ibid.* pp. 46–7.

[71] 'Man muss jede tüchtige und materielle Kraft im ganzen Staate aufsuchen, man muss sie suchen in der niedern Hütte des polnischen Juden wie in den Prachtpalästen des ritterlichen Adels, und jede muss man dem Ganzen und seinen grossen Zwecken dienstbar machen, mit Allen insgesammt den Neubau vollenden.' *Ibid.* p. 50.

which bound him to the Jewish community, so that he could make his contribution to the new state of the future in which it seemed that all, not only the Jews, would receive the education necessary 'um erst recht Menschen zu werden'. For Jaques then, as for most assimilated Jews, Jeiteles' problem that *Bildung* did not bring equality could be regarded as irrelevant, for in their eyes the Jewish strategy of assimilation through *Bildung* was also the goal of the whole of society. In the new humanity of the future all would be educated regardless of what was the case in the present.

THE NEW HUMANITY

It was the idea of *Mensch*, the possibility of a humanity which would be united beyond the old divisions of religion and social class, which was the basic building block of assimilationist thought among Jews, at least at the beginning. In 1849 von Mosenthal asserted in his play *Deborah* that 'our home' was Austria, not Jerusalem. He could say this because he looked forward to a time when the new society would have arrived: 'And Christian and Jew will be – human-beings.'[72] This type of vocabulary appears throughout the period and was plainly a cliché of liberal thought. A typical use of the term is that of Pflugfelder in Schnitzler's play, *Professor Bernhardi*, when he talks of Bernhardi's action in providing for the dying 'Menschenkind' a happy death: 'It takes an incredible falseness to regard the case in any other than purely human terms [menschlich]. Where is the person [Mensch] whose religious feelings could truly be injured by Bernhardi's action?'[73] Schnitzler here, as Lessing before him, was putting *Menschheit* above the truths – such as the need for last rites – of organized religion.

The idea of *Mensch* created a plane of action above the supposedly absolute truths of religion, or if not above, at least independent from their control. It was not a purely fictitious idea, but provided the Jews with a real opportunity in the nineteenth century to live in society regardless of race or creed, 'einfach als Mensch zu gelten', to be regarded simply as human beings.[74] The influence of such ideas seems to have been particularly

---

[72] 'Und Christ und Jude werden – Menschen sein.' Salomon Hermann Mosenthal, *Deborah* (Leipzig 1908) p. 62 cf. Häusler, 'Toleranz, Emanzipation', p. 107. Also see Sacher-Masoch, *Der Mann ohne Vorurtheil* (Berne 1877) for a vivid example of the ideology of *Menschheit*, esp. p. 32.

[73] 'Was für eine ungeheuere Verlogenheit gehört dazu, um den ganzen Fall anders anzusehen als rein menschlich. Wo existiert der Mensch, dessen religiösen Gefühle durch das Vorgehen Bernhardis in Wahrheit verletzt worden wären?' Arthur Schnitzler, *Professor Bernhardi*, in vol. 6 of *Dramen* (Frankfurt-on-Main 1962) p. 206. NB this echoes Mosenthal, *Deborah*, p. 54: 'Bin ich nicht auch ein Menschenkind? Ist Liebe / Nicht aller Eigentum wie Luft und Licht?'

[74] See Ardelt, *Friedrich Adler*, p. 21. Cf. August Bondi, *Autobiography* (Galesburg, Ill. 1910) p. 10.

strong in the Bohemian crownlands, which were at the same time the homelands of the more sophisticated Jewish immigrants to Vienna and also the home of what William Johnston has called Bohemian Reform Catholicism. Here Jews could experience at first hand a tolerant, humane, humanist attitude even from the Catholic Church.[75]

In such an atmosphere one's Jewishness could become, in Theodor Gomperz's words, "un pieux souvenir de famille"; but the advantage to the individualistic organization of society which the concept of *Mensch* provided was that religion, or at least faith, could become irrelevant to the social world. This was expressed amongst assimilated Jews in the formula: 'men like others in the street, but Jews at home'.[76] Heinrich Jaques developed this idea at length in differentiating between *Logos* and *Ethos*. The former was the set of beliefs of any religion, which were absolutes, but metaphysical. *Ethos*, however, was temporal and concerned totally with human action, with inter-personal relations. The world we live in, therefore, was a matter for the psychological, relative *Ethos*, whereas *Logos* 'is relatively indifferent to such matters'. Differences in the sphere of *Logos* were thus not relevant to social forms. Only the *Ethos* decided the compatibility of two religious groups, and even if they disagreed in doctrine their standards of morality could be identical. As the example of the coexistence of Christian sects in a state showed, a common morality could be shared by different faiths, and Jaques argued that the same was true of Judaism and Christianity.[77]

All this was by 1859 fairly old hat, but it illustrates the way in which the Jews, to make assimilation possible, sought to take the question of truth out of the empirical world, out of the argument, by internalizing it, by making it a matter for the individual alone. The Platonic claim of the Church on absolute truth *in* the world was thus opposed in this kind of thought by a double assault. From below, society could continue regardless of doctrine by the recognition of the rights of man (*Mensch*), while, from above, the idea of religious truth being divorced from inter-subjective reality meant that the individual did not need to be told what to believe. Jaques was right to claim the support of Kant, Schopenhauer and Fichte, despite their antisemitism, because the tenets of German idealism contained the one vital prerequisite to assimilationist theory, the autonomy of the will; 'philosophische Bildung' made *all* religion unnecessary to human action, and so what one believed became a matter outside society,

---

[75] William M. Johnston, *The Austrian Mind: an Intellectual and Social History 1848–1938* (Berkeley 1972, pb. 1983) pp. 278ff. Also Guido Adler, *Wollen und Wirken* (Vienna 1935) pp. 3, 75; Gomperz, *Essays*, pp. 14–15.

[76] Quoted in Arendt, 'Privileged Jews' in *JSS* 1946, p. 7. Also, Harald Leupold-Löwenthal, 'Freud und das Judentum' in *Sigmund Freud House Bulletin*, vol. 4, nr. 1, 1980, p. 34.

[77] Jaques, *Denkschrift*, pp. 30–1.

ultimately outside language, as it was later to be defined.[78] The integration of the Jews into nineteenth-century Austrian society was thus based on the principle that religion was a matter of individual faith – not a part of the inter-subjective world.

This idea, naturally enough, had a devastating effect on the outward signs of Judaism in the assimilated community, and it could lead to the total abandonment of belief in traditional religious forms. Apart from preserving family traditions, there seemed little point in continuing in a religious faith one did not hold, and for many, such as Josef Popper-Lynkeus or the Gomperzes, religion was just not an issue any more.[79]

What was important was the moral goodness of the individual, not his religion.[80] For assimilated Jews this was especially important, for if religion did happen to be more important *in* the world than the value of the individual, then they, being neither in one religious camp nor the other, would be excluded from both. Hence the great admiration for the heroes of human liberation, whether they were Joseph II, Lincoln or Zola, was not only due to a real faith in moral progress, but also to an attempt to guarantee the assimilation. In this respect it is worth noting that a great number of Viennese Jews around 1900, including Freud, Theodor Gomperz and Emil Zuckerkandl, supported Lamarck against Darwin, mainly because the Lamarckian theory of the inheritance of acquired characteristics offered the prospect, among humans, that the Jewish race would one day become just like the German, that it would change for the better.[81] The aim of the progressives in Austrian society was thus to destroy completely a separate Jewish identity.

BEYOND THE JEWISH IDENTITY

There is a great danger when handling this question of identity to react, with hindsight, with outrage at this attempted obliteration. The charge cannot be denied. The assimilation was about leaving the Jewish past behind.[82] Yet this ought to be understood in context. Assimilationists

[78] *Ibid.* p. cxiv, for Jaques's attitude to Kant *et al.*
[79] Ingrid Belke, *Die sozialreformerischen Ideen von Josef Popper-Lynkeus 1838–1921* (Tübingen 1978) p. 112; on the Gomperzes, see the comments of R. A. Kann, in Gomperz and Kann, eds., *Josephine von Wertheimstein*, p. 13.
[80] Stella Klein-Löw's grandfather put it thus: 'Die Religion ist nicht so wichtig wie ein gutes Herz und ein heller Kopf.' See Stella Klein-Löw, *Erinnerungen: Erlebtes und Gedachtes* (Vienna 1980) p. 13.
[81] R. W. Clark, *Freud: the Man and the Cause* (London 1980) p. 381; *Theodor Gomperz: ein Gelehrtenleben im Bürgertum der Franz-Josephszeit*, eds. H. Gomperz and R. A. Kann (Vienna 1974) pp. 356–7.
[82] Typical expressions of this charge are to be found in: Scholem, *Jews and Judaism in Crisis*, p. 63; Ardelt, *Friedrich Adler*, p. 15; Lohrmann, *1,000 Jahre*, p. 335 (on Wessely).

welcomed the demise of the religio–cultural complex dependent on Jewish tradition, which can be seen as the 'Jewish identity'. They may well have thought, however, that the disappearance of that type of Jewishness was necessary in order for the new world of Enlightenment to enable the implementation of the true spirit of the Jewish faith: that Jewishness and enlightenment, far from being antagonists, were actually allies in the triumph of light, for in this lay also the triumph of the essence of God's law. By being a part of the enlightenment, Jews were in fact continuing the mission of the Jews to be a 'light among the nations'. The Haskalah and the assimilation did not destroy the Jewish identity, but took it up into the new world.

This is a common theme among Jewish thinkers. Moses Mendelssohn identified Judaism as 'revealed law', as natural religion based on the principles of reason. Hermann Cohen, in turn, could proclaim that Kant was the philosopher of the Jews, that Jews had become the carriers of the 'idealistic' mission because not of this world.[83] Wilhelm Jerusalem, a Viennese example, came up with similar arguments: that Judaism was essentially ethical monotheism, and, as such, could easily form the basis of belief in a scientific world unlike more hidebound religions.[84] Although it is not something that can be unequivocally stated, it does seem true that Judaism, and Jewish thought, contain a strong vein of rationalism. As Friedrich Heer wrote, the great Jewish philosophers (by descent at least), Philo, Maimonides, Spinoza, Mendelssohn, Cohen and Freud, do seem to be connected by the identification of God with the *Logos* of rationality.[85]

It is important to realize, however, that the existing rational aspects of Judaism were made much more evident because it was precisely those rational elements which entered western culture, assimilated into the society, and contributed to the culture, leaving the rest part of the traditional way of life, outside European society though in its midst. Rabbi Boruch stayed in his shtetl, but his great-grandson, Manès Sperber, took that part of his heritage which could be divorced from tradition and used it in the modern world, converting, for example, hope for the coming of the Messiah into revolutionary activity.[86]

The devotion to science, knowledge and the faith in the ethical

---

[83] Hans Liebeschütz, 'Jewish Thought and its German Background' in *LBIY* 1956, p. 222.

[84] Wilhelm Jerusalem, *Gedanken und Denker: gesammelte Aufsätze*, new series (Vienna 1925) pp. 9–10.

[85] Heer, *God's First Love*, pp. 224, 238; also Jürgen Habermas, 'Der deutsche Idealismus der jüdischen Philosophen' in *Philosophisch-politische Profile* (Frankfurt-on-Main 1971) pp. 37–46, cited in Ivar Oxaal, *The Jews of Pre-1914 Vienna: Two Working Papers* (Hull 1981) p. 29.

[86] Manès Sperber, *Die Wasserträger Gottes* (Munich 1983) p. 23.

autonomy of the individual, which were the leading principles of the Enlightenment, were, as we have seen, also familiar to a large number of Jews, if not in exactly the same forms. Just as the social and economic structure of the Jewish community lent itself to the new structures of the capitalist economy, with its destruction of hierarchical barriers, and the transformation of the whole of society into the Third Estate, so too, when the Enlightenment proclaimed the need for *Bildung*, and the independence of the individual from religious constraints in the world which were not *natural*, then there were a great number of Jews not only in the west, but also in the east, who could recognize their own ideas and attitudes, who could identify with the new concept of man. Heinrich Jaques could make the point that the Jews had the same morality as the Christians.[87] Sigmund Mayer, himself quoting Berthold Auerbach, could go further: 'When it comes to pure humanity [reines Menschtum] the Jews are superior.'[88] By this he meant that Jews had no need for drinking laws or orphanages because such problems did not exist in the Jewish community. When it came to 'pure humanity' the Jews were already better than the surrounding community, more ready for the Enlightenment than the carriers of the Enlightenment themselves.

The assimilated Jews were indeed the 'Kerntruppe' of Austrian liberalism; not only did they depend for their life's meaning on the principles for which liberalism stood, they also brought to the movement a fervour for the creation of a new type of man which only they, who had most radically accomplished the sloughing off of the traditions of the past, could bring. It is impossible to do justice to the assimilationists unless their naïve faith in the future is fully recognized. This was a common denominator between people as politically apart as Victor Adler and Theodor Gomperz.[89] Gomperz's whole rationale rested on the belief that one day there would be a united humanity. His principles were 'Bildung und Aufklärung', but also mankind's unity.[90] It was 'unity and fraternity' which were needed, not obstinate separation.[91] Gomperz saw *any* differentiation within society as merely an opportunity for division: 'Alles, was die Menschen unterscheidet, scheidet sie auch.'[92] In the 'fight against arbitrariness' it was therefore the duty of Jews to 'melt into' the surrounding populace.[93]

The views of people such as Gomperz were common currency among

---

[87] Jaques, *Denkschrift*, p. 31.   [88] Mayer, *Ein jüdischer Kaufmann*, p. 48.

[89] Ardelt, *Friedrich Adler*, p. 64, on Adler's belief in technological progress.

[90] *Gomperz: ein Gelehrtenleben*, p. 16.

[91] *Ibid.* p. 173.

[92] 'Everything which makes men different separates them from each other as well.' Gomperz, *Essays*, p. 198.

[93] *Ibid.* pp. 34–5; *Gomperz; ein Gelehrtenleben*, p. 173.

assimilated Jews in Vienna throughout the period. At the beginning had been Sonnenfels. Criticizing Hans Tietze for seeing in Sonnenfels some kind of inferiority complex in adopting enlightenment culture and the Catholic faith, R. A. Kann made the point that 'both Judaism and Enlightenment, in earlier modern times, shared the belief in a universal law of reason by virtue of which the new era was expected to last forever'.[94] Sonnenfels would therefore have felt no insuperable barrier between Jewish and enlightened thought, and the identification of the two was common in nineteenth-century Vienna.[95] Jellinek, the preacher of the Viennese Kultusgemeinde, interpreted Jewish law in a universalist spirit, as the law of reason without the need for 'petty externalities, inessential minutiae [and] antiquated customs'.[96] Freud's religious instructor, Samuel Hammerschlag, held similar views: for these people there was no contradiction between the essence of the Jewish message and the ideas of the Enlightenment.[97]

As the century progressed this simple identity and faith in a society united on principles of the 'new type of humanity' became increasingly difficult to sustain, though the offspring of assimilated Jews did their utmost to continue it, as in the revival of the encyclopaedists' tradition by Otto Neurath.[98] The reasons for such difficulties came not so much from the Jewish side as from the failure of the environment to live up to expectations.[99] As time went on it appeared that, far from the Jews being the ones who were in need of education, it was the rest of the populace who had to be changed for the better.[100] Speaking to the antisemites in the Viennese Gemeinderat, Sigmund Mayer put the Jewish view succinctly: 'The Jews are already ripe for their emancipation – the ones who are not are unfortunately you, the Christians.'[101]

The Jews thus began to see themselves as the real bearers of the Enlightenment. Where before they had thought themselves entering a

---

[94] R. A. Kann, *A Study in Austrian Intellectual History* (London 1960) p. 254, cited in Oxaal, *The Jews of Pre-1914 Vienna*, p. 31.

[95] For instance, Ardelt, *Friedrich Adler*, pp. 16–17, on the attraction of the French Enlightenment to an Orthodox Jew in Lipnik, Bohemia. Also see ÖW 15 January 1897 pp. 41–3.

[96] Klein, *The Jewish Origins of the Psychoanalytic Movement*, p. 4.

[97] *Ibid.* pp. 43–4. Cf. Bondi, *Autobiography*, p. 10: 'Enthusiastic Jew and lover of humanity.'

[98] Otto Neurath, *Empiricism and Sociology* (Dordrecht 1973) p. 53.

[99] See the comments of Belke, *Popper-Lynkeus*, p. 101: 'Popper war ein Spätschüler der grossen französischen Aufklärung, und das in einem Land, in dem liberalen und fortschrittlichen Ideen, demokratisches Denken und Bildungsstreben nie recht Wurzel gefasst haben.'

[100] Cf. the speech of Gundaccar von Suttner, reprinted in NFPm 26 February 1895 p. 3: 'Die Lösung [des Problems des Antisemitismus] liegt nur in der Erziehung. Wissenschaft und Ethik sollen in allen Formen der Menge zugänglich und erreichbar sein.'

[101] Mayer, *Ein jüdischer Kaufmann*, p. 91.

civilization in which the goals of their Jewish commandments could be realized for all, by the end of the period of assimilation with the threat of antisemitism to the future society all too obvious, they began to realize that they alone were carrying the standard of enlightenment. By 1902, when Salomon Ehrmann gave a speech to the B'nai B'rith, the argument was as follows: a 'glorious period' for mankind could still be envisaged, but instead of this being a liberal future, of which Jews were to be allowed to be a part, now it was a Jewish future. With the creation of the new era 'not only the B'nai B'rith but all of Judaism will have fulfilled its task. They will disappear as a self-contained community, because all of mankind will have been judaized [*verjudet*] and joined in union with the B'nai B'rith.'[102] Here the triumph of enlightened thought had come to be seen completely as a triumph of the teachings of Judaism. *Verjudung* meant *Aufklärung*.

The Enlightenment had demanded from Jews, in return for the prospect of living in a free and equal society, the sacrifice of their separate identity. Jews, in turn, attracted by what many saw as the triumph of Jewish traditions of rationality, individual freedom and education, accepted this call in large numbers, a quite disproportionate reaction to that of the rest of the populace, who, as mostly Catholic peasants, did not have the same kind of affinity to liberal ideas. While the stereotype of 'the Jew' became a symbol of all that the assimilation had overcome, the assimilated Jews themselves evolved a tradition, as Kraus had demanded, of assimilating into the *Menschenadel* which the Enlightenment had foretold. So powerful was the attraction of this idea of the new humanity, so central to the whole theory of assimilation that, when the rest of society began to reject it, many assimilated Jews came to claim it as their own. What had once been seen as an Austrian mission of civilization came to be seen by Jews, as early as 1900, as a Jewish mission, to be a light among the nations, to achieve *Verjudung*. The values of humanity which Jews had cherished in their religion thus came to be safeguarded in the new forms which the Enlightenment had offered. In this way assimilation came to be the continuation of Judaism by other means beyond the Jewish identity.[103]

---

[102] Klein, *The Jewish Origins of the Psychoanalytic Movement*, p. 147.
[103] See for Germany, George L. Mosse, *German Jews beyond Judaism* (Bloomington, 1985); David Sorkin, *The Transformation of German Jewry* (Oxford 1987).

⟫ 10 ⟪

German culture

GERMAN JEWS IN AUSTRIA

Having decided to assimilate into western society, the Jewish families which were to form part of the cultural élite in Vienna chose to do this through German, not Austrian, culture. In the nineteenth century Austria was a German state. The state language was German; the capital city, Vienna, was German. Vienna's university was one of the foremost places of German learning.[1] Germans headed the bureaucracy, the constitution was based on the principle of 'Staatsdeutschtum' (State Germandom) – Germans in Austria were the ruling class.[2] Franz Joseph was 'a German prince', the monarch of *Österreich*, a name which was a constant reminder that it had once been the *Ostmark*, the eastern march of the Holy Roman Empire of the Germans, of which the Habsburgs had been emperors for centuries.

The Germans in Austria saw themselves as pioneers, bringing civilization to the barbarians of the east and south. The Austrian mission had once been to defend Christendom against the Turks; in the eighteenth century it became a mission of enlightenment of the benighted masses, with German being adopted as the language of administration under Joseph II. The schools which were set up in his reign and the bourgeoisie which was to have created the economic growth which he wanted were German.[3] The towns of Bohemia and Moravia were German islands in a sea of Czech peasantry, and the further east one went, the more did German appear to be a synonym for western progress. Josef Redlich in the

---

[1] It was commonplace for a graduate of Vienna to study for his doctorate at another German university. Among those who did this were Hans Kelsen, Martin Buber, Otto Neurath and Käthe Leichter.

[2] W. J. Cahnman, 'Adolf Fischhof and his Jewish Followers' in *Leo Baeck Institute Yearbook* (*LBIY*) 1959, p. 111.

[3] For instance, Max Beloff, *The Age of Absolutism* (London 1954) pp. 121–2; George Rudé, *Revolutionary Europe 1983–1815* (Glasgow 1964) pp. 37–8; P. Mitrofanov, *Joseph II: seine politische und kulturelle Tätigkeit* (Vienna 1910) vol. 1, pp. 252–68.

1900s still saw Austria's mission as the spreading of 'German culture' to the east.[4]

It is not too difficult to see, therefore, why the Jews of the Habsburg Monarchy for the most part chose German as the vehicle of assimilation into western society.[5] Many prominent Jewish families, such as the Wittgensteins and Gomperzes, had in any case come from Germany only a few generations before, bringing with them an already acquired German culture.[6] Jews from the Austrian provinces, if they were *Ashkenazim*, as the vast majority were, had also come originally from Germany, if many centuries back. The Yiddish which Jews in the eastern parts of the Monarchy spoke, though written in Hebraic lettering and laced with words from Hebrew and the Slavonic languages, remained a dialect of medieval German.[7] In the western parts of the Monarchy by the beginning of the nineteenth century Jews spoke a language even closer to German, known pejoratively as *Mauscheldeutsch*.[8] German was thus the language with the most affinities for Jews.

In the Bohemian crownlands these linguistic affinities were enhanced by a recognition of social and cultural affinities. Most Jews were traders and the like. They therefore had much more in common with the German middle classes in the towns than the Slav peasants who were their customers. Jews also saw the Germans here as their emancipators, as the enlightened element, as can be seen in the work of Leopold Kompert. Jews and Germans, as the middle class, were seen as standing together against the reactionary Czech peasantry.[9] Jews therefore adopted the German culture of Bohemia, something which expressed itself in the great trouble

---

[4] Josef Redlich, *Schicksalsjahre Österreichs 1908–1919: das Politische Tagebuch Josef Redlichs*, ed. F. Fellner (Vienna 1953), p. 166.

[5] R. A. Kann, 'German-speaking Jewry during Austria-Hungary's Constitutional Era' in *Jewish Social Studies (JSS)* x, 1948, pp. 239–50; Jakob Thon, ed., *Die Juden in Österreich* (Berlin 1908) p. 93. Also see J. S. Bloch, 'Deutschtum und Judentum in Österreich' in *Österreichische Wochenschrift. Centralorgan für die gesammten Interessen des Judentums (ÖW)* 8 January 1886 (III.2) p. 13, where Bloch recognizes the great identification of Jews with German and German culture.

[6] *Theodor Gomperz: ein Gelehrtenleben im Bürgertum der Franz-Josephszeit*, eds. R. A. Kann and H. Gomperz (Vienna 1974) p. 21; Allan Janik and Stephen Toulmin, *Wittgenstein's Vienna* (New York 1973) p. 170.

[7] Bloch, 'Deutschtum und Judentum' in *ÖW* 8 January 1886, p. 13.

[8] Fritz Mauthner, *Erinnerungen* (Munich 1918) p. 33. Cf. Michael A. Riff, 'Jüdische Schriftsteller und das Dilemma der Assimilation im böhmischen Vormärz' in W. Grab and H. Schoeps, eds., *Juden im Vormärz und in der Revolution von 1848* (Stuttgart 1983) pp. 68–78; Eduard Goldstücker, 'Jews between Czechs and Germans around 1848' in *LBIY* 1972 (XVII), p. 65.

[9] Kompert spoke of 'dieser Zug innerer Verwandschaft' between Jews and Germans which had brought about the emancipation of the Jews, cited in Bernhard Denscher, 'Vergessene jüdische Literatur' in K. Lohrmann, ed., *1,000 Jahre österreichisches Judentum* (Eisenstadt 1982) pp. 213–4; also see Leopold Kompert, *Zwischen Ruinen* (Leipzig 1887) pp. 120, 133; Kann, 'German-speaking Jewry', *JSS* x, p. 250.

that was taken to learn the finest German.[10] Prague Jews became notorious in this respect.[11]

The culture, the world in which the assimilating Jews of the Bohemian crownlands lived, was that of the Germans, with Czechs in the background as maid or nurse. In the case of Gustav Mahler, according to Guido Adler, the environment in Iglau where he grew up 'crystallized about the figure of the old German man-at-arms'.[12] The young Mahler in Vienna was a convinced German nationalist.[13] Jews such as he simply regarded themselves as German. In the middle of the terrible riots in Moravia at the end of 1899, caused by the Polna affair and the rescinding of the language ordinances, the *Neue Freie Presse* proclaimed in outrage that it was dangerous nonsense to suggest that the Jews of Moravia, the main target of the Czech riots against German oppression, were simply the fellow travellers of the German ruling classes. The truth was that the Jewish community of Moravia was 'by upbringing, education, and centuries of tradition, German'. The Jews had not chosen their German culture, but had been born into it.[14] The newspaper should have known: both its chief editors, Bacher and Benedikt, came from that background.[15]

The Jews in the east had even more reason to look to Germany as the great hope for progress. Until well into the nineteenth century German was the only form of western culture available to those Jews in Galicia and Hungary who wanted to assimilate. The espousal by Jews of Magyar language and culture in Hungary only occurred, in many cases, after those Jews had become German.[16] In Galicia there was a small group of Jews who assimilated into Polish society, and some were given the pejorative nickname of 'Talmi-Polen'.[17] However, the reactionary style of

[10] *Käthe Leichter: Leben und Werk*, ed. Herbert Steiner (Vienna 1973) p. 240; Mauthner, *Erinnerungen*, p. 33; cf. Christoph Stölzl, *Kafkas böses Böhmen: Zur Sozialgeschichte eines Prager Juden* (Munich 1975) pp. 24–8.

[11] Sigmund Mayer, *Ein jüdischer Kaufmann, 1831–1911: Lebenserinnerungen* (Leipzig 1911) p. 151. On Prague Jewry generally, see Gary B. Cohen, 'Jews in German Society: Prague, 1860–1914' in *Central European History, vol. x*, 1977, pp. 28–54; also Cohen, *The Politics of Ethnic Survival: Germans in Prague, 1861–1914* (Princeton 1981) pp. 76–83, 224–5.

[12] Cited in Kurt Blaukopf, *Mahler: a Documentary Study* (London 1976) p 149.

[13] William McGrath, *Dionysian Art and Populist Politics in Austria* (New Haven 1974) p. 89.

[14] *Neue Freie Presse*, morning edition (*NFPm*) 12 November 1899 p. 1; also see *ÖW* 6 November 1896 (xiii.45) pp. 887–8, where the innate loyalty of Moravian Jews to German culture is recognized and praised.

[15] Bacher was born in Postelberg, Bohemia. Benedikt was born in Hradisch, Moravia. A. Wandruczka, *Geschichte einer Zeitung: das Schicksal der 'Presse' und der 'Neuen Freien Presse' von 1848 zur Zweiten Republik* (Vienna 1958) pp. 93–9.

[16] See Ludwig Hatvany, *Bondy Jr.* (Munich 1929) pp. 61, 99, 125f, 442. Herzl's mother was a perfect example of a German Pest Jew, see Alex Bein, *Theodore Herzl* (London 1957) p. 10; also Leon Kellner, *Theodor Herzls Lehrjahre* (Vienna 1920) pp. 16–17.

[17] For instance, Joseph S. Bloch, *Erinnerungen aus meinem Leben* (Vienna 1911) p. 287.

the Poles and the backwardness of the Ruthenian peasantry, meant that most assimilating Jews who followed the dictates of the Enlightenment had to do so through German. The schools which Homberg tried to set up in Galicia, and into which the *Maskilim* of Brody lured the sons of the Hasidim, were, as a matter of course, German schools.[18]

It was natural that these people come to identify Germany with the new world which they were entering. Franzos was captivated by the type of world the school in Czernowitz promised, whose 'tolerant, humane spirit remained his whole life long an ideal of German civilization and tolerance'.[19] It was thus fitting that the hero of Franzos' book, *Der Pojaz*, should seek freedom from the Hasidim by joining a troupe of (Jewish) German actors.[20] Joseph Ehrlich began to learn German in his teens. Through the reading primers he read at the new Jewish school he learnt of a totally different world, where children were allowed to go strawberry picking and where fathers went walking with their children in the woods instead of to the synagogue. He fell in love with the world in which 'Franz' and 'Anna' lived, and this fabulous land had a name: 'this world was called Germany'.[21]

The identification of German as the culture of the assimilated Jews meant that in places where Jews were, so was German culture, even if there were hardly any Germans.[22] Jews came to be the pioneers for German culture in certain districts of the Monarchy, as with the Jewish schools in various parts of Bohemia.[23] Certainly their votes here and in Moravia, despite German antisemitism, were what kept the Germans with a sizeable part of the area's political representation.[24] One could say that the identification of a great number of the Monarchy's Jews with German culture created a class in the outlying areas which became attached first to the Monarchy as the bringer of German civilization and order, and only secondly to the environment in which they lived. Jews thus became the *Staatsvolk* of the empire, as long as it remained a bastion of German civilization.

[18] Lohrmann, *1,000 Jahre*, p. 335; Joseph R. Ehrlich, *Der Weg meines Lebens* (Vienna 1874) pp. 32–4.

[19] Denscher, 'Vergessene jüdische Literatur', p. 217.

[20] Karl Emil Franzos, *Der Pojaz* (Berlin 1950) pp. 75ff; Denscher, 'Vergessene jüdische Literatur', p. 220.

[21] Ehrlich, *Der Weg meines Lebens*, p. 56.

[22] Cf. Ernst Topitsch, 'Wien um 1900 – und heute' in P. Berner, E. Brix and W. Mantl, eds., *Wien um 1900: Aufbruch in die Moderne* (Vienna 1986) p. 20.

[23] Cf. a report of the meeting of the Deutsche Schulverein in the Leopoldstadt, where it was pointed out that in some areas Jewish schools were the only ones still to offer a German education, *NFPm* 26 April 1896 p. 3.   [24] See *NFPm* 19 June 1896 p. 1.

LAND OF POETS AND THINKERS

Joseph Ehrlich described his life's career as 'leading from the gloomiest depths of superstition and orthodoxy to the purest summit of German philosophy and art'.[25] It is impossible to understand how a Jew could say such a thing unless the events of the twentieth century are swept from our minds, and the awe with which Jews must have regarded German culture in the middle of the nineteenth century is recognized. The German culture which they saw was the brilliant Germany of 'poets and thinkers', a new nation, whose philosophers saw themselves as providing the theoretical counterpart of the French Revolution. German culture meant Beethoven, Kant, Schiller, Goethe and Lessing. This culture had a faith in reason and a cosmopolitan preference for personality over nationality.[26] It was universalist in nature, the culture which produced the two great hymns to freedom and reason, *Fidelio* and *Die Zauberflöte*. Before 1870 Germany was a cultural entity, a set of ideas which included some of the greatest products of enlightened thought, the secret to the freedom of the individual, the autonomy of the will, the categorical imperative. For a Jew trying to make his way in a new world such ideas were wellnigh irresistible.

To become Germans, Jews in Austria undertook a cultural assimilation.[27] The German nation into which Viennese Jews were assimilating was a cultural phenomenon, which could be acquired by reading.[28] Arthur Schnitzler insisted that he was German, a German poet.[29] As far as Schnitzler was concerned, there would have been no such thing as an Austrian writer, separate from a German one, because the language was the same. Viennese writers such as himself were Germans, members of German culture, people who spoke German and shared the literature. To be German, it followed, was to take part in a linguistic culture, which, just as the universalist traditions of German humanism, was separate from political boundaries or allegiances. Schnitzler was wont to describe himself as 'a European Jew of German culture'.[30] The Germany into which the Jew assimilated was a Germany he had read of in books.

---

[25] Ehrlich, *Der Weg meines Lebens*, p. ix.

[26] Cf. Ludwig Speidel's review of *Nathan der Weise*, in *NFPm* 20 January 1895 p. 1.

[27] Cf. R. Ardelt, *Friedrich Adler: Probleme einer Persönlichkeitsentwicklung um die Jahrhundertwende* (Vienna 1984) pp. 21, 239.

[28] Joseph Kareis, Jewish deputy for the Leopoldstadt, said the following in a Reichsrat speech: 'Meine Erziehung war eine deutsche, ich habe die Geistesschätze der deutschen Literatur nach meinen Kräften angesammelt.' Reprinted in *NFPm* 8 October 1897 p. 3.

[29] See Schnitzler's letter on this, reprinted in translation in Sol Liptzin, *Germany's Stepchildren* (Philadelphia 1944) p. 136.

[30] Olga Schnitzler, *Spiegelbild der Freundschaft* (Vienna 1962) p. 96.

The culture of the Viennese Jews was not exclusively German, but was set in a general European context. The classics played a great rôle in shaping the outlook of pupils in the Gymnasien and were an unquestioned assumption of Viennese culture.[31] Jewish liberals, such as Freud and Theodor Gomperz, were also drawn to other sources of enlightenment thought, perhaps more so than their non-Jewish counterparts. England was admired for its political system and its positivist tradition.[32] Francophilia was rife in many parts of liberal society and especially among Jews.[33] It was, for instance, the family of Moritz Szeps, editor of the *Neue Wiener Tagblatt*, connected by marriage to the Clemenceaus, which provided the core of the movement to lessen Austrian dependence on Wilhelmine Germany in favour of liberal France.[34] Even here, however, there were cultural ties to Germany, Szeps being an honoured guest at Bayreuth.[35] There was no reason, indeed, why there should be any conflict between cultural loyalties, even if political allegiances were at odds.[36] France was the indisputable centre of European culture in the nineteenth century, and for Jews assimilating into European high culture it was impossible not to admire the French achievement.[37]

By the late nineteenth century, however, German culture could provide a vocabulary to rival its western neighbour. When the reporter for the *Neue Freie Presse* described a victory for the Dreyfusards, he could celebrate this in terms which expressed higher cultural loyalties: 'Soon Zarastro will be the victor, night's realm will sink, and the finale will sound in powerful unison.' The affair had taught, continued the report, 'that there are still swan-knights among us'.[38] The articulation of a victory of the French

---

[31] Theodor Gomperz was a prominent protagonist in keeping the status of the classics in the educational system, Gomperz, *Essays und Erinnerungen* (Stuttgart 1905) p. 214; also W. Johnston, *The Austrian Mind: an Intellectual and Social History 1848–1938* (Berkeley 1972, pb. 1983) pp. 6ff. On Freud's classical background, see R. W. Clark, *Freud: the Man and the Cause* (London 1980) p. 17. A book such as Otto Weininger's *Geschlecht und Charakter* (Vienna 1903, 1919) simply assumes a reading knowledge of the classics.

[32] Clark, *Freud*, p. 38; *Gomperz: ein Gelehrtenleben*, pp. 13–14. Another great admirer of England was Herzl, see Kellner, *Herzls Lehrjahre*, pp. 13–14.

[33] Sigmund Mayer recalled how in his childhood in the Pressburg ghetto 'Paris war der Himmel, zu dem wir aufblickten.' Mayer, *Ein jüdischer Kaufmann*, p. 83.

[34] See Berta Zuckerkandl's two sets of memoirs, *Ich erlebte fünfzig Jahre Weltgeschichte* (Stockholm 1939), and *Österreich Intim: Erinnerungen 1892–1942* (Frankfurt 1970), and her memoir of Clemenceau, *Clemenceau tel que je l'ai connu* (Algiers 1944).

[35] Berta Zuckerkandl, *Ich erlebte fünfzig Jahre*, pp. 110–2.

[36] Thus the *Neue Freie Presse*, a staunchly pro-German newspaper, could nevertheless admire French culture, *NFPm* 23 February 1899 p. 1.

[37] Gomperz admired Comte, Gomperz, *Essays*, p. 36–7. Freud was a pupil of Charcot, Clark, *Freud*, p. 70–4. Neurath admired the Encyclopaedists, Otto Neurath, *Empiricism and Sociology* (Dordrecht 1973) p. 53.

[38] 'Bald siegt Sarastro, das Reich der Nacht versinkt, und im gewaltigen Unisono erklingt das Finale.' 'Dass noch Schwanenritter unter uns wallen', *NFPm* 10 June 1899 p. 1.

Enlightenment was thus expressed in terms of two operas by German composers, Mozart and Wagner. The German Enlightenment could stand on its own merit and pass judgement on the French.

While people such as Freud or Gomperz could be Anglophile and Francophile, they still remained Germans, belonging to the 'deutsche Kulturgemeinschaft' (body of German culture). Freud remained, despite himself, a 'German provincial'.[39] While some, such as Stefan Zweig, devoted themselves to the ultimate goal of a general European culture, entry into it was easily available through German high culture, which was intricately connected to it.[40] (Shakespeare and Dante were regarded almost as German classics, so widespread was the habit of reading other literatures in translation.) Furthermore, the Germans, and hence the German Jews, possessed by the mid nineteenth century a cultural tradition which could stand up to that of anyone else. Jews in Austria who wanted to be educated in the great European culture of the nineteenth century had on their doorstep a tailor-made cultural tradition of reason and individual freedom, and they had one of the great exponents of the thought of the Enlightenment in verse: Schiller.

Schiller was the national poet of Germany into the twentieth century. He was even more of an idol for the assimilated German Jews of which the Viennese were no exception. Schiller dominated the childhood experience of many in Vienna's cultural élite and was quoted freely by liberals such as Heinrich Jaques.[41] His fame extended from the most assimilated in Vienna to the shtetls of Galicia, at least the one in which Manès Sperber grew up: 'The educated usually decorated their excessively long speeches with quotes from the poetical works, which did not always exactly fit but that was not really the point. The most revered poet was Schiller – he was the sublime poet of ideals.'[42] Hans Tietze, historian of the Viennese Jews, saw in Schiller the spark which ignited the Jewish wish to join German culture and the Enlightenment. As he put it, in the *Judenstrassen* of the Austrian provinces the works of Schiller were a necessary part of every Jewish household with the Torah. For him Schiller as the 'singer of

[39] Clark, *Freud*, p. 73.

[40] D. A. Prater, *European of Yesterday: a Biography of Stefan Zweig* (Oxford 1972) p. 8.

[41] Ardelt, *Friedrich Adler*, pp. 30, 239; H. H. Stuckenschmidt, *Schoenberg: his Life, World and Work* (London 1977) p. 18; Felix Braun, *Das Licht der Welt* (Vienna 1962) pp. 68, 94–5; Richard Kola, *Rückblick ins Gestrige: Erlebtes und Empfundenes* (Vienna 1922) p. 20; Heinrich Jaques, *Denkschrift über die Stellung der Juden in Österreich* (Vienna 1859) p. cxix. See also, Hatvany, *Bondy Jr.* pp. 16–17; Moritz Benedikt, *Aus meinem Leben: Erinnerungen und Erörterungen* (Vienna 1906) pp. 4, 29.

[42] 'Die Gebildeten schmückten gewöhnlich ihre zu langen Reden mit Zitaten aus Werken der Dichter, welche nicht immer genau passten; aber darauf kam es nicht so sehr an. Am meisten verehrte man Schiller – er war der sublime Dichter der Ideale.' Manès Sperber, *Die Wasserträger Gottes* (Munich 1983) p. 17.

freedom' provided the rationale for the Jewish adoration of German culture.[43] Gershom Scholem has said much the same about the way the lofty idealism of Schiller gave Jews an all too favourable picture of the Germans, making the penetrating remark that: 'For many Jews the encounter with Friedrich Schiller was more real than their encounter with actual Germans.' The weight of evidence points to confirmation of Tietze and Scholem: the German culture to which a Jew who came to Vienna devoted himself was the culture of Schiller 'for this was music that spoke to his depths'.[44]

For the Jew Schiller was more real than actual Germans. This idea is central to any understanding of the great admiration, the love Jews showed for things German. In the idealism which Schiller represented Jews could find not only the emotional justification for the idea of a new society of individual freedom, but also their own Jewish values, only stripped of all religious form and presented in enlightened dress. It was not only that, as Tietze would have it, the Jews saw Schiller as providing release from their prison, but also, as I take Scholem to be hinting, that his work offered Jews a new version of an old faith, retaining the belief in an absolute moral law and in the ability of the individual human being – the image of God – to act for the good. It was because Schiller provided this secular version of what the Jews of the ghetto or shtetl must have regarded as Jewish values, that he gained such a massive following in what supposedly must have been still largely unassimilated communities. To paraphrase Scholem, Schiller spoke a language which Jews already understood – *before* they entered German culture. Schiller was telling them what they already knew, but in a way which stirred their imagination. Thus he came to be a symbol for them of what Germany really stood for, what it would one day become, when the culture of Schiller was available to all. In this way Schiller really was 'more real' than actual Germans, for it was his culture and not the culture of actual Germans which Jews adopted.[45]

German became a synonym among Jews for all that was liberal, just and progressive; it was the virtue of the German people on which the hopes of Jews rested. In the homes of assimilated Viennese Jews it was with Lessing's parable of the rings that fathers ended talks with their children.[46] Germans were looked up to as the epitome of a civilized nation, 'German science' the summit of learning.[47] In the middle of the Dreyfus affair, the *Neue Freie Presse* published a leader on Goethe's 150th birthday. It

---

[43] Hans Tietze, *Die Juden Wiens* (Vienna 1935) pp. 165ff.
[44] Gershom Scholem, *Jews and Judaism in Crisis* (New York 1976) p. 79.
[45] Cf. J. P. Stern, *Hitler: the Führer and the People* (London 1984) pp. 205–7.
[46] *Käthe Leichter*, p. 262.
[47] Israel Jeiteles, *Die Kultusgemeinde der Israeliten in Wien mit Benützung des statistischen Volkszahlungsoperates v. J. 1869* (Vienna 1873) p. 78.

complained that the reactionaries on the city council (the Christian Socials) had done nothing to mark this auspicious date. The German way must be defended against the 'new heathens', and though it might have been tarnished and corrupted by evil men, it was still the ideal: 'On the other hand, it is a comfort to think that, despite the difficulty of fighting simultaneously for Germandom and liberty, being liberal and thinking liberal is not a fashion, but rather the realization of the human ideal, and truly German [echt deutsch].'[48] 'Echt deutsch' meant for the people who read the *Neue Freie Presse*, and that included the Viennese Jewish cultural élite, belief in progress and liberty. This is what lay behind the pride in being German so prevalent in figures such as Freud or Schoenberg.[49]

LOOKING TO THE NORTH

For most Jews who came to Vienna the culture into which they wanted to assimilate was the culture of Lessing and Schiller, the German Enlightenment. It was not the culture of any specifically Austrian tradition. There was an Austrian tradition of baroque splendour, but this was not what most Jews were interested in. In the Bohemian crownlands there were even traces of a distinctly pro-Prussian and anti-Habsburg bias among some Jews. The Germany which Jews admired was the Protestant north of the Prussians, not the 'reactionary' Catholic south of the Habsburgs. Austria lay very much at the periphery of the German Enlightenment.[50]

Many confusions of loyalties were possible in mid century. When as a *Gymnasiast* in Brünn Theodor Gomperz marched to Vienna in 1848, the Studentenkorps of which he was a member tried to devise colours for itself. This was no easy task. There was the black, red and gold to consider first (Germany), but then there was also a need to consider the colours of Austria, and then what about Moravia? The solution at the time was to include all the colours in a rainbow. The students thus marched to Vienna as Germans and Austrians and Moravians.[51] This kind of generosity with one's allegiances was not so easy later for Austria ceased to be a part of

[48] 'Andererseits ist uns der Gedanke, so schwer der gleichzeitige Kampf für Deutschtum *und* Freiheit ist, tröstlich, dass liberal zu sein und zu denken, nicht Mode, sondern Verwirklichung des Menschen-Ideals und echt deutsch ist.' *NFPm* 27 August 1899 p. 1.

[49] Stuckenschmidt, *Schoenberg*, p. 277; Clark, *Freud*, p. 368.

[50] H. Gomperz and R. A. Kann, eds., *Briefe an, von und um Josephine von Wertheimstein* (Vienna 1981) p. 14; Hilde Spiel, 'Jewish Women in Austrian Culture' in Josef Fraenkel, ed., *The Jews of Austria: Essays on their Life, History and Destruction* (London 1967) p. 104. Sigmund Mayer likened the relationship of Austria to Germany to that of South America to Spain, as a colonial appendage, Mayer, *Die Wiener Juden: Kommerz, Kultur, Politik 1700–1900* (Vienna 1918) p. 392.   [51] Gomperz, *Essays*, p. 19.

Germany. In the crisis of the 1860s many Bohemian Jews continued to hold fast to Germany against the Catholic Habsburgs. In 1866 the families of people such as Josef Pick made their homes available not to the Austrian forces but to the Prussians, for it was the Prussians who were the hope of Germany.[52]

In 1844 Samuel Hirsch had written: 'It is only natural that today's Judaism regards itself to be permeated by a spirit similar to Protestantism.'[53] Despite living in a Catholic state, this was also true of the Jews in the Habsburg Monarchy. In a state where Protestants were a tiny minority there was a remarkable number of Jewish converts to Protestantism, accounting for about a quarter of all Jews leaving Judaism in Vienna.[54] Among the more famous converts to Protestantism were Victor Adler, Alfred Adler, Peter Altenberg, Egon Friedell, Schoenberg and Otto Weininger. Such conversion was not merely because, as has been suggested, Jews could convert more easily to Protestantism than to Catholicism, but was also a sign of the full identification with the traditions of North Germany.[55] The *Neue Freie Presse* made this clear in its commemoration of Goethe: 'the capital itself did nothing to celebrate the day, for the spirit of Rome rules in city hall and casts its spell over the great new heathens'. It spoke of 'the deep chasm between German culture [Bildung] and Roman conviction', Rome, the Catholic Church, thus being identified as the enemy of *Bildung*. The conclusion was obvious: 'We share with Germany the treasures of our culture and customs.'[56] Not with Catholic Rome and by implication not with Catholic Austria. In the pages of the *Neue Freie Presse* Austria was continually being admonished in the light of the shining example set by her northern neighbour.[57]

In 1894 Heinrich Jaques died and his friend Theodor Gomperz gave the funeral address. Heinrich Gomperz criticized his father for having called Jaques first a German and only second an Austrian. The father replied: 'To take offence at putting the German before the Austrian is something of which only someone born after 1866 could think. Our generation still lives in the lands of the old German Confederation.'[58] Even for many born after 1866 this was often true, that Germany was taken to include German

[52] *Käthe Leichter,* p. 239; also see Paul Schick, *Karl Kraus* (Hamburg 1965) pp. 10–11.

[53] Quoted in Carl Cohen, 'The Road to Conversion' in *Leo Baeck Institute Yearbook (LBIY)* 1961, p. 265.

[54] Thon, *Die Juden in Österreich,* p. 71.

[55] For evidence that it was easier to convert to Protestantism, see Siegfried Trebitsch, *Chronik eines Lebens* (Zurich 1951) pp. 242–3. [56] *NFPm* 27 August 1899 p. 1.

[57] For instance, *NFPm* 8 March 1895 p. 1, where the rectitude of the German government on the Jewish question is contrasted with the pussy-footing of the Austrians.

[58] 'An den Deutschen vor dem Österreicher Anstoss zu nehmen, kann nur einem nach 66 Geborenen in den Sinn kommen. Wir Älteren leben eben immer noch in den alten deutschen Bundes-Ländern.' *Gomperz: ein Gelehrtenleben,* p. 251.

Austria as well. Even when people such as Theodor Gomperz denied the 'grossdeutsch' solution to the problems of the Monarchy, there was still a great deal of ambiguity in their attitude.[59] This was a result of the failure of the revolution of 1848 to achieve unification of Germany as a liberal, national and constitutional state.

In 1848 there had been little doubt among liberals and Jews that the Habsburg dynastic state stood in the way of German unity and freedom, progress being identified with the unification of the German peoples.[60] For Jews 1848 had a double significance, for if the revolution meant national liberation for the Germans, it also meant emancipation for the Jews. The success of the former meant, indeed, the achievement of the latter.[61] It was therefore to be expected that Jews would take a leading rôle in the struggles of 1848, and that they came to idealize the events of that year, for in taking part in the German struggle for freedom they felt they were earning their own.[62]

The problem with this was that 1848 only lasted a few months, and, until 1866, the same Habsburgs continued to stand in the way of German unification, a unification which, when it did come, was quite different from the liberal *grossdeutsch* solution of 1848. The result of 1866 was the exclusion of the Austrian Germans from the German heartland; it also left the Habsburgs in charge. While the liberals obtained a leading rôle in the new constitutional state, they nevertheless had to share power. Franz Joseph was far from being an impotent constitutional monarch on western lines, and the bureaucracy, while sympathetic to liberal ideas, was still independent of real control.[63] As time went by, moreover, it became increasingly clear that, far from extending German civilization in the Monarchy, the German Liberals were going to be swamped electorally by the resurgent nationalities. While this was compensated for by the alliance with Germany, Germans and German Jews were on the defensive by the late nineteenth century, the attempt to create a 'second German empire'

[59] Gomperz, *Essays*, p. 30.

[60] See the reminiscences of 1848 by Eduard Neusser, reprinted in *NFPm* 20 February 1898 pp. 23–6; also August Bondi, *Autobiography* (Galesburg, Ill.) pp. 22–4; Benedikt, *Aus meinem Leben*, p. 18.

[61] The slogan among Jewish students in March 1848 was: 'Freiheit für alle, Gleichheit für uns Juden!' Quoted in Mayer, *Ein jüdischer Kaufmann*, p. 138.

[62] *Ibid.* pp. 136–7; Gomperz, *Essays*, p. 19; Wolfgang Häusler, 'Toleranz, Emanzipation und Antisemitismus' in N. Vielmetti, Drabek, Häusler, Stuhlpfarrer, *Das österreichische Judentum* (Vienna 1974) p. 101, on Joseph Unger's attitude to 1848; on the presence of Jews in the 1848 leadership, Lohrmann, *1,000 Jahre*, pp. 208, 210, 347, 364; John W. Boyer, *Political Radicalism in Late Imperial Vienna* (Chicago 1981) p. 12. Also see Karl Goldmark, *Erinnerungen aus meinem Leben* (Vienna 1922) pp. 27ff, on his brother Josef and his experiences in 1848.

[63] Carl E. Schorske, *Fin-de-Siècle Vienna: Politics and Culture* (London 1980) p. 5; A. J. May, *The Habsburg Monarchy* (London 1965) pp. 90ff; McGrath, *Dionysian Art*, pp. 9ff.

having failed.[64] Faced with this reality, liberals and Jews came to support the Habsburg state as a way of preserving German superiority in Austria, rather than out of any innate loyalty to the dynasty as such, which was far from their ideal in many respects.[65] Remaining true to the German cause within Austria was the first priority.

The idea of defending German ideals within the Monarchy formed the basis of the liberal and Jewish compromise with the Habsburg dynasty. Yet the ideals of 1848 still lurked beneath the surface: a Germany united in the principles of freedom and democracy. Hence the (Jewish) leadership of Austria's socialists was convinced that, if the Monarchy were one day to collapse under its own contradictions, the only reasonable thing to do would be for the Germans in Austria to join their fellow Germans in the Reich, that is to say, to effect an *Anschluss*.[66] To many Jews in Vienna this must have seemed eminently logical, for it would have been the realization of an ideal which had been put to one side, but never forgotten, since the defeat of 1848. Germany was, after all, the paragon of progress, was it not?

JEWISH GERMAN NATIONALISTS

One of the Viennese Jews most dedicated to the German cause was Victor Adler. He too was an ardent supporter of the idea of *Anschluss*. There was an element in his admiration of the German cause, however, which was of a different order to that of other Jews so far discussed here. Karl Kautsky recalled meeting Adler and his circle in 1892. They were socialist, and most in the circle were Jewish, but: 'they were inspired nationalists, many of them outright chauvinists... While wanting to have nothing to do with the Habsburgs, they were all the more enthusiastic about the Hohenzollerns. The Jews of Austria were at that time the most passionate advocates of the *Anschluss* which Bismarck decisively rejected.'[67] This was

---

[64] May, *The Habsburg Monarchy*, pp. 130–43; Mayer, *Die Wiener Juden*, p. 392.

[65] This is certainly the impression given by reading the *Neue Freie Presse* in the 1890s. Described as the 'chief German-Jewish organ' by Wickham Steed, the newspaper, which had the reputation of being the only real *Weltblatt* in the Monarchy, consistently took the German side, supporting the parliamentary obstruction of Badeni's language ordinances in 1897, to cite one case. *NFPm* 6 November 1897 p. 1; Henry Wickham Steed, *Through Thirty Years* (London 1924) p. 305. For the Jewish opposition to the government out of loyalty to their German identity during the Taaffe era, see Bloch, *Erinnerungen*, p. 20, 167.

[66] Otto Leichter, *Otto Bauer: Tragödie oder Triumph?* (Vienna 1970) pp. 80–1, 323; *Gomperz: ein Gelehrtenleben*, p. 27, on Heinrich Gomperz.

[67] Translation in McGrath, *Dionysian Art*, p. 211, from Karl Kautsky, *Erinnerungen und Erörterungen* (The Hague 1960) pp. 530–1. NB Kautsky uses the ambiguous phrase 'durch die Bank' to describe the extent to which Adler's circle was Jewish. It is unclear whether this means 'mostly' or 'almost entirely', although McGrath chooses the former.

something more than thinking of Germany as the great liberal hope. The circle which Kautsky described has been researched by William McGrath. It included such people as Heinrich Friedjung, Engelbert Pernerstorfer, Siegfried Lipiner and Gustav Mahler. They were full-blooded German nationalists (so to speak), who spoke the same language which Schönerer was to use that would so impress the young Hitler. If, as I have tried to show, Jews assimilated into the culture of Schiller, how was it that many in the circle around Adler were initially part of the cultural and political movement which was to lead to Hitler – the other, darker side to German culture?

People such as Victor Adler still identified with the culture of Schiller. His father, Salomon, had named him after Victor Hugo. He named his first son Friedrich (after Schiller) Wolfgang (after Goethe) – Schiller came first.[68] The problem with Adler's generation had been that, having grown up in the German enlightenment culture which their fathers had embraced, they saw that these very fathers had betrayed the promise of that culture and thus came to see the culture itself as a sham. They objected to the type of liberal rhetoric which has so far graced these pages, because they looked at what was really going on and saw that it bore little relation to the things which their fathers, quoting Schiller or whomever at them, were saying. There were good grounds for this revolt among youth, and especially Jewish youth, in the 1870s.

The Adler family is a perfect example, as Rudolf Ardelt has shown. The father, Salomon, responded to the failure of 1848 by building a large enough fortune for his children to enjoy the kind of intellectual career which he had been denied by the reaction. While he still spouted the rhetoric of 1848, his children would have seen him as collaborating with the authorities, playing along in the tradition of the Jew as moneymaker. When in 1867 the liberals gained power by default, at the expense of being cut off from the German nation, he adjusted to the 'arrangement'. Salomon, as a speculator on the stock exchange, had in the eyes of his children betrayed the original attempt to escape the shackles of Jewishness and compromised their German upbringing. For Victor then the culture of the father was ruled out by association.[69]

Seen from the political level rather than the biographical, there was much to feed the disenchantment of the generation growing up in the 1870s. The 1866 Prusso-Austrian settlement, on which the triumph of liberalism in Austria was founded, had signalled the death knell of the idea of a united Germany. Compared to the hopes aroused by 1848, the new liberal ministry was very much second best. The ministry did nothing in the eyes of the teenagers in Adler's circle to enhance this initially flawed

[68] Ardelt, *Friedrich Adler*, p. 239.   [69] *Ibid.* pp. 6–11.

reputation. While the ideology spoke of a new humanity, the reality was that the Interior Minister, Giskra, denied that there was a social problem in Austria. Then there was the crash of 1873, followed by the notorious Ofenheim trial. This revealed a moral poverty in the liberal Establishment which outraged these idealistic young radicals, already disillusioned by the way in which the Liberals had settled down so comfortably with their old arch-enemy, the Habsburg state. Adler and his friends came to the conclusion that something else had to be found to replace this unfeeling and unjust system.[70]

What replaced it for the circle around Adler was the thought of the German irrationalists: Schopenhauer, Wagner and Nietzsche. These thinkers' ideas provided the philosophical justification for a radical, nationalist and socialist critique in the spirit of 1848 which the group had already evolved.[71] German irrationalism strove to replace the old liberal emphasis on rationality, individualism and analysis by a stress on synthesis, wholeness and feeling. Politically this expressed itself in the ideology of the *Volk*.[72] It could also be aesthetic, as in Wagner's *Gesamtkunstwerk*, or ethical, as in Schopenhauer's overcoming of the will, or a combination, as in the book which had the greatest influence on Adler and his friends, Nietzsche's *The Birth of Tragedy*. The world of feeling would be restored to its rightful place and would provide the kind of emotional cement which liberalism lacked; the new Wagnerian culture would reunite a national society shattered by the onslaught of rational modernization.[73]

Such ideas, and the Wagnerian culture they produced, met an enthusiastic response from a sizeable number of Viennese Jews. Guido Adler was one of the first Viennese Wagnerians and a founder of the Akademischer Wagnerverein.[74] The first composer in Vienna to emulate Wagner was a Jew, Karl Goldmark.[75] Wagnerianism was especially warmly received among assimilated Jewish youth.[76] To an extent this was

[70] McGrath, *Dionysian Art*, pp. 17–52.

[71] Victor Adler wrote to Pernerstorfer during the Franco-Prussian War: 'All around me here are friends of France – out of opportunity, out of loyalty to Austria, or much more to imperial banknotes. I must be black-red-gold. Surely the red, the one red – with the blood of my heart I would like to colour all flags red.' McGrath comments that this meant that socialism (red) would regain Austria (black-yellow) for Germany (black-red-gold), *Dionysian Art*, p. 26; also see Ardelt, *Friedrich Adler*, p. 24.

[72] George L. Mosse, 'The Influence of the Völkisch Idea on German Jewry' in *Germans and Jews: the Right, the Left, and the Search for a 'Third Force' in Pre-Nazi Germany* (London 1971) pp. 78–90. This deals with a rather later period, but describes the same type of response as that of Adler and his circle.   [73] McGrath, *Dionysian Art*, pp. 53–83.

[74] Guido Adler, *Wollen und Wirken* (Vienna 1935) pp. 10–12.

[75] Goldmark, *Erinnerungen*, p. 77.

[76] Among Jewish Wagnerians were: Moritz Szeps, see Zuckerkandl, *Ich erlebte fünfzig Jahre*, pp. 110–12; Käthe Leichter's father, see *Käthe Leichter*, p. 254; Weininger and

only following the general trend. *Völkisch* ideas were common currency among German youth and indeed in society generally.[77] It even seems to have affected the thought of Jewish theologians, such as Buber, and, according to Hans Kohn, the main force behind intellectual Zionism was also the same *völkisch* ideology of the search for roots.[78] Even Jewish concerns were thus linked to the new culture, so it is hardly a surprise to see totally assimilated Jews following the trend.[79]

Yet it would be too simple to dismiss the German nationalism of Jews in Vienna and elsewhere as just following the trend of the rest of society. Jews had their own reasons for becoming nationalists of the 'new key'. When youths such as Adler became interested in it, the *völkisch* movement was not yet virulently antisemitic. By joining the counter-culture of the radical German Nationalists, Jews were also assimilating into a culture: their very rejection of their Jewish fathers should prove their credentials, that they had ceased to be Jews and had become part of the great German *Volk*.[80] Until Jews were denied the possibility of 'rising above their Jewishness' there was no reason why they should not take the holistic alternative of becoming the member of a (cultural) nation.[81]

Assimilating into the *Volk* was just as good, in their eyes, as entering a universal human society. After all, the *Volk* continued to be regarded even by the liberals as something that could do no wrong, an ideal entity; in fact the *Volk* was just as much an idealization of what was really going on in Germany as the idea of Germany as the carrier of liberal civilization.[82] Jews in other countries acted no differently, as Dreyfus' unceasing devotion to the 'patrie' shows.[83] Serving the nation was the best way of gaining acceptance (or thinking one had). Jews who died for their country thus received the 'Bluttaufe' (baptism of blood), as if they had been baptized into being German.[84] This kind of thinking, this kind of national

Weininger's father, see David Abrahamsen, *The Mind and Death of a Genius* (New York 1946) pp. 8–9; Felix Braun, *Das Licht der Welt*, p. 133. Admirers of Nietzsche included: Otto Rank, see Dennis B. Klein, *The Jewish Origins of the Psychoanalytic Movement* (New York 1981) p. 111; Max Reinhardt, see Gottfried Reinhardt, *Der Liebhaber* (Munich 1975) pp. 177–80. Also see Vicki Baum, *Es war alles ganz anders* (Berlin 1962) p. 60.

[77] See Hans Kohn, *Bürger vielen Welten* (Vienna 1965) p. 88.
[78] Mosse, 'The Influence of the Völkisch Idea', pp. 86ff; Kohn, *Bürger vielen Welten*, p. 92.
[79] Cf. George Clare, *Last Waltz in Vienna* (London 1981) p. 190.
[80] McGrath, *Dionysian Art*, p. 6.   [81] Mosse, *Germans and Jews*, p. 19.
[82] Cf. Pflugfelder's confession in Schnitzler's *Professor Bernhardi*: 'Ich glaube an ein elementares Rechtsgefühl in juridisch unverbildeten Köpfen, an den ursprünglich gesunden Sinn des Volkes.' Cyprian retorts: 'Zum Volk willst du sprechen? Zu unserer Bevölkerung!' Arthur Schnitzler, *Professor Bernhardi*, in vol. 6 of *Dramen* (Frankfurt-on-Main 1962) pp. 212–3.
[83] See the reports in the *NFPm* 3 June 1899 p. 1; 4 June 1899 p. 1. Also see Michael Marrus, *The Politics of Assimilation: the French Jewish Community at the Time of the Dreyfus Affair* (Oxford 1971) p. 284.   [84] *NFPm* 8 March 1895 p. 1.

assimilation into the people, was shared by liberals and nationalists among Jews. It was just a question of what that people stood for that divided the camps.

One might say that the Jewish German nationalists such as Adler were following the same ends as their fathers, but along different paths. The goal of the first generation of assimilation had been to become part of a Germany of *Bildung* and rational individualism. Their sons were grappling with the problem of how culture could integrate the individual into society, which was just an irrationalist version of their fathers' aim. The individual was still central, only now it was a question of how he could escape his alienation from man and nature. The new philosophical heroes (Nietzsche) were, in their own way, just as concerned with the ethical question of the individual as their predecessors (Kant).[85] The early Nietzsche, so heavily influenced by Schopenhauer, was concerned with what the individual could do to regain his link with the 'world will'. The means was self-transcendence:

Everyone who possesses culture is, in fact, saying: 'I see something higher and more human than myself above me. Help me, all of you, to reach it, as I will help every person who recognizes the same thing...so that finally the man may again come into being who feels himself infinite in knowing and living, in seeing and ability, and who with all his being is a part of nature.'[86]

The person who, according to McGrath, articulated the views of the Adler circle and thus of their view of Nietzsche, Schopenhauer and Wagner most clearly was Siegfried Lipiner in books such as *The Unbound Prometheus*, *Adam* and *Hippolytos*. He was totally devoted to the idea of self-transcendence in the Nietzschean sense.[87] He had, however, been born Salomon Lipiner in Jaroslau in Galicia. He went to the same school as Freud when he came to Vienna from the Gymnasium in Tarnow. His mother was by then a widow.[88] Although not identical this background looks very similar to that of Joseph Ehrlich, who also came from the wilds of Galicia to make good in Vienna, as a German poet. As we have seen, Ehrlich was swept up in the Haskalah's veneration of nature, coming to think of himself as 'part of a higher world'. The combination of the deep religiosity of his Hasidism and the enlightened love of nature culminated in a metaphysical view of the world: 'Thus I experienced the world as a moral whole, as the most actual, that which should be, and is not.'[89] Such

[85] See McGrath, *Dionysian Art*, pp. 48–51; Kohn *Bürger vielen Welten*, p. 88.
[86] McGrath, *Dionysian Art*, p. 66.
[87] *Ibid.* pp. 87ff; Ardelt, *Friedrich Adler*, p. 28.
[88] Siegfried Lipiner, letter to K. E. Franzos, 23 July 1882, MS in Wr. Stadtbibliothek, I.N. 63648; *Maturaprotokoll* of the Sperlgymnasium for 1975.
[89] 'So empfand ich bloss die Welt als sittlich Ganzes, als das Eigentlichste, was da sein soll und nicht ist.' Ehrlich, *Der Weg meines Lebens*, p. 101.

a sentiment could have been taken directly from Nietzsche, but it was actually the response of an *Ostjude* to the Haskalah, just as Wilhelm Neurath was a mystic and Siegfried Lipiner was a follower of Schopenhauer and Nietzsche. It is thus a possibility that Lipiner's deep religiosity, which affected his close friend Mahler so greatly, had roots in his Jewish experience long before he made contact with the thought of Nietzsche.[90]

The acceptance by Jews of German irrationalist thought can thus be viewed as a variant of the mainstream assimilation, stemming from the same kind of Jewish experience, the same Jewish values, only interpreted differently. In fact, people such as Adler were much nearer to the cosmopolitan German tradition than might at first appear. The books which he and his friends read in their youth were not only Schopen-hauer, but also Mill, Owen, Saint-Simon, Fourier, Proudhon, Lassalle and Marx.[91] Adler himself was never completely a German nationalist, with unquestioning obedience to the German cause.[92] When German nation-alism of the type of Schoenerer showed its true colours, so did Adler, ending up as the honoured leader of rationalistic socialism in Austria, although he did retain an admiration for the culture of German irrationalism and used it to further his now socialist aims.[93]

There was no absolute dividing line between German liberals and German nationalists (irrationalists) among the Viennese Jews. Szeps and Pick went to Bayreuth. Adler admired Goethe, Beethoven and Jean Paul.[94] The dominant theme in the history of the Germans in Austria, and

---

[90] Lipiner does seem to have cut a very Jewish figure, and his 'profundity' was attributed to his Jewish background by Pernerstorfer. Blaukopf, *Mahler: a Documentary Study*, p. 157; Vorwort by Paul Natorp, in Lipiner, *Adam: ein Vorspiel* (Berne 1974, facsim.) pp. 4–12; Paul Natorp, 'Siegfried Lipiner' in *Biographisches Jahrbuch und deutscher Nekrolog*, ed. Anton Bettelheim, vol. XVIII (1913) (Berlin 1917) pp. 284–90; Leonie Gombrich Hock, 'Einige persönliche Erinnerungen an Anna Bahr-Mildenburg', MS pp. 7–10, which discusses Lipiner's circle and Mahler's leading rôle, as well as describing Lipiner's appearance as that of 'ein alttestamentarischer Prophet'.

[91] Ardelt, *Friedrich Adler*, p. 23.

[92] Kautsky thought that Adler and Heinrich Braun were the least nationalistic in Adler's circle, Kautsky, *Erinnerungen*, p. 531. A letter from Adler to Heinrich Friedjung is also enlightening about the young Adler's attitude to German nationalism. In it he distances himself from treating the nation as an absolute good, unlike his friend Pernerstorfer, and stresses that the really important goal is to have a free state: 'Wenn ich Bürger eines freien Staates bin, so steht es mir frei dieser oder jener Nation meine Sympathien zuzuwenden wie es mir frei steht Jude oder Katholik zu sein. Wenn ich als Österreicher frei bin so bin ich zufrieden wenn auch Österreich kein deutsch-nationaler Staat ist.' He goes on to say that what is really needed is a social revolution against the government and its new bourgeois allies to achieve universal suffrage and majority rule. All this in 1870! Letter to Heinrich Friedjung, 12 March 1870, Ober-Döbling, MS in Wr. Stadtbibliothek, I.N. 163.440.　　　　[93] McGrath, *Dionysian Art*, pp. 208–37.

[94] *Ibid.* p. 214; Max Graf recalled how Adler would always appear at the performance of Beethoven's Ninth Symphony in the Musikvereinsaal and listen intently to the final movement and the words, 'Alle Menschen werden Brüder' (from Schiller's *Ode to Joy*), see Max Graf, *Jede Stunde war erfüllt* (Vienna 1957) p. 130.

thus also of the Jews, is one of confusion. On the one hand, German nationalists in Austria could be much more ferociously German than Germans in the Reich, because at the margin, due to the Bismarckian settlement, the identification with Grossdeutschland could take on a radical, democratic and revolutionary meaning which German patriotism in the Reich could not. On the other hand, elements could survive in Vienna which were unwanted in an increasingly imperialistic Germany. 'Austria' thus came to symbolize for many a better alternative, which preserved enlightened ideals. The old cosmopolitan openness to western ideas was seen as being preserved in Vienna, when in Germany a liberal approach had been abandoned in favour of a patriotic adherence to the idealist system-builders.[95] In politics as well Austria afforded an independent base, where the views of what Germany *ought* to be, as opposed to what it was, could be more freely aired, notably in the pages of Moritz Szeps' *Neue Wiener Tagblatt*.[96]

If Austria thus afforded room for an alternative Germany, there were very many different views as to what should be made of it. Its identity was problematic. Should it be German progressive, German irrationalist, Austrian enlightened or, as the aristocracy would have wanted, Austrian reactionary? Individuals such as Otto Bauer were constantly flitting back and forth between an Austrian and a German identity for German Austria.[97] Even when they made the choice, there was still the question of what *kind* of Germany or Austria? Germany could be progressive or reactionary, Austria a model of coexistence or the oppressor of nations, depending on how you saw it, which tradition you believed. The labels had a multitude of meanings.

It is clear that Jews in Austria saw German nationalism, for the most part, in a quite different light from most of their Aryan colleagues. The sense of the individual's need to overcome himself had more meaning for people who did indeed have to overcome what they saw as their Jewish selves.[98] This was not a problem for an Aryan nationalist, who was simply defending his own innate superiority when he supported Schönerer. While Jews such as Adler and Friedjung cherished the idea of a united Germany because of the social and cultural goals this would realize, Schönerer and his supporters were fighting a histrionic battle to preserve the kind of society, and German domination, which capitalism threatened; they were interested in preserving a pre-capitalist system, rather than creating a post-capitalist one. In this they were prepared to define their

---

[95] Ludwig von Mises, *Erinnerungen* (Stuttgart 1978) p. 23; Neurath, *Empiricism and Sociology*, p. 301–2; cf. Kurt Rudolf Fischer, 'Zur Philosophie des Wiener Fin de Siècle' in H. Nagl-Docekal, ed., *Überlieferung und Aufgabe: Festschrift für Erich Heintel*, p. 159.

[96] Zuckerkandl, *Ich erlebte fünfzig Jahre*, pp. 17, 32–44.

[97] Leichter, *Otto Bauer*, p. 76.   [98] Reinhardt, *Der Liebhaber*, p. 177.

Germanness in a way which forestalled any threat to their inherited cultural superiority, which prevented any outsiders invading their exclusive claim to be the ruling class.[99] They made being German a racial quality. Through antisemitism the differences within the nationalist camp were made crystal clear. Jews had thought they were joining a movement of cultural and social revolution to create a Germany united in the new culture. Now they were confronted with a movement which believed in the *Gemeinschaft* of the blood alone.

The turning point for the Jewish German nationalists came with the drafting of the famous Linz Programme. Jews had drafted the main points of the manifesto, but already Schönerer was turning to the racial option.[100] By 1885 antisemitic clauses had been added to the programme.[101] Jews such as Adler had made one big mistake. They had not recognized that the Germany of the nationalists was not like the cultural Germany of Goethe and Schiller, or even Nietzsche, but was now a unity based on the principle of descent, where Jews did not belong.

JEWISH GERMANS?

The Jewish reaction to this was to look elsewhere to realize their goals of social and cultural change, but also to preserve, independently of political nationalism, the values they had adopted as their own. Adler became a socialist. Mahler, a convinced German nationalist in his youth, stayed true to the culture of German irrationalism, while identifying the *Volk* with Adler's working class.[102] Guido Adler saw himself as staying true to his idol Wagner while rejecting the Wagnerians.[103] The creators of the culture were greater than the result.

It proved almost impossible for Jews who had once been in love with Germany ever to break the spell completely. Even Freud, who recognized early on the dangers of German nationalism, could not totally destroy the love of things German which he had acquired as a student nationalist.[104] The irony of the situation was that by the early twentieth century German high culture was strongly Jewish; Goldstein's famous article of 1912 spoke of the 'virtual management of German culture' by Jews.[105] As we have

[99] Albert Fuchs, *Geistige Strömungen in Österreich 1867–1918* (Vienna 1949) pp. 163ff. See above, note 90.
[100] McGrath, *Dionysian Art*, p. 170. [101] Lohrmann, *1,000 Jahre*, p. 409.
[102] McGrath, *Dionysian Art*, pp. 157–62; Blaukopf, *Mahler: a Documentary Study*, p. 241.
[103] Adler, *Wollen und Wirken*, p. 79.
[104] E. L. Freud, ed., *Letters of Sigmund Freud 1873–1939* (London 1961) p. 216; Klein, *The Jewish Origins of the Psychoanalytic Movement*, pp. 54–7; Harald Leupold-Löwenthal, 'Freud und das Judentum' in *Sigmund Freud House Bulletin*, vol. 4. nr. 1, 1980, p. 32.
[105] Discussed in Roy Pascal, *From Naturalism to Expressionism: German Literature and Society 1880–1918* (London 1973) pp. 77–8.

seen, this was especially true in Vienna and it was resentfully recognized by the non-Jewish population.[106] The result was that many progressive 'German' organizations in Vienna were almost exclusively Jewish.[107]

In 1897 Joseph Kareis, the Jewish, Liberal deputy for the Leopoldstadt, contrasted the Jewish devotion to German with the thanks they received from the Germans themselves:

When you consider the way in which the poor Jews strive to gain your favour in the ranks of the Germans, how they try to accumulate the treasures of German culture, how they work in the sciences, some perhaps dying young as a result – and all the thanks they get is that they are not even accepted as human-beings.[108]

For most Jews it was impossible to believe that the Germans had rejected them in this way, that the Germany of real life was not that of Schiller. As Friedrich Heer put it: 'German Jews in 1933 still *saw* the Germany of Goethe, Schiller and Mendelssohn'.[109] Some Jews saw what was happening much earlier. Schnitzler, like Freud, saw that the word 'German' had come to mean something very different from the image it had acquired in the first days of the assimilation.[110] Yet he could but remain true to his Germany. In January 1915 Schnitzler made a few short notes which sum up all the ambiguities of the Jewish relationship to the Germans. He described how he had often come to ask, as a Jew, why the Germans had always refused to accept him and his kind. Though he denied that he had been affected by this rejection, there was a great air of sadness in what he wrote. His point was that now, in the war, the Germans were experiencing the same unjust hatred that the Jews had suffered for so many centuries from the Germans. Yet he was experiencing this hatred he wrote, 'as a German, as a member of the German people'. He wrote of 'the great Germany... of which I, of Jewish descent, an Austrian, have always felt a part, with equal rights and equal responsibility'.[111] Schnitzler, an Austrian

---

[106] Lohrmann, *1,000 Jahre*, p. 365, shows a cartoon from *Kikeriki* in 1883, where on one side there is a group of kaftanned *Ostjuden*, and on the other the 'Redaction' of an obviously 'verjudet' newspaper. The caption reads: 'So, und nicht anders haben ihre Väter ausgesehen! Und die Söhne von solchen polnischen Juden wollen uns Wiener heute im Deutschtum unterrichten!'

[107] *Käthe Leichter*, p. 332, on the *Jugendbewegung* in Austria; Harry Zohn, *Wiener Juden in der deutschen Literatur* (Tübingen 1964) p. 89, on Robert Neumann's 'German-Liberal' student society.

[108] 'Wenn ihr dagegen haltet, wie die armen Juden sich bemühen eure Gunst in den Reihen der Deutschen zu erlangen, wie sie streben die deutschen Geistesschätze anzusammeln, wie sie in der Wissenschaft arbeiten, Manche vielleicht jung darüber zu Grunde gehen, und als Dank dafür haben sie, dass man sie nicht als Menschen anerkennt.' *NFPm* 8 October 1897 p. 3.

[109] Friedrich Heer, *God's First Love* (London 1970) p. 258.

[110] See Arthur Schnitzler, *Der Weg ins Freie*, in vol. 4 of *Romane* (Frankfurt-on-Main 1978) p. 202.

[111] H. Schnitzler, R. Urbach and C. Brandstätter, eds., *Arthur Schnitzler: sein Leben, sein Werk, seine Zeit* (Frankfurt-on-Main 1981) p. 274.

Jew, felt himself to be as much a German as the rest, even though he knew he was unwanted.

What these Jews felt for Germany and German culture was not something which could be rationally explained away as the attempt to get on in the world, to fit in. They were not escaping their Jewish fate so much as entering, crossing over, into a promised land of freedom. Historical circumstance was such that for a vast number of Jews in Germany and outside this promised land happened to be Germany. It came to sum up, to symbolize, all their great desires and came, like liberalism, to be desired in itself. In 1942 in America the Viennese Jew, Max Reinhardt, still wrote about his 'yearning, as a racially alien, not in any sense native [bodenständigen] Jew, for the – in spite of everything, everything – deeply loved German language'.[112] Germany simply meant something other than the empirical collection of individuals known as the German people, and while Germans had rejected their own humanistic heritage by allowing Hitler to take power, Jews, even Galician Jews, continued the tradition. A Jew such as Joseph Roth came to see the Jews as the true carriers of the German message: 'The east European Jew sees Germany, for example, still as the land of Goethe and Schiller, of the German poets, whom every eager Jewish youth knows better than our Nazi *Gymnasiast.*'[113] The German culture and values which the Jews in the Austrian Empire worshipped were something other than reality. They had assimilated into a great and glorious culture but the society for that culture did not exist.

[112] Reinhardt, *Der Liebhaber*, p. 128.

[113] 'Dem Ostjuden ist Deutschland zum Beispiel immer noch das Land Goethes und Schillers, der deutschen Dichter, die jeder lernbegierige jüdische Jüngling besser kennt, als unser hakenkreuzlerischer Gymnasiast.' Josef Roth, *Juden auf Wanderschaft*, in vol. 3 of *Werke* (Cologne 1956) p. 629. Cf. Claudio Magris, *Weit von wo?* (Vienna 1974) p. 163. Also see Berthold Feiwel, 'Die Juden in Mähren' in *Die Welt*, 177 June 1898, no. 24, p. 8.

≫ 11 ≪

Vienna

THE ARRIVAL IN A GERMAN CITY

The Jews who came to Vienna carried with them the same conceptions of western society and German culture as other central European Jews, and in coming to Vienna they thought that the ideals which had led them to leave the ghetto (or the shtetl or the *Gasse*) would now be realized in the capital of the sprawling Habsburg Monarchy. Their expectations were partly to be fulfilled, but in certain critical aspects they were to be severely disappointed. Out of the complex responses and reactions to their unique Viennese environment, these Jews became something quite different from Jews in the German Reich or even in other parts of the Monarchy. They emerged as a special phenomenon, reflecting the specific qualities of their city, but in a way quite different from the rest of the Viennese population. They became Viennese Jews.

Vienna acted like a magnet on a large part of the Jewish population, carrying great prestige even in traditional communities.[1] One of its great attractions, especially for assimilating Jews, was that apart from being the imperial capital it was a German city, the last bastion of German culture in southern central Europe. Even in 1873 it was being seen as a safe port for Germans in the nationalities' struggles.[2] We have already touched upon the character of Vienna and Austria, politically, as German. Culturally, it was still regarded as completely German long after the trauma of 1866, with some reason. Schoolboys learnt that the *Nibelungenlied* related events which had taken place on the Danube in Lower Austria.[3] Vienna was the home of the tradition of German classical music. The dramatic German spoken in the Burgtheater was the best in all

---

[1] Manès Sperber, *Die Wasserträger Gottes* (Munich 1983) p. 90; M. Sperber, *Masks of Loneliness: Alfred Adler in Perspective* (New York 1974) p.x.

[2] Israel Jeiteles, *Die Kultusgemeinde der Israeliten in Wien mit Benützung des statistischen Volkszahlungsoperates v.J. 1869* (Vienna 1873) p. 5.

[3] William McGrath, *Dionysian Art and Populist Politics in Austria* (New Haven 1974) pp. 32ff.

Germany.[4] The Viennese School of Medicine was the most prestigious of any German university.[5] The schools, due to a characteristic shortage of adequately trained native teachers, had largely been staffed by teachers from the Reich in the expansion of the 1850s and 1860s. The university, despite the efforts of Count Leo Thun, became a bastion of German liberalism.[6] The Vienna of the Liberals was very pro-German and welcomed the last wave of German 'pioneers', who brought their Protestant values with them. They included the Wittgensteins.[7] The *Neue Freie Presse* in 1895 could still talk of 'this old German city' in terms which suggested a larger version of a German Bohemian town.[8] Many Jews found this irresistible.

Jews flocked to this German city as soon as they were allowed. According to the official census returns (unreliable until 1880), the Jewish presence in Vienna, a mere 1·3 per cent in 1857, had risen to 10 per cent in 1880, and reached 12 per cent in 1890.[9] This compared to a figure of roughly 4·7 per cent in Cisleithania as a whole.[10] Economic opportunity undoubtedly played the largest rôle in this immigration. Even before 1848, when officially only 179 'Tolerierten' had permission to reside in the city, there was a large unofficial Jewish population engaged in the textile trade.[11] The economic impulse lay behind the migration of many of the fathers of the cultural élite.[12] Vienna also acted as a great lure for those who had already made their fortune, especially for the industrial barons from the Bohemian crownlands. Their families could enjoy the cultural luxuries of Vienna while the factories in Nachod, or wherever, produced the means of payment. Initially a case of spending the winter social season

---

[4] Gottfried Reinhardt, *Der Liebhaber* (Munich 1975) p. 174; Leonhard M. Fiedler, *Max Reinhardt* (Hamburg 1975) p. 15; also see Margret Dietrich, ed., *Das Burgtheater und sein Publikum* (Vienna 1976).

[5] William M. Johnston, *The Austrian Mind: an Intellectual and Social History 1848–1938* (Berkeley 1972, pb. 1983) p. 224; Peter Gay, *Freud, Jews and Other Germans* (Oxford 1978) p. 33.

[6] Hans Lentze, *Die Universitätsreform des Ministers Graf Leo Thun-Hohenstein* (Vienna 1962) pp. 79–131, 272.

[7] Allan Janik and Stephen Toulmin, *Wittgenstein's Vienna* (New York 1973) p. 167–71. On North German immigrants, see *Neue Freie Presse*, morning edition (*NFPm*) 29 October 1899 p. 1.   [8] *NFPm* 31 March 1895 p. 1.

[9] Figures quoted in Ivar Oxaal, *The Jews of Pre-1914 Vienna: Two Working Papers* (Hull 1981) p. 60.

[10] Wolfdieter Bihl, 'Die Juden' in *Die Habsburgermonarchie 1848–1918*, eds. A. Wandruszka and P. Urbanitsch (Vienna 1973–) vol. 2, part 2, p. 882.

[11] Sigmund Mayer, *Ein jüdischer Kaufmann 1831–1911: Lebenserinnerungen* (Leipzig 1911) pp. 116–30. Mayer estimated that the true Jewish population of Vienna in 1848 was 12,000!

[12] Rudolf Ardelt, *Friedrich Adler: Probleme einer Persönlichkeitsentwicklung um die Jahrhundertwende* (Vienna 1984) p. 16–17; Manfred Durzak, *Hermann Broch* (Hamburg 1966) p. 12; R. W. Clark, *Freud: the Man and the Cause* (London 1980) pp. 13–14; R. A. Métall, *Hans Kelsen: Leben und Werk* (Vienna 1969) p. 1.

in the capital, this often led to a permanent shift over generations.[13] It was not only Bohemian Jews who followed this pattern. Hungarian families, such as the Gutmann-Gelseys, felt the pull of the capital, as did Jewish families as far away as Rumania.[14] Here, in Vienna, proper western German culture could be enjoyed, away from all those Czechs, Slovenes and the like, who provided most of the labour for the economic success of these families.

Young Jews were attracted to Vienna by its German university. A sizeable number were packed off, or came of their own accord, to acquire a German education.[15] While some came at an earlier stage of education, the university was the main attraction. Indeed, the original wave of antisemitism in Vienna was the result of Billroth's speech complaining of the hordes of Galician Jews coming to study medicine at Vienna.[16] Other young Jews, such as Wilhelm Neurath, came to Vienna not merely for its cultural importance, but also because the city offered an environment quite different from their home towns.[17] Whereas other towns had a tradition of a Jewish community, and hence a ghetto, Vienna had virtually none. Jews had been expelled in 1669, and only a few 'Tolerierten' were ever officially allowed back until 1848. An official Kultusgemeinde was only recognized after 1848. Although there was an informal organization before then, it seems true that in the early nineteenth century there was far less of an infrastructure than in other Jewish centres such as Prague.[18]

The result was, as Sigmund Mayer relates, that Jewish individuals felt much more free and easy than they had in ghettos such as in Pressburg, both with regard to the non-Jewish society and culture and their own Jewish traditions.[19] The distance from the patriarchal regimentation of the ghetto led to large-scale secularization. The Viennese Jews gained the reputation in the provinces for being 'godless'.[20] Put another way, for a

[13] *Käthe Leichter: Leben und Werk*, ed. Herbert Steiner (Vienna 1973) pp. 240–1; the presence of industrialist families in Vienna also had a material basis, in that government regulations encouraged the establishment of headquarters in the capital for Bohemian firms, see Joseph C. Pick, 'The Economy' in *The Jews of Czechoslovakia: Historical Studies and Surveys* (Philadelphia 1968) vol.1, pp. 359–60.

[14] Interview with Erika Czuczka, Vienna, 7 June 1983; *Käthe Leichter*, pp. 245–6.

[15] *Käthe Leichter*, p. 243; Karl Goldmark, *Erinnerungen aus meinem Leben* (Vienna 1922) p. 18; Kurt Blaukopf, *Mahler: a Documentary Study* (London 1976) pp. 151–2; Elias Canetti, *Die gerettete Zunge: Geschichte einer Jugend* (Frankfurt-on-Main 1979) pp. 31, 36–7.

[16] Klaus Lohrmann, ed., *1,000 Jahre österreichisches Judentum* (Eisenstadt 1982) p. 162.

[17] Otto Neurath, *Empiricism and Sociology* (Dordrecht 1973) p. 3.

[18] Nikolaus Vielmetti, 'Zur Geschichte der Wiener Juden im Vormärz' in Lohrmann, *1,000 Jahre*, pp. 93–103; Mayer, *Ein jüdischer Kaufmann*, p. 115.

[19] Sigmund Mayer, *Die Wiener Juden: Kommerz, Kultur, Politik 1700–1900* (Vienna 1918) pp. 209–15, 273–80.

[20] *Ibid.* pp. 298–300; anon. *Der jüdische Gil Blas* (Leipzig 1834) p. 204.

young Jew wanting to free himself from the shackles of tradition, Vienna looked a good bet. As a result Vienna received a large surplus of the most enterprising young Jewish men of the provinces, whose liberality in turn perpetuated Vienna's reputation as a prime escape route from the ghetto, as a centre of assimilation.[21]

It would be wrong to think that the Jewish population of Vienna during the latter half of the nineteenth century entirely followed the path described above. Just as there is no 'Jewish mind', so there was no 'Viennese Jew' who summed up all Jews in Vienna. There was a great deal of stratification in the Jewish community in Vienna from the ultra-assimilated *Hofjuden* to Galician Hasidim. Indeed the degree to which the Viennese Jews did not assimilate has recently been shown by Marsha Rozenblit.[22] We, however, are only interested in the background of the cultural élite, at the leading edge of the (cultural) assimilation. While, therefore, much of the later immigration to Vienna was of Jews who stayed more or less true to their traditions, it is the earlier form of the immigration with its assimilationist impulse, as described above, which interests us directly.[23] If we look at the origins of the central cultural figures, we can see whence this cultural élite came.

Some came from families long-established as 'Tolerierten' in Vienna, Hofmannsthal being the most famous.[24] Others came from the traditionalist communities of Galicia, bringing the cultural turmoil of a Lipiner or Joseph Roth.[25] The Hungarian half of the empire provided figures such as Herzl.[26] By far the most important contribution to the cultural élite, however, was that of the areas which Sigmund Mayer identified as the source of the original, pre-1848 immigration: Germany and the Bohemian crownlands.[27] A list of Viennese Jews with this

---

[21] Mayer, *Die Wiener Juden*, pp. 208–9; Hans Tietze, *Die Juden Wiens* (Vienna 1935) p. 165.

[22] The main purpose of Marsha Rozenblit's book, *The Jews of Vienna 1867–1914: Assimilation and Identity* (Albany 1983) is to point out how little Jews really integrated into the city. See especially pp. 195–6.

[23] On the motives and structure of immigration, see Oxaal, *The Jews of Pre-1914 Vienna*, p. 59–73.

[24] Hermann Broch, *Hofmannsthal und seine Zeit*, in Broch, *Schriften zur Literatur 1* (Frankfurt-on-Main) pp. 178ff. Schnitzler, through his mother, was also connected to this background. Hartmut Scheible, *Schnitzler* (Hamburg 1976) pp. 13–15.

[25] On Roth, see David Bronsen, 'Austrian versus Jew: the Torn Identity of Joseph Roth', in *Leo Baeck Institute Yearbook (LBIY)* 1973, pp. 220–7.

[26] Ironically, many of the 'Hungarian' Jews were fairly recent immigrants from the Bohemian crownlands. See Ludwig Hatvany, *Bondy Jr,* (Munich 1929) p. 1. Herzl's mother was a fanatical German culturist. Alex Bein, *Theodore Herzl* (London 1957) p. 10.

[27] Mayer, *Die Wiener Juden*, p. 462; also see Y. 'Die Juden in Wien' in *Die Welt*, 30 September 1898, no. 39, p. 5; anon., *Die Juden in Böhmen und ihre Stellung in der Gegenwart* (Prague 1863) p. 45.

background provides one of the most impressive collections of cultural talent in Europe at that time.[28]

The Bohemian crownlands were the industrial heartland of the Monarchy, and there prevailed in the social system of this area an attitude to work quite different from that in most supposedly Catholic countries.[29] The atmosphere in the German areas of the crownlands resembled in many respects the North German rather than that of South German Vienna. Rudolf Sieghart, himself born in Austrian Silesia, described the special character of the region: 'There, in Bohemia, Moravia and Silesia, a way of life prevailed based on hard work and success in business, a frugal lifestyle and the careful accumulation of wealth.'[30] This type of Puritanism, which appears to have been a real characteristic of the Germans in the Bohemian lands, contrasted sharply with the Viennese lifestyle, as described by Sieghart, but it was very similar to that of Jewish families, especially of the most assimilated.[31] The environment in which Josephine von Wertheimstein and Theodor Gomperz were brought up was quite different from the aristocratic, baroque, hedonistic culture of Vienna, and was marked by 'worldly Puritanism'.[32] The families of Otto Bauer and Victor Adler are instances of the same austere atmosphere.[33] The up-bringing which the Wittgenstein children received from their Protestant father is also in the same mould: 'Life as a task.'[34]

There was thus a very strong tradition amongst a certain group of Jews in Vienna which was quite different from the image of the *parvenu* that has often been used to discredit the Jewish bourgeoisie. While the latter

[28] Those with a German or Bohemian (Moravian) background included the socialist leaders, Victor Adler, Otto Bauer; the writers, Richard Beer-Hofmann, Hermann Broch, Egon Friedell, Karl Kraus, Stefan Zweig; Freud; in music, Guido Adler, Gustav Mahler; Otto Neurath (a German Protestant mother); Ludwig Wittgenstein. Max Reinhardt, Arnold Schoenberg and Otto Weininger also had family connections with the Bohemian crownlands. It may also be noted that the school data for 1870–1910 discussed earlier also shows that of those Jewish *Gymnasiasten* born outside Vienna, 48 per cent came from the Bohemian crownlands, 15 per cent from Hungary and only 19 per cent from Galicia.

[29] A. J. May, *The Habsburg Monarchy* (London 1951) p. 202.

[30] 'Dort in Böhmen, Mähren und Schlesien waltete ein auf harte Arbeit und geschäftlichen Erfolg, auf bescheidene Lebensführung und bedächtige Ansammlung von Wohlstand abgestelltes Dasein...' Rudolf Sieghart, *Die letzten Jahrzehnte einer Grossmacht* (Berlin 1932) p. 262; cf. Alfred Ableitinger, *Rudolf Sieghart 1866–1934* (Graz Univ.diss. 1964) p. 25. It might be noted that Sieghart is explicitly referring to the 'deutschen Bürgertum' of what he calls the 'Sudetenländern'.

[31] On the Bohemian/Alpine (Viennese) contrast, Sieghart, *Die letzten Jahrzehnte*, pp. 261–2. On the reputation of the German Bohemians, see Gregor von Rezzori, *Memoirs of an Anti-Semite* (London 1983) p. 88.

[32] Theodor Gomperz, *Essays und Erinnerungen* (Stuttgart 1905) p. 9.

[33] Otto Leichter, *Otto Bauer: Tragödie oder Triumph?* (Vienna 1970) p. 23; Ardelt, *Friedrich Adler*, pp. 17–18.

[34] Paul Engelmann, *Letters from Wittgenstein; with a Memoir* (Oxford 1967) p. 79.

type plainly existed, the Jews from the Bohemian crownlands, to a large extent, brought with them to Vienna a way of life which was very close to a type of Weberian Calvinism.[35] The city to which they brought this was, however, not quite what they might have imagined; it was anything but a city suited to the Puritan ethic and German culture.

GERMAN DREAM, BAROQUE REALITY

Vienna as a centre of German culture must have been a great disappointment for German Jewish immigrants by the end of the nineteenth century. As late as 1859 a statue could be put up in Vienna to commemorate Archduke Charles as 'the steadfast defender of Germany's honour'.[36] After 1866, however, the German character of Vienna began to pall. The bright start of the German Liberals, with its campaign against the Church, soon slowed as it became clear that the Germans were far from being alone in having a say in how the Monarchy was run. The onset of Taaffe's 'Iron Ring' with its encouragement of the Slavs, and then the tragedy of Mayerling, dimmed liberal hopes, producing a divided and near powerless German liberal bourgeoisie, a potential ruling class which now found itself one interest group among others.[37] This demise of German liberal political hegemony had its cultural consequences. The historian of the Austrian system of education complained bitterly of the Slavicization which had started under Taaffe.[38] Strakosch-Grassmann also complained of the appalling standard of education when compared to Prussia.[39] The law of 1883 was seen as encouraging illiteracy and as an agent of the Catholic Church.[40] The Josephinist mission of bringing German culture to the east had been halted and was now in retreat.[41]

The *Neue Freie Presse* in 1899 complained in a similar vein that there was a drain of the best talent away from Vienna back to Germany.[42] It was talking about university academics, but this was part of a shift in personnel which was already occurring before the First World War from Vienna to

---

[35] Cf. *Käthe Leichter*, p. 247. It might be added that Käthe Leichter likened her father's manner and posture to Max Weber himself (one of her teachers), *ibid*, p. 258.

[36] This dedication is still on the statue in the Heldenplatz, Vienna.

[37] McGrath, *Dionysian Art*, p. 22; Ilsa Barea, *Vienna* (London 1966) pp. 248, 312; May, *The Habsburg Monarchy*, pp. 194, 339; Frederic Morton, *A Nervous Splendour: Vienna 1888/9* (London 1979) p. 37. The degree to which Germans were a potential ruling class is perhaps gauged by the fact that in 1900 Germans comprised 36 per cent of the Cisleithanian population, held 45 per cent of the seats in the Reichsrat, but contributed 63 per cent of tax revenue; this is according to Emil Brix, 'Der Gleichheitsgedanke in der Sprachenpolitik' in P. Berner, E. Brix and W. Mantl, eds., *Wien um 1900: Aufbruch in die Moderne* (Vienna 1986) p. 183.

[38] Gustav Strakosch-Grassmann, *Geschichte des österreichischen Unterrichtswesens* (Vienna 1905) pp. 331ff.

[39] *Ibid*. pp. 310–15.

[40] *Ibid*. p. 298.

[41] Mayer, *Ein jüdischer Kaufmann*, p. 237.

[42] NFPm 10 May 1899 p. 1.

Berlin.[43] Vienna was becoming a marginal German city.[44] Seen from another perspective, what was now happening was that a side of Vienna's character was reasserting itself which had been effectively repressed during the all too short liberal era.[45] This other side had never really gone away, but had simply not been seen in the liberals' rosy view of the city as a progressive centre of German culture and *laissez faire*. This was not what the real Vienna was like.

Let us start with the ruling house: it did not fit at all easily into the rôle befitting a constitutional monarchy. Francis Joseph, more Francis I than Joseph II, was not by the widest stretch of the imagination a model liberal monarch; he had goals which were quite independent of the constitution and put *Hausmacht* above all else.[46] Moreover, the empire over which this man ruled was a travesty of what the liberals had hoped it would be: 'the wildest mixture of all European systems of government subjects us to an official polyarchy and anarchy which appears impossible to comprehend and take hold of'.[47] This was the view of a socialist, Friedrich Austerlitz, in 1905. It is likely, however, that liberals from his background, Jewish German Bohemian, would have shared his opinion; the political and constitutional mess of the pre-war period certainly confirms it.

Vienna came increasingly to reflect this ramshackle and self-contradictory empire, rather than to live up to her reputation as a German city. As the *Haupt- und Residenzstadt* of the international Habsburg dynasty, Vienna had always been a far more cosmopolitan city than most, taking talent where she could find it.[48] She was also a city of international immigration, especially in the late nineteenth century from the Czech lands.[49] Her population was, therefore, only very dubiously German; the Viennese spoke German, after a fashion, but were Viennese rather than German. Sigmund Mayer described this in terms of the Viennese being like a cloth which was finished then dyed, while the true Germans of Germany and German Bohemia were 'dyed in the wool'.[50] The Viennese developed

[43] Viennese emigrés to Berlin included Max Reinhardt, Samuel Fischer, Arnold Schoenberg and Oskar Kokoschka. Fiedler, *Reinhardt*, pp. 24ff.; H. H. Stuckenschmidt, *Schoenberg: his Life, World and Work* (London 1977) pp. 47ff.

[44] See Barry Smith, 'The Production of Ideas: Notes on Austrian Intellectual History from Bolzano to Wittgenstein' in B. Smith, ed., *Structure and Gestalt: Philosophy and Literature in Austria-Hungary and her Successor States* (Amsterdam 1981) pp. 224ff. where Smith discusses various aspects of Vienna's marginality. Also see Paul Vasili, *Die Wiener Gesellschaft* (Leipzig 1885) p. 296.

[45] Cf. E. W. 'Arbeiterschaft und Bürgerthum' in *Die Wage*, 23 July 1899, no. 30, p. 515.   [46] Barea, *Vienna*, pp. 263–6.

[47] Quoted in Blaukopf, *Mahler: a Documentary Study*, p. 240.

[48] Hilde Spiel, 'Jewish Women in Austrian Culture' in Josef Fraenkel, ed., *The Jews of Austria: Essays on their Life, History and Destruction* (London 1967) p. 104.

[49] Mayer, *Ein jüdischer Kaufmann*, p. 280; Barea, *Vienna*, p. 335.

[50] Mayer, *Die Wiener Juden*, p. 320. Also see L. A. Frankl's letter to Anastasius Grün 22 July 1866, reprinted in B. Zeller, L. Greve and W. Volke, ed., *Jugend in Wien: Literatur um 1900* (Stuttgart 1974) p. 16.

into something which was German only in name. The attitude amongst most Viennese to the greater German nation, to the Germany of Berlin and Prussia, was a mixture of apathy and antipathy.[51] The masses in Vienna and the surrounding countryside were both, in their own way, developing an Austrian identity which went right against all that German Liberals imagined Vienna to be.

Vienna was also the capital of a staunchly Catholic monarchy, which based itself on the heritage of the Counter-Reformation. Protestants were a tiny minority, and to a large degree the Monarchy was still dominated by the alliance which had effected this situation: the Church, the Habsburgs and the high aristocracy – the cultural expression of which, baroque, dominated Vienna's inner city.[52] When the Christian Socials were voted into power in 1895 it was thus natural for the *Neue Freie Presse* to identify them with the clericalism which had proven so dominant in Austria's past; Vienna was, one might say, simply reverting to type.[53] This was, after all, a society in which the theories of Darwin could be hushed up by telephone.[54] It was the Liberals, not the Christian Socials, who were going against the traditions of Vienna, the Catholic, supra-national and baroque seat of the Habsburgs.

The history of the *Ringstrasse* symbolized the fate of German liberalism's Vienna. It had started as a symbol of liberation and modernization. Vienna was freed from the medieval straitjacket of her city walls, just as the architects were freed from the uniformity imposed by the authorities.[55] The resulting menagerie of historicist styles was seen as progressive by none other than Burkhardt, who saw Vienna as well on the way to outshining Paris. When he came back to the city twelve years later, however, he felt the unreality of the magnificent form compared to the crippled content of Austrian liberal society.[56] By 1884 the whole thing had already begun to look like a nineteenth-century version of Disneyland, Loos' Potemkin

---

[51] May, *The Habsburg Monarchy*, p. 309; Albert Fuchs, *Geistige Strömungen in Österreich 1867–1918* (Vienna 1949) p. 171.

[52] Thon puts the size of the Protestant community at less than one per cent of the Cisleithanian population: Jakob Thon, ed., *Die Juden in Österreich* (Berlin 1908) p. 71. May quotes a figure of 589,000 in 1910: May, *The Habsburg Monarchy*, p. 189. On the alliance of Church and State, see Johnston, *The Austrian Mind*, pp. 11ff, 56; May, *The Habsburg Monarchy*, p. 186.

[53] *NFPm* 14 May 1895 p. 1.

[54] Berta Zuckerkandl, *Österreich Intim: Erinnerungen 1872–1942* (Frankfurt-on-Main 1970) p. 132.

[55] Carl E. Schorske, *Fin-de-Siècle Vienna: Politics and Culture* (London 1980) pp. 24–111; Barea, *Vienna*, p. 239; Vasili, *Die Wiener Gesellschaft*, p. 4.

[56] Jakob Burkhardt, *Briefe* (Basle 1963, 1974) vol. 5, p. 173 (7 July 1872), vol. 8, p. 228 (14 August 1884); cf. review of Schorske's book in *Freibeuter* 16 (Berlin 1983) p. 146.

City.[57] Yet it was not only the architecture which revealed liberalism's weakness. It was also the *Ringstrasse's* very position, a thin riband between the medieval old city of the *ancien régime* and the *Vorstädte* of the officials and artisanry. The *Ringstrasse* lay uneasily between these older parts of the city, surrounding the medieval core without ever getting to its heart, something which might well have happened if the Liberals had remained in power on the city council, but which was foiled by the victory of the Christian Socials.[58]

By the turn of the century Vienna was not shaping up to be the great centre of capitalist enterprise it had once promised to be. In commercial terms it was beginning to lose out to Budapest, and in the structure of its industry the small craftsman remained the predominant form.[59] This relative economic backwardness was reflected in the social composition of the city, where the society of the *Ringstrasse* was far from being the dominant force. Vienna was first and foremost the seat of the Habsburgs, not an industrial centre. The beginnings of a capitalist bourgeoisie had disappeared during the Counter-Reformation. There was, it is true, a native liberal bourgeoisie, comprising the most successful craftsmen such as Lobmeyer and Bösendorfer. There was also the liberal tradition of Josephinism among officialdom.[60] However, the true significance of my figures from the Gymnasien is not to be found so much in the size of the Jewish presence in the 'liberal bourgeois sector', as in the very poor showing of Catholics, only 29 per cent, with Protestants comprising 5 per cent. Much work must still be done to obtain a true picture of the ethnic and religious composition of the upper middle-class society of the *Ringstrasse*, but these figures do seem to confirm the impressions of contemporaries – that this society of the capitalist middle class was a largely Jewish phenomenon, isolated and without native support of any substance, existing in a society hostile to its values.[61]

[57] Cf. Hermann Bahr's comments on the unreality of the *Ringstrasse*, in Hermann Bahr, *Wien* (Stuttgart 1907) pp. 115–6, and also Hermann Bahr, *Selbstbildnis* (Berlin 1923) pp. 106–10; cf. Gotthart Wunberg, ed., *Die Wiener Moderne* (Stuttgart 1981) p. 110.

[58] It was proposed by the engineer Riehl to build a new avenue from the *Stephansdom* to the *Prater* (the Leopoldstadt), which would have destroyed much of Vienna's medieval heart. Liberal opinion, though divided, was generally favourable, but the Christian Socials were vehemently against the plan, seeing it as a Jewish plot. *NFPm* 15 March 1895 p. 1; *NFPm* 22 March 1895 p. 7; *NFPe* (evening edition) 1 August 1895 p. 3; *NFPm* 19 January 1898 p. 6. Cf. Karl Kraus' comments on the Christian Socials' attitude, in Karl Kraus, *Frühe Schriften II, 1897–1900* (Munich 1979) pp. 166–7.

[59] Barea, Vienna, p. 333.   [60] *Ibid.* p. 290–3.

[61] Cf. Burkhardt's comments (see note 55 above); Bahr's comments in *Wien* pp. 115–6; Olga Schnitzler, *Spiegelbild der Freundschaft* (Vienna 1962) p. 114; Mayer, *Die Wiener Juden*, p. 450; Vasili, *Wiener Gesellschaft*, pp. 402–3, 450. To what extent the *Ringstrassengesellschaft* was Jewish remains unclear, despite the great degree of

The liberal and capitalist society of the *Ringstrasse* confronted an established social structure of, on the one side, aristocracy and, on the other, a guild-based artisanry, which, in a Catholic and hierarchically-minded culture, had no need of a capitalist bourgeoisie to mediate between them, depending instead on the bonds of deference and what Broch called the 'Gallertdemokratie' (jelly democracy) evident in such events as the *Fiakerball*.[62] Broch contrasted the English and Austrian forms of nobility: whereas the *Gentleman*, with his essentially Protestant values, could easily be adapted as a bourgeois model, the Austrian bourgeoisie, if it wanted to adopt the leading model in society, had to imitate the far less suitable image of the *Cavalier*, which, typically for Austria, was a matter of style rather than substance. The lower middle class, well-schooled in baroque manners, felt no such compunction, entering fully into a *style democracy* with the aristocrats.[63] It is not really true that the bourgeoisie was dependent on Austrian aristocratic style – it got its fashions from England and France – but what it did lack was a style of its own.[64] The presence of people such as Lobmeyer could not disguise the fact that the bourgeoisie in Vienna was isolated, that it did not fit into an already pre-existent social structure, and could thus be felt to be a foreign, imported element.[65]

This had not seemed an irremediable situation at the beginning of the liberal era. In 1848 it seemed for a fleeting moment as though the artisanry would be part of the progressive coalition.[66] This was illusory. The decision to restrict the franchise to the *Grossbürgertum* permanently alienated the lower middle classes from the liberals in Vienna, thus splitting the *Bürgertum*.[67] Yet it has to be doubted whether the artisan classes would ever have been enthusiastic liberals. Socially conservative and hierarchically minded, they defined *Bürgertum* in terms of guild protection and hereditary right (son succeeds father in the business).[68]

attention which the *Ringstrasse* has received recently, cf. Elisabeth Lichtenberger, 'Wirtschaftsfunktion und Sozialstruktur der Wiener Ringstrasse' in R. Wagner-Rieger, ed., *Die Wiener Ringstrasse* (Vienna 1969 et seq.) vol. VI. Also see Roman Sandgruber, 'Der Grosse Krach' in R. Waissenberger, ed., *Traum und Wirklichkeit: Wien 1870–1930* (Vienna 1985) catalogue, p. 69.

[62] Morton, *A Nervous Splendour*, p. 72; Johnston, *The Austrian Mind*, p. 44; Broch, *Hofmannsthal und seine Zeit*, p. 167.

[63] Broch, *Hofmannsthal und seine Zeit*, p. 167.

[64] Morton, *A Nervous Splendour*, p. 69.

[65] Broch, *Hofmannsthal und seine Zeit*, p. 167; Bahr, *Wien*, pp. 65–7; for a different view, from a contemporary, which stresses the strength and influence of the bourgeoisie, see Vasili, *Die Wiener Gesellschaft*, pp. 418–9, 448–9.

[66] Barea, *Vienna*, p. 189.

[67] John W. Boyer, *Political Radicalism in Late Imperial Vienna* (Chicago 1981) pp. 12ff.

[68] *Ibid.* pp. 27–67; J. W. Boyer, 'Lueger and the Viennese Jews' in *Leo Baeck Institute Yearbook (LBIY)* 1981, pp. 131–3; Mayer, *Die Wiener Juden*, pp. 387–90; Vasili, *Die Wiener Gesellschaft*, pp. 402–3, 415.

This may have been 'bürgerlich', but it was not bourgeois, and certainly not liberal.[69]

While the Viennese bourgeoisie failed to bring the lower classes over to its way of thinking, it also failed to come to terms, or to overcome, the social dominance of the aristocracy. By all accounts this was largely due to the great reluctance of the aristocrats to be seen socializing with their social inferiors, thus excluding the kind of osmosis effected in England.[70] Instead they chose to leave the cultural field to the bourgeoisie, rather than meet them on that ground.[71] Nevertheless, they remained socially very powerful, and when they wanted could through the institution of *Protektion* – the operation of government and patronage on the basis of personal preference rather than merit or the rules – wield enormous influence over the cultural world, often to the detriment of more progressive elements.[72] The bourgeoisie, effectively excluded from this society, could do little but look on in a state of enraged impotence.

Vienna was simply not the capital of a liberal state or even of a rational autocracy. Everything was done with a touch of *Schlamperei*: Wickham Steed noted that nowhere else had he seen a culture which had so many words to express the idea of 'slovenliness'[73] Nothing was done quite as it should be. This was Kafka's state. Kraus spoke of 'Bürokretinismus', nothing ever quite worked out the way foreseen.[74] It was another manifestation of the same system which allowed *Protektion*. If you knew the ropes, if you were on the inside, everything was easy.[75] Problems began when you were not one of the initiated, when you operated on the written laws rather than the unwritten ones. Jews had had full experience of how the system operated in Vienna before 1848, and the experience was not good.[76]

The necessary concomitant of *Schlamperei* was what is affectionately

---

[69] For a brief discussion of the problems of interpretation with such words as 'Bürgertum' and 'bürgerlich', Julius Carlebach, 'The Forgotten Connection: Women and Jews in the Conflict between Enlightenment and Romanticism' in *LBIY* xxiv 1979, p. 110.

[70] Cf. the comments of Frances Trollope in the 1830s, reprinted in Lohrmann, *1,000 Jahre*, p. 98; Vasili, *Die Wiener Gesellschaft*, pp. 357–9, 422, for the 1880s; and Henry Wickham Steed, *Through Thirty Years* (London 1924) p. 195.

[71] Morton, *A Nervous Splendour*, p. 123; Mayer, *Die Wiener Juden*, pp. 297ff.; *Die Wiener Gesellschaft*, pp. 295, 422.

[72] Johnston, *The Austrian Mind*, p. 43; one of the most notorious instances of this was the removal of Schnitzler's *Der grüne Kakadu* from the Burgtheater programme, due to the protest of an archduchess at its supposedly revolutionary sentiments, see O. Schnitzler, *Spiegelbild*, p. 41; Zeller, *Jugend in Wien*, p. 346.

[73] Steed, *Through Thirty Years*, p. 195.

[74] Quoted in Johnston, *The Austrian Mind*, p. 48.

[75] Cf. Joseph Roth, *Die Kapuzinergruft* (Munich 1967) p. 57.

[76] Vielmetti, 'Zur Geschichte der Wiener Juden' in Lohrmann, *1,000 Jahre*, pp. 93–6; Mayer, *Die Wiener Juden*, pp. 244–6.

referred to as *Wiener Schmäh*, which is essentially the talent for telling lies in an attractive manner. It was only a verbal form of the kind of baroque architecture where all marble was really exquisitely painted wood, or of social manners, where a student would be addressed by the waiter as 'Herr Doktor'. In the bureaucracy everyone was given the title of the job above them. Everyone knew this, but all played the game. Flattery was institutionalized, and appearance counted far more than the facts.[77] It did not matter what you said but how you said it, preferably in as many languages as possible.[78]

This all culminated in an enormous self-satisfaction, which quite contradicted the facts of Viennese existence.[79] The truth was often an extreme poverty, terrible housing conditions, and the hysterical nastiness of social groups such as the artisanry, who felt threatened by new developments.[80] The reverse side of the sickening self-adulation in songs such as *Wien, Wien, nur Du allein* was a cynical realization of the mess the empire had become, and the impotence of the ruling classes to do anything about it. According to Broch, the aristocracy had given up trying to do anything constructive after the disaster of 1859. They were 'driven by a mood of decline to partake in the most fleeting of life's pleasures' with no belief any more in their State. Their response he called 'the flight into the apolitical'.[81] This flight was a theme running throughout Habsburg Viennese society in its closing years. It has been suggested that part of Viennese fatalism is to be traced back to the forcible re-Catholicization of the Protestant populace in the seventeenth century, which created a cynicism in religion and politics, which saw living the good life as the only sensible approach.[82] Be that as it may, all Vienna's classes seemed to be affected by political apathy.[83]

The rider to this was that Vienna became known as the city of hedonism and 'official gaiety'.[84] Wickham Steed described the Viennese as a people, who had been deliberately taught for generations that their one duty was

[77] Johnston, *The Austrian Mind*, p. 116; see also Sieghart, *Die letzten Jahrzehnte*, pp. 262–3; Bahr, *Wien*, pp. 45–64.   [78] Barea, *Vienna*, p. 356.

[79] Alexander Girardi, one of the most popular 'Viennese' comic actors of the late nineteenth century born in Graz, said of his portrayal of the Viennese: 'The way I play a Viennese for them isn't what they are, it's just what they'd like to be...If I'd been born a Viennese, I'd never have managed it.' Barea, *Vienna*, p. 320.

[80] Janik and Toulmin, *Wittgenstein's Vienna*, pp. 50–2.

[81] Broch, *Hofmannsthal und seine Zeit*, p. 169.

[82] This point is made by Allan Janik in Creative Milieux: the Case of Vienna' in Janik, *How not to Interpret a Culture* (Bergen 1986) p. 115; Barea, *Vienna*, pp. 44–57; Bahr, *Wien*, pp. 25–6, 43–4.

[83] See the leader of *NFPm* 3 March 1895 p. 1; Broch, *Hofmannsthal und seine Zeit*, pp. 170–1.

[84] Johnston, *The Austrian Mind*, p. 115; Edward Crankshaw, *Vienna: the Image of a City in Decline* (London 1976) p. 54.

to eat, drink and be merry and to leave the affairs of State to the management of the dynasty and its servants'.[85] This was a fair assessment. Music had been encouraged as an art form precisely because it was not politically dangerous.[86] Nestroy had been covertly very political, but he gave way to operetta in popular entertainment.[87] The most famous operetta, *Die Fledermaus*, written after the 1873 *Krach*, took the usual Viennese line:

> Glücklich ist, wer vergisst,
> Was nicht mehr zu ändern ist.[88]

This kind of aesthetic fatalism was common to all Viennese cultural groups including the bourgeoisie, who, as Broch says, were sucked into the 'Fröhliche Apokalypse' along with everyone else.[89]

To a North German Jew such as Jakob Wassermann Vienna offered a most peculiar picture around 1900. Whereas Germany was 'impossible to misunderstand in any respect', everything in Austria was 'open to question'. It combined hollow superficiality, indiscipline, frivolity and a sense of 'conscious inadequacy' with an undeniable charm in its culture and scenery. Most seriously, however: 'Whosoever sought a path leading away from the trivial and the popular became an outlaw, and every activity that aimed at deeper, less immediate results was aspersed or simply derided.'[90] There was a darker side to the city's hedonistic style, a virulent form of philistinism, which made Vienna the 'Capua der Geister', a city which destroyed the mind.[91] Kraus spoke of 'des österreichischen Ungeistes'.[92] The essence of the Austrian way of life, *Gemütlichkeit*, symbolized this in its rejection of any serious thought or culture; the reaction to Mahler (and by implication Schoenberg) was 'nur Gemütlichkeit, nur keine Aufregung!'[93] Music was to be enjoyed, not taken seriously.[94]

[85] Steed, *Through Thirty Years*, p. 328; also see Adam Müller-Guttenbrunn, *Im Jahrhundert Grillparzers: Literatur- und Lebensbilder aus Österreich* (Vienna 1893) p. 9.

[86] Janik, 'Creative Milieux', p. 113. L. A. Frankl relates how the censors under Francis changed a line in the finale of Don Juan from 'Es lebe die Freiheit' to 'Es lebe die Fröhlichkeit'. See L. A. Frankl, *Erinnerungen* (Prague 1910) pp. 146–7.

[87] Barea, *Vienna*, p. 260.

[88] 'Happy is he, who forgets, / What no more can be altered.' Quoted in Zeller, *Jugend in Wien*, p. 35.

[89] Broch, *Hofmannsthal und seine Zeit*, pp. 173–5.

[90] Jakob Wassermann, *My Life as German and Jew* (London 1934) pp. 139–41. See also J. Wassermann, *Hofmannsthal der Freund* (Berlin 1930) pp. 14–5.

[91] Johnston, *The Austrian Mind*, p. 124; see also Steed, *Through Thirty Years*, p. 328.

[92] Quoted in Norbert Leser, ed., *Das geistige Leben Wiens in der Zwischenkriegszeit* (Vienna 1981) p. 256.

[93] Zuckerkandl, *Österreich Intim*, p. 38; cf. Julius Bab and Willi Handl, *Wien und Berlin: Vergleichendes zur Kulturgeschichte der beiden Hauptstädte Mitteleuropas* (Berlin 1918) p. 296.   [94] O. Schnitzler, *Spiegelbild*, p. 108.

The *feuilletoniste* Kürnberger summed up Vienna thus: 'laziness, frivolity, vulgarity, moral degradation, unmanly childishness, wicked lust after pleasure, panting after smut, worship of filth, hatred of culture [Bildungshass], callous, dissolute, self-glorifying, absolute shabbiness'.[95] This does not sound like the seat of high culture that it was supposed to be. There was hedonistic enjoyment of music and the arts, but there was also 'Bildungshass'. Vienna was an especially aesthetic environment in the sense of sensuousness alone, for to contemporaries the reputation of Vienna was of a place where culture was an opiate, to be enjoyed, not taken seriously. It needed outsiders to do that.

JEWISH STRATEGIES OF RESPONSE

The kind of Vienna described in the last few pages must have come as quite a shock to Jewish families coming to Vienna as a seat of German culture. In coming to terms with the situation there were many strategies which could be employed, involving varying degrees of acceptance and rejection of this Vienna. Elements of acceptance could be, for many Jews, very strong. They identified themselves with the city's whole tradition, not only its German side.[96] The problem was how to integrate into a city as baroque in style and social structure as Vienna.

In certain ways, as Ivar Oxaal has pointed out, Vienna's cosmopolitan nature should have helped Jewish integration into the city, for the pluralistic approach allowed Jews to be just one more 'hyphenated nationality' among others.[97] The problem was that the Jews, in the cultural élite at least, did not want to be integrated, but assimilated, absorbed by the majority group. Hence Berlin, with its emphasis on cultural uniformity, could be preferred because there 'the Jew' was not a set character as in Vienna.[98] The aim was assimilation, not integration.

The best way of doing this appeared to be to acquire a title of nobility, undergo the usually prerequisite conversion to Catholicism, and adopt the appropriate lifestyle. Many of the wealthiest Jewish families followed this pattern.[99] Often this led to the next generation being totally indis-

---

[95] Quoted in Zeller, *Jugend in Wien*, p. 27; for a similar view see E. W. 'Wiener Volksgeist' in *Die Wage*, 1 January 1899, no. 1, p. 1.

[96] Franziska von Wertheimstein thus spoke of Vienna as her 'Vaterstadt' which must say something about the peculiarity of the relation of Vienna's *haute bourgeoisie* to the rest of Austria. Quoted in Mayer, *Ein jüdischer Kaufmann*, p. 44.

[97] Oxaal, *The Jews of Pre-1914 Vienna*, p. 51; also see Friedrich Torberg's speech in 1975 to the B'nai B'rith in *B'nai B'rith 1895–1975* (Vienna 1975) pp. 48–9.

[98] Reinhardt, *Der Liebhaber*, p. 176; also interview with Joan Campbell (Stolper), Hamilton, Ontario, 9 October 1987. For a different view, see Bab and Handl, *Wien und Berlin*, pp. 263–70.

[99] On conversion among the Jewish nobility see Hanns Jäger-Sunstenau, 'Die geadelten Judenfamilien im vormärzlichen Wien' (Vienna Univ. diss. 1950) pp. 64ff.; also Broch, *Hofmannsthal und seine Zeit*, pp. 178–9.

tinguishable from their counterparts, apart, as Kraus quipped, from the great emphasis they put on that very fact.[100] It depended where you were on the road to assimilation as to which aristocratic lifestyle you chose. Käthe Leichter, still bourgeois, saw the ennobled *Hofrat* as the Austrian ideal.[101] Wassermann, a German Jew, saw Hugo von Hofmannsthal as '*the* Austrian man', but Hofmannsthal himself saw quite clearly that as the son of a banker, though ennobled, he was far from being at the summit of the Austrian social pyramid, no matter how hard he strove to overcome this fact by consorting with a nobility into which he was *not* born.[102] The *real* nobility generally held aloof from the *parvenus* of the *Geldadel*, thus leaving the assimilation through ennoblement only partially successful.[103] Indeed, the Jewish nobility remained very small and socially isolated, with only 4·3 per cent of families ennobled from 1701–1918, the *new* aristocracy, being of Jewish descent.[104] In any case, the option of assimilation into the nobility was an option offered and taken only by a chosen few in the Jewish community.

On a more general level, Viennese Jews adapted themselves well to the more superficial aspects of Viennese life, taking part in the easy-going atmosphere, and dedicating themselves to Austrian cultural institutions such as Grillparzer.[105] Jews tried, almost literally, to merge into the landscape. When Freud and his daughter Anna went on a walk in the woods while on holiday they would be dressed in the appropriate peasant costume of *Lederhosen* and feathered hat for him, dirndl for her.[106] Similar things happened in Vienna. Käthe Leichter made a conscious effort, when she was a child, to dress like her non-Jewish schoolmates.[107] This was just an anticipation of what adult Jews were doing, learning all the complicated social rules, speaking the proper *Schönbrunnerdeutsch*, going to all the balls during Carnival, playing the dissolute young aesthete, sitting in the coffeehouse talking about nothing very much, only very cleverly, going to the operetta or opera to be seen. Jews did, to a remarkable extent, blend into the style and adopt the attitudes of the other Viennese. Vienna was more easy-going, softer, and so were its Jews.

The kind of symbiosis which went on in Vienna between Jews and Gentiles was expressed quite wittily by Alfred Polgar: describing the Viennese *feuilleton*, he said that it was a mixture 'of the melancholy of the

---

[100] Karl Kraus, *Eine Krone für Zion* (Vienna 1898) p. 27.

[101] *Käthe Leichter*, pp. 278–9, 306.

[102] Wassermann, *Hofmannsthal der Freund*, p. 16; Siegfried Trebitsch, *Chronik eines Lebens* (Zurich 1951) p. 165; Broch, *Hofmannsthal und seine Zeit*, pp. 203–210.

[103] Vasili, *Die Wiener Gesellschaft*, pp. 357–9.

[104] Jäger-Sunstenau, 'Die geadelten Judenfamilien', pp. 86–8. There was a total of 444 Jewish families ennobled between 1701 and 1918 out of 10,414.

[105] See Zeller, *Jugend in Wien*, pp. 19–20, for Kürnberger's description of Grillparzer's funeral.

[106] Clark, *Freud*, p. 307.   [107] *Käthe Leichter*, p. 308.

synagogue and the alcoholic mood of Grinzing', the misery of the Diaspora was being drunk into oblivion in the Heurigen. The *feuilleton*, he
continued, 'possesses a sensitive intellect and a remarkably intelligent
sensitivity'.[108] While being part of Vienna, the Jews were thus bringing
their mental ability to interpret to the Viennese their own way of life. Jews
did indeed play a great part not only in high culture, but also in popular
culture, with even a tendency to 'überwienern', be more Viennese than
the Viennese.[109] The *Fiakerlied* was after all written by a Jew, Adolph
Pick.[110] It might even be the case that in the lower strata it was quite
possible to achieve total assimilation, to become an invisible Jew.[111]

Once one started going up the social scale, however, problems of
consciousness and subtlety began to complicate matters, social failings
being revealed through a mere stage direction by an observant play-
wright.[112] No matter how Viennese one was, consciousness that others
saw you as a Jew could destroy any sense of being totally accepted. The
hero of Leopold Hichler's novel, *Der Sohn des Moses Mautner: ein Wiener
Roman*, discovers the vanity of thinking himself Viennese when, having
sung in perfect Viennese dialect, he is congratulated by a man in the
audience, who adds that he never knew Jews could sing Viennese songs so
well. Do what he can, he is still not Viennese.[113]

While many Jews in Vienna tried assimilating into Vienna as they found
it, others set up Vienna and Austria as ideals, and tried to make the
ramshackle empire and its capital serve their liberal purposes. The supra-
national character and cosmopolitan tradition of the Habsburg Monarchy
made it seem to someone like Stefan Zweig a model for European co-
operation.[114] Vienna's situation meant that its cultural groups, such as
Young Vienna, were, at least in their beginnings, very receptive to the
latest ideas from Berlin, London and especially Paris.[115] Vienna, because it
lay between everywhere else, could provide a good ground for a synthesis
of the rest of European culture, with someone such as Schnitzler mingling
the influence of the French *décadents* with a revived Austrian baroque and
a love of German.[116] This had a political parallel in the francophile group

[108] Alfred Polgar, *Sperrsitz*, ed. U. Weinzierl (Vienna 1980) p. 36.
[109] Tietze, *Die Juden Wiens*, p. 233.   [110] *B'nai B'rith 1895–1975*, p. 49.
[111] Cf. Friedrich Torberg, *Die Erben der Tante Jolesch* (Munich 1981) p. 149.
[112] In *Professor Bernhardi* Schnitzler gives this stage direction for the Jewish convert Dozent
       Schreimann: 'Auffallend tiefes, biederes Bierdeutsch mit plötzlich durchschlagenden
       jüdischen Akzenten.' Schnitzler, *Professor Bernhardi*, in vol. 6, *Dramen* (Frankfurt-on-
       Main 1962) p. 182.
[113] Leopold Hichler, *Der Sohn des Moses Mautner: ein Wiener Roman* (Vienna 1927)
       p. 310.
[114] D. A. Prater, *European of Yesterday: a Biography of Stefan Zweig* (Oxford 1972) p. 6.
[115] Wunberg, ed., *Die Wiener Moderne*, pp. 49. 57; Zeller, *Jugend in Wien*, pp. 103, 112.
[116] See Rudolf Lothar's description of Schnitzler reprinted in Zeller, *Jugend in Wien*, p. 182;
       Harry Zohn, *Wiener Juden in der deutschen Literatur* (Tübingen 1964) p. 40. Theodor
       Herzl, reviewing Bahr's *Das Tschaperl*, had the following to say about the *Jung Wien* group:

around Crown Prince Rudolph, which also tried to make the best of the idea of an Austria quite independent from Germany and acting as a model of international harmony.[117] For them and others Austria came to be an idea, representing tolerance and national understanding.[118] Although not a specifically Jewish idea, many Jews were attracted to it for fairly obvious reasons and, as Claudio Magris points out, when the 'Habsburg Myth' arose after the First World War, it was mainly Jewish writers who fostered it.[119] Before 1914 the political message of someone such as Moritz Szeps had little impact, the francophile tradition continuing more in the salon of his daughter Berta Zuckerkandl than in the political world.[120]

There has been much talk of the Jews as the *Staatsvolk* of the Monarchy, as the only supra-national group, whose situation made them loyal to the emperor first. There is some truth in this, as shown in the editorials of the Jewish newspaper in Vienna, the *Österreichische Wochenschrift*.[121] Yet it would be wrong to think that this meant loyalty to the concept of Habsburg dynasticism which lay at the heart of baroque Vienna. If Jews were loyal to the Monarchy, it was to a constitutional monarchy, not to a dynasty. It was the Austria of the 'Verfassungspartei' (constitutional party) which attracted Jews, not old ideas of apostolic majesty.[122] Loyalty to the ruling house did not mean belief in aristocratic values, and there are many cases where a title of nobility was refused by someone because he did not think it proper.[123] Indeed, as we have seen, there was considerable anti-Habsburg feeling amongst the generation of Victor Adler and Freud.[124] If most Jews were loyal to the Monarchy it was because the liberties it guaranteed were better than nothing. It was thus to be expected that it was only really after the empire's demise that most Jews realized how 'Austrian' they had been.

Underneath the elegant Viennese exterior which many Jews adopted there remained the same values that they had brought with them from the

'Die neuesten Spielereien von Montmartre sind ihnen gerade recht, und gleichzeitig sind sie altwienerisch barock...es sind eher empfangende als zeugende Individuen.' *NFPm* 7 March 1897 p. 1.

[117] Berta Zuckerkandl, *Ich erlebte fünfzig Jahre Weltgeschichte* (Stockholm 1939) p. 44.
[118] For instance, Ernst Lothar, *Der Engel mit der Posaune* (Salzburg 1947) p. 644.
[119] Magris' ideas are discussed by Johnston in *The Austrian Mind*, p. 32.
[120] See Zuckerkandl's memoirs, *Ich erlebte fünfzig Jahre* and *Österreich Intim*, especially the *cultural* consequences of the Dreyfus affair, in *Ich erlebte*, pp. 185–9.
[121] Joseph S. Bloch, *Der nationale Zwist und die Juden in Österreich* (Vienna 1886) is a collection of some of the more successful of his leaders in the *Österreichische Wochenschrift*.
[122] Joseph Kareis gave a characteristic definition of being Austrian: 'Österreicher sein heisst, die Staatsgrundgesetze hochhalten.' Reported in *NFPm* 8 October 1897 p. 3. See also Stella Klein-Löw, *Erinnerungen: Erlebtes und Gedachtes* (Vienna 1980) p. 28.
[123] For instance, *Theodor Gomperz: ein Gelehrtenleben im Bürgertum der Franz-Josephszeit*, eds. H. Gomperz and R. A. Kann (Vienna 1974) p. 10; Engelmann, *Letters from Wittgenstein*, p. 120 (on Karl Wittgenstein); Stefan Zweig, *Die Welt von Gestern* (Frankfurt-on-Main 1982) p. 22 (on Moritz Zweig).
[124] Ardelt, *Friedrich Adler*, p. 24; McGrath, *Dionysian Art*, p. 21; Clark, *Freud*, pp. 33–4.

provinces. For all their *viennoiserie* they were just as German in many respects as they had been when they came to Vienna. Schnitzler, we have seen, regarded himself as German. Young Vienna itself started as a response to the new German literature, and was identified by Ernst Mach as a reaction to the trauma of separation from Germany, as the product of alienated German intellectuals.[125]

The *haute bourgeoisie* of Vienna and the more liberal bureaucrats had as their newspaper the *Neue Freie Presse*, by far the most prestigious newspaper in Vienna and the mouthpiece for the educated élite.[126] If we are to regard its opinion as representative of its readership, then we must conclude that the educated élite of Vienna continued to be very pro-German and continued to claim Vienna as a German city, with all that that entailed. The paper defended the Protestant Germans in Vienna even more stoutly than it defended Jews, a characteristic sign; Vienna would continue to be German until the Danube ceased flowing from the Black Forest: 'This city will remain German as long as the Germans themselves, in character and conviction, do not sink to the level of moral cripples.'[127] The real Vienna, as far as the *Neue Freie Presse* was concerned, was still German Vienna, German because liberal and decent. For its German Bohemian editors, Bacher and Benedikt, the baroque Vienna was, at least in the editorials, something which should not be allowed to spoil the real, liberal Vienna, the centre of German culture.

The other Vienna was hated by liberal Jews. Sigmund Mayer, as Boyer has remarked, revealed a perfect contempt for the *Kleinbürgertum* which comprised such a large part of Vienna's population.[128] The lower middle class was, for him, the rabble.[129] His view of the classes above him was not much more respectful. He viewed the high aristocracy as having retreated into an exclusive shell, where culture was without substance and conversation banal.[130] This disrespectful attitude was repeated in the views of Ludwig von Mises, himself the son of an ennobled Jewish engineer, who blamed the demise of the Monarchy on the magnates of the Sudetenland.[131] The *Neue Freie Presse*, for all its character as part of the Establishment,

---

[125] Zuckerkandl, *Österreich Intim*, p. 80.

[126] Adam Wandruczka, *Geschichte einer Zeitung: das Schicksal der 'Presse' und der 'Neuen Freien Presse' von 1848 zur Zweiten Republik* (Vienna 1958) pp. 99–101. Cf. Zweig, *Welt von Gestern*, pp. 122ff.; George Clare, *Last Waltz in Vienna* (London 1981) p. 85; Canetti, *Die gerettete Zunge*, p. 36.

[127] 'Diese Stadt wird deutsch bleiben, so lange nicht die Deutschen selbst in Charakter und Gesinnung bis zur Gemeinheit verkrüppeln.' *NFPm* 18 July 1899 p. 1. On Protestants, *NFPm* 29 October 1899 p. 1.

[128] Boyer, *Political Radicalism*, pp. 82–3.

[129] Mayer, *Ein jüdischer Kaufmann*, pp. 249–52; Mayer, *Die Wiener Juden*, pp. 379–80.

[130] Mayer, *Die Wiener Juden*, p. 297.

[131] Ludwig von Mises, *Erinnerungen* (Stuttgart 1978) pp. 17–18.

was nevertheless opposed to the 'aristocratic principle'.[132] What it and its readership admired was not *Adel*, but *Menschenadel*. In fact, as Ilsa Barea pointed out, there was a tendency among Jews to regard any aristocrat as slightly stupid, as is Georg von Wergenthin's fate in *Der Weg ins Freie*.[133] Jews of the educated élite in Vienna were not the enthusiastic imitators of aristocratic culture they have sometimes been made out to be. Far from acceding to Vienna's hedonism, the liberal press was constantly trying to restore the bourgeois tradition in Vienna.[134] Faced with the other Vienna, Jews tried to preserve the German city to which they had come.

COEXISTING CULTURES

In a sense they were right because the Vienna that was liberal and devoted to German culture existed side by side with the other Catholic, feudal and hedonistic Vienna. As Polgar intimated, it was the atmosphere of the Heuriger which typified the 'Urariertum' of Vienna.[135] The inns in Grinzing or the other small surrounding villages were the perfect setting for Ödön von Horváth's play *Geschichten aus dem Wienerwald*, where *Gemütlichkeit* only thinly veiled the hatred, prejudice and small-mindedness of the Viennese *Kleinbürgertum*.[136] Jews, on the other hand, were mainly to be found in the coffee-house. While it is wise not to over-estimate here, it does seem that, as we have seen, in several of the more famous literary coffee-houses in the inner city and in most of the coffee-houses of the Leopoldstadt, Jews made up a majority of customers.[137] While the coffee-house itself could seem like a 'Capua of the mind' to someone such as Herzl, it was undoubtedly bourgeois in its style with desks for businessmen, its array of newspapers, and above all its tradition of witty conversation, all of which put it worlds away from the Heuriger.[138] The one was the characteristic preserve of the Jewish bourgeoisie, the other that of the rest.

The Vienna into which Jews assimilated was also different from that which a Czech immigrant would meet. Karl Renner includes in his memoirs the biography of a Viennese landlord, who had come to the city as a shoemaker's apprentice from Bohemia, married a cook with savings,

---

[132] Morton, *A Nervous Splendour*, p. 167; *NFPm* 7 August 1895 p. 1.

[133] Barea, *Vienna*, p. 329; Arthur Schnitzler, *Der Weg ins Freie* (Frankfurt-on-Main 1978) pp. 129–30.

[134] For instance, *NFPm* 3 March 1895 p. 1.   [135] Polgar, *Sperrsitz*, p. 36.

[136] Ödön von Horvàth, *Tales from the Vienna Woods* (London 1977).

[137] See the report on the Christian Social riot in the Leopoldstadt, *NFPm* 3 December 1895 p. 6; also *NFPm* 23 March 1897 p. 2.

[138] On Herzl's attitude, see *NFPm* 7 March 1897 p. 1; on the bourgeois style of the coffee-house, *Das Wiener Kaffeehaus*, with an introduction by Hans Weigel (Vienna 1978) p. 29.

and set up his own shop. Through clever speculation on the land market he had become a wealthy *Hausbesitzer*. He then settled down to the life of a typical Viennese *Bürger*, sending his sons off to Gymnasium to become reserve officers and *Beamten*. They had been taught to play the violin as the daughter had been taught to play the piano. The family had also acquired a villa. For aesthetic pleasures there was the occasional visit to the Burgtheater, but the real source of their aesthetic satisfaction was the singer at the Heuriger, and nothing more demanding than that.[139] This kind of bourgeoisie was not the *Bildungsbürgertum* which provided Vienna at the turn of the century with its audience, and it was quite different from the Jewish bourgeoisie, whose form of assimilation put more emphasis on high culture and on entry into the liberal professions rather than official-dom.[140] The Jewish and non-Jewish bourgeoisie followed different patterns of social mobility, and in that sense were separate social entities.

This again raises the question of the accuracy of Schorske's claim that the Jewish assimilation into Viennese society and culture was merely a special case of a general phenomenon, or whether it was something quite different from the experience of other groups assimilating into Vienna.[141] Schorske, as I understand him, claims that the educated bourgeoisie in Vienna, including the Jews, assimilated into a 'pre-existing aristocratic culture of grace', albeit in distorted form, and that the Jewish dedication to culture was really only a consequence of their belonging to the Viennese bourgeoisie.[142] Although much is a matter of language and emphasis, this approach seems to me a sophisticated misunderstanding of events. As we have seen, the salon culture of Vienna was actually a Jewish import from Berlin, independent of the Austrian aristocracy. Further, the Jews had an independent drive to learning, to all that was *das Geistige*. Stefan Zweig had no trouble including aesthetics here, and it was his opinion that Jews had blossomed in Vienna because the environment had allowed them to develop their already present cultural ambitions.[143] There was a Jewish element.

While charitable interpretations of Schorske might find no basic contradiction here, there is still the vexed question of whether the culture of the bourgeoisie was really based on an aristocratic model, and also whether it is true that the values of the *Jewish* bourgeoisie were really only the same as the rest of bourgeois Vienna. Schorske relates how the children of the liberal bourgeoisie in Vienna acquired a great aesthetic culture:

---

[139] Barea, *Vienna*, p. 322.
[140] Mayer, *Ein jüdischer Kaufmann*, pp. 249–50; Ardelt, *Friedrich Adler*, pp. 21, 239.
[141] Schorske, *Fin-de-Siècle Vienna*, p. 149.
[142] *Ibid.* pp. 10, 148.   [143] Zweig, *Welt von Gestern*, p. 25.

Beginning roughly in the 1860s, two generations of well-to-do children were reared in the museums, theatres, and concert halls of the new Ringstrasse. They acquired aesthetic culture not, as their fathers did, as an ornament of life, or a badge of status, but as the air they breathed.[144]

That may well be true, but which culture did they acquire? Viktor Weisskopf, in recounting his childhood and that of the Jewish liberal bourgeoisie in general, has said:

What was most important was what was called 'Bildung'. That is to say a detailed knowledge of and emotional relation to the treasures of German culture, the works of Goethe, Schiller and Lessing, and the music of Bach, Mozart and Beethoven. We often went to the museum of classical art: we were force-fed the traditional Victorian values.[145]

The world of the cultured liberal Jewish bourgeoisie was thus not an aristocratic culture of hedonism, nor that of the Heuriger, but precisely the culture which they had wanted to enter in the first place: German classical culture. The connections and apparent similarities to a culture of grace were superficial. This culture remained a culture of the mind rather than of the senses. Schorske himself sees how Herzl took aristocratic forms and used them for rational goals.[146] The former were superficial, the latter were what counted.

Schorske sees the ground for the cultural blossoming of *fin-de-siècle* Vienna in what he terms the 'second society', which included *haute bourgeoisie* and high officialdom.[147] Certainly the *Hofrat*, the symbolic figure of the latter group, came much closer to the Jewish ideal of social prestige *and* education than most other Viennese models. It is true that there was a non-Jewish educated élite, especially within the higher bureaucracy which shared the Jewish dedication to culture as *Bildung*.[148] Yet even this group was not going to be the source of any great cultural explosion. The bureaucrat in Vienna, while he might be cultured, regarded his culture as part of his social standing, nothing more. The *Hofrat* too, though cultured, was also a party to the Viennese predilection not to think – he followed rules, like all bureaucrats.[149]

This was quite different from the attitude of the Jewish bourgeois, as was evident when the daughters of the two groups went to the same school,

[144] Schorske, *Fin-de-Siècle Vienna*, p. 298.

[145] 'Das wichtigste war, was man "Bildung" nannte, nämlich eine ausführliche Kenntnis und emotionelle Beziehung zum deutschen Kulturgut, die Werke von Goethe, Schiller, Lessing und die Musik von Bach, Mozart und Beethoven. Man ging viel in die Museen der klassischen Kunst; kurz und gut, man wurde mit den traditionellen viktorianischen Werten getränkt.' Viktor F. Weisskopf, 'Einige persönliche Eindrücke von Österreich', speech given at Schloss Duino, 20 September 1983 (MSS) p. 2.

[146] Schorske, *Fin-de-Siècle Vienna*, p. 165.   [147] *Ibid.* p. 45.

[148] Cf. Schorske, *Fin-de-Siècle Vienna*, pp. 289ff.

[149] Cf. Peter F. Drucker, *Adventures of a Bystander* (London 1979) pp. 33–4.

the Beamtentöchterschule, which Käthe Leichter attended. She describes the way in which the bureaucrats' daughters were intentionally kept childlike and brought up to be above all well-ordered, as their fathers had to be, their exercise books as spotlessly clean as officials' documents. The Jewish girls, though totally assimilated, were quite different. At first the difference was to be seen only in the way that the Jewish girls were slightly better dressed. Then the Jewish girls experienced puberty earlier, and this physical difference was soon followed by a totally different attitude to culture, the officials' daughters reading girls' books, the Jewish girls reading Wilde and Schnitzler. Leichter lived in both these worlds, but saw the immense gulf between them: 'With my friends I discussed "last things", shared with them my experiences from books, poetry, nature and music. With the officials' daughters I played "mother and child".'[150] The indications are that this kind of difference remained when these girls grew up. If this is a fair reflection of the lifestyle of *hofrätlich* society in comparison to the Jewish bourgeoisie, then the claim that Jews shared the same set of values with this group cannot be accepted.[151] Though closer than the aristocratic attitude to culture, the *hofrätlich* approach was still worlds apart from the Jewish.

Many Jews rejected out of hand the aspects of Vienna which went against the set of values which they had brought with them from the provinces. There was a feeling that they were defending the values of Vienna's German civilization against the Viennese. Figures such as Julius Ofner and Otto Bauer sniped at the institutionalizing of *Schlamperei*, as did Mahler.[152] Kraus, from Bohemia, lambasted everyone involved for their connivance in the travesty of a society and state called Austria, and for the existence of a moral sewer called Vienna, where nothing and no one was honest, where everything was a charade.[153]

In the same manner, if you came from a traditional Jewish background such as that of Manès Sperber, there was only one real response to Vienna. As he was watching the grand procession which accompanied the funeral

---

[150] 'Mit meinen Freundinnen diskutierte ich über letzte Dinge, teilte mit ihnen Erlebnisse mit Büchern, Lyrik, Natur und Musik. Mit den Beamtentöchtern spielte ich Mutter und Kind...' *Käthe Leichter*, pp. 306–9.

[151] Cf. Bahr, *Selbstbildnis*, pp. 21–2, on an official's attitude to his daughter's upbringing.

[152] On Ofner, *Käthe Leichter*, p. 356; on Bauer, Richard Kola, *Rückblick ins Gestrige: Erlebtes und Empfundenes* (Vienna 1922) p. 273; on Mahler, Alma Mahler, *Gustav Mahler: Memories and Letters* (London 1968) p. 115.

[153] Janik, 'Creative Milieux', p. 106, classes Kraus as a 'professional anti-Viennese'. On Kraus' views on Viennese hierarchism and the 'ethos of *Gemütlichkeit*', see Edward Timms, *Karl Kraus: Apocalyptic Satirist: Culture and Catastrophe in Habsburg Vienna* (London 1986) pp. 212–4, 331. For Victor Adler's view of *Gemütlichkeit* see Josef Weidenholzer, 'Trinkende und denkende Arbeiter' in A. Pfabigan, ed., *Ornament und Askese im Zeitgeist des Wien der Jahrhundertwende* (Vienna 1985) pp. 286–7.

of Francis Joseph in 1916, he began to get bored with all the impressive finery and glittering costumes, and he was reminded of his past:

While my tired eyes apathetically followed the progress of the Magyar nobles from Slovakia, I thought with pride of my great-grandfather, who had refused all honours, but who nevertheless had been respected by all, even the Ukrainians, and strangers as well. He had despised everything which was mere appearance and not authentic. And now I had seen the splendour of centuries go by, and it had in the end bored me. I now realized that this was not what was important, for it could only have a superficial meaning.[154]

As he says elsewhere, the Jews had seen Vienna as a new Jerusalem; 'now reality had unmasked and destroyed the dream'.[155]

Sperber, in rejecting 'die Vermengung von echt und unecht', was following a great tradition of Jews, brought up in the same puritan tradition, who demanded the separation of what was real from what was illusion. Vienna, in offering a model of a culture and society which went against the principles of truth, moral responsibility and integrity which the Jews had transferred to their German culture and brought with them to Vienna, provided the necessary environment out of which the thought of Kraus or Weininger, Freud or Schoenberg or even Schnitzler could spring. In the end, what we call Viennese culture is hardly that at all. The truly great contribution to modern thought, the work of Freud or Kraus, is nothing other than a culture which was produced *against* its Viennese environment. Individuals such as Freud were, in many ways, trying to counter the threat to the life of the mind which Vienna symbolized. Before we can discuss how they did this, it would be as well to round off our picture of Vienna with another of its central aspects: antisemitism.

[154] Sperber, *Die Wasserträger Gottes*, p. 137.   [155] Sperber, *Masks of Loneliness*, p. x.

≫ 12 ≪

Antisemitism

AN ENDEMIC HOSTILITY

In coming to terms with Vienna, Jews after 1895 had to face one salient fact: Vienna was the only European capital at the time to have an elected antisemitic municipal government.[1] Vienna was not only not German, it was also anti-Jewish. There had always been hatred of the Jews in central European culture since the Middle Ages. Until the Enlightenment the Jews were a feared and despised people.[2] While with the triumph of liberalism the legal oppression of the Jews disappeared, the antipathy to them did not. The Jew continued to be stereotyped as the evil instrument of Mammon to the point where he became almost an archetype.[3] When Richard Kola went to the Prater in 1885 it was a matter of course that the finale of the puppet show would be Hanswurst beating 'den Juden' to death.[4] This could appear to Kola at the time as harmless fun, but such symbolism did point to an antipathy which ran right through the whole of society.[5] It only needed careful exploitation to produce results.

In Austria antisemitism of a very mild form, but still antisemitism, began at the top. Austria was a Catholic land and the Habsburg Establishment intended it to remain so. This expressed itself in the higher bureaucracy, the army and the diplomatic service by a virtual ban on professing Jews, despite on paper the Jews having gained full rights in 1867.[6] Even the Liberals appear to have been chary of employing Jews in government posts

---

[1] Cf. *Neue Freie Presse*, morning edition (*NFPm*) 24 September 1895 p. 1.

[2] Friedrich Heer, *God's First Love* (London 1970) pp. 23ff; Hans Kohn, *Kraus, Schnitzler und Weininger: aus dem jüdischen Wien der Jahrhundertwende* (Tuebingen 1962) p. 25.

[3] Cf. Herzl's comment in 1887: 'nowadays the Jew is despised only for having a crooked nose, or for being a plutocrat even when he happens to be a pauper'. Quoted in Alex Bein, *Theodore Herzl* (London 1957) p. 57.

[4] Richard Kola, *Rückblick ins Gestrige: Erlebtes und Empfundenes* (Vienna 1922) p. 38.

[5] Felix Braun, *Das Licht der Welt* (Vienna 1962) pp. 35–6.

[6] A. J. May, *The Habsburg Monarchy* (London 1951) p. 180; Ilsa Barea, *Vienna* (London 1966) p. 302; Joseph S. Bloch, *Erinnerungen aus meinem Leben* (Vienna 1922) pp. 160–2; Peter F. Drucker, *Adventures of a Bystander* (London 1979) p. 34.

for fear of antagonizing their voters.[7] Jews were definitely affected by this sort of unofficial official religious antisemitism. Theodor Gomperz had seen his academic career suffer an artificial caesura due to the Concordat of 1855, and in 1872 he still doubted his acceptability as a Jew in what he insisted were still basically denominational German universities (including Vienna).[8] Mahler, Herzl and Freud all had similar experiences in their careers; being Jewish was not good if you wanted to get on.[9]

The simple remedy for this was conversion. In the legal profession there were a great many conversions, and in the army the evidence suggests a definite link between conversion and promotion.[10] The same was true in the academic world and it was plain that conversion was a great boost to any career.[11] Many a young student would naturally consider this move seriously, but more often than not, as in the case of Sigmund Mayer, obstacles of family tradition prevented the move from being carried through.[12] To convert was not such an easy thing for Jews to do.[13]

[7] John W. Boyer, *Political Radicalism in Late Imperial Vienna* (Chicago 1981) p. 84; Sigmund Mayer, *Die Wiener Juden: Kommerz, Kultur, Politik 1700–1900* (Vienna 1918) pp. 476–9; also see *NFPm* 13 March 1895 p. 1.

[8] Theodor Gomperz, *Essays und Erinnerungen* (Stuttgart 1905) p. 24; *Theodor Gomperz: ein Gelehrtenleben im Bürgertum der Franz-Josephszeit*, eds. H. Gomperz and R. A. Kann (Vienna 1974) pp. 65–8. Also see S.T. 'Verjudet' in *Die Welt*, 22 December 1899, no. 51, p. 2.

[9] Kurt Blaukopf, *Mahler: a Documentary Study* (London 1976) p. 200; Bein, *Herzl*, p. 47; R. W. Clark, *Freud: the Man and the Cause* (London 1980) pp. 202–10; Carl E. Schorske, *Fin-de-Siècle Vienna: Politics and Culture* (London 1980) pp. 184–6; Drucker, *Adventures*, pp. 86–8.

[10] Franz Kobler, 'The Contribution of Austrian Jews to Jurisprudence' in Josef Fraenkel, ed., *The Jews of Austria: Essays on their Life, History and Destruction* (London 1967) p. 29; Boyer, *Political Radicalism*, p. 86. On the army, my own calculations from the lists of personnel in Moritz Frühling, *Biographisches Handbuch der in der k.u.k. österr.ungar. Armee und Kriegsmarine aktiv gedienten Offiziere, Ärzte, Truppen-Rechnungs-Führer und sonstigen Militärbeamten jüdischen Stammes* (Vienna 1911), show the following: in the army's top four ranks 58 per cent of Jews were converts; in the next four ranks, from *Major* to *Leutnant*, only 25 per cent; amongst army doctors figures are 19 per cent for the top four ranks, 8 per cent for lower ranks; in the army administration 20 per cent for the top three ranks, 7 per cent for the lower four. These figures may well be affected by the fact that being in a lower rank provides a greater anonymity, but they are an indication of the general trend.

[11] Bloch, *Erinnerungen*, p. 261; Blaukopf, *Mahler: a Documentary Study*, p. 208. Siegfried Lipiner wrote to his friend Moritz Necker the following: 'Es ist für dich gerade jetzt höchst wünschenswert und unter Zuständen von entscheidender Wichtigkeit, dein verfluchtes Judentum loszuwerden. Ich habe dir bereits gesagt, wie du das kannst, ohne deinem Gewissen irgendwie Gewalt anzuthun. Ich bitte dich: denke daran. Bei jedem Gesuche, sei es in Salzburg oder in Wien oder wo immer, ist diese schmerzliche "Confessions" rubrik verhängnisvoll.' Lipiner, letter to M. Necker, 26 August 1885, in Wiener Stadtbibliothek, I.N.142.540.

[12] Sigmund Mayer, *Ein jüdischer Kaufmann 1831–1911: Lebenserinnerungen* (Leipzig 1911) p. 159.

[13] Cf. Heinrich Jaques, *Denkschrift über die Stellung der Juden in Österreich* (Vienna 1859) pp. 40–2.

Although there were those who, either out of conviction or to improve career prospects, did take the formal step of baptism, for most Jews it was too much to expect; among many it was bitterly resented that they should sacrifice their heritage, or even their freedom of choice, for a position which was rightfully theirs.[14] Some saw it as merely too difficult socially; others saw conversion as a betrayal, a surrender to the pressures of Gentile society.[15] The consequence of such attitudes was that, although Vienna was far ahead of every other city in the Monarchy in this respect with over 9,000 conversions in the period 1868–1903, most Jewish families remained Jewish.[16]

Most Jews were happy to go along with the system. Although the civil service was largely closed to them, there was the flourishing liberal press and there were the liberal professions. In the 1860s and 1870s Jews could consider becoming politicians, and all kinds of opportunities existed for the enterprising young man in the Austrian economy, despite the *Krach* of 1873.[17] Money made there could be enjoyed in one of the major cultural centres of Germany and Europe in an atmosphere of peaceful co-existence and prosperity, with the added joy of seeing the new age of progress materialize before one in the *Ringstrasse*. Above all, the Jewish question was hardly mentioned, as Sigmund Mayer emphasized.[18] The lull afforded the Jews did not last long. By the early 1880s Jew-hatred had resurfaced in the modern form of antisemitism; it was no longer a petty bureaucratic annoyance or an endemic but harmless instinct, but something which was to destroy the whole fabric of the assimilation.

FROM CULTURAL TO RACIAL ANTISEMITISM

The first form of antisemitism to make a real impact on Austrian politics was the German nationalist variant of Schönerer and the student radicals from the late 1870s onwards.[19] It stemmed from the cultural antisemitism which has already been mentioned in the context of the Jewish wish for assimilation. Cultural German antisemitism based itself on the concept of the Jew as an idea, going back at least to the theories of Grattenauer

---

[14] Paul Lazarsfeld refused conversion (in order to get a good post in the artillery during the First World War) simply on the principle of not being forced against his will to do something. Interview with Paul Neurath, 17 May 1983, Vienna. (Neurath was a pupil of Lazarsfeld.)

[15] Braun, *Das Licht der Welt*, p. 36; Stella Klein-Löw, *Erinnerungen: Erlebtes und Gedachtes* (Vienna 1980) p. 13; *Gomperz: ein Gelehrtenleben*, p. 24.

[16] Jakob Thon, *Die Juden in Österreich* (Berlin 1908) pp. 69–70; Ivar Oxaal, *The Jews of Pre-1914 Vienna: Two Working Papers* (Hull 1981) p. 95.   [17] Clark, *Freud*, pp. 27–8.

[18] Mayer, *Ein jüdischer Kaufmann*, pp. 236, 289; Boyer, *Political Radicalism*, p. 77.

[19] Mayer, *Ein jüdischer Kaufmann*, p. 280; Wolfgang Häusler, 'Toleranz, Emanzipation und Antisemitismus' in N. Vielmetti, Drabek, Häusler, Stuhlpfarrer, *Das österreichische Judentum* (Vienna 1974) p. 112; Ilsa Barea, *Vienna*, p. 312.

around 1800. There developed an image of the Jew as all that the Germans hated, and by the process of making Jewishness 'a psychological quality' the actual empirical Jew could be brushed aside as irrelevant.[20] 'Jewish' came to be shorthand for capitalist and rationalist and 'the Jew' became a commonplace in German culture, appearing in the work of Wagner, Schopenhauer and others.[21]

The point about cultural antisemitism for a Jewish individual was that, because Jewishness was a psychological quality, it was there to be overcome. If one really wanted to be German, there was no obvious barrier to this: as far as 'Aryans' such as Wagner and H. S. Chamberlain were concerned, it was quite possible for the Jewish individual to overcome 'the Jew' in himself.[22] For many of the central figures in Viennese culture at the turn of the century their Jewish character was something bad. According to this type of cultural antisemitism, however, it could be overcome.[23] To be a 'Jewish self-hater' was not, therefore, necessarily the hopeless situation which it has usually been described as being.

The problem for these people was that cultural antisemitism was replaced by racial antisemitism in the circles which counted, the German National Burschenschaften. Antisemitism in these student bodies is supposed to have been sparked off by a speech in 1875 by the unfortunate Theodor Billroth.[24] Having acquired such slogans as 'Überfremdung der Universität', the Burschenschaften started expelling Jewish members from as early as 1877.[25] In 1881 this racial antisemitism received its theoretical backbone in Eugen Dühring's *Die Judenfrage als Racen-, Sitten-, und Kulturfrage* [sic], which denied the possibility of Jews ever becoming Germans.[26] It was a death blow to the Jewish involvement in German Nationalism. During the early 1880s all those Jews such as Adler,

[20] Hannah Arendt, 'Privileged Jews' in *Jewish Social Studies (JSS)* VIII 1946, p. 27.

[21] George L. Mosse, *Germans and Jews: the Right, the Left and the Search for a 'Third Force' in Pre-Nazi Germany* (London 1971) p. 37; William McGrath, *Dionysian Art and Populist Politics in Austria* (New Haven 1974) p. 6; P. G. J. Pulzer, *The Rise of Political Antisemitism in Germany and Austria* (New York 1964) p. 26; Heer, *God's First Love*, pp. 218–9.

[22] On Wagner it may be noted that one of Wagner's closest associates, Hermann Levi, was, as his name suggests, Jewish by descent: Sigmund Kaznelson, *Juden im deutschen Kulturbereich* (Berlin 1962) p. 193. A figure of note is that of Ernst von Wolzogen, the Berlin impresario, who was a strong antisemite but reserved a softspot for 'Jews of talent' with the result that many of his employees and his main collaborator, Oskar Straus, were Jewish: H. H. Stuckenschmidt, *Schoenberg: his Life, World and Work* (London 1977) p. 52. Also see Mosse, *Germans and Jews*, p. 19.

[23] Cf. the description of Hermann Schwarzwald by Peter Drucker in *Adventures*, pp. 32–3.

[24] Klaus Lohrmann, ed., *1,000 Jahre österreichisches Judentum* (Eisenstadt 1982) pp. 161–2, 252; Rudolf G. Ardelt, *Friedrich Adler: Probleme einer Persönlichkeitsentwicklung um die Jahrhundertwende* (Vienna 1984) p. 27; Dennis B. Klein, *The Jewish Origins of the Psychoanalytic Movement* (New York 1981) p. 52.   [25] Ardelt, *Friedrich Adler*, p. 27.

[26] See Herzl's reaction, quoted in Ruth Burstyn, 'Theodor Herzl – Krisenzeit und Selbstbesinnung' in Lohrmann, *1,000 Jahre*, p. 229; Bein, *Herzl*, pp. 36–7.

Friedjung, Herzl and Freud who had once been members of German National organizations either resigned or were kicked out.[27] Antisemitic clauses were added to the Linz Programme in 1885 and in 1896 came the greatest insult of all, when the *Waidhofener Beschluss* declared all Jews by descent to be 'satisfaktionsunfähig' because born without honour.[28] The admirers of the German *Volk* had been excluded by the very group who should have been their closest ally, the German national intelligentsia.

The emergence of a strong racial antisemitism was a nightmare for the young men of the Jewish cultural élite, for it meant, as Schnitzler graphically described in the case of Herzl, a total rejection by their social peers.[29] Much has been made of the political weakness and insignificance of Schönerer's brand of racial antisemitism, and it is true that it never posed a serious threat to Austria's Jews. Yet to dismiss the racial antisemites thus as unimportant would be to disregard the fact that they were very powerful at exactly the most crucial point, as far as Jews in the cultural élite were concerned, in the student body of the German university – the group of future teachers and officials.[30] German National antisemitism tore the cultural élite apart. When it is added that the other great area of German National antisemitism was in the German Bohemian borderlands, then it will be plain that racial antisemitism not only took away the chance of the Jews to assimilate into the society of which they had dreamed, but also destroyed the empirical basis of that society.[31] By the end of the Monarchy the hope of a German-Jewish symbiosis on the lines which Kompert had envisaged was faced with the fact that, in exactly those groups which had stood for the progress of freedom and reason, the Sudeten Germans and the German intelligentsia of the university, appeared the greatest support for the idea which threatened all the true values of German culture – racial antisemitism.

[27] Jonny Moser, 'Von der antisemitischen Bewegung zum Holocaust' in Lohrmann, *1,000 Jahre*, p. 253–4; McGrath, *Dionysian Art*, pp. 175–6, 197–8; Klein, *The Jewish Origins of the Psychoanalytic Movement*, pp. 54–5; Bein, *Herzl*, p. 40.

[28] Moser, 'Von der antisemitischen Bewegung', p. 253; Arthur Schnitzler, *Jugend in Wien* (Frankfurt-on-Main 1981) pp. 152–3; *NFPm* 13 March 1896 p. 5.

[29] Schnitzler, *Jugend*, p. 153; also see Friedrich Heer's comments in Norbert Leser, ed., *Das geistige Leben Wiens in der Zwischenkriegszeit* (Vienna 1981) p. 302.

[30] Cf. the comments of Schalit, leader of *Kadimah*: 'diese deutsch-nationalen Studenten werden ja einst die Jugend erziehen, sie werden Recht sprechen, sie werden in der Verwaltung sitzen, sie repräsentieren die künftige Gesellschaft'. Reported in *NFPm* 17 March 1896 p. 6.

[31] Mayer, *Die Wiener Juden*, p. 473; Pulzer, *The Rise of Political Antisemitism*, pp. 207–11. Also see Berthold Feiwel, 'Die Juden in Mähren' in *Die Welt*, 17 June 1898, no. 24, p. 8.

CHRISTIAN SOCIAL ANTISEMITISM

In Vienna racial antisemitism in its pure form was not very successful, but this was because Vienna's own brand of antisemitism, that of the Christian Socials, was tremendously successful. John Boyer has written a comprehensive account of the social history of the political movement.[32] He tells how social and economic grievances formed the basis of the movement's electoral success; the details of this do not directly concern us here. What is important to note is that all the anger and sense of grievance which the movement channelled was directed against one group above all: the Jews.

From its inception in 1880 with Buschenhagen's meeting to protest against the threat to business from Jewish pedlars, the Christian Social movement was openly antisemitic.[33] It was the use of the native Jew-hatred which provided Lueger and his allies with the crucial lever against the Liberals in Vienna. Antisemitism was the one way to unite the polyglot populace of Vienna, for it offered a way in which the Viennese could themselves assimilate and unify while denying the Jews the right to belong.[34] When immigrants came to Vienna they could hide behind the picture of the Jew as an outsider and thus see themselves as on the inside. Eduard Suess made just this point in 1895, that antisemitism was a result of the assimilation of the whole city, a fact to which Schnitzler also alluded in *Der Weg ins Freie*.[35] Although many Viennese might really be 'entnationalisiert' Czechs, they shared with other Viennese the anti-semitism native to Austrian, Ruthenian, Hungarian and Polish society where they had originated.[36] If this antisemitism could be used intelligently it could galvanize the city. Antisemitism was the common denominator with which all members of the rag-bag Christian Social coalition, renegade Liberals, Democrats, German Nationals, Clericals, artisans' leaders, could agree. The favourable response in wide swathes of the electorate meant that it was the exploitation of this pre-Enlightenment prejudice which was the main tool in destroying the Liberals.[37] The 'key' of politics may have been a new one but the tune was very old indeed.[38]

[32] John W. Boyer, *Political Radicalism in Late Imperial Vienna* (Chicago 1981).
[33] *Ibid.* p. 62.
[34] Cf. Manes Sperber, *Die Wasserträger Gottes* (Munich 1983) p. 154, for this phenomenon in his Ruthenian teacher.
[35] Suess is reported in *NFPm* 29 March 1895 p. 5; Arthur Schnitzler, *Der Weg ins Freie* (Frankfurt-on-Main 1978) p. 92.
[36] Mayer, *Ein jüdischer Kaufmann*, p. 281.
[37] Cf. *NFPm* 19 June 1896 p. 1; Brunner's comments in *NFPm* 10 July 1897 p. 6; Friedrich Kick's comments in *NFPm* 16 May 1899 p. 2; cf. Christoph Stölzl, *Kafkas böses Böhmen: Zur Sozialgeschichte eines Prager Juden* (Munich 1975) pp. 45–6.
[38] Cf. Schorske, *Fin-de-Siècle Vienna*, p. 116.

The nature of Christian Social antisemitism reflected its constituency, and since that constituency was so varied, so was the antisemitism. This led to a great deal of confusion, then and now. Whereas the Waidhofen type of antisemitism was at least clear, Viennese antisemitism was true to its place of origin in its total ambiguity. It has been said that it was a religiously based antisemitism, but it was initially antagonistic to the Catholic hierarchy, and its main base of support in the Church, the lower clergy, reflected not the official antisemitism of the Establishment (already discussed), but that of the Austrian peasantry.[39] However, this endemic variety had apart from the stereotype no clear idea of what a Jew actually was. It was typical of Christian Socials that, while one wing accepted conversion as a qualification to join the movement (a logical conclusion, if this was religious antisemitism), another did not.[40] Conversion certainly did not protect one from the antisemitic press, if, like Mautner-Markhof, one was the owner of a brewery – then economic antisemitism could take on a racial tinge.[41]

While it is true that moderate Christian Socials, such as Lueger, were not racial antisemites, one wing of the party, essential to the electoral success of the movement, came directly from the German Nationalist movement and retained an explicitly racial antisemitic attitude; this wing was tolerated by the leadership for many years.[42] It certainly seemed to the liberal press that racial hatred was far from being an insignificant part of the support for the Christian Socials, the *Neue Freie Presse* using the word *Racenhass* [sic] to explain Christian Social victories in the First Curia.[43] Christian Social antisemitism could be very confusing. A typical case is afforded by Pfarrer Deckert, a Catholic priest who openly preached rabid racial antisemitism to his flock in Währing.[44] Yet Deckert, the racial antisemite, had as his lawyer the (converted) Jew, Dr Max Löw. The liberal press picked up on the obvious inconsistency, but for the Viennese this did not seem to matter.[45] Nor was Deckert, in his racialist approach, an unacceptable face of Viennese antisemitism: in October 1899 the Christian Social-dominated Gemeinderat conferred on him the highest honour it could, the *Salvatormedaille*.[46]

The kind of confusion which Deckert's case exemplifies led some

[39] Boyer, *Political Radicalism*, pp. 167–82.
[40] For instance, the argument about Löw, the leader of the Christian Social railway workers' association, reported in *NFPm* 22 July 1897 p. 6.
[41] *NFPm* 2 September 1896 p. 6. [42] Boyer, *Political Radicalism*, pp. 237, 218ff.
[43] *NFPm* 27 September 1985 p. 1; on occasion the Christian Socials did display what can only be interpreted as a racial definition of who was a Jew, as in their attacks on the 'Jew' Eduard Suess, *NFPm* 5 January 1895 p. 4, and in their proposal to ban all Jews, by descent or religion, from the Landtag's committees, *NFPm* 30 December 1896 p. 1.
[44] Lohrmann, *1,000 Jahre*, pp. 396–400.
[45] *NFPm* 15 January 1896 pp. 1,7.   [46] *NFPm* 29 October 1899 p. 1.

Christian Socials to attempt a clarification. The Arbeiter Reformverein met in April 1899 to discuss proposals for a new electoral system. One speaker declared that their continued antisemitism took precedence over their being Christian Socials. Some compromise on the Jewish question was necessary, so two curiae were proposed for the electorate, a Jewish and a Christian; as for converted Jews, they would be included in the Christian curia, but they would only have an active vote, not a passive one. In other words, they could not stand as candidates. They were not exactly second-class citizens, but nor were they first-class.[47]

Most Christian Socials never went to the trouble of definition because the great advantage of Viennese antisemitism for its adherents was precisely that it left it to one's discretion whom one regarded as Jewish, that is to say whom one wanted to attack, and left one free to ignore what was happening in the rest of the party.[48] The inherent ambivalence in this antisemitism gave great scope for political manoeuvring. When Lueger said: 'Wer ein Jud' ist, bestimme ich' (I decide who is a Jew), he found a superb way of keeping the opposition on the run, for whom, if anyone, was he attacking? He could protest innocence of or claim credit for being antisemitic, always depending on whether it suited him.[49] At one point, in a speech full of the cleverest hypocrisy, he could even deny totally that his party had ever attacked the Jewish religion, despite their support of Deckert among other things.[50] Mark Twain, in a brilliant satire on this speech, came to the conclusion that the only proper response was 'Hoch Lueger! Hoch die Juden!'[51] Everyone knew that the real situation was the reverse: it was just that Lueger was milking the ambiguities of Viennese anti-semitism for all they were worth.

On the basis of speeches such as the one mentioned above, Lueger and his followers have often been regarded as a moderate, almost harmless form of antisemitism.[52] In the case of Lueger, the supreme opportunist, there is some truth in this: he did have Jewish friends and could be at times quite accommodating.[53] Yet his main characteristic was his opportunism,

[47] *NFPm* 25 April 1899 p. 2.
[48] Stella Klein-Löw reports an example of this kind of discretionary antisemitism in that the family maid was antisemitic 'nur waren wir für sie keine Juden'. Klein-Löw, *Erinnerungen*, p. 13. Such an approach allowed Lueger to canvass the support of *Ostjuden*, as opposed to the real enemy, the capitalist assimilants, while a prominent member of his party, Gregorig, could attack these very *Ostjuden*. *NFPm* 7 November 1896 p. 4; *NFPm* 19 January 1898 p. 6.
[49] Cf. George Clare, *Last Waltz in Vienna* (London 1981) pp. 21–3.
[50] *NFPm* 16 October 1897 p. 7.   [51] *NFPm* 17 October 1897 p. 6.
[52] Hannah Arendt, *Die verborgene Tradition* (Frankfurt-on-Main 1976) p. 79; M. Z. Rosensaft, 'Jews and Antisemites in Austria at the End of the Nineteenth Century' in *Leo Baeck Institute Yearbook (LBIY)* 1976, pp. 71–83; Boyer, *Political Radicalism*, p. 88.
[53] Mayer, *Die Wiener Juden*, p. 475; Guido Adler, *Wollen und Wirken* (Vienna 1935) p. 109.

and, if he did have Jewish friends, he also had political allies who acted as if all Jews were sub-human.[54] In the party as a whole there is evidence that a certain degree of co-operation was possible, in such things as guild politics and the administration of charitable foundations.[55] Strobach, the stand-in for Lueger as mayor, sent a wreath to the funeral of the president of the Jewish Kultusgemeinde, Gustav Simon, in January 1897.[56] These reassuring signs were, however, matched by others which gave no indication of any qualitative change in the attitude of Christian Socials to the Jews.[57] What the *Neue Freie Presse* called the 'Terrorismus der Rohheit' continued unabated after the electoral triumphs of 1895–7, with figures such as Gregorig, Schneider and Deckert demanding the annihilation of the Jews, and the deputy mayors, Strobach and Neumeyer, revealing an only marginally less extreme contempt and hatred for them.[58] The same attitudes were still present at the end of 1899 when, at the antisemitic meeting held in the Musikverein, the speakers claimed that Dreyfus' acceptance of his pardon signalled his guilt and that the Polna affair was based on a real ritual murder.[59] While it may well be true that the actions of the Christian Socials were pragmatic, the words they used were calculated to shock and it was these that the newspapers of the cultural élite reported.

The effects of this kind of rhetoric on the public at large were to be expected. The violence of the language did not, as is sometimes asserted, satisfy the antisemitic drives of the populace and was matched by violence in the streets. There were no mass murders, but for a Jewish child in Vienna the chances were that at one stage or another he was going to be beaten up because he was a Jew, and this was so even for children from fairly well-to-do families.[60] In adult life antisemitism meant an annoying, but defeatable, economic boycott, and the impossibility of getting any

---

[54] Barea, *Vienna*, p. 318; Bloch, *Erinnerungen*, pp. 240–2.

[55] Boyer, *Political Radicalism*, pp. 74–6; on charitable foundations, *NFPm* 19 November 1896 p. 1; *NFPm* 6 January 1897 p. 7; Joseph Oppenheimer exacted a certain degree of humour out of the situation by having the chairman of an imaginary Gemeinderat greet the donation of a Baron Hönigsmann with the following words: 'Ich glaube den Intentionen aller zu entsprechen, wenn ich den edlen Spender, welcher allerdings einer verworfenen Rasse angehört, den tiefgefühlten Dank ausspreche.' *NFPm* 2 June 1895 p. 6.

[56] *NFPm* 17 January 1897 p. 6.   [57] Cf. Braun, *Das Licht der Welt*, p. 90.

[58] *NFPm* 23 January 1895 p. 1; for Gregorig's rhetoric, see *NFPe* (evening edition) 8 January 1895 p. 2; *NFPm* 14 February 1896 p. 3; for Schneider, *NFPm* 14 February 1896 p. 3; *NFPm* 6 February 1895 p. 2; on Deckert, *NFPe* 20 May 1895 p. 1; on Strobach and Neumeyer, *NFPe* 21 December 1897 p. 2; *NFPe* 11 October 1897 p. 3.

[59] See *NFPm* 28 September 1899 p. 7.

[60] Braun, *Das Licht der Welt*, pp. 73, 90; Gottfried Reinhardt, *Der Liebhaber* (Munich 1976) p. 174; Klein, *The Jewish Origins of the Psychoanalytic Movement*, pp. 48–9; Barea, *Vienna*, p. 305.

contracts from the city council or of getting promoted, which hit families such as the Klaars.[61] Jews were banned from the Stadtrat, and the Gemeinderat denied the Freiwillige Rettungsgesellschaft (voluntary first-aid society) funds unless it dismissed its very large Jewish membership.[62]

These were all niggling restrictions, which did not affect the more wealthy very much. Yet the atmosphere created by the success of antisemitism was not good, and an avid reader of the *Neue Freie Presse* could find a whole catalogue of small incidents which revealed a very sad story of popular antisemitism, with people getting beaten up just because they were Jews and the judicial system doing precious little in their defence.[63] There were riots in Vienna against Jewish property and periodic cases of discrimination.[64] In 1898 there were large-scale anti-Jewish riots in Galicia, in 1899 riots against the 'pro-German' Jews in Bohemia, and then the beginning of the Polna affair.[65] When one considers that the Dreyfus affair was also filling the pages of the newspaper, then it becomes clear that the Jewish problem was a very considerable matter in the consciousness of the readership of the *Neue Freie Presse*, for they could not help but be reminded of it every time they picked up the newspaper.[66] The success of the Christian Social brand of antisemitism meant that it was now very difficult for Jews to ignore the Jewish problem.

A VIENNESE PHENOMENON

None of the physical results of antisemitism, the riots and the beatings, had much to do with the cultural élite in Vienna. The probable reaction to reading about such things in the paper would have been to think how fortunate one was not to be in the lower classes where most of the popular antisemitism appeared. Yet, while one could ignore what was going on in the Leopoldstadt, it was well-nigh impossible to disregard the fact that the

[61] Clare, *Last Waltz*, pp. 21–3; see *NFPe* 11 October 1897 p. 3; *NFPm* 4 March 1899 pp. 4–5.

[62] *NFPm* 28 May 1896 p. 1; *NFPm* 17 July 1896 p. 1.

[63] A variety of such cases can be found in the *Neue Freie Presse* on the following pages: 5 May 1895m p. 9; 7 June 1895m p. 6; 16 July 1895e p. 1; 27 July 1895m p. 7; 19 September 1895m p. 7; 4 October 1895m p. 1; 20 August 1896m p. 3; 22 August 1896e p. 31; 24 October 1896m p. 6; 30 March 1899e p. 1.

[64] See the following pages of the *Neue Freie Presse*: 29 June 1895m p. 10; 13 July 1895m pp. 6–7; 18 August 1895m pp. 3–4; 3 December 1895m p. 6; 4 November 1896e p. 3; 23 February 1897m p. 8; 23 March 1897m p. 2; 15 December 1897m p. 8; 6 July 1898e p. 2; 12 August 1898m p. 6.

[65] See the following pages of the *Neue Freie Presse*: 25 May 1898e p. 3 (and following days); 6 April 1899m p. 8; 22 September 1899m p. 7; 24 October 1899m p. 1. On the Polna (Hilsner) affair, see Ernst Rychnovsky, ed., *Masaryk und das Judentum* (Prague 1931) *passim*.

[66] Needless to say the Dreyfus affair is major news in the *Neue Freie Presse* from roughly October 1897 to September 1899.

new rulers of Vienna represented everything about the city which Jewish immigrants despised. Not only were they antisemitic, they were also Viennese in the worst sense, as far as German liberals were concerned, and they set about destroying the German liberal establishment in Vienna.

There was a definite air of philistinism about the Christian Socials with an innate distrust of the value of *Bildung*.[67] In 1896 they cut off the funds of the Volksbildungsverein (society for popular education) and continued to harass this attempt to spread 'Aufklärung' among the people.[68] They also attacked the independence of the teaching profession, even though the teachers had been one of their most important bases of support.[69] Not only was there an air of ignorance about the new rulers, they also held a far from unambiguous attitude to their, supposedly, German heritage. While a wing of the party had come from the German Nationalists, the party was also interested in gaining Czech votes. The result was that in October 1897 Lueger gave a ferociously German Nationalist speech in the Gemeinderat, and at the same time supported Badeni's language ordinances, the bane of German Nationalists and Liberals alike, in the Reichsrat.[70] Even worse than this betrayal of the German nation was the hostility to German culture, which expressed itself in the cutting off of funds to the Deutsche Schulverein (society for German schools) in May 1898, the sacred cow of German liberalism.[71]

The Christian Socials were Viennese in other respects. Lueger himself was the epitome of fine appearance, 'der schöne Karl', allied with a huge talent for hypocrisy and doublespeak, one of the great exponents of *Wiener Schmäh*.[72] For the liberal press, and hence for the liberal bourgeoisie, the Christian Social administration was seen as grossly inefficient and the agents of clerical reaction, the 'reactionary secret agents from Kalksburg'.[73] The Christian Social victory was seen as putting an end to the history of Vienna as a centre of progress, and jeopardizing the achievement of 'the wealth-producing Viennese bourgeoisie [Bürgertum]'.[74] German culture was threatened by the 'deutschfeindlich' Clericals, and Lueger's Germanness regarded as a sham.[75]

[67] Friedrich Heer, *Land in Strom der Zeit* (Vienna 1958) p. 295.
[68] *NFPm* 24 June 1896 p. 1; *NFPm* 15 October 1899 p. 1.
[69] *NFPm* 18 February 1898 p. 4; *NFPm* 24 February 1899 p. 1; also *NFPm* 23 September 1897 p. 5; *NFPm* 28 September 1897 p. 5.
[70] *NFPm* 23 October 1897 p. 7 (Lueger's speech); *NFPm* 17 July 1897 p. 6 (reluctance of the Gemeinderat to support Germans in Bohemia); *NFPm* 30 October 1897 p. 7 (Mittler's critique of Lueger's ambivalence).
[71] *NFPm* 18 May 1898 p. 1; *NFPm* 24 May 1895 p. 1.   [72] Barea, *Vienna*, p. 318.
[73] *NFPm* 23 September 1897 p. 5; *NFPm* 25 February 1899 p. 1; quotation comes from *NFPm* 4 July 1896 p. 1.
[74] *NFPm* 18 September 1895 p. 1; *NFPm* 29 November 1898 p. 1; *NFPm* 14 May 1895 p. 1.
[75] On the perceived threat of clericalism, see *NFPm* 2 July 1899 p. 1; *NFPm* 11 May 1899 p. 1; *NFPm* 23 August 1896 p. 1. On Lueger, *NFPm* 23 September 1897 p. 5.

Yet it was culture and civilization in general which the *Neue Freie Presse* claimed was under attack from the forces of reaction, of which the Viennese were only a part, but a large part.[76] When Philippovich was attacked in the Lower Austrian Landtag as a 'Geistesprotz' the *Neue Freie Presse* was scathing in its condemnation of the Christian Social attackers: 'Philistinism senses that it is the majority, therefore: Let us rid ourselves of culture! Away with science! Down with the teachers!'[77] In May 1895 the same newspaper saw the growth of the antisemitic movement as a huge plot to destroy freedom and all that was dear to the newspaper's heart. The aim was simply: 'to take every free institution, the influence of the middle classes, the political fruits of the progressive sciences, the moral effect of culture, and destroy them all'.[78] All that the Jews had ever come to Vienna for was disappearing before their very eyes.

The attitude of a Jewish liberal to the Viennese antisemites was well expressed by Joseph Oppenheimer in a satire which he wrote for the Sunday edition of the *Neue Freie Presse* in June 1895 called *Die letzte Sitzung*. It was a short skit on the dissolution of the Gemeinderat by the authorities in that month. Its target was the new majority on the council, the Christian Socials. It began with a description of the street violence and the hatred of the bourgeoisie which Lueger had unleashed, but this had its Viennese side to it. When you gave money to a beggar, the reply was a Viennese one: 'Every beggarwoman to whom you give a coin thanks you with the words: "Thank you most kindly, most honoured bloodsucker!"' Vienna's elaborate manners in this interpretation were just a charade. Then, when the antisemitic councillors arrive, they are addressed by the chairman (Lueger) in the broadest Viennese, but the minutes are taken down in *Hochdeutsch*. These people were not really proper Germans was the implication. When it comes to voting for a rise in teachers' pay the Liberals are for it, but the antisemites say: 'Go jump in the lake, we don't need any teachers, the children learn too much as it is.' The chairman tells them to shut up, reminding them that teachers are also voters. The clear message was that the Christian Socials were against culture and education, but they needed the teachers' votes and so were prepared to dissimulate. It was all very shabby and very Viennese.[79]

---

[76] *NFPm* 14 May 1895 p. 1 (use of the word *Bildungsfeindlichkeit*); *NFPm* 20 January 1898 p. 1 – the root of the reaction in Europe is seen as 'jene finstere Macht, welche in allen Ländern die Zwietracht nährt, um auf den Trümmern der Bildung und Cultur [sic] ihre eigene Herrschaft aufzurichten.'

[77] 'Die Unbildung fühlt sich in der Majorität, darum: Hinaus mit der Bildung! Fort mit der Wissenschaft! Kampf den Lehrern!' *NFPm* 11 May 1899 p. 1.

[78] 'Alle freien Einrichtungen, den Einfluss des Bürgerthums [sic], die politischen Früchte der fortschrittlichen Wissenschaften, die moralische Wirkung der Cultur [sic] auf das öffentliche Leben zu zerstören.' *NFPm* 31 May 1895 p. 1.

[79] 'Jede Bettlerin, der man eine Kupfermünze reicht, bedankt sich schon mit den Worten: Küss' die Hand, gnädiger Blutsauger!' 'Gengen's baden, mir brauchen keine Lehrer, die

In identifying the antisemites with all the worst characteristics of the Viennese Oppenheimer was only reflecting the shift in political identity which the triumph of the Christian Socials effected. Seen obversely, what had happened was that, through the power of antisemitic prejudice, the Christian Socials had been able to destroy and divide the liberal establishment by identifying 'Jew' in the mind of the electorate with all that their opponents stood for.[80] Anyone could be discredited by being associated with the Jews, a tactic sometimes used in the most absurd contexts, as with Bielohlawek's accusation that Schönerer was being financed by the Jews.[81] Usually, however, it was targeted on the Liberals, who were continually being called *Judenknecht* in the various representative chambers.[82] This tactic led the *Neue Freie Presse* to call the city council the place 'where every lesson of science and experience is routed by one word: Jew-slave'.[83] If the target was actually Jewish or of Jewish descent then the task was all the easier, for he could be discredited without having done or said anything and was thus at an automatic disadvantage.[84]

Such rhetorical identification of Liberal with Jew when coupled with large economic grievances had a devastating effect on Liberal support, as Boyer has shown. As discussed earlier, the electoral triumph of the Christian Socials was based on support not only from the lower-middle classes, but also among the bourgeois intelligentsia of teachers and officials, non-Jewish small shopkeepers and even among landlords, who voted in the First Curia. If Boyer's contentions are correct, then the non-Jewish part of the bourgeois classes voted largely for the Christian Socials, leaving the Jews and the remaining Liberal voters isolated.[85] According to my figures from the Gymnasien, moreover, the well-educated part of this out-group was largely Jewish.[86] It was thus Jews who stood in the forefront of the group most affected by the change in allegiance of what had seemed a Liberal ruling class. As the *Neue Freie Presse* noted in September 1895, it was 'the same citizenry' that had voted for liberalism which had now turned against it, with the teachers and officials leading the betrayal of

Kinder lernen eh zu viel.' Published in *NFPm* 2 June 1895 pp. 6–7. The young Karl Kraus also commented on the poor German of the Christian Socials, see *Die Wage* 29 January 1898, no. 5, p. 90.

[80] See Bloch, *Erinnerungen*, p. 247.   [81] *NFPe* 18 December 1897 p. 2.

[82] For instance, *NFPm* 2 June 1895 p. 7; *NFPm* 5 January 1895 p. 4.

[83] *NFPm* 4 August 1895 p. 1. Also see S.T. 'Verjudet' in *Die Welt*, 22 January 1899, no. 51, p. 2.

[84] See Ludwig von Mises, *Erinnerungen* (Stuttgart 1978) p. 17; Arthur Schnitzler, *Professor Bernhardi*, in *Dramen* vol. 6 (Fischer 1962) p. 156.

[85] Boyer, *Political Radicalism*, pp. 307, 349–57, 396–403; *NFPm* 2 April 1895 p. 1; *NFPm* 8 May 1895 p. 4.   [86] See above, p. 52 ff.

the cause.[87] The Jews had not changed, but the rest of the Viennese bourgeoisie had – or had they merely reverted to type?

JEWISH REACTIONS – THE FAILURE OF ASSIMILATION

Liberalism in Vienna had fallen apart because its electorate, for whatever reason, was quite prepared to sacrifice Liberal principles of freedom and equality and vote for a party which openly embraced discrimination against an ethnic minority, the Jews. The effect on the Jewish community was shattering. As Bloch put it, after having worshipped the goddess of liberalism for decades, tolerated her flirts with the opposition: 'One day he awoke to hear shrill, ugly tones which shocked him, like the bellowing of beasts. He looked around and saw his divine, revered protectress lifeless on the ground.'[88] While Jews had been far from happy with the Liberals' behaviour in Vienna, the latter's defeat meant that it was the Jews from the late 1880s onwards who were in the political wilderness, and this meant a social isolation as well which was in some eyes worse than before the emancipation.[89] Sigmund Mayer reported: 'Between the tables at which Christians sat, and those at which Jews sat, there was an invisible dividing line.'[90] Social intercourse between Jews and Christians came to a sudden stop. This expressed itself in the exclusion of Jews from Burschenschaften, or from cycling associations, and in the fact that children did not mix at school, nor even take the same hiking trails.[91] The cumulative effect was to separate the Jews from the rest of society.[92]

The result of these changed circumstances was to make the Jewish problem unavoidable for Jews.[93] The Jewish community at large responded in various ways. There was great anger, as shown by the near lynching

---

[87] *NFPm* 18 September 1895 p. 1; *NFPm* 24 September 1895 p. 1; cf. Kronawetter's letter reprinted in *NFPm* 11 March 1898 p. 4.

[88] 'Eines Morgens erwachte er, schrille, gehässige Töne erschreckten sein Ohr, gleich dem Gebrüll wilder Bestien; er blickte um sich, und seine angebetete Schutzgöttin lag entseelt auf dem Boden.' *Österreichische Wochenschrift. Centralorgan für die gesammten Interessen des Judentums* (*ÖW*) 2 January 1885 (II.1) p. 3. Note how early the death of liberalism was evident, 1885 rather than 1895.

[89] On dissatisfaction with the Liberals, see *NFPm* 31 January 1896 p. 1; *NFPm* 1 October 1895 p. 5. On social isolation, see the obituary of Arnold Hirsch in *NFPm* 25 November 1896 p. 5.

[90] 'Zwischen den Tischen, an welchen Christen und denen, an welchen Juden sassen, war ein unsichtbar Trennendes.' Mayer, *Die Wiener Juden*, pp. 469–70.

[91] O. Schnitzler, *Spiegelbild*, p. 81; *NFPe* 14 December 1896 p. 5; interview with Ann Unger, Berkeley, summer 1983.

[92] Cf. Paul Vasili, *Die Wiener Gesellschaft* (Leipzig 1885) pp. 226–7, where the rise of antisemitism is attributed to a *pre-existent* tendency of Jews and non-Jews not to mix socially.   [93] Cf. Schnitzler, *Der Weg ins Freie*, p. 61.

of the socialist Jewish renegade Ellenbogen at a Liberal electoral meeting in the Leopoldstadt in 1896.[94] There was also a feeling among many Jewish Liberals, such as Mayer and Alfred Stern, that the Jews would have to retreat from the political and social world which rejected them.[95] Many Jews fell back on their Jewish identity and religion. New temples and synagogues were built reflecting what has been described as a 'strengthening of their solidarity'.[96] Jewish pride was rediscovered, but as a reaction to the collapse of the assimilation.[97] Jewish student societies such as the Jüdisch-akademische Lesehalle (founded in 1894) and the Lese- und Redehalle jüdischer Hochschüler (founded in 1900), although both Zionist, nevertheless saw themselves as preserving the western heritage against the reaction, as in a way Herzl himself saw Zionism doing.[98] Much of Jewish pride was in fact a pride in their acquired liberal heritage, which for them had become indistinguishable from their Judaism, especially compared with the rest of society.

It is true that Jewish consciousness could also mean a rejection of liberalism and the retreat to a specifically Jewish cultural and ethnic identity, such as was embodied in the Jewish National Party.[99] The Jewish response of Zionism produced an unstable mixture of liberal, ethnic and traditionalist motives whereby the initiating liberal ideas gradually lost out to other principles.[100] Yet neither the Nationalist nor the Zionist option was ultimately acceptable to the cultural élite, despite the sympathies of many. Jewish organizations such as the Österreichisch-Israelitische Union remained assimilationist in their political views.[101] The aim was to counter antisemitism, not to surrender to it. Jews had to remain within the bounds of western society.[102] The Jewish question was to be resolved as a personal matter by the individual within society, so that the 'integration into the full cultural life of the whole populace' would not be upset.[103] Someone such as Sigmund Mayer saw that a personal Jewish identity could not be

[94] *NFPm* 26 February 1896 p. 7.
[95] Mayer, *Ein jüdischer Kaufmann*, p. 300; *NFPm* 1 October 1895 p. 5.
[96] Mayer, *Die Wiener Juden*, p. 464.
[97] For example, Freud, see Klein, *The Jewish Origins of the Psychoanalytic Movement*, pp. 22–9. Also see O. Schnitzler, *Spiegelbild*, p. 81.
[98] Klein, *The Jewish Origins of the Psychoanalytic Movement*, pp. 23–5. Cf. Nike Wagner, 'Theodor Herzl ou la Vienne delivrée' in *Vienne 1880–1938; l'apocalypse joyeuse* (Paris 1986) pp. 154–62.
[99] Lohrmann, *1,000 Jahre*, pp. 362–4.
[100] Schorske, *Fin-de-Siècle Vienna*, pp. 146–75; Bein, *Herzl*, pp. 84, 116; also see Theodor Herzl, 'Judenthum' in *ÖW* 13 November 1896 (xiii.46) pp. 921–4. Also the speeches by Amos Elon and Shlomo Avineri at the conference, *Versunkene Welt: die Welt von Gestern*, Vienna 19–22 November 1984.
[101] Marsha Rozenblit, *The Jews of Vienna 1867–1914: Assimilation and Identity* (Albany 1983) pp. 154–61.
[102] Mayer, *Ein jüdischer Kaufmann*, p. 259.   [103] Mayer, *Die Wiener Juden*, pp. 465–8.

objected to in this respect.[104] Other, more radical assimilationists, such as Theodor Gomperz, refused to make any concessions at all to a Jewish identity, seeing it as a threat to the unity of mankind. Gomperz saw Jewish Nationalism and Zionism as a surrender to the antisemites, an acceptance of their anti-liberal beliefs in the incompatibility of races.[105] Antisemitism should be overcome, not accepted, the assimilation continued. The argument was essentially the same in Karl Kraus' *Eine Krone für Zion* (1898), where Herzl was described as 'the ultimate executor of the will of the Christian Socials'.[106] Assimilation was the only real answer to the plight of the Jews, and socialism, due to its universalism, would save the day. The Jews would not go to Palestine, because 'another red sea, social democracy, will bar their way there.'[107]

The biggest argument against Zionism before the First World War was that in physical terms the situation was actually not that bad. If society was hostile, at least Jews could insist on their rights as *Menschenrechte* in a state which still upheld the constitution and was headed by a monarch who despised the new antisemitism.[108] Ironically, while the former Liberal coalition became largely antisemitic, the house of Habsburg, or at least Franz Joseph, became *relatively* philosemitic.[109] Jews thus came to see Franz Joseph in a different light as a defender of the constitution and their rights, instead of as a Catholic Habsburg, and became very loyal as a result.[110]

There was even a sense in which, despite the spread of antisemitism, Jews in Austria and in Vienna could look with some confidence into the future. The economic boycotts failed, as did the attempts to keep Jews out of public life.[111] Käthe Leichter could write that the liberal Jewish bourgeoisie was hardly affected by Lueger and Schönerer.[112] All the threats of the antisemites did not, apart from the occasional riot, endanger the Jewish bourgeoisie. The state protected life and livelihood; pre-war Vienna could be, in Zweig's words, a 'world of security'.[113] What was missing was the idea that the Jews were accepted by society as equals. This, the goal of the assimilation, had been shown to be an illusion. While the Jews could live more or less at ease, the social reality was there, even

---

[104] *Ibid.* p. 464.
[105] *Gomperz: ein Gelehrtenleben*, p. 445; Gomperz, *Essays*, pp. 196–9.
[106] Karl Kraus, *Eine Krone für Zion* (Vienna 1898) pp. 3–5.
[107] *Ibid.* p. 30. [108] Barea, *Vienna*, p. 303.
[109] May, *The Habsburg Monarchy*, p. 310; Häusler, 'Toleranz, Emanzipation', p. 118; *NFPe* 11 December 1899 p. 3.
[110] *NFPm* 8 October 1899 p. 8; William M. Johnston, *The Austrian Mind: an Intellectual and Social History 1848–1938* (Berkeley 1972, pb. 1983) p. 40.
[111] Mayer, *Die Wiener Juden*, pp. 475–8.
[112] *Käthe Leichter: Leben und Werk*, ed. Herbert Steiner (Vienna 1973) p. 238.
[113] Stefan Zweig, *Die Welt von Gestern* (Frankfurt-on-Main 1982) pp. 14ff.

among what remained of the non-Jewish bourgeoisie. There was the suspicion that even one's business colleagues and friends were secretly quite happy to see the antisemites in power.[114] Antisemitism had become 'hoffähig', and it was quite clear that Jews were not living in the best of all possible worlds, but were indeed strangers in their own home.[115] To be called 'Fremdling', stranger, was what really hurt and no amount of economic prosperity could wash that away.

Many individuals understood the Jewish predicament and people such as Count Wilczek could show great sympathy for them, as did Gundaccar von Suttner, Marie von Ebner-Eschenbach, Nothnagel, Hermann Bahr (after a change of heart), Robert Musil and Anton Wildgans (both of whom married Jewesses), Engelbert Pernerstorfer and others.[116] These people stood out because of what they were, exceptions. Mayer commented that it was 'nur die allerbesten, nämlich die den intellektuellen Kreisen angehörenden Kollegen' who resisted the alienation from the Jews, yet even among intellectuals support for the Jews was not good enough, as far as Jews were concerned.[117] In the crisis of 1899, which saw the Dreyfus affair in its later phases and the Polna affair producing all kinds of nasty revelations of what Czechs and Germans really thought of the Jews, the cry rang out that Austria needed her own Zola.[118] This was taken up by Rabbi Güdemann in his speech to the Jewish meeting in the Musikverein in October of that year. Making an allusion to the German crowning ceremony, he proclaimed: 'Therefore we Jews have come to ask, in the face of this terrible blood libel, "Is there no Zola here?"' But we have asked in vain.' Ignoring the efforts of Masaryk in Prague, Güdemann was saying that the battle of the Gentile intellectual class for progress, which the Dreyfusards embodied in France, was non-existent in Austria outside the ranks of the Jews themselves. He even went on to claim that the Jews alone were defending truth, the seal of God. There was no Austrian Zola.[119]

Part of the reason why the Gentiles in the cultural élite were not more forthcoming was that even they were not unaffected by antisemitic ideas. Brahms, for instance, good North German liberal that he was, would

---

[114] Mayer, *Die Wiener Juden*, p. 471.
[115] *NFPm* 28 April 1896 p. 1; *NFPm* 8 October 1899 p. 8, where Heinrich Steger is quoted as saying: 'Ist es nicht eine Judenverfolgung, wenn man es wagt jüdische Staatsbürger Fremdlinge zu nennen, deren Eltern und Voreltern hier gelebt, trotzdem wir uns mit Gut und Blut dem Staate zur Verfügung stellen und mit allen Fasern des Herzens an unserem österreichischen Heimatslande hängen!'
[116] May, *The Habsburg Monarchy*, p. 180, on Wilczek.
[117] Mayer, *Die Wiener Juden*, p. 471.
[118] Cf. *NFPm* 2 July 1899 p. 1.
[119] 'So hat sich uns Juden angesichts dieser infamen Blutbeschuldigung die Frage auf die Lippen gedrängt: "Ist kein Zola da?" Aber die Frage war eine vergebliche.' Reported in *NFPm* 8 October 1899 pp. 7–8.

occasionally indulge a slight cultural antisemitism.[120] Max Burckhard, a good friend of Schnitzler, the model for Hofrat Winkler in *Professor Bernhardi*, is reported by Alma Mahler-Werfel to have advised against marrying Mahler on the following grounds: 'A fine girl like you – and racially so pure.'[121] Rilke showed much the same attitude when he advised Sidhonie von Nadherny against marriage with Karl Kraus, talking of a 'last ineradicable difference' between her and Kraus, the implication being that this was because Kraus was Jewish.[122] Even a liberal such as Bernatzik could reveal an innate prejudice by advising Hans Kelsen against an academic career because he was a Jew, not realizing or taking into account the fact that Kelsen had converted.[123]

It is a myth to suppose, as many converts did, that they could escape the social stigma of being a Jew by conversion, or even by being only partly Jewish. How one regarded oneself did not have much effect on what others thought of one, and it was very rare never to get an inkling of what even one's best friends might think. The convert Kelsen was told that he would not get a teaching post at the university because of the racial antisemitism of the students he would have to teach.[124] Nor could Hofmannsthal remain oblivious to the fact that antisemitic newspapers could criticize his version of *Oedipus* as being written in 'a Jewish German'.[125] He himself was aware that one of the main reasons for the impossibility of Reinhardt becoming President of the Salzburg Festival was that he was a Jew.[126] Hofmannsthal's friend, Leopold von Andrian, was known in the War Ministry as 'the sweet Semite', due to his mother's descent.[127] Antisemitic prejudices were everywhere, virtually impossible to avoid; while Austrian antisemitism was not as clearly racist as the German Nationalist version, this was only because, like all things Viennese, no one had bothered to clarify it. This did not mean that it could not be applied, where necessary, in just as far-reaching a manner as its racist counterpart, if not more so.

Arthur Schnitzler wrote in a sketch for his autobiography:

It was impossible, especially for a Jew in the public eye, to ignore the fact that he was a Jew, for the others did not, the Christians not, and the Jews even less. One had the choice of being regarded as insensitive, pushy and arrogant, or

[120] Karl Goldmark, *Erinnerungen aus meinem Leben* (Vienna 1922) p. 87; Blaukopf, *Mahler: a Documentary Study*, p. 231.

[121] 'Sie sind ein so schöner Mensch und eine so gute Rasse!' Alma Mahler, *Gustav Mahler: Erinnerungen und Briefe* (Amsterdam 1940) p. 27. The translation in the English version, Alma Mahler, *Gustav Mahler, memories and letters* (London 1968) p. 18, uses the word 'pedigree' for 'Rasse'.

[122] Paul Schick, *Karl Kraus* (Hamburg 1965) p. 74.

[123] R. A. Métall, *Hans Kelsen: Leben und Werk* (Vienna 1969) p. 10.   [124] *Ibid.* p. 13.

[125] Alfred Polgar, *Sperrsitz*, ed. U. Weinzierl (Vienna 1980) p. 109.

[126] Gottfried Reinhardt, *Der Liebhaber* (Munich 1975) p. 205.

[127] Information from John Leslie, Bristol.

hypersensitive, shy and paranoid. And even when one could control one's internal and external behaviour to the point that one avoided appearing as either of these, it was quite impossible not to be affected. It was like asking someone to remain indifferent when he had received a local anaesthetic but had to watch with his own eyes dirty knives scraping, cutting into his skin, until the blood ran.[128]

The Jews had the unique experience of being excluded for a second time from the rest of society. They could act as part of that society, physically unmolested, but it was quite clear to them that they were not full members, that they were 'strangers, excluded, who did not belong',[129] Singled out to be the outsiders of society, they now had to provide answers to the failure of assimilation, to the problem of being Jewish.

[128] 'Es war nicht möglich, insbesondere für einen Juden, der in der Öffentlichkeit stand, davon abzusehen, dass er Jude war, da die andern es nicht taten, die Christen nicht und die Juden noch weniger. Man hatte die Wahl, für unempfindlich, zudringlich, frech oder für empfindlich, schüchtern, verfolgungswahnsinnig zu gelten. Und auch wenn man seine innere und äussere Haltung so weit bewahrte, dass man weder das eine noch das andere zeigte, ganz unberührt zu bleiben war so unmöglich, als etwa ein Mensch gleichgültig bleiben könnte, der sich zwar die Haut anästhesiren liess, aber mit wachen und offenen Augen zusehen muss, wie unreine Messer sie ritzen, ja schneiden, bis das Blut kommt.' Arthur Schnitzler, *Jugend in Wien* (Frankfurt-on-Main 1981) p. 322.
[129] O. Schnitzler, *Spiegelbild*, p. 81; Arendt, *Die verborgene Tradition*, p. 87; Braun, *Das Licht der Welt*, p. 90.

The ethics of outsiders: the cultural response

PARIAH STRATEGIES

Gustav Mahler occupied one of the most prestigious posts in the Viennese cultural world, as *Hofoperndirecktor*. In 1902 he married the very Austrian Alma Maria Schindler. He became Catholic in 1897. As far as the outer trappings of assimilation went, he had gone as far, perhaps further, than any person of Jewish descent could expect to get. Yet it was Mahler who said: 'I am rootless three times over: as a Bohemian among Austrians, as an Austrian among Germans, and as a Jew everywhere in the world. Everywhere I am regarded as an interloper, nowhere am I what people call "desirable".'[1] Even the greatest social success could not disguise the fact that the hopes of the emancipation and assimilation had been dashed – that Jews remained, as they always had, outsiders in the society in which they lived. What Schnitzler called the 'Sicherheitswahn' (illusion of security), that Jews were accepted, had proven to be a chimera.[2] Jewish individuals had to face up to the fact that they were still in what Hannah Arendt called the 'hidden tradition' of the Jew as pariah.[3] Those in the cultural élite responded to this in several ways, which will be described here. In turn these responses affected the way they saw the world and their work. It is the purpose of this chapter to suggest the possible ways in which the situation of being Jewish in an antisemitic environment, combined with the remnants of the traditions of Judaism and assimilation, could have acted decisively in shaping the cultural achievements of Vienna at the turn of the century.

Responses to their predicament were greatly complicated by the

[1] 'Ich bin dreifach heimatlos: als Böhme unter den Österreichern, als Österreicher unter den Deutschen und als Jude in der ganzen Welt. Überall bin ich Eindringling, nirgends "erwünscht".' Quoted in Alma Mahler, *Gustav Mahler: Erinnerungen und Briefe* (Amsterdam 1940) p. 135; also Kurt Blaukopf, *Mahler: a Documentary Study* (London 1976) p. 214.

[2] Arthur Schnitzler, *Der Weg ins Freie* (Frankfurt-on-Main 1978) p. 203.

[3] Hannah Arendt, *Die verborgene Tradition* (Frankfurt-on-Main 1976) p. 47.

ambivalent attitude of Jewish individuals in the cultural élite to their Jewishness, a situation which produced several ironies. Herzl and Freud, for instance, both took a positive view of their Jewishness – eventually. Yet, whereas Herzl wanted to free the Jews from what he saw as the debilitating state of being outsiders in a hostile society, and hence make Jews normal as it were, Freud's pride as a Jew was firmly based on the marginal character of the Jews.[4] As he explained to the B'nai B'rith in 1926: 'Because I was a Jew, I found myself free of many prejudices which restrict others in the use of the intellect: as a Jew, I was prepared to be in the opposition and to renounce agreement with the "compact majority".'[5] With this image of the Jew as being free of what has been called the 'Hemmungsschwelle' of the rest of the population with regard to new ideas Freud was making a virtue of the process of assimilation.[6] His view that the Jewish predicament offered opportunities of experience and insight which were unavailable to others was thus in direct antithesis to Herzl's wish to destroy the Jews' social alienation.

Freud's model certainly makes sense of much of Jewish participation in modern culture in Vienna. Since they were outside the 'compact majority', Jews could not hope to assimilate into the status quo, but might be able to make alliances with other outsiders in the hope that they would become the arbiters of the future. Psychoanalysis itself, in its emphasis on the power of sexual instinct, was in some way making a political attack on Viennese society by an alliance of scientific rationality with instinct against the irrationalism (perhaps irrationality) of Vienna's baroque culture with its strong associations of the sensual.[7] The Jewish domination of the socialist leadership can be seen in the same way. Confronted with exclusion from bourgeois politics, Jews looked to the other outsiders, the workers, for help.[8] Socialism was, after all, the last major political theory

[4] On Herzl, see Carl E. Schorske, *Fin-de-Siècle Vienna: Politics and Culture* (London 1980) pp. 146–75; Alex Bein, *Theodore Herzl* (London 1957) pp. 29–105; Desmond Stewart, *Theodor Herzl: Artist and Politician* (London 1974) pp. 177–8.

[5] 'Weil ich Jude war, fand ich mich frei von vielen Vorurteilen, die andere in Gebrauch ihres Intellektes beschränkten, als Jude war ich dafür vorbereitet, in die Opposition zu gehen und auf das Einvernehmen mit der "kompakten Majorität" zu verzichten.' Quoted in *B'nai B'rith 1895–1975* (Vienna 1975) p. 53; translated in Josef Fraenkel, ed., *The Jews of Austria: Essays on their Life, History and Destruction* (London 1967) p. 198.

[6] The word 'Hemmungsschwelle' (inhibition threshold) was suggested to me by Dr Helmut Andics, Eisenstadt, 14 February 1984.

[7] This is one interpretation of the motto of Die Traumdeutung: 'Flectere si nequeo superos, Acheronta movebo.' See Schorske, *Fin-de-Siècle Vienna*, pp. 200ff; Ilsa Barea, *Vienna* (London 1966) p. 304; Paul Roazen, *Freud and his Followers* (London 1976) p. 102 (comments of Hanns Sachs); Albert Fuchs, *Geistige Strömungen in Österreich 1867–1918* (Vienna 1949) p. 246.

[8] Sigmund Mayer, *Ein jüdischer Kaufmann 1831–1911: Lebenserinnerungen* (Leipzig 1911) pp. 310–22; Sigmund Mayer, *Die Wiener Juden: Kommerz, Kultur, Politik 1700–1900* (Vienna 1918) p. 470; Walter B. Simon, 'The Jewish Vote in Austria' in *Leo Baeck Institute Yearbook (LBIY)* 1971, p. 107.

after liberalism's demise in which Jews could hope to be seen as equals.[9] Kraus had seen this in contrast to Zionism, and it also made sense that, when German Nationalism failed them, people such as Victor Adler and Gustav Mahler should look to socialism and the workers as the new counter-culture.[10] It was a question of belonging to the new society, even if, as with Otto Neurath, identification meant wearing a worker's cap.[11] It also made sense that the Austrian party should be so well known for its emphasis on education, *Bildung*, for in many ways the assimilated Jewish leadership was trying to realize in the workers the kind of Enlightenment dreams scotched by antisemitism.[12]

There were other groups in Vienna outside the pale of society which Jews could court. There were cultural rebels who could be encouraged, thereby perhaps promoting a counter assimilation. Robert Waissenberger thus has suggested that Jewish patrons of the *Sezession* sought to rival established art, and hence come, one day, to be accepted as the doyens of the new art.[13] It was a cultural variant of the Jewish motivation in socialism, the attempt to assimilate into the future rather than the present. The epitome of such an attempt might well be viewed in the career of Eugenia Schwarzwald. Firstly she led the struggle for women's education at university by founding her school, then she staffed her school with most of the leading lights of the avant garde including Loos and Kokoschka. On the assumption that this élite would one day form the new canons of taste, Eugenia Schwarzwald could thus think of herself as an insider of the future society.[14]

It is ironic that while all these outsiders acted much as Freud described, their tactic of alliance with the people and ideas of the future was, in the main, the result of trying desperately not to identify themselves as isolated outsiders. It was the image of a future in which they would cease to be regarded as different, that is, cease to be Jews, which spurred them on, just as it had spurred on their fathers. Far from identifying with the rôle of the Jewish outsider, as Freud did, they were attempting to overcome and

---

[9] Cf. the comments of Felix Frankl in Ingrid Belke, *Die sozialreformerischen Ideen von Josef Popper-Lynkeus 1838–1921* (Tübingen 1978) p. 240. Also Frederick Wyatt, interview, London, 30 October 1986.

[10] Karl Kraus, *Eine Krone für Zion* (Vienna 1898) p. 30; Rudolf G. Ardelt, *Friedrich Adler: Probleme einer Persönlichkeitsentwicklung um die Jahrhundertwende* (Vienna 1984) pp. 34ff.; Blaukopf, *Mahler: a Documentary Study*, pp. 225, 241.

[11] Otto Neurath, *Empiricism and Sociology* (Dordrecht 1973) p. 47.

[12] Cf. Karl Popper, *Unended Quest* (Glasgow 1976) pp. 35–6; Belke, *Popper-Lynkeus*, p. 19; Fuchs, *Geistige Strömungen*, pp. 109, 146 (on Ludo Hartmann); Norbert Leser, ed., *Das geistige Leben Wiens in der Zwischenkriegszeit* (Vienna 1981) p. 303 (including the comments of Friedrich Heer); cf. Leopold Hichler, *Der Sohn des Moses Mautner: ein Wiener Roman* (Vienna 1927) p. 259.

[13] Interview with Robert Waissenberger, 24 February 1984, Vienna.

[14] Hilde Spiel, 'Jewish Women in Austrian Culture' in J. Fraenkel, ed., *The Jews of Austria*, p. 109.

suppress the whole problem of being Jewish, if not in the present then in the future.

The policy of outright assimilation was one which the older and younger generations shared. Antisemitism was evil, but mainly because it stood in the way of the complete obliteration of a specifically Jewish identity. An instance of such attitudes in the older generation is afforded by Theodor Gomperz in his correspondence. Gomperz hated antisemitism, making a point of dining with Captain Dreyfus as a symbolic act.[15] Yet it was plain to him that there was much in the social behaviour of Jews which made antisemitism all too understandable.[16] Further, Gomperz believed, as his essay of 1904 *Über die Grenzen der jüdischen intellektuellen Begabung* reveals, that the Jewish mind lacked the darker side to thought which was necessary for genius. As he put it: 'for certain kinds of creative endeavour Jewish minds are too bright'. He attributed this to acquired characteristics (after Lamarck) and perhaps to racial traits. Yet his major point was that such generic explanations could not apply to the individual: 'People are, after all, people, and in any individual an element which is foreign to most of his people can be mightily developed.' He added: 'There are no limits to the potential of genius.'[17] Gomperz was, in effect, echoing his friend, Heinrich Jaques, that Jews should not be cut off from society for this would prevent the man of talent or genius from overcoming his Jewish background, whether acquired, racial, social or cultural. That was the goal.

As such, the whole process of overcoming one's Jewishness was, in Vienna, a peculiarly Jewish phenomenon. While other groups in Vienna might also be assimilating in their own way, the exposed position of Jews and the special nature of their assimilation, meant that Jewish assimilants were different from the other Viennese, as well as other Jews. The assimilation process in itself made them stand out.[18]

Assimilation, whether into the present or future society, entailed parting with what we would call 'roots'. The socialist leader, Victor Adler, was just as much trying to 'disappear' into the working class as he was allying with the workers to overthrow the status quo. The rôle of 'Überläufer' (deserter) was a way of forgetting, getting rid of, a Jewish heritage that was a complete embarrassment.[19] As Friedrich Adler was later to recall, the

---

[15] *Theodor Gomperz: ein Gelehrtenleben im Bürgertum der Franz-Josephszeit*, eds. H. Gomperz and R. A. Kann (Vienna 1974) p. 351.

[16] *Ibid.* p. 263, for instance.

[17] 'Mensch ist schliesslich Mensch, und in einem Einzelnen kann immer ein der Mehrzahl seiner Volksgenossen fremdes Element mächtig entwickelt sein. 'Genialen Möglichkeiten sind keine Grenzen gesetzt!' *Ibid.* pp. 384–9.

[18] See Hans Mayer, *Aussenseiter* (Frankfurt-on-Main 1981) pp. 350–79; as Dorothy Parker said: 'The Jews are like everyone else, only more so.' Quoted in Friedrich Torberg, *Die Tante Jolesch, oder der Untergang des Abendlandes in Anekdoten* (Munich 1977) p. 213.

[19] Ardelt, *Friedrich Adler*, pp. 37ff.

century is that they were motivated by a search for fame through art to force acceptance, as celebrities, in the cultural élite, if not in society at large. The Viennese *fin de siècle* is to be seen largely, in her opinion, as a Jewish search for fame.[33] In this she is supported by a contemporary satire, which appeared in the *Neue Freie Presse*. The author is again Joseph Oppenheimer, and the piece is entitled *Wie wird man berühmt?* The general theme of the article is the sudden surge of young writers who want to have their plays performed at the Burgtheater. Oppenheimer comments that soon it will be easier to be known for *not* writing a play than vice versa. The article is full of such witty quips, but underneath the humour lay more sinister aspects, which Oppenheimer saw as the causes for this search for fame. Listing the ways of becoming famous, he remarks on the story of an American paying to have a planet named after him. Oppenheimer's comment reveals the state of mind of the cultural élite in 1899:

It must be a wonderful feeling, as an ordinary citizen already during one's lifetime to reign between Venus and Mars; but who knows whether everyone in our society, regardless of religion, would be allowed to name a star after himself, and wear this heavenly medal, without official permission. Especially nowadays, when the religious divisions are so exacerbated. One cannot really expect that an unsuspecting Catholic girl, who is saying her nightly prayer to the starry heavens, should have suddenly to see with horror an unforeseen Löwy twinkling there.[34]

The implication was that the drive for fame was somehow a reaction to the antisemitic environment, and it is certainly true that most of the writers were Jewish.

The theatre offered an arena which was free of the antisemitism of the outside world. Reviewing a performance of L'Arronge's *Pastor Brose* in October 1895, the reporter for the *Neue Freie Presse* remarked on the enthusiasm with which attacks on antisemitism in the play had been greeted. He added: 'Im Theater ist der Liberalismus noch in der Mehrheit.'[35] This social fact, repeated by Karl Kraus in 1899, goes far to explaining the hordes of young men wanting to be playwrights.[36] In Oppenheimer's language, there was no fear in the theatre of causing offence by being called Löwy. This contemporary evidence suggests that

---

[33] Arendt, *Die verborgene Tradition*, p. 79.

[34] 'Es müsste ein köstliches Gefühl sein, da oben als einfacher Mitbürger schon bei Lebzeiten zwischen Venus und Mercur zu thronen, aber wer weiss, ob es bei uns Jedermann, ohne Unterschied der Religion, erlaubt wäre, ein neues Gestirn auf seinen Namen zu taufen, und diesen himmlischen Hausorden ohne behördliche Bewilligung zu tragen? Zumal heutzutage, wo die confessionellen Gegensätze sich so verschärft haben. Man kann wahrlich nicht verlangen, dass ein ahnungsloses katholisches Fräulein, welches sein Nachtgebet zum gestirnten Himmel richtet, dort mit Entsetzen plötzlich einen unvorhergesehenen Löwy schimmern sehen soll.' Joseph Oppenheimer, 'Wie wird man berühmt? in *Neue Freie Presse*, morning edition (*NFPm*) 21 May 1899 pp. 8–9.

[35] *NFPm* 20 October 1895 p. 7.   [36] Quoted in Schorske, *Fin-de-Siècle Vienna*, p. 8.

it was antisemitism, and not a general social crisis as such, which was acting as the main spur to the retreat into culture which the search for fame embodied.[37]

As to the nature of the culture into which these people retreated, it is far from self-evident that it was, as Schorske insists, some kind of aesthetic *Gefühlskultur*, at least as far as Jews were concerned. Schnitzler, for instance, seems to have seen a clear distinction between the Jewish and non-Jewish approach to art and culture. In *Der Weg ins Freie* he has Heinrich Bermann make the distinction between those who are to be beautiful and those who are geniuses, life being much simpler for the former. It is clear that Bermann, the Jew, is fated to be the genius and not beautiful.[38] The Jewish world of culture was not an aesthetic one, in Schorske's understanding, but the world of intellect, something of a different order: the world of *Bildung*, of *Geist*. Thus, when Karl Kraus sought a sanctuary from racial prejudice, it was to the world of *Geist* that he turned.[39] In attempting to escape the problem of being Jewish, Jewish individuals retreated into the same world as their ancestors had inhabited, that of the intellect. In this way the Jewish tradition was continued almost against the will of its heirs, but it was continued. There was more than one 'hidden tradition' among Vienna's cultural élite.

JEWS IN THE CULTURAL ÉLITE

The situation of the assimilated cultural élite in Vienna became a very anomalous one. On the one hand they had left behind their former identity as Jews. They had dispensed with their inherited, historical *Eigenschaften* (characteristics), becoming a *tabula rasa*. On this basis they had developed an elaborate structure of *Bildung*, in order to become members of what they saw as the society and culture of a new, just and free world. They had been rejected by what they had taken to be that society. The result was now that they were no longer really Jews, but neither were they Germans nor Austrians. They lacked a collective identity.[40] The denial of the past, a precondition of assimilation, now produced not a group of people, but only a 'sum of individuals', dependent solely on their own resources and their education, not their heritage.[41] They were left, as it were, with a culture which was not theirs, nor anybody else's. In that sense it became very much theirs alone, for this cultural world was the one thing which

[37] Cf. Barea, *Vienna*, p. 301.

[38] Schnitzler, *Der Weg ins Freie*, p. 38.   [39] Kraus, 'Er ist doch e Jud', p. 362.

[40] Cf. Ardelt, *Friedrich Adler*, pp. 14ff; also see J. P. Stern, *Hitler: the Führer and the People* (London 1984) pp. 204–7.

[41] The phrase 'sum of individuals' is from Jakob Wassermann, quoted in Sol Liptzin, *Germany's Stepchildren* (Philadelphia 1944) p. 119.

could still give them some sense of identity when society could not. Culture came to be a substitute for background — roots – as the only bond between individuals. The cultural élite became a set of radical individualists, 'anarchists of personality', a society of collective individualism, aracial and asocial. The coffee-houses where they met became a 'surrogate totality' to replace a social world which they did not have.[42]

Was this a Jewish phenomenon? Clearly the coffee-house was not a Jewish institution. Even those which counted, such as Griensteidl, Central and Herrenhof, had among their more famous clientèle many figures who were not Jewish, and, moreover, shared the same milieu as outsiders. Kokoschka and Loos are good examples. In any case, it would be foolhardy to see the Jews as being the *only* source of modern high culture in Vienna around 1900. It is plain, however, that assimilated Jews were drawn to this type of lifestyle in considerable numbers, while in others it represented an exceptional state of affairs by 1900. To be a Jewish *Kaffeehausliterat* was a common event, 'natural'; to be a non-Jewish one was increasingly uncommon. The social and cultural pressures were such that the lifestyle outlined here, of the alienated, individuated intellectual, had become typical of the assimilated Jewish community, but atypical for the others.

Jews had not always dominated Viennese liberal high culture.[43] Before Ludwig von Mises the Austrian School of Economics was exclusively led by non-Jews. Leading writers of the 1880s had been non-Jews, such as von Saar and Bauernfeld. In music Brahms dominated. There was nothing magical about the Jews. They did not do everything. Nevertheless they became increasingly important as time went on, exactly in the realm where they thought they could not be touched, liberal, modern high culture, the world of *Geist*. As we have seen, they were predominant in almost all the major intellectual fields by 1914, even more so by 1934.[44] The explanation for this appears to be that Jews assimilated into social and cultural groups, only to find that the others, originally the vast majority, disappeared, leaving Jews among Jews. Part of this, as Marsha Rozenblit has shown, was due to the social dynamics of assimilation by which Jews tended to stick together, even in their assimilation.[45] Yet the major reason

[42] See Berta Zuckerkandl, *Ich erlebte fünfzig Jahre Weltgeschichte* (Stockholm 1939) p. 307; *Das Wiener Kaffeehaus*, with an introduction by Hans Weigel (Vienna 1978) pp. 33, 67–8; on Peter Altenberg, the paragon of a *Kaffeehausmensch*, see Albert Ehrenstein, 'Peter Altenberg' in Ehrenstein, *Menschen und Affen* (Berlin 1925) p. 68: 'Altenberg war ein Urwiener und doch heimatlos als er starb; der Boden unter seinen Füssen grüsste ihn nicht. Er war ein Jude. Ahasverisch lief sein Leben von Hotelzimmer zu Hotelzimmer, von Café zu Café.'

[43] However, some sources do talk of Jewish predominance as early as the 1880s. See Paul Vasili, *Die Wiener Gesellschaft* (Leipzig 1885) pp. 403, 450.   [44] See above, pp. 14–32.

[45] Marsha Rozenblit, *The Jews of Vienna 1867–1914: Assimilation and Identity* (Albany 1983) pp. 122–5; cf. Vasili, *Wiener Gesellschaft*, pp. 226–7.

for the paucity of non-Jews in the cultural groups, I would suggest, has to do with the prevailing antisemitic atmosphere in Vienna. For any non-Jew who was interested in modern and liberal culture there was always the threat that he would be convicted by association, be regarded as 'verjudet' or a 'Judenknecht', by being identified with groups or movements in which Jews were involved.[46] Although not all were affected, there does seem to have been a parallel in the cultural élite to the falling away from the Liberal coalition evident in the political world. The claim that culture was 'verjudet' became a self-fulfilling prophecy, as non-Jews were warned off from all but the most conservative forms of culture.

The art of the *Sezession* could thus be called 'le goût juif', although the painters were not Jewish. Whether as cause or effect, it became true that their patrons, apart from the State, came largely from the Jewish bourgeoisie.[47] Before 1848 it had been the Jews who had gone to the coffee-house to seek out the resident Viennese intellectuals.[48] By the 1920s, if an aspiring journalist such as Milan Dubrovic wanted to enter the world of the intellectuals, he had to go to the coffee-house where the Jewish intellectuals met.[49] Jews started to assimilate into a world that was already Jewish. The financier Castiglioni attempted to gain respectability in what he took to be high society by financing Max Reinhardt's restoration of the Theater in der Josefstadt; but the people who would have been impressed by such patronage of a Jew like Reinhardt were most likely to have been other Jews.[50] The Schwarzwaldschule, if it had originally been intended to produce a new female élite to destroy old social barriers, became in the words of one witness 'in effect the premiere school of the Jewish bourgeoisie'.[51] The cultural sphere, the neutral ground on which the assimilation could be achieved, was becoming a Jewish world.[52]

Jews found themselves in a situation at the centre of culture but the

---

[46] E.g. *NFPm* 9 May 1899 p. 1. See also the report of student clashes in *NFPe* 14 March 1896 p. 2, where the Jewish societies clash with the antisemites. As the reporter described it: 'An diese [jüdischen] Verbindungen gliederten sich die übrigen liberalen, sowie sozial-demokratischen Studenten.' That is, the polarity is not social, but ethnic: Jew/antisemite.

[47] See pp. 27–9.   [48] Mayer, *Ein jüdischer Kaufmann*, pp. 115–6.

[49] Interview with Milan Dubrovic, 29 September 1983, Vienna.

[50] Gusti Adler, *Aber vergessen Sie nicht die chinesischen Nachtigallen* (Vienna 1980) pp. 141–2.

[51] *Käthe Leichter: Leben und Werk*, ed. Herbert Steiner (Vienna 1973) p. 305; cf. *Statistisches Jahrbuch der Stadt Wien* 1910 (Vienna 1911) p. 400, which shows 113 out of 164 pupils at the school (69 per cent) being of the Jewish religion.

[52] The realization of this fact among Jews led to the use of *Renommiergoyim* to improve the image of the various cultural groups, see Belke, *Popper-Lynkeus*, p. 239. The most famous instance is Jung, see R. W. Clark, *Freud: the Man and the Cause* (London 1980) pp. 252, 298–9. The socialist party also laboured under the fact that most of its leadership was Jewish, see Ardelt, *Friedrich Adler*, p. 66.

edge of society, which could produce new insights not readily available to the rest of society.[53] In reaction to their situation they had to ask new questions. As Fritz Wittels said of Freud: 'The prevalence of antisemitism creates in the minds of the Jews a passionate "Why?" In favourable circumstances, this urgent questioning may have results of considerable scientific importance.'[54] Jewish individuals, in response to their environment, achieved a far higher consciousness of themselves and that environment, because they were forced to come to terms with things in a way others, generally, were not.[55] There was thus in a sense a special rôle for Jews, one might say a secular version of the chosen people, and this was recognized in the literature of the time, by Jews. Kraus, though he attacked the Zionists for wanting to divide the Jews from others, had a rather ambiguous attitude to assimilation. While, as we have seen, he wanted complete assimilation externally, he envisaged that Jews would still have a mission: 'Fated to dissolve entirely into their surrounding cultures, and nevertheless still to remain a ferment.'[56] Schnitzler (perhaps consciously) repeated Kraus' thought almost verbatim when he had Heinrich Bermann say: 'That we, we Jews I mean, have been a sort of ferment of humanity – that will perhaps be the verdict of generations a thousand, or two thousand years from now.'[57] In the same book he described the Jews as the people 'in whose souls the future of humanity was preparing itself'.[58] By being forced to question their relationship with the world through the fact of antisemitism, Jews, Kraus and Schnitzler seemed to be saying, had taken over the rôle of the cultural avant-garde. Forced outside, they had gained insight into the problems of the present and the shape of the new.

Schnitzler's most comprehensive picture of the cultural élite of Vienna is provided in his one major novel, *Der Weg ins Freie*. Most of the characters are Jewish. Everyone in the novel, Jew and non-Jew, is looking to escape his or her stalemated existence. There are Jewish and non-Jewish solutions. The novel is as much about the parting of the ways in the cultural élite between Jew and non-Jew, as it is about the common predicament. Non-Jews go off and become antisemitic German Nationalists, that is insiders, while it is the Jews who have to seek a 'way out'. Zionism, socialism,

---

[53] Cf. Mary Gluck, *George Lukacs and his Generation, 1900–1918* (Cambridge, Mass. 1985) p. 74 and *passim* for the Budapest parallel.

[54] Fritz Wittels, *Sigmund Freud* (London 1924) p. 247.

[55] Cf. Hans Tietze, *Die Juden Wiens* (Vienna 1935) pp. 256, 262.

[56] 'Bestimmt in allen umgehenden Culturen [sic] unlösbar aufzugehen und dennoch immerdar Ferment zu bleiben.' Kraus, *Eine Krone für Zion*, p. 23.

[57] 'Dass wir, wir Juden, mein ich, gewissermassen ein Menschheitsferment gewesen sind – ja, das wird vielleicht herauskommen in tausend bis zweitausend Jahren.' Schnitzler, *Der Weg ins Freie*, p. 205.   [58] *Ibid.* p. 94.

conversion, the coffee-house, none of these provide the promised salvation. The way to freedom seems blocked on all sides.

The most famous passage in the book, much quoted in present literature, is the point where Heinrich Bermann explains to the aristocrat, Georg von Wergenthin, the only real way to freedom: 'I believe that such wanderings into the open do not lend themselves to a collective approach...for the ways to that goal are not on the land out there but rather in ourselves. Everyone must find his own inner way.'[59] This is one of the clearest expressions of the retreat into the self as a way out of the cul-de-sac of Vienna at the turn of the century. It could be seen as confirmation of the idea of a retreat into the aristocratic, aesthetic world of *Gefühlskultur*. Yet a close reading of the text shows this is not what Schnitzler meant. Georg, the aristocrat of the novel, reacts to Bermann's speech by thinking that he is 'just as sick as his father'. He also thinks that Bermann's speech shows how Jewish he is: 'He feels solidarity with all Jews, and with the last of them more than with me.'[60] Thus the representative of the aristocratic, aesthetic principle regards Bermann's tactic of seeking freedom in knowledge of the self as a Jewish affair. For Schnitzler, Jews represented a separate way of thinking in Vienna's cultural élite.

AN ETHICAL PURSUIT

Schnitzler saw this tactic of introspection not as a retreat into aesthetics, but rather as an ethical pursuit, a search for truth and for real values. It is often thought that he was an aesthete, a rebel against the liberal values of his father's generation. There is much in this, but like all half-truths it masks a more important truth, which is that within an aesthetic form Schnitzler retained the essence of those values, only taking them out of the political sphere. It was quite clear to him that liberalism as a political ideology had failed. It had done so because its optimism about the social world had been sadly misplaced.[61] In *Professor Bernhardi* he made abundantly clear the way in which liberalism's promise of the ultimate victory of light and truth was illusory: against the perplexing nature of the Austrian State and society, the only wise counsel was one of retreat, 'nicht hineinmischen'.[62] Yet this does not mean that he gave up the values of his

---

[59] 'Ich glaube überhaupt nicht dass solche Wanderungen ins Freie sich gemeinsam unternehmen lassen...denn die Strassen dorthin laufen ja nicht im Lande draussen sondern in uns selbst. Es kommt nur für jeden darauf an, seinen inneren Weg zu finden.' *Ibid.* p. 205.

[60] *Ibid.* p. 205.   [61] O. Schnitzler, *Spiegelbild*, p. 48.

[62] Arthur Schnitzler, *Professor Bernhardi*, in Schnitzler, *Dramen*, vol. 6 (Frankfurt-on-Main 1962) p. 253.

youth, but rather, I would argue, he preserved those values within the cultural world.[63]

The *Neue Freie Presse* in May 1895 wrote of 'the moral effect of culture', and it was through culture that Schnitzler wanted to create a moral effect.[64] His aestheticism, his fine style, were, as Schorske recognizes, only the smooth veneer of a great moralist.[65] His attitude to the old liberals was, at least by 1908, one of nostalgia, and in many of his works it is as the defender of the basic values of liberal, and by implication, Jewish thought that Schnitzler appears.[66] His prime aim was to be truthful. In works such as *Professor Bernhardi, Reigen, Grüne Kakadu, Das Weite Land* and *Leutnant Gustl* his aim appears to be the uncovering of society's hypocrisies; as early as his first great success, *Liebelei*, first performed in 1895, it was as the bringer of truth that he was described. Ludwig Speidel called him 'the independent-minded, courageous man' who had shown the truth about Viennese society. He continued: 'Here the purpose is not to be clever, but rather truthful.'[67] Schnitzler's need for truth, and to be true to the self, meant that for contemporaries he resembled far more the Nordic writers than other Viennese.[68] Indeed, when summing up her husband's attitude to art, Olga Schnitzler borrowed a saying from Ibsen: 'Poetry means: judging yourself.'[69]

Freud, Schnitzler's *Doppelgänger* in so many respects, shared this basic goal for much the same reasons. Psychoanalysis was another means of safeguarding the principle of intellectual honesty from the institutionalized dishonesty which the Viennese environment provided.[70] By realizing the illusions of liberal ideology about human motivation, Freud wanted to

[63] For a more detailed study of this point, and what follows, see Norbert Abels, *Sicherheit ist nirgends: Judentum und Aufklärung bei Arthur Schnitzler* (Königstein 1982).

[64] *NFPm* 31 May 1895 p. 1.

[65] Schorske, *Fin-de-Siècle Vienna*, pp. 10–15; Barea, *Vienna*, pp. 326–7.

[66] See Arthur Schnitzler, *Aphorismen und Betrachtungen*, vol. 4 of Schnitzler, *Gasammelte Werke* (Frankfurt 1967) p. 18 and *passim*. Also Hans Kohn, *Kraus, Schnitzler und Weininger: aus dem jüdischen Wien der Jahrhundertwende* (Tübingen 1962) p. 27.

[67] 'Allein es kommt hier gar nicht darauf an, geistreich, sondern wahr zu sein.' *NFPm* 13 October 1895 p. 1.

[68] Alfred Polgar called Schnitzler 'Ibsen in Wienerwaldes Luft', see H. Schnitzler, R. Urbach and C. Brandstätter, eds., *Arthur Schnitzler: sein Leben, sein Werk, seine Zeit* (Frankfurt-on-Main 1981) p. 137. Schnitzler himself is quoted as saying: 'ich weiss nicht, ob die Neigung, wahr gegen mich selbst zu sein, von Anfang an in mir lag. Sicher ist, dass sie sich im Laufe der Jahre gesteigert hat, ja, dass mir diese Neigung heute die lebhafteste und beständigste Regung meines Innern zu sein scheint.' Quoted in O. Schnitzler, *Spiegelbild*, p. 48. Also cf. Schnitzler, *Aphorismen*, p. 51.   [69] O. Schnitzler, *Spiegelbild*, p. 47.

[70] Heinz Politzer, in likening Schnitzler's *Bernhardi* to Freud, justifies this by saying: 'weil sein Verstehen dem Glauben der Herrschenden zuwiderlief'. Quoted in H. Schnitzler *et al.* eds., *Arthur Schnitzler*, p. 106. Also see Claudio Magris, *Weit von wo?* (Vienna 1974) p. 162.

restore the ability of individuals to gain control over themselves.[71] Thus, after a successful session, Freud would show his patient an engraving of Oedipus: not *Oedipus Rex*, but *Oedipus and the Sphinx*.[72] By recognizing man's true nature, and his flaws, the power of darkness which the sphinx represented could, Freud seemed to be intimating, be overcome. The phrase 'Freud the moralist' is thus far from being the *non sequitur* which many of his critics would have us believe.

The wish to be true to the self, which lay behind both Freud and Schnitzler, is one of the great themes of the European *fin de siècle*, and so it was in Vienna. Far from being a world of illusion, the world of 'aesthetes' such as Schnitzler, was a world where illusions were recognized and revealed, where dreams were brought out into the light of day, where music was to express the inner landscape of man rather than delight the ear.[73] That Austrian culture has been so prominent in revealing to us the darker side of the human personality has as much to do with the fact that there were people there to search out the facts, as that the facts were there. That those discoverers were nearly all Jewish was no coincidence, for people such as Schnitzler and Freud were simply applying the standards of their forebears to their social and psychological predicament. Their aesthetics was only a very thinly disguised ethical impulse to truth. What Bermann is really suggesting in his speech about the inner way to freedom only becomes apparent in its continuation: 'Moreover it is of course necessary to look into yourself as clearly as possible, to shed light on the deepest recesses; to possess the courage to follow your own nature; not to let yourself be misled. Yes, that must be the daily prayer of every decent person: never to let yourself be misled.'[74] The search for freedom is the search for inner certainty, complete honesty with oneself.

Here, however, Schnitzler and his generation came up against what seemed an insuperable problem. Though they recognized the real need for a self which possessed free will, they saw too that such a self did not actually exist, that the empirical psyche was not the unity which theories of free will assumed. It was plain to Schnitzler that the assumption of free will was a necessity if there was to be any meaning to life, for the assumption that the individual was not responsible for his acts would, in his words, destroy morality, explode the moral self and reduce tragedy and comedy to mere farce.[75] Schnitzler remained true to a metaphysics of truth

[71] Cf. Schorske, *Fin-de-siècle Vienna*, p. 201.

[72] Fritz Wittels, *Sigmund Freud*, p. 114.

[73] See Allan Janik and Stephen Toulmin, *Wittgenstein's Vienna* (New York 1973) pp. 108–10; Moritz Csaky, 'Die sozial-kulturelle Wechselwirkung in der Zeit des Wiener fin de siècle', in P. Berner, E. Brix and W. Mantl, eds., *Wien um 1900: Aufbruch in die Moderne* (Vienna 1986) pp. 143ff. [74] Schnitzler, *Der Weg ins Freie*, p. 205.

[75] Schnitzler, *Aphorismen*, p. 32; cf. O. Schnitzler, *Spiegelbild*, p. 138.

and the freedom of the will, incorporated in the idea of a moral self, even if this essentially liberal view was limited to the internal world. Yet Schnitzler also saw that such a moral self was far from self-evident. He and his fellow writers believed in Ernst Mach's concept of 'das unrettbare Ich' (the irretrievable self). Here, instead of forming a unity, the self was composed of a sum of sensations, nothing more.[76] Looking inward, in the end, would also not provide the moral certainty it had promised. Schnitzler put this well, again in *Der Weg ins Freie*, when Bermann remarks that whether one is guilty depends on the level of the self one is on, and even when all levels are illuminated it is still unclear what the real verdict is. Bermann asks: 'What use is it to me, in the end, that the lights are shining on all levels of my psyche? What use is my knowledge of men and my wonderful understanding? Nothing...less than nothing.'[77] This dilemma, for Schnitzler a Jewish one, meant that there was no fixed point in the moral universe anymore. This was a moral as well as a cultural crisis.

Yet Schnitzler remained ambiguous about the possibility of a moral order. He did see the necessity of the moral self, and at one point he seems to suggest a self beyond the empirical. Addressing Georg von Wergenthin, Bermann states: 'When I want to have a well-ordered world, I must create one myself. That is hard for someone who is not God himself.[78] What this meant was that value had to be created by the individual. Yet it could be created, as God had created the world. Hence a self beyond the old value systems was assumed, for how else could value be created?[79] It was another Jew, Otto Weininger, who at the beginning of the century gave the clearest answers to the questions Schnitzler was raising, and in his work can be seen the intimate way in which the attempt to solve the Jewish problem intermeshed with the general cultural crisis.

JEWS, VALUE AND THE SELF

Otto Weininger has been seen as the best pathological example of the Jewish assimilation in Vienna. He is known as the Jewish self-hater *par excellence*.[80] Yet within Weininger's view of the world lie many of the

---

[76] See William Johnston, *The Austrian Mind: an Intellectual and Social History 1848–1938* (Berkeley 1972, pb. 1983) pp. 184–6.

[77] 'Was hilft's mir am Ende, dass in allen meiner Stockwerken die Lichter brennen? Was hilft's mir mein Wissen von den Menschen und mein herrliches Verstehen? Nichts... Weniger als nichts.' Schnitzler, *Der Weg ins Freie*, pp. 329–30.

[78] 'Ich, wenn ich eine wohlgeordnete Welt haben will, ich muss mir immer selbst erst eine schaffen. Das ist anstrengend für jemanden, der nicht der liebe Gott ist.' *Ibid.* p. 330.

[79] For Schnitzler's own attempted explanation see Schnitzler, *Aphorismen*, pp. 30–1.

[80] For instance, Theodor Lessing, *Der jüdische Selbsthass* (Berlin 1930) pp. 80ff; Peter Gay, 'Encounter with Modernism: German Jews in German Culture 1888–1914' in *Midstream*, Feb. 1975, vol. XXI, no. 2, p. 58.

attitudes prevalent in Vienna's Jewish community, and what is remarkable about his work is the way in which the connection between his attempt to master the Jewish problem and his philosophy in general is so clearly displayed. It is clear that many of his views stemmed directly from his upbringing. He came from a background of Bohemian, Hungarian and Viennese Jewry. As such he was born Jewish and was given the Jewish name of Schlomo at his circumcision.[81] Yet his father, Leopold, can fairly be described as a Jewish antisemite. Although the father remained Jewish until very near his death, evidence from the family suggests that he despised other Jews, and, as with so many other Viennese Jews, was a great admirer of Wagner with all that that entailed.[82] Weininger thus grew up with the tension between a Jewish background and a hatred of things Jewish.

To complicate the matter further, the father displayed attitudes which seem to be survivals of his Jewish heritage. He was a strict patriarch in the home, but more importantly he did all he could to encourage Otto's early signs of intelligence by flooding him with books and more books.[83] It was thus natural that Otto should seek to resolve and overcome the inner contradictions between his Jewishness and his hatred of Jews in the world of the mind, of books. There was a ready model in the tradition of German philosophy, the idea of self-overcoming. We have already discussed the attraction of the concept of an ethical self capable of overcoming the empirical self for assimilating Jews in the example of Joseph Ehrlich and others. Indeed the whole strategy of the assimilation depended on the idea of the autonomous self, for without this the idea of breaking with the past and forming a new society was not feasible. Yet it was just this self which was now seen as illusory by Schnitzler among others. The self was reduced to a collection of warring selves, which could not provide the decisiveness needed for a clean break with history. To achieve this, Weininger would have to restore the idea of Kant's 'intelligible self', while taking into account the theories of empirical psychology which denied the moral self as such.

This is what he did in his notorious book, *Geschlecht und Charakter*. His answer to Mach's 'irretrievable self' was a metaphysical order of selves on a Schopenhauerian model, which he labelled in sexual terms.[84] Man represented a version of Kant's 'intelligible self'; Woman represented an amalgam of Lombroso's views on women, Freud's idea of a sexually driven psyche and Mach's 'irretrievable self'.[85] Weininger stated that the real self,

[81] David Abrahamsen, *The Mind and Death of a Genius* (New York 1946) pp. 6–16.
[82] *Ibid.* pp. 8, 57.   [83] *Ibid.* p. 15.
[84] Otto Weininger, *Geschlecht und Charakter* (Vienna 1903, 1919) pp. 9–10, 469.
[85] *Ibid. passim* esp. pp. 93–99, on Kant, pp. 202ff.

mankind's meaning, was embodied in Man, in his perfect form the genius.[86] Since this was an imperfect world, however, we were all to some degree 'bi-sexual', composed of male and female plasma, and thus possessing aspects of both the male and female ideals. This explained why men were sexual, but Man was the antithesis of sexuality.[87] If only the higher self within all of us could overcome the empirical, female self, we could attain moral perfection.[88]

Much attention has been given to Weininger's admittedly shocking misogyny.[89] This has meant that the other side of his equation, the concept of Man, has been neglected. This is unfortunate, for Weininger's purpose becomes much clearer when this side of his thought is recognized. The system of character types which he employs turns out to be an attempt to provide an apolitical solution to the battle of the sexes. As in Schnitzler the only real solution is a personal, ethical and asocial one – a radically stoic position. Man's inner meaning is the genius, pure consciousness.[90] Weininger is quite clear that the purpose of Man is not Nietzsche's Will to Power, but the Will to Value.[91] This is a purely ethical goal outside the social or political realm.[92] Man's purpose was to be a genius, which meant omniscience, the ideal of which was identical with God.[93] Logic and memory were also to be identified with God, so the only possible conclusion was that the pursuit of knowledge and logical thought were the *ethical* goals of Man.[94] Knowledge, moreover, began with self-knowledge, and the self was the root of all logic – due to the law of identity.[95] Therefore logic and ethics were in effect equivalent to being true to the self: 'However logic and ethics are at base one and the same – duty to one's self.'[96] The pursuit of inner knowledge had become the goal of ethics. Furthermore, Weininger developed the idea that beauty, erotic and aesthetic, was but the projection of the ethical self onto the object of contemplation or creation.[97] Thus 'all aesthetics is a product of ethics'.[98] There was no absolute aesthetics, everything depended on the ethical self. While this kind of philosophical construction was common in German philosophy, many of the ideas were also in complete accord with Weininger's puritanical upbringing, and look for all the world like a secularized version of Jewish stoicism.

The irony is that Weininger was using the concept of the ethical self, the

---

[86] *Ibid.* pp. 126–39.   [87] *Ibid.* pp. 13–50.   [88] *Ibid.* pp. 451–61.
[89] For instance, Jacques Le Rider, *Le Cas Otto Weininger* (Paris 1982) pp. 137–66.
[90] Weininger, *Geschlecht und Charakter*, pp. 137, 145.
[91] *Ibid.* pp. 167ff.   [92] *Ibid.* pp. 189, 218–9.   [93] *Ibid.* p. 215.
[94] *Ibid.* pp. 198, 228–9.   [95] *Ibid.* pp. 191–99.
[96] 'Logik und Ethik aber sind im Grunde nur eines und dasselbe – Pflicht gegen sich selbst.' *Ibid.* p. 200.   [97] *Ibid.* p. 316.
[98] 'alle Ästhetik ein Geschöpf der Ethik bleibt.' *Ibid.* p. 320.

genius, as an antidote for the contemporary society which he regarded as tainted not only with female sexuality, but also with Jewish nihilism. A long chapter in his book is devoted to the theme of *Das Judentum*.[99] From this it becomes quite clear that Weininger regarded the quality of Jewishness as an idea or principle with disgust. All that Weininger saw as wrong with society and culture is blamed on the Jews.[100] Or rather, the Jew, for throughout the chapter Weininger is careful to point out that the idea of Jewishness and individual Jews must not be confused.[101] The reason for this becomes evident towards the end of his diatribe, when he makes his largest accusation: 'The Jew is the unbeliever.'[102] Around this claim Weininger builds his solution to the problem which Schnitzler recognized, the lack of identity.

In Weininger's view, belief was the fundament of all form, of everything which allowed of thought. It was belief in the truth of God which allowed belief in the self, which in turn lay beneath the laws of logic. The existence of the law of logic could not be proven because, said Weininger, it was not possible to prove in thought that which formed the basis of that very thought. It was necessary to believe, if one wanted to retain any validity for thought at all.[103] The Jew as non-believer was thus for Weininger a symbol of the nihilism of modern culture. The Jew believed in nothing, not even himself. Worse still, whereas the Aryan always had a clear view of every situation, the Jew always saw various possibilities, for there was no unity to his character. He lacked the 'Einfalt' of belief; instead 'Inner multiplicity...is absolute Jewishness.'[104]

This was exactly Schnitzler's complaint. Weininger was offering a solution through the recognition of the existence of value and the self above – beyond – the empirical evidence. This could restore the way to freedom through the inner self. What is more, Weininger was also seeing this as a Jewish problem for the Jewish individual to solve. The spread of disbelief and the loss of identity were not to be solved by mass movements, least of all antisemitism or Zionism. 'Therefore the Jewish question can only be solved individually.'[105] At base this Jewish question was one of how to regain belief. The solution to the Jewish question was thus the solution to the general malady of mankind. The answer was self-overcoming.

It is quite clear in Weininger's work that it is 'the Jew' who is the one who battles with the problems raised by modernity. The Aryan genius is born with belief in God and the self. Yet the truly great genius for

---

[99] *Ibid.* pp. 399–442.   [100] *Ibid.* pp. 406ff.   [101] *Ibid.* pp. 402–5, 14.
[102] 'Der Jude ist der ungläubige Mensch.' *Ibid.* p. 427.   [103] *Ibid.* pp. 193–8, 427.
[104] 'Innere Vielfältigkeit...ist das absolute Jüdische.' *Ibid.* pp. 427–32.
[105] 'Darum kann die Judenfrage nur individuell gelöst werden.' *Ibid.* p. 415.

Weininger is the religious genius, the founder of religion, and this must be a Jew, for to become a saviour of mankind it is first necessary to overcome the self, as Jesus Christ did in his forty days in the wilderness.[106] The Jewish religion now takes on a different light. Ancient Judaism is praised. What happened was that Christianity, one of the two possibilities inherent in the religion, separated from Jewishness, which is its mutual negation. Christianity is thus a product of Judaism's inner dialectic. Christ had to be 'Jewish' to overcome himself and be pure: 'Judaism is the abyss over which Christianity is built.' The theological purpose of the survival of Jewishness in the world is thus that other 'Jews', following Christ, can overcome their Jewish nature and become themselves redeemers.[107] Weininger's hope for the world lies in the self-overcoming of a Jew.

There is a great deal of irony in this conclusion. Weininger, the 'self-hater', nevertheless saw the hope for the future as coming from within the Jewish people, for, though it was possible for someone such as Wagner to be a 'Jew' despite his Aryan birth, it was the Jews who possessed the greatest degree of 'Jewishness'.[108] It was just that the Jew had to leave his Jewish self behind, by believing in the validity of the self, logic and God. The Jew thus came to play the central rôle in Weininger's whole theory of cultural decadence and its remedy. Schnitzler's problematic is solved by the reassertion of the existence of the moral self, out of necessity. The greatest irony is that Weininger's solution, faith in the self, in inner truth and value, looks very much like a variant of the tradition of Jewish stoicism with its emphasis on the individual's relation to God. What Weininger was decrying as 'Jewish' was very much the result of the original 'self-overcoming', the assimilation, which religious Jews were already in the 1880s blaming for the irreligiosity – and Jewish antisemitism – of the new generation.[109] Weininger's overcoming of the Jew was a response, in a way, to the predicament caused by the assimilation in the first place.[110] What seemed an attack on the Jewish tradition was, as at least one commentator saw, in many ways a return, though unwitting, to that tradition.[111] This interpretation is speculative; what is clear, however, is that Weininger's solution to being Jewish in an antisemitic society rested on the belief in a world of absolute values lying not in the social sphere,

---

[106] *Ibid.* pp. 433–7.   [107] *Ibid.* pp. 438–40.   [108] *Ibid.* pp. 440, 402.

[109] Cf. J. S. Bloch, 'Wie gebieten wir Einhalt dem rapiden Verfall des religiösen Geistes?' in *Österreichische Wochenschrift. Centralorgan für die gesammten Interessen des Judenthums* (*ÖW*) 15 October 1884 (1.1) pp. 3–5. Bloch blamed religious apathy among parents for the 'religiöser Nihilismus' of Jewish youth, which in turn was leading them to Schönerer, and creating 'jüdischer Antisemitismus'.

[110] Cf. Willi Handl, *Die literarische Welt: Erinnerungen* (Munich 1960) pp. 29–32.

[111] Georg Klaren, *Otto Weininger: der Mensch, sein Werk und sein Leben* (Vienna 1924) p. 203.

but within; he had made the Jew the one who would, in overcoming himself, realise those values. Religion thus provided the ultimate refuge for the Jewish self-overcomer for that was his world.

It might be thought that Weininger with his misogyny and Jewish self-hatred was a marginal figure in the cultural élite of Vienna in the first years of this century. This was not the case. Weininger was one of the most influential figures of his time, especially among Jews in the cultural élite. He was a central topic of conversation in the literary coffee-houses, and even someone such as Stefan Zweig regarded Weininger as a genius.[112] Most important was the recognition which Weininger received from cultural radicals around Karl Kraus. Not only Kraus himself, but also Schoenberg and Wittgenstein professed their admiration for him.[113] The younger Hermann Broch and Franz Kafka also seem to have taken much of what Weininger said to heart.[114]

What is important is not so much the degree of influence, but the fact that such people were attracted to Weininger's way of thinking in the first place. It cannot simply be put down to the *succès de scandale* of Weininger's suicide. These people were attracted to Weininger partly because they too were thinking along similar lines, especially with regard to the place of ethics and religion within culture.[115] There was a religious undertone to much of Viennese culture which was only thinly disguised by modern forms. Many conversions, for instance, were not undertaken due to considerations of expediency, but out of deep religious conviction. Many agreed with Weininger that Judaism as it was could not serve as a proper religion, that it was, in Theodor Gomperz's words 'hollow and redundant', 'lacking almost any ethical nourishment'.[116] Many Jewish individuals came to their new religion looking for a new faith.[117] Yet someone such as Kraus was not coming to his adopted religion simply for the dogma of the Church. When he tried to explain why he had left Judaism, 'the last thing that ties me to the literary swindlers', for Catholicism he could only say

[112] See Hartmut Binder, 'Ernst Polak – Literat ohne Werk' in *Jahrbuch der deutschen Schiller Gesellschaft* 1979 (23) (Stuttgart 1979) p. 384; *Das Wiener Kaffeehaus*, p. 76; also Milan Dubrovic, 'Joseph Roth und der "Querulant"' in *Spectrum, Die Presse*, 3 March 1984; Stefan Zweig, *Europäisches Erbe* (Frankfurt 1960) pp. 223–6.

[113] Janik and Toulmin, *Wittgenstein's Vienna*, pp. 73–4; Arnold Schoenberg, *Harmonielehre*, 7th edn (Mainz 1966) p. vi, where in the original foreword Schoenberg wrote: 'Oder wie Weininger und alle andern die ernsthaft gedacht haben.' Wittgenstein, *Culture and Value*, p. 19.

[114] Manfred Durzak, *Hermann Broch* (Hamburg 1966) p. 43; Le Rider, *Le cas Otto Weininger*, p. 223; also paper given by Gerd Stieg, *Langue maternelle, langue marâtre: Karl Kraus et Franz Kafka*, at the Austrian Institute, Paris, 9 October 1984, in the conference *Vienne 1880–1938: Fin de Siècle et Modernisme*.

[115] Cf. Hermann Bahr, *Selbstbildnis* (Berlin 1923) p. 263, on the relation of Jews and religion.   [116] *Gomperz: ein Gelehrtenleben*, p. 173.

[117] For instance, Alma Mahler, *Gustav Mahler*, p. 126.

that it was not to follow the Church's dogma.[118] Kraus plainly had his own idea of what the true values were and, when the Church transgressed these by its collusion with Reinhardt, Kraus gave up Catholicism.[119] Religion was above doctrine, above any single version of it.

Kraus' attitude to religion was a radically individualistic one in the mould of Weininger. Wittgenstein, according to Paul Engelmann, shared this idea of religion being essentially the affair of the individual alone with his faith. The externalities of religion were redundant, what mattered was the search for inner truth, the attainment of identity between the outer moral imperatives and the inner will.[120] Wittgenstein's was a stoic version of what religion meant, and this was a view shared by many in the cultural élite.[121]

It was also clear to some whence the religious side to Viennese culture had come. Hermann Broch in his novel, *Die Schlafwandler*, characterized the Jew as the herald of abstract, unworldly religion, in contrast to the Christian-Platonic vision of a world filled with values.[122] This theme is continued in a note he made in 1938, where he stated that the non-religious Jew was absolutely evil because the complete opposite of his true self.[123] In other words, the Jew was *the* religious man. Theodor Hertzka could appeal to the same idea in the 1890s when he talked of the Semitic spirit being ethical, while the Aryan spirit was technological.[124] In such discussions the point was often made that Christ had been a Jew. Freud took this line when he tried to explain antisemitism not as the result of the fact that Christ had been crucified by the Jews, but rather because Christ himself had been Jewish: antisemitism was the revenge for Christianity's repression of the instinctual life of the heathen peoples. Christianity itself was somehow Jewish.[125]

The fact that Christ was a Jew was something which was often used by members of the cultural élite, in the same way as Weininger, to provide Jewish converts a special status and meaning. Franz Werfel is said to have viewed Christ as a kind of rabbi.[126] Kraus saw Christ as the epitome of the Jew without Jewish qualities.[127] Wittgenstein also seems to have been

[118] Paul Schick, *Karl Kraus* (Hamburg 1965) p. 68.
[119] *Ibid.* p. 110.
[120] Paul Engelmann, *Letters from Wittgenstein; with a Memoir* (Oxford 1967) pp. 70–81.
[121] Cf. Jakob Wassermann, *My Life as German and Jew* (London 1934) pp. 147–8.
[122] Hermann Broch, *Die Schlafwandler* (Frankfurt-on-Main 1978) pp. 580–2.
[123] Durzak, *Broch*, p. 17.
[124] Theodor Hertzka, 'Arischer und semitischer Geist' reported in *ÖW* 20 January 1893 (x.3) pp. 37–40.
[125] Quoted in Wolfgang Häusler, 'Toleranz, Emanzipation und Antisemitismus' in N. Vielmetti, Drabek, Häusler, Stuhlpfarrer, *Das österreichische Judentum* (Vienna 1974) p. 121.
[126] Interview with Milan Dubrovic, 29 September 1983, Vienna.
[127] Kraus, 'Er ist doch e Jud', p. 362.

alluding to a Weiningerian idea when he wrote: 'Amongst Jews "genius" is to be found only in the holy man.'[128] Jews were, whether out of their own nature or the antithesis of that nature, fated to be the carriers of the religious idea, identified as the kind of ethical truth achieved through self-overcoming and the totally ethical view of the world, or so it seemed to some in the cultural élite.

How true was this idea that the religious and ethical emphasis of these individuals stemmed from a Jewish background? It would be foolish to claim that the religio-ethical aspect of Vienna was *exclusively* Jewish. There was, after all, Adolf Loos, who was extremely close to the thought of someone such as Kraus in many respects.[129] Nevertheless, most of the central figures in the group around Kraus were Jewish. The question is, did *their* attitudes mirror their situation as Jews, or was this irrelevant to their work? Was it their Jewish heritage and their being Jews which led them to this attitude, or were they in the same situation as Loos, with only Moravian and Viennese influences to be accounted for, as well as those of modern European culture in general?

Such questions cannot be answered definitively, but some salient facts can be pointed out. Karl Kraus, for instance, came from a fairly typical Jewish manufacturer's family which had moved from Bohemia to Vienna when he was a child.[130] Just as with many Jewish children, he was offered all that education could provide, and when he started to publish his periodical, *Die Fackel*, his father provided the capital and moral support. Displaying a certain independence of mind, Jakob Kraus was proud of his son, even when he was attacking the bourgeois society of which he, the father, was a member.[131] This indicates, I would suggest, that Kraus' individualist attitude was not foreign to the family tradition.

It is often suggested that Kraus's stance, as prophetic defender of the Word, fits very well into some sort of Jewish intellectual tradition.[132] Such claims could easily be denied but for the fact that Kraus himself confirmed this. In February 1934 he wrote that he

thankfully recognizes in the spiritual scorn which he possesses in liberal measure, in the veneration for desecrated life and defiled language, the natural force of an incorruptible Judaism, which he loves above everything: as something which,

[128] Wittgenstein, *Culture and Value*, p. 18.
[129] Janik and Toulmin, *Wittgenstein's Vienna*, pp. 89, 112; but see also Burkhardt Rukschcio and Roland Schachel, *Adolf Loos: Leben und Werk* (Salzburg 1982) p. 295, for the degree to which Loos was part of a 'Jewish' world.
[130] Schick, *Kraus*, pp. 10–13.	[131] *Ibid*. pp. 37, 43.
[132] Frank Field, *The Last Days of Mankind* (London 1967) p. 22–3; Ernst Lothar, *Das Wunder des Überlebens* (Vienna 1966) p. 370; Erich Heller, 'Karl Kraus: Satirist in the Modern World', in *The Disinherited Mind* (London 1952, 1975) pp. 233–54, among many others.

untouched by race, money, class, ghetto or the masses, in short by any sort of hatred between troglodytes and profiteers, exists in and of itself.[133]

This was a man defying fate in the times of Hitler. It was also, however, a very strong statement, and what it identifies as Jewishness is precisely the kind of ethical tradition which has been outlined here. If Kraus really meant what he said, then the idea of him as a kind of prophet within the Jewish tradition gains credence. His ethical stand then becomes a Jewish one.[134]

A similar story can be told of Arnold Schoenberg. He, like Kraus, left the Jewish faith becoming a Protestant.[135] Yet his great love of biblical themes stemmed from his Jewish youth.[136] He could simply continue his already acquired values in his adopted religion. He had a typical Jewish lower-middle class upbringing in the Leopoldstadt, surrounded by Jewish friends such as David Bach.[137] He was very much an outsider in Viennese society from the start. His idols were North Germans, not Austrians.[138] He must have cut a fairly Jewish figure in cultural circles; in any case, from the 1920s Schoenberg began returning to Judaism, as a direct response to personal experience of antisemitism.[139] By the time he had come to write *Moses und Aron*, his opera against opera, he could comment that this opera confirmed his thinking of himself as Jewish.[140]

With Wittgenstein it is not possible to establish any direct Jewish influence, for he was too far away from the tradition. Yet the signs of indirect influence are considerable. The family history was a catalogue of strong-willed individuals breaking with the way things were. The grandfather, Hermann, started this by breaking away from his Jewish family in the ghetto, eventually converting to Protestantism with his wife. The family moved to Vienna, where they married into the higher reaches of non-Jewish society, a successful assimilation. Yet Hermann's eldest son,

---

[133] 'in der freien Verfügung geistigen Hohns, in der Ehrerbeitung für das geschändete Leben und die besudelte Sprache die Naturkraft eines unkompromittierbaren Judentums dankbar erkennt, und über alles liebt: als etwas das von Rasse und Kasse, von Klasse, Gasse und Masse, kurz jeglichem Hasse zwischen Troglodyten und Schiebern unbehelligt in sich beruht.' Karl Kraus, 'Warum die Fackel nicht erscheint' in *Die Fackel* (Munich 1973) vol. 39, end of July 1934, xxxvi, Nr.890–905, p. 38; quoted in Schick, *Kraus*, p. 131.

[134] Cf. Timms, *Kraus*, pp. 241–3 on Kraus's Catholic and Jewish identity.

[135] H. H. Stuckenschmidt, *Schoenberg: his Life, World and Work* (London 1977) p. 34.

[136] *Ibid.* pp. 26, 107.   [137] *Ibid.* pp. 22ff.   [138] *Ibid.* p. 35.

[139] Mahler's nickname for Schoenberg and Zemlinsky was 'Eisele und Beisele', *ibid.* p. 106. On the effect of antisemitism, see Josef Rufer, '*Hommage à Schoenberg*' in Arnold Schoenberg, *Berliner Tagebuch* (Frankfurt 1974) p. 54.

[140] Schoenberg stated this in at least two letters: one to Berg, 16 October 1933, reproduced in Ernst Hilmar, ed., *Arnold Schoenberg*, catalogue (Vienna 1974) p. 125; in translation in Arnold Schoenberg, *Letters*, ed. E. Stein (London 1964) p. 184; another to Joseph Rufer, 24 July 1935, repr. in Hilmar, *Schoenberg*, p. 329.

Karl, was equally as self-willed as his father, going off to America, and then marrying a half-Jewish girl, Leopoldine Kalmus, which was not looked upon approvingly in the family. This was a typical example, albeit a very successful one, of the processes of Jewish emancipation and assimilation. Karl even displayed certain tendencies which were evidently handed down from the father, but which, far from being something 'Protestant', resemble the stoic inheritance of the ghetto from which the grandfather came. Karl Wittgenstein refused a title and in 1898, when the government started to interfere in his business dealings, and for no other apparent reasons, resigned all his directoral positions and retired from active business life at the age of fifty-two. This was the action of a man confident that social values, the keeping up of appearances, were not the true ones.[141]

The ethos of the Wittgenstein family can be summed up in the words: 'Life as a task.' There was a massive emphasis on the duty of the individual to fulfill his responsibilities. This extended to the aesthetic world. Here, if we are to believe Janik and Toulmin, the family identified their Jewish heritage as a type of 'aesthetic idealism'.[142] In other words, the view of the aesthetic world as a world of responsibility was credited to the Jewish tradition. This is the kind of milieu in which Wittgenstein grew up with a stress on the ethical quite foreign to most of Viennese society.[143] On the other hand, when Wittgenstein ended up in the Moravian town of Olmütz during the First World War, there was an almost immediate understanding between him and the circle of friends around Paul Engelmann, all Jewish.[144] It is speculation, but it does seem that – with Kraus, Weininger and Schoenberg – Wittgenstein and these people saw the world through the same 'moral spectacles'. Although an Adolf Loos could also do this, he was exceptional, whereas the others were part of a sizeable group, which shared the 'family resemblances' of their Jewish background. Not all Jews thought like this, and a few non-Jews belonged, but the historical developments and experience within the various groups meant that, within Viennese culture, such a view of the world was more or less restricted to people from a Jewish background. It remains for us to make a few speculative suggestions as to how this religio-ethical approach manifested itself in Viennese culture.

[141] Lecture by Bryan McGuinness, 14 June 1984, in the School for Slavonic and East European Studies, London; Janik and Toulmin, *Wittgenstein's Vienna*, pp. 169–71; Engelmann, *Letters from Wittgenstein*, pp. 120, 137–8.
[142] Janik and Toulmin, *Wittgenstein's Vienna*, pp. 172–3.
[143] Cf. Frederick Morton, *A Nervous Splendour: Vienna 1888–9* (London 1979) pp. 70–1.
[144] Engelmann, *Letters from Wittgenstein*, pp. 60–9.

THE ETHICS OF AESTHETICS – A FEW SPECULATIONS

We have already seen the way in which people such as Freud and Schnitzler retained an ethical approach. In Weininger we saw the explicit claim that aesthetics was nothing more than a reflection of the ethical self. Further, Weininger's emphasis on the need for belief has been seen to have a broad resonance in the rest of Vienna's avant-garde. This is equally true of Weininger's tendency to conflate ethics and aesthetics – with each other and with the metaphysical self. One might say that for much of Vienna's cultural élite, especially the Krausians, culture became the ground for the ethical pursuit of the individual, divorced from society.

Paul Engelmann in his memoirs on Wittgenstein wrote: 'Kraus was (after Weininger) the first to raise an earnest voice of warning, reminding an epoch given to judging life as well as art by one-sided aesthetic canons that the morality of an artist is vital to his work.'[145] The mention of Weininger is not fortuitous. It is true that Kraus disagreed with Weininger's attitude to Woman, regarding the female principle as the fount of all creation, to be adored and not denied. Yet there was much to the form of Weininger's theorizing with which Kraus agreed. The idealization of the sexes, a radically individualistic approach to society, but most of all the ethical nature of artistic creation were points on which Kraus and Weininger were in accord. Though creative inspiration, for Kraus, was female and extra-moral, the artist in transforming inspiration into art was performing a male function. He was thus subject to the ethical imperative of being true to his inspiration. The approach was not identical to Weininger's, but it was in the same vein.[146]

Paul Schick makes much of Kraus' idea of the moral responsibility of the artist; he concludes that for Kraus: 'Ethics and aesthetics were... inseparable.' Pure aestheticism was worthless; in Kraus' words: 'The aesthete's attitude to beauty is the same as the pornographer's to love, or the politician's to life.'[147] In other words, Kraus saw it was the artist's duty to express the truth of his creation. The aesthetic product was not to be judged on grounds of how pleasing it was, but on the ethical grounds of truth. It was the imperative of being true to creation, which for the poet meant language, the Word, which ruled Kraus.[148] We have seen that at one point at least Kraus attributed his reverence for language to his Jewishness. His vicious attacks on the Viennese, 'Jewish' press could thus

[145] *Ibid.* pp. 125–6.
[146] Janik and Toulmin, *Wittgenstein's Vienna*, pp. 73–4; Field, *The Last Days of Mankind*, pp. 57–8; Heller, *Kraus*, pp. 250–1; on Kraus as an individualist, Belke, *Popper-Lynkeus*, p. 200.   [147] Schick, *Kraus*, p. 66.
[148] Janik and Toulmin, *Wittgenstein's Vienna*, pp. 67–91; Field, *The Last Days of Mankind*, pp. 26–7.

be understood as his condemnation in the spirit of the prophets, of the prostitution of language, which journalism represented, from within the Jewish tradition. It was precisely because the Jews were betraying their true Jewishness by destroying the Word that Kraus attacked them.[149] His whole career can be seen as the attempt to preserve the ethical truth of language within the aesthetic world.

Arnold Schoenberg had the same kind of approach as Kraus and Weininger.[150] He was concerned, as Kraus was, with the problem of how art could serve as the expression of inner inspiration. The musical thought, 'der Gedanke', should be expressed in an authentic way.[151] Schoenberg regarded music as a logical medium, which communicated 'thoughts'; it was not a beautiful sound.[152] His problem was, given the breakdown of the conventions of tonality within western music, how were these 'Gedanken' to be expressed?[153] He initially moved to atonality, then adopted the idea of the twelve-tone scale.[154] Yet it was always composition, and not any particular mechanics of composition which mattered to him, 'twelve-tone *composition*, not *twelve-tone* composition'. He wanted to enable the composer to compose in a way which freed him from the phrase, from social convention, so that the composition was the composer's own creation, and hence his own ethical responsibility.[155] This was the same as Kraus' emphasis on the need for authenticity, the matching of personality and creation, the same individualistic approach.

Schoenberg for much of his career appears to have been completely German in his approach, to the extent that one can talk of such national distinctions in music. Yet there was always this religious undercurrent in him, which though latent for a long time from the 1920s became increasingly obvious. By the time he wrote *Moses und Aron*, his religiosity, in a Jewish form, was plain.[156] It is this opera which expresses Schoenberg's

---

[149] See Field, *The Last Days of Mankind*, pp. 22–3; Berthold Viertel's comments in Harry Zohn, *Wiener Juden in der deutschen Literatur* (Tübingen 1964) p. 69; Schick, *Kraus*. pp. 37–40.

[150] Schoenberg wrote in the copy of the *Harmonielehre* which he gave to Kraus: 'I have learnt more from you, perhaps, than a man should learn, if he wants to remain independent.' Quoted in Janik and Toulmin, *Wittgenstein's Vienna*, p. 102.

[151] *Ibid.* pp. 106ff; lecture by Professor Alexander Goehr at the Edinburgh Festival 1983, 25 August 1983.

[152] Cf. Stuckenschmidt, *Schoenberg*, p. 385.

[153] *Ibid.* p. 420; Charles Rosen, *Schoenberg* (Glasgow 1976) pp. 26ff.

[154] Stuckenschmidt, *Schoenberg*, p. 263; Rosen, *Schoenberg*, pp. 41ff; Janik and Toulmin, *Wittgenstein's Vienna*, p. 250.

[155] *Ibid.* pp. 108–12, 250.

[156] Schoenberg, in his letter to Berg, 16 October 1933, pointed out that his work had shown Jewish influences since 1922, notably in *Der biblische Weg* (started 1922, finished 1926–7), and in his *Credo*, p. 27, of 1926. Schoenberg, *Letters*, p. 184; Peter Gradenwitz, 'Mahler and Schoenberg' in *LBIY* 1960, p. 270 (translation of the *Credo*); Stuckenschmidt, *Schoenberg*, pp. 310, 370 (letter to Webern, 4 August 1933, on *Moses und Aron*

ideas about the relationship between truth, ethics and aesthetics in most detail. It has been called the opera of Austrian Expressionism.[157] Be that as it may, the opera's argument harks back to a much older cultural tradition. The central argument is that the ethical truth of God's Word can be known by the ethical man – Moses – but cannot be expressed by him nor communicated to the masses. Aaron's rôle is thus to put truth into aesthetic form, music, which the masses can understand. Yet Aaron, in the sensuous joy of the singer, distorts God's message. His song is further perverted by the masses into a cult of sensuality and excess, idolatry. The only place where unity with God can be achieved is in the wilderness.[158] Only without sensuality, outside a world of hedonistic aesthetics, in a desert without figurative form, alone, can man find true understanding and faith. This was virtually identical with Jewish attitudes to idolatry. Instead of a baroque drama, the culminating work of Vienna 1900 was a modern version of the legend of the golden calf, the origin of Jewish anti-aestheticism.[159]

The reason why music distorts God's Word in the opera is because Aaron indulges in the beauty of song. What if music could be made to be true and not beautiful? Schoenberg's answer to this question, according to Schorske, was to make music into a logical construction which ignored canons of aesthetics – that made logic the arbiter of musical form regardless of beauty.[160] Underneath the apparent wilderness of the music, the logical truth would become manifest. Weininger had thought that logic was at the base of ethics and aesthetics. Another Viennese Jewish thinker, Broch, had similar ideas.[161] He also thought logic to be identical to the *Logos*, the Word of God.[162] In *The Death of Virgil*, which itself was about artistic integrity, he described the Word of God as a pure music.[163] For someone such as Broch, then, Schoenberg, by making logic the base of his musical language, was returning music to its original function, as

as a Jewish work). Also see the brilliant analysis of *Moses und Aron* by George Steiner, 'Schoenberg's "Moses and Aaron"' in *Encounter*, June 1965 (24) pp. 40–46.

[157] Cf. Schorske, *Fin-de-Siècle* Vienna, pp. 360–2.

[158] *Ibid.* pp. 360–1; Gradenwitz, 'Mahler and Schoenberg' in *LBIY* 1960, pp. 276–82. The last words of the third act, spoken by Moses are: 'Aber in der Wüste seid ihr unüberwindlich und werdet das Ziel erreichen: Vereinigt mit Gott.' Arnold Schoenberg, *Moses und Aron: Textbuch* (Mainz 1957) p. 32.

[159] Cf. Peter Gradenwitz, 'Jews in Austrian Music' in Fraenkel, ed., *The Jews of Austria*, p. 24.

[160] Schorske, *Fin-de-Siècle* Vienna, p. 362.   [161] Durzak, *Broch*, p. 86.

[162] Erich Kahler, *Die Philosophie von Hermann Broch* (Tübingen 1962) pp. 20ff.

[163] Hermann Broch, *The Death of Virgil* (Oxford 1983) pp. 414–6. The book ends with the lines 'the word without speech'. The original reads 'trotzdem immer noch Wort: er konnte es nicht festhalten, und er durfte es nicht festhalten; unerfasslich unaussprechbar war es für ihn, denn es war jenseits der Sprache'. H. Broch, *Der Tod des Vergil* (Frankfurt-on-Main 1976) p. 454; cf. Steiner, *Moses and Aaron*, p. 45.

the expression of God's Word. Is it fair to say that that is what he felt he actually was doing? In any case, Schoenberg is an obvious example of the invasion of the world of aesthetics by the ethical impulse of truth, and it does not seem improbable that this stemmed from attitudes whose origins lay in his Jewish background.[164]

Wittgenstein shared with Kraus and Schoenberg the idea of the artist's ethical responsibility. He demanded 'veracity' for all forms of cultural expression – the agreement between feeling and form.[165] His *Notebooks* of 1914–16 show a deep concern with ethical problems, and Engelmann claims he shared the same personal view of religion.[166] Above all there are striking similarities between his views on logic, ethics and aesthetics with those of the others so far discussed here. Janik and Toulmin's book, *Wittgenstein's Vienna*, is at base concerned merely with what was meant by Wittgenstein's enigmatic claim: 'Ethics and aesthetics are one and the same.'[167] They have traced how this was connected with the ideas of Kraus and others, including Weininger.[168] Here I would like to point out other similarities between the thought of Wittgenstein and Weininger, which are connected to this enigmatic quotation.[169] They concern the attitude of both to the problem of the self.

Weininger had seen that any positivist denial of the self was misguided, for it was not something which could be proved or disproved; it just was. Proof could only be conveyed in language, but language and logic assumed identity; yet, for Weininger, the law of identity already made evident (*dartun*) the existence of the self.[170] This could not be proven, because its assumption lay at the base of language itself.[171] Weininger said of the self:

[164] Cf. Steiner, *Moses and Aaron*, pp. 42–3, where Schoenberg is seen as a Jew defending artistic morality against the libertinage of such as Richard Strauss.

[165] Engelmann, *Letters from Wittgenstein*, pp. 82–9; also see Erich Heller, 'Karl Kraus und die Ethik der Sprache' in W. Kudszin and H. C. Seeba, eds., *Austriaca: Beiträge zur österreichischen Literatur* (Tübingen 1975) p. 306.

[166] Ludwig Wittgenstein, *Notebooks 1914–16* (Oxford 1961) pp. 73–87; Engelmann, *Letters from Wittgenstein*, pp. 70–81.

[167] See Janik and Toulmin, *Wittgenstein's Vienna*, pp. 167–201. Quotation, p. 193.

[168] *Ibid.* pp. 199–200, on Kraus' influence.

[169] Connections between Weininger and Wittgenstein have been made, especially by Allan Janik: see Janik, 'Wittgenstein and Weininger' in *Second Kirchberg Wittgenstein Symposium 1977* (Vienna 1978) pp. 25–8; Janik, 'Wittgenstein, Ficker and Der Brenner' in, C. G. Luckhardt, ed. *Wittgenstein: Sources and Perspectives* (Ithaca 1979) pp. 172–5. Also see Rush Rhees, ed., *Recollections of Wittgenstein* (Oxford 1984) pp. 177–87 for a refutation of any major intellectual connection.

[170] Otto Weininger, *Geschlecht und Charakter*, pp. 190–204.

[171] *Ibid.* p. 193: 'Der Satz der Identität...vermehrt nicht einen Reichtum der er vielmehr gänzlich erst begründet.' Also: 'Die Norm des Denkens kann nicht im Denken selbst gelegen sein.'

The existence of the subject cannot be deduced, here Kant is quite correct in his critique of rational psychology. But it can be demonstrated (dartun), where this existence appears clearly and unambiguously, in logic. One does not need to regard the intelligible self as a mere possibility of thought, which is only necessary to ensure the validity of the moral law, as Kant does.[172]

He also stated that the law of identity 'will by its own self-evidence reveal the existence of the subject'.[173]

Wittgenstein's ideas in the *Tractatus Logico-Philosophicus* are very close to this approach. Here the true self is the 'metaphysical subject' which is 'the limit of the world – not a part of it'. The self, though existent, could not be expressed in the world of language – *the* world. It was thus beyond criteria of proof; rather it made itself manifest by the fact of the world as 'my world'.[174] Wittgenstein, and Weininger, had thus taken the self out of the world of language, of inter-subjectivity. It had become an absolute which was untouchable, either by the soul merchants or any accident of birth. Most importantly: 'The sense of the world must lie outside the world.'[175] Meaning became independent of the vagaries of existence. Weininger had said that the genius (the metaphysical self) saw things as they gave meaning (bedeuten) separately from the scientist who only saw how they could make sense (sinnfähig sein).[176] Wittgenstein now said the same: value was a matter for the self, beyond all inter-subjectivity. This was extreme ethical individualism, or ethical universalism, but nothing in between.[177] Ethics and aesthetics were the same because they were both expressions of a self independent of the world.[178] Wittgenstein, in his ethical stance, his religious concept of absolute value, and his radical individualism was very much in the mould of the other potential Jewish stoics discussed here.

But was Wittgenstein a *Jewish* stoic? Was a Jewish background really important in producing this stoic attitude? It would be speculative to answer this question positively *or* negatively. Yet seen in the context in which he lived, of the people in Vienna he admired and by whom he was influenced, I would say that the Jewish element was far from irrelevant.

---

[172] 'Die Existenz des Subjektes lässt sich nicht ableiten, hierin behält Kantens Kritik der rationalen Psychologie vollkommen recht. Aber es lässt sich dartun, wo diese Existenz streng und unzweideutig auch in der Logik zum Ausdruck gelangt; und man braucht nicht das intelligible Ich als blosse Denkmöglichkeit hinzustellen, die uns allein das moralische Gesetz völlig zur Gewissheit zu machen geeignet sei, wie Kant dies tat.' *Ibid.* p. 198.

[173] 'Wird durch seine Evidenz also die Existenz des Subjektes offenbaren.' *Ibid.* p. 197.

[174] Ludwig Wittgenstein, *Tractatus Logico-philosophicus* (London 1961) axiom 5.641. Cf. axiom 5.5421: 'This shows too that there is no such thing as the soul – the subject etc. – as it is conceived in the superficial psychology of the present day.'

[175] *Ibid.* axiom 6.41.   [176] Otto Weininger, *Geschlecht und Charakter*, p. 214.

[177] Engelmann, *Letters from Wittgenstein*, pp. 109–10.

[178] Cf. Wittgenstein, *Tractatus*, axiom 6.421.

Wittgenstein was, after all, ultimately a product of the multi-faceted and extremely complex process of the Jewish assimilation.[179] As such he shared attitudes with people from the same background, attitudes which had a decisive impact on much of Viennese culture. This can be seen in the retreat into the self and the ethical nature of the retreat. Seen from the perspective of the failure of any true assimilation and the survival of some sort of Jewish secularized tradition, we can explain this retreat as both a reaction to an antisemitic environment and, though diverted into aesthetics, the continuation of a pre-assimilationist emphasis of Jews on the world of the mind. Further, from the Jewish perspective, it makes sense that these cultural figures should see in the aesthetic realm not any way of avoiding truth, by living dreams, but rather that they should have brought to the temple of art the fervent and iconoclastic search for truth which had so marked their ancestors: the only difference was that now these people were finding truth *through* art.

One might describe much of Vienna's cultural thematic as the attempt to make aesthetics the ethical realm of the individual. Aesthetics, for Weininger or Schoenberg, was no longer so much a realm of beauty as the central battleground of the individual's struggle for the meaning of existence – ethical truth. What lay behind *this* approach, I would suggest, was a tradition which stretched back far beyond the German Enlightenment to people in the mould of Rabbi Boruch and Lazar Auspitz; what we see in Vienna in the first decades of this century, in the radical ethical individualism of Kraus or Wittgenstein, owed the great weight of its influence to a radically transformed Judaism, all the more powerful for being a hidden, perhaps unconscious factor.

Wittgenstein, in his enmeshing of aesthetics with ethics, in his attempt to put the source of all value, the self or the moral universe, outside the world of inter-subjectivity, was following the logic of the Jewish experience in Vienna. If society refused to see the neutral *Mensch* and insisted on seeing individuals in racial or ethnic terms, then *one* of the solutions was to create a world outside that society within a metaphysical self. Here the ethical pursuit of truth, of honesty, could continue, despite a society which contradicted such aims. In this way the attempt to escape being Jewish also saw the transfer of Jewish stoic attitudes to this now extra-racial sphere. Wittgenstein was, in the end, not a Jewish stoic, but a stoic *tout court*. There were also other sources for this stoicism. Yet it is not too outlandish to say that within this stoicism lay the remains of the Jewish

---

[179] Cf. Engelmann, *Letters from Wittgenstein*, p. 119: Wittgenstein was 'the greatest offspring and antithesis of that closing epoch of Viennese-Jewish culture during the first quarter of our century when the light of European intellect shone with full brilliance for the last time, up to the present.'

tradition, and that, in the conflation of the attempt to achieve assimilation with the survival of a vague Jewish ethical tradition, Wittgenstein was also a part of the phenomenon of the Jewish influence within Viennese culture. And if that is true of Wittgenstein it was also and more definitely true of all the others we have discussed here.

Conclusion – Vienna and the Jews in perspective

The purpose of this study has not been to prove that culture in Vienna was an exclusively Jewish affair to be completely explained by the Jewish experience outlined in the preceding pages. It is clear other aspects were involved. There was, for instance, the Josephinist legacy, which bred a certain type of enlightened attitude among some members of the bureaucracy. In addition, it can be argued that, in a sense, everyone was an 'outsider' in the Habsburg Monarchy, a decaying empire that lacked a centre.[1] Musil's Vienna, therefore, also existed, at least in theory. The Jewish experience of Vienna did not hold a total monopoly in modern Viennese high culture.

What this study has attempted to show, however, is that the immense Jewish presence in Viennese culture around 1900 was neither accidental nor incidental to that culture's character and results, as seen in the work of individual members of its élite. It was not accidental that most of this culture's major figures were Jewish, because, as the study of the Gymnasien has shown, the liberal bourgeois educated classes in Vienna were predominantly Jewish. It looks very much as though the old stories are true, and that the educated liberal bourgeoisie was a Jewish bourgeoisie. Nor was the Jewishness of the cultural élite incidental, for the effect of the Jewish tradition, and the fact of being Jewish, can be seen to have had a major impact on the way that the Jewish element of Viennese culture responded to the events of the turn of the century, even though this expressed itself in a huge variety of forms, of which only the survival of ethical individualism has received concentrated attention in this study. The evidence collected here suggests, at the very least, that the Jewish

---

[1] See Micheal Pollak, 'Cultural innovation and social identity in *fin-de-siècle* Vienna,' in I. Oxaal, M. Pollak and G. Botz, *Jews, Antisemitism and Culture in Vienna* (London, 1987) pp. 59–74; also, Michael Pollak, *Vienne 1900: une identité blessée* (Paris 1984); Edward Timms, *Karl Kraus: Apocalyptic Satirist: Culture and Catastrophy in Habsburg Vienna* (London 1986) pp. 12ff.

experience was a decisive influence on the attitude of Jewish individuals in the cultural élite to their work, and hence on that work itself.

This is all very well, and, as I hope I have shown, it is possible to create a cogent, if speculative, conceptual framework in which the Jewish experience is given a decisive rôle. In the general Viennese context, however, there is the question of how non-Jews, such as Hermann Bahr, Adolf Loos, Kokoschka or Musil, could have held views virtually identical with those of their Jewish colleagues, without the 'Jewish background' of which so much has been made in this study. If the conceptual framework offered here is to survive in a more general context this question must be satisfactorily answered. There are at least two approaches which appear to me to accomplish this. One is the question of interpretation within the Viennese context; the other looks to the wider historical and geographical context to provide support for my argument.

The first approach is to accept the fact that people who were not from a Jewish background could hold similar views, but to point out the need to investigate this by looking at the backgrounds of those individuals in the light of the Jewish experience. This would be to say: the influence of the Jewish background on Jewish individuals in Vienna's cultural life has been shown; now the background of the others must be described to see how they obtained their similar views. If we accept the effect of ethnic, religious and cultural factors for Jews, then we can, perhaps must, do the same for non-Jews. The framework suggested here for the Jewish experience looks as if it might well serve for non-Jews, with different variables. There are aspects of the Jewish experience which, plainly, are not confined to the Jews. The Enlightenment and the admiration for the West were traditions shared with Jews by people such as Bahr and Loos. Loos' architectural theory was, after all, a result of his experience of the United States of America and of English furniture-making.[2] Bahr got most of his ideas from his many expeditions abroad, especially to France.[3] Similarly both men started out as pronounced Germans. Bahr came from a family which was originally Silesian, and he later became a staunchly German Nationalist (and antisemitic) student, before becoming an Austrian patriot.[4] Adolf

---

[2] On Loos and the United States, see Emil Szittya's comments reproduced in *Das Wiener Kaffeehaus* with an introduction by Hans Weigel (Vienna 1978) p. 90; William M. Johnston, *Vienna: the Golden Age 1815–1914* (New York 1981) p. 207; on furniture-making, see Loos' article in the *Neue Freie Presse* morning edition, 19 June 1898 p. 16.

[3] See William M. Johnston, *The Austrian Mind: an Intellectual and Social History 1848–1938* (Berkeley 1972, pb.1983) pp. 119–20.

[4] See Hermann Bahr, *Selbstbildnis* (Berlin 1923) pp. 7–11; Olga Schitzler, *Spiegelbild der Freundschaft* (Vienna 1962) p. 114.

Loos made his name as a stern German Moravian moralist outsider in Vienna.[5] Both men shared an essentially antagonistic attitude to the Viennese Establishment.[6] Thus there were parallels.

It could be argued that many apparent parallels between the ideas and background of Jewish and non-Jewish figures were deceptive. Although Klimt and Mahler were in many ways parallel figures of the *fin de siècle* – exact contemporaries and both, according to Schorske, the victims of social rejection – in their attitudes to the world and to culture they were worlds apart: Klimt the lover of pure hedonism and the erotic, and Mahler, though emotional, the completely intellectual composer for whom music became a religious duty. It is not too difficult to trace the differences between them to their totally different backgrounds.[7] This can also be done in the case of the two 'discoverers' of the twelve-tone scale, Schoenberg and Josef Matthias Hauer. That a Catholic from Wiener Neustadt should discover Schoenberg's 'Jewish' tonal scale is a huge irony, but the impact of this is greatly lessened when it is realized that Hauer's view of the scale was quite different from Schoenberg's.[8]

It could even be argued that neither Bahr nor Loos, the two figures with most in common with the 'Jewish' part of Viennese culture, were ever really in full accord with their Jewish colleagues. Edward Timms has, for instance, pointed out the great difference in attitude, especially in ethical attitude, implied by the respective fields chosen by Loos and Kraus. Whereas Loos, in architecture, never really went far beyond building buildings, Kraus, in the world of language, was involved directly in the very processes of thought on a much higher intellectual and ethical plane.[9] Hermann Bahr's autobiography also shows some interesting divergences from the usual Jewish response. He describes himself as a person who never really felt any moral responsibility for his actions.[10] Although he discovered the existence of an eternal realm of values, it is the realm of beauty. The aesthetic realm leads him, it is true, eventually to

[5] See *Das Wiener Kaffeehaus*, p. 90.

[6] On Bahr, O. Schnitzler, *Spiegelbild*, pp. 114–5; on Loos, Ilsa Barea, *Vienna* (London 1966) p. 257; B. Zeller, L. Greve and W. Volke, eds., *Jugend in Wien: Literatur um 1900*, catalogue (Stuttgart 1974) p. 312.

[7] Cf. Carl E. Schorske, 'Mahler and Klimt: Social Experience and Artistic Evolution' in *Daedalus*, vol.III, no.3, summer 1982, pp. 29–50. Also Maria Bisanz-Prakken, 'Programmatik und subjektive Aussage im Werk von Gustav Klimt, in R. Waissenberger, ed., *Traum und Wirklichkeit: Wien 1870–1930* (Salzburg 1984) pp. 110–19. It is interesting in this context that Kirk Varnedoe has written of the relative failure of Vienna's visual arts in comparison to Freud and Schoenberg. See Varnedoe, *Vienna 1900: Art, Architecture and Design* (New York 1986) p. 220.

[8] See H. H. Stuckenschmidt, *Schoenberg: his Life, World and Work* (London 1977) pp. 263–4; on further instances of differences see Paul Engelmann, *Letters from Wittgenstein; with a Memoir* (Oxford 1967) pp. 17–19; Stuckenschmidt, *Schoenberg*, p. 157.

[9] Timms, *Kraus*, pp. 121–3.   [10] Bahr, *Selbstbildnis*, p. 85.

God, but not, it would seem, by way of ethics.[11] Bahr was not at one with the other members of Young Vienna.[12]

That even within the élite of modern high culture there were such differences in approach, especially concerning the place of ethics in aesthetics, is interesting, and would be a confirmation of my speculations concerning the survival of some kind of Jewish approach. Yet one does not have to go that far. Even if their views were identical, all that would have to be asserted is that those non-Jewish members of the élite were drawn to their ideas from certain aspects of their background, which happen to be similar to parallel aspects in the Jewish background. The latter would continue to be an independent factor.

This first approach receives much of its justification from considerations involved in the second, and, I think, more cogent approach to the problem of putting the Jews in context. Let us start with the premiss, already assumed in the first approach, that no cultural complex can produce ideas that are exclusive to that culture or cultural experience. In other words, no culture or cultural group can ever claim a monopoly on any idea; hermetic exclusivity is an impossibility in the history of ideas. Therefore it is only reasonable that non-Jews could have, from whatever background, somehow or other acquired a way of looking at the world which has been described here as the product of the Jewish experience. Yet this does not invalidate the idea that the Jewish experience was important.

While individuals such as Musil, Loos and Bahr shared ideas with Jewish colleagues, the point about them is that they were exceptions in the group from which they came. Musil came from an official's family and retained the air of a civil servant even when he was writing *The Man without Qualities*.[13] How many architects went over to the United States? How many writers from Vienna who were not Jewish travelled across Europe? While it is true that outstanding cultural figures are always going to be marginal by definition, there is a sense in which these non-Jewish figures were exceptional products of the margin whereas their Jewish counterparts were not. As we have seen, the situation of Jews in Vienna was such that it would have produced certain attitudes as a matter of course, and, at the margin, would have forced the more sensitive among the assimilated Jewish community to come to terms with the problems of the isolated individual. The Jewish experience did not produce a way of looking at the

---

[11] *Ibid*, pp. 80–2, 226–8. It is of note that Kokoschka in his autobiography also denied any interest in the moral aspect of his painting, see Oskar Kokoschka, *My Life* (London 1974) pp. 36, 67.

[12] Pollak, *Vienne 1900*, p. 122, talks of Bahr as outside the central group of Hofmannsthal, Andrian, Schnitzler and Beer-Hofmann.

[13] Wilfried Berghahn, *Robert Musil* (Hamburg 1973) pp. 9ff; the description of Musil as a typical civil servant is that of Stella Ehrenfeld, interview 25 March 1984, Surrey.

world which was exclusively Jewish, but I think it can be said that, in the Viennese context, the views outlined above were seen at the time by Jew and antisemite alike as *typically* Jewish.

One can perhaps go even further in this direction for it is remarkable to what extent non-Jewish figures became attached to the 'Jewish' cultural élite. One way in which this occurred was obvious: marriage. We have already come across various instances of this, such as Franz Brentano marrying a von Lieben, and Kolo Moser marrying a Mautner von Markhof. Similarly, the wife Musil so admired, Martha Heimann, was of Jewish descent.[14] Two of Loos' wives were Jewish also. Loos' career provides an illustration of another means by which non-Jews could, as it were, be co-opted. At one point, when Loos needed work, his supporters suggested to him that he ought to go to Palestine to build houses there. Loos would have none of it, but the suggestion was understandable given the ethnic composition of his group of supporters.[15] That is to say, even when a member of the cultural élite was not Jewish, he often either shared his life with a person from that background, or received much of his support, encouragement and advice from such people.

Then again, there is the question of how non-Jewish figures became involved in modern culture. In the case of Bahr, he tells us that the person who introduced him to the 'intellectual life of Vienna' was none other than his uncle, S. Robiczek, who happened to be a Jewish dentist.[16] Could one not suggest from such instances that, in the cultural élite at least, one is witnessing what has been called a 'double assimilation'? That is to say, the Jews might have been assimilating themselves into what they saw as western culture, but at the same time they were, consciously or not, assimilating the surrounding society, which knew little of western culture as such, to a new set of values.[17]

Much of what Schorske says about Jews 'sharing' the values of northern Protestants is, as will have become evident from the discussions above of the Enlightenment and German culture, unexceptionable.[18] What needs to be stressed, and what Schorske and others like him, at least in print, do not fully acknowledge, is that, even if there had been absolutely no difference between the Jewish and Protestant/liberal bourgeois value systems, the Jewish background to Vienna's cultural élite would still be of the utmost importance, because it was only on account of the Jews that

[14] See Berghahn, *Musil*, p. 68.

[15] Burkhardt Rukschcio and Roland Schachel, *Adolf Loos: Leben und Werk* (Salzburg 1982) p. 295.

[16] Bahr, *Selbstbildnis*, pp. 118ff.

[17] Karl Kraus made exactly this point in yet another diatribe against the *Neue Freie Presse*. See Kraus, *Die Fackel*, no.71, mid-March 1901, p. 1.

[18] Carl E. Schorske, *Fin-de-Siècle Vienna: Politics and Culture* (London 1980) p. 148.

Vienna had a liberal bourgeoisie of the character it did. The non-Jewish liberal bourgeoisie, which Schorske assumes, to all intents and purposes did not exist. The 'Protestants' in Vienna were the Jews.

The best way of putting the Viennese Jews in context is to put Vienna itself at the turn of the century in context. In the introduction the problems with the historiography of Vienna 1900 were briefly discussed, and the point made that what is really remarkable is that Vienna during this period suddenly became a major centre of intellectual innovation, whereas before it had only been known for music. This view of Vienna's place in modern cultural history allows us a large insight into the rôle of Jews in the city's cultural life. If my interpretation is correct, the greater intellectuality of Viennese culture during this era can be explained largely by the Jewish tradition of respect for the mind and learning. The correlation between the process of assimilation and the emergence of a powerful intellectual tradition in Vienna is just too obvious to be accidental.

Taking up another idea suggested in the introduction, it can fairly safely be remarked that *fin-de-siècle* Vienna was not quite the birthplace of the modern cultural world that is supposed. Yet it did produce important premonitions of the problems in culture and society which we now face. There is a point in Schorske's view that it was in Vienna that liberalism and western ideology met first demise.[19] Yet consider the rôle of the Jewish element in this. Liberalism was defeated politically by an avowedly antisemitic coalition, for which the non-Jewish middle classes voted in a large majority. Would this have happened if the most articulate and influential part of the liberal bourgeoisie had not been Jewish? Would antisemitism and with it reactionary mass politics have had anything like the same effect? I doubt it. Therefore the Jewish question was integral to the conditions of the *fin de siècle* and the collapse of liberalism. It could be argued that the Jews were simply filling a vacuum left by the effects of the Counter-Reformation on any nascent capitalist class in Vienna. Yet this is beside the point, for it was the specific nature of the Jewish populace and their historical place in Austrian society which were decisive in undermining liberalism's support among non-Jews and creating a mass politics which, unlike the western democracies, combined political radicalism with particularist discrimination.

The importance of Vienna around 1900 stems largely from the fact that it possessed a cultural élite which, because it came from a Jewish background, could be isolated from the rest of society in a way which would have been impossible in late nineteenth-century Europe if it had been merely Protestant or Catholic Liberal. This isolation, this exposure to

[19] *Ibid.* p. xxvi–xxvii.

the darker side of nineteenth-century society, allowed Jews in the cultural élite to observe and record the nature of post-liberal society and the crisis of the individual with an intensity and in a form which only emerged later in other societies. In those societies these problems had appeared only marginal, whereas for the Jews of Vienna they had become central.

The Jews of Vienna combined a type of approach similar – though not necessarily identical – to that of liberals elsewhere with a fundamental fragility in their social position directly due to their Jewishness. It was this fragility which made them prime candidates for expressing the predicament of the isolated individual in mass society. Furthermore, it was their Jewishness which meant that the liberal bourgeoisie continued to uphold liberal principles, even after liberalism's political collapse, in other forms such as socialism and culture. In the assimilated Jews Vienna possessed a group of people who could not abandon faith in the basic values of freedom of the individual and equality of rights, for to abandon those beliefs would have been to destroy their *raison d'être*. If Vienna was important around 1900, it was due to the crisis of confidence in liberal culture, and this crisis was largely a Jewish crisis. It was the Jewish problematic which powered Vienna's cultural innovation. As for the others, the non-Jews, they merely shared the values of the Jewish cultural élite. The Jewish element, the bulk of that élite, provided the leading ideas and principles of modernism in Vienna and it was the others who followed.

With this second approach can be seen the significance of the Viennese Jews in a Viennese and European context. They were not the sole inventors of the modern world. One need only look at other cultural centres to realize that the Jews of Vienna were only one of the major forces in the European avant-garde around 1900. I would argue, however, that the Jewishness of the cultural élite in Vienna gave the capital of the Habsburg Monarchy a cultural and intellectual importance for that time which it had never known before and certainly no longer possesses. The awkward but inescapable conclusion seems to be that it was indeed its Jews which made Vienna what it was in the realm of modern culture.

Bibliography

1. ARCHIVAL SOURCES

Archive and file index of the *Bibliographica Judaica*, Frankfurt-on-Main.
Geburts- und Todesbücher of the *Israelitische Kultusgemeinde* (copies) in the possession of the city authorities.
File index of Dr Hanns Jäger-Sunstenau, Vienna.
Verzeichnis der im Wiener Gemeindegebiete wohnhaften Wähler für die Wahlen in den Kultusvorstand und der Vertrauensmänner im Jahre 1910 (Vienna 1910).

2. SCHOOL RECORDS

Hauptkataloge and *Maturaprotokolle* of the Akademisches, Franz-Josephs-, Josefstädter-, Mariahilfer-, Schotten-, Sophien-, Sperl- and Wasa- (Maximilians-) gymnasien, 1870–1910 (or from the first *Matura* year of the school).
Maturaprotokolle of the Landstrassergymnasium.
Jahresberichte of the above schools and of the Gymnasium der theresianischen Akademie and the Elisabethsgymnasium.
(With the kind permission of the Wiener Stadtschulrat, Oberrat Dr Wieser and Dr Anzböck.)

3. STATISTICAL SOURCES

Bihl, Wolfdieter, 'Die Juden' in A. Wandruszka and P. Urbanitsch eds., *Die Habsburger Monarchie 1848–1918* (Vienna 1973–) vol. 2, part 2, pp. 880ff.
Frühling, Moritz, *Biographisches Handbuch der in der k.u.k. österr.ungar. Armee und Kriegsmarine aktiv gedienten Offiziere, Ärzte, Truppen-Rechnungs-Führer und sonstigen Militärbeamten jüdischen Stammes* (Vienna 1911).
Cohen, Gary B., 'Die Studenten der Wiener Universität von 1860 bis 1900: ein soziales und geographisches Profil' in R. G. Plaschka and K. Mack, eds., *Wegenetz europäischen Geistes II: Universitäten und Studenten* (Vienna 1987), pp. 290–316.
Goldhammer, Leo, *Die Juden Wiens: eine statistische Studie* (Vienna 1927).
Heuer, Renate, *Bibliographica Judaica* (Frankfurt-on-Main, 1982).
Jäger-Sunstenau, Hanns, 'Die geadelten Judenfamilien im vormärzlichen Wien' (Vienna Univ. Diss. 1950).
Leitner, Helmut, 'Alphabetisches Register wissenschaftlich bedeutender Mediziner

jüdischer Abstammung in Österreich (mit Einschluss der Emigranten)' (typed manuscript).

Maderegger, Sylvia, *Die Juden im österreichischen Ständestaat 1934–38* (Vienna 1973).

Ruppin, Arthur, *Sociologie der Juden* (Berlin 1930), 2 vols.

Schimmer, G. A. 'Die Juden in Österreich' in *Statistiche Monatschrift*, 7 (1881) pp. 489–503.

Statistisches Jahrbuch der Stadt Wien (Vienna 1883–1911).

Stern, Julius, *Werden und Walten der Concordia: Festschrift* (Vienna 1909).

Thon, Jakob, ed., *Die Juden in Österreich* (Berlin 1908).

Öffentliche Vorlesungen an d. kk. Universität Wien, Sommer 1910 (Vienna 1910).

Windt, Berthold, 'Die Juden an den Mittel- und Hochschulen Österreichs seit 1850' in *Statistische Monatschrift*, 7 (1881) pp. 442–57.

4. NEWSPAPERS

Deutsche Wochenschrift, ed. H. Friedjung, 1884–8.

Freies Blatt: Organ zur Abwehr des Antisemitismus, 1894–5.

Neue Freie Presse, 1895–1900 (*NFP*).

Die Neuzeit: Wochenschrift für politische, religiöse und Cultur-Interessen, 1861–7, 1895–1900.

Österreichische Wochenschrift: Centralorgan für die gesammten Interessen des Judenthums, ed. Dr Bloch, 1884–1900 (*OeW*).

Die Wage: eine Wiener Wochenschrift, ed. R. Lothar, 1898–1900.

Die Welt, ed. T. Herzl, 1897–1900.

Wiener Tagblatt: Demokratisches Organ, ed. M. Szeps, 1886–95.

Die Zeit, 1894–6.

5. MANUSCRIPTS

Adler, Victor: letter to Heinrich Friedjung, 12 March 1870.

Friedell, Egon: 'Rezension über Geschlecht und Charakter', (1904).

Lipiner, Siegfried: letter to Moritz Necker, 26 August 1885.

Neurath, Wilhelm: letters to L. A. Frankl, 3 July 1889, 2 February 1890, 4 November 1893.

Zuckerkandl, Berta: letter to Josef Hoffmann, February 1912.

6. INTERVIEWS

Browne, Professor Martha Steffy, New York, 12 September 1987.

Campbell, Joan, (Stolper), Hamilton, Ontario, 9 October 1987.

Czuczka, Erika, Vienna, 7 June 1983.

Dubrovic, Milan, Vienna, 29 September 1983.

Ehrenfeld, Stella, Surrey, 25 March 1984.

Ehrlich, Bettina, London, 4 January 1984.

Faust, Marcel, Vienna, 2 May 1983.

Federn, Ernst, Vienna, 30 October 1982.

Frei, Bruno, Klosterneuburg, 13 October 1982.

Fuchs, Ernst, Vienna, 15 May 1984.

Hacker, Iwan, President of the Israelitische Kultusgemeinde Wiens, Vienna, 12 April 1984.

Häussermann, Ernst, Vienna, 27 October 1982.

Heinz, Ella, Berkeley, August 1983.
Hofmannsthal, Frieda von, London, 31 May 1984.
Kraus, Professor Walther, Vienna, 25 November 1983.
Lauterbach, Professor Albert, Vienna, 15 October 1982.
Neurath, Paul, Vienna, 17 May 1983.
Rudolf Ray-Rappaport, London, 4 January 1984.
Schnitzler, Lily, Vienna, 27 October 1987.
Spiel, Hilde, London, 31 May 1984, Vienna, 15 March 1985.
Stern, Dr Michael, Vienna, 23 January 1984.
Sussmann, Heinrich, Vienna, 7 June 1983.
Thalberg, Hans, Vienna, 22 March 1987.
Tischler, Manina, Venice, 1 May 1985.
Unger, Ann, Berkeley, August 1983.
Wellesz, Emmy, Vienna, 12 March 1985.
Wyatt, Professor Frederick, London, 30 October 1986.

7. PRIMARY SOURCES

Adler, Guido, *Wollen und Wirken* (Vienna 1935).
Anon. *Der jüdische Gil Blas* (Leipzig 1834).
Bahr, Hermann, *Selbstbildnis* (Berlin 1923).
Bauer, Otto, *Die Nationalitätenfrage und die Sozialdemokratie* (Vienna 1907).
Baum, Vicki, *Es war alles ganz anders* (Berlin 1962).
Benedikt, Dr Moritz, *Aus meinem Leben: Erinnerungen und Erörterungen* (Vienna 1906).
Bettauer, Hugo, *Die Stadt ohne Juden* (Vienna 1980), reprint.
Bloch, Dr Joseph S. *Der nationale Zwist und die Juden in Österreich* (Vienna 1886).
    Erinnerungen aus meinem Leben (Vienna 1922).
Bondi, August, *The Autobiography of August Bondi, 1833–1907* (Galesburg, Ill. 1910).
Braun, Felix, *Das Licht der Welt: Geschichte eines Versuches als Dichter zu leben* (Vienna 1962).
Braunthal, Julius, *Auf der Suche nach dem Millenium* (Vienna 1964).
Broch, Hermann, *Der Tod des Vergil* (Frankfurt-on-Main 1976).
    Die Schlafwandler (Frankfurt-on-Main 1978).
    The Death of Virgil (Oxford 1983).
Burckhardt, Jakob, *Briefe*, vol. 5 (Basle 1963), vol. 8 (Basle 1974).
Canetti, Elias, *Die gerettete Zunge: Geschichte einer Jugend* (Frankfurt-on-Main 1979).
Clare, George, *Last Waltz in Vienna* (London 1981).
Daviau, D. G., ed., *The Letters of Schnitzler to Hermann Bahr* (Chapel Hill 1978).
Drucker, Peter F., *Adventures of a Bystander* (London 1979).
Dubrovic, Milan, 'Im Milieu der fliessenden Übergänge' in *Spectrum, Die Presse*, 14 May 1983.
    'Joseph Roth und der "Querulant"' in *Spectrum, Die Presse*, 3 March 1984.
    Veruntreute Geschichte: die Wiener Salons und Literatencafés (Vienna 1985).
Eckstein, Friedrich, *Alte unnennbare Tage!* (Vienna 1936).
Ehrenstein, Albert, *Menschen und Affen* (Berlin 1925).
Ehrlich, Joseph R., *Der Weg meines Lebens* (Vienna 1874).
Engelmann, Paul, *Letters from Wittgenstein; with a Memoir* (Oxford 1967).

Ewart, Felice (Marie Exner), *Zwei Frauenbildnisse – Erinnerungen* (Vienna 1907).
Frank, Philipp, *Between Physics and Philosophy* (Cambridge, Mass. 1941).
Frankl, L. A., *Erinnerungen von Ludwig August Frankl* (Prague 1910) ed. S. Hock.
Franzos, Karl Emil, *Der Pojaz* (Berlin 1950).
Freud, Sigmund, *Die Traumdeutung* (Frankfurt-on-Main 1942).
  Letters of Sigmund Freud 1873–1939 (London 1961) ed. E. L. Freud.
Friedell, Egon, *Kulturgeschichte der Neuzeit*, 2 vols. (Munich 1976).
Goldmark, Karl, *Erinnerungen aus meinem Leben* (Vienna 1922).
Gomperz, H. and Kann, R. A., eds., *Briefe an, von und um Josephine von Wertheimstein* (Vienna 1981).
Gomperz, Julius von, *Jugend-Erinnerungen* (Bruenn 1903).
Gomperz, Theodor, *Essays und Erinnerungen* (Stuttgart 1905).
Theodor Gomperz: ein Gelehrtenleben im Bürgertum der Franz-Josephszeit, ed. H. Gomperz and R. A. Kann (Vienna 1974).
Gomperz-Bettelheim, Caroline von, *Biographische Blätter* (Vienna 1915).
Graf, Max, *Jede Stunde war erfüllt* (Vienna 1957).
Grossmann, Stefan, *Ich war begeistert: eine Lebensgeschichte* (Berlin 1931).
Haas, Willy, *Die literarische Welt: Erinnerungen* (Munich 1960).
Hatvany, Ludwig, *Bondy Jr.* (Munich 1929).
Herdan-Zuckmayer, Alice, *Genies sind im Lehrplan nicht vorgesehen* (Frankfurt-on-Main 1981).
Hichler, Leopold, *Der Sohn des Moses Mautner: ein Wiener Roman* (Vienna 1927).
Hofmannsthal, Hugo von, Arthur Schnitzler, *Briefwechsel* (Frankfurt-on-Main 1983).
Horváth, Ödön von, *Tales from the Vienna Woods* (London 1977).
Jaques, Dr Heinrich, *Denkschrift über die Stellung der Juden in Österreich* (Vienna 1859).
Jeiteles, Israel, *Die Kultusgemeinde der Israeliten in Wien mit Benützung des statistischen Volkszahlungsoperates v. J. 1869* (Vienna 1873).
Jerusalem, Wilhelm, *Gedanken und Denker: gesammelte Aufsätze* (Vienna 1925) new series.
Kautsky, Karl, *Erinnerungen und Erörterungen* (The Hague 1960).
Klein-Löw, Stella, *Erinnerungen: Erlebtes und Gedachtes* (Vienna 1980).
Kohn, Hans, *Bürger vielen Welten* (Vienna 1965).
Kokoschka, Oskar, *My Life* (London 1974).
Kola, Richard, *Rückblick ins Gestrige: Erlebtes und Empfundenes* (Vienna 1922).
Kompert, Leopold, *Zwischen Ruinen* (Leipzig 1887).
Kraus, Karl, *Eine Krone für Zion* (Vienna 1898).
  Worte in Versen (vol. 7 of *Werke* (Munich 1959–)).
  Die Fackel (Munich 1968–), nos. 1,11,13.
  Frühe Schriften II, 1897–1900 (Munich 1979).
  'Er ist doch e Jud' in *Untergang der Welt durch schwarze Magie* (Vienna 1922), pp. 360–7.
  'Warum die Fackel nicht erscheint' reprinted in *Die Fackel* July 1934, (36) no. 890–905, vol. 39 (Munich 1973).
Käthe Leichter: Leben und Werk, ed. Herbert Steiner (Vienna 1973).
Lessing, Gotthold, E. *Nathan der Weise* (Stuttgart 1982).
Lipiner, Siegfried, *Adam, ein Vorspiel; Hippolytos, Tragödie* (Berne 1974, facsim.).
Lothar, Ernst, *Das Wunder des Überlebens: Erinnerungen und Ergebnisse* (Vienna 1966).
Lothar, Ernst, *Der Engel mit der Posaune: Roman eines Hauses* (Salzburg 1947).

Mahler, Alma, *Gustav Mahler: Erinnerungen und Briefe* (Amsterdam 1940).

Mauthner, Fritz, *Erinnerungen* (Munich 1918).

Mayer, Sigmund, *Ein jüdischer Kaufmann 1831–1911: Lebenserinnerungen* (Leipzig 1911).

Mayreder, Rosa, *Das Haus in der Landskrongasse* (Vienna 1948).

Mises, Ludwig von, *Erinnerungen* (Stuttgart 1978).

Mosenthal, Salomon Hermann, *Deborah* (Leipzig 1908).

Musil, Robert, *The Man without Qualities* (London 1979) 3 vols.

Neurath, Otto, *Empiricism and Sociology* (Dordrecht 1973).

Polgar, Alfred, *Sperrsitz*, ed. U. Weinzierl (Vienna 1980).

Popper, Karl, *Unended Quest: an Intellectual Autobiography* (Glasgow 1976).

Redlich, Josef, *Schicksalsjahre Österreichs 1908–1919: das politische Tagebuch Josef Redlichs*, ed. F. Fellner (Vienna 1953).

Roth, Joseph, *Juden auf Wanderschaft*, in *Werke*, vol. 3 (Cologne 1956) pp. 625–90. The original appeared in 1927.

    Die Kapuzinergruft (Munich 1967).

    Radetzkymarsch (Munich 1981).

    Hiob (Cologne 1982).

Sacher-Masoch, *Der Mann ohne Vorurtheil* (Berne 1877).

Salten, Felix, 'Der junge Hofmannsthal: das Bild eines Dichters' in *Neue Volkszeitung*, date unknown (press cutting in the Steininger Bequest, archive of the *Bibliographica Judaica*).

Schnitzler, Arthur, *Professor Bernhardi*, in vol. 6 of Schnitzler, *Dramen* (Frankfurt-on-Main 1962) pp. 127–253.

    Aphorismen und Betrachtungen, vol. 6 of Schnitzler, *Gesammelte Werke* (Frankfurt-on-Main 1967).

    Leutnant Gustl, in vol. 2 of Schnitzler, *Romane* (Frankfurt-on-Main 1977) pp. 207–36.

    Der Weg ins Freie (Frankfurt-on-Main 1978).

    Jugend in Wien (Frankfurt-on-Main 1981).

Schnitzler, Olga, *Spiegelbild der Freundschaft* (Vienna 1962).

Schoenberg, Arnold, *Moses und Aron: Textbuch* (Mainz 1957).

    Letters, ed. E. Stein (London 1964).

    Harmonielehre, 7th edn (Mainz 1966).

    Berliner Tagebuch (Frankfurt-on-Main 1974).

Sieghart, Rudolf, *Die letzten Jahrzehnte einer Grossmacht* (Berlin 1932).

Sperber, Manès, *Die Wasserträger Gottes* (Munich 1983).

Steed, Henry Wickham, *Through Thirty Years* (London 1924).

Torberg, Friedrich, *Die Tante Jolesch, oder der Untergang des Abendlandes in Anekdoten* (Munich 1977).

    Die Erben der Tante Jolesch (Munich 1981).

Trebitsch, Siegfried, *Chronik eines Lebens* (Zurich 1951).

Vasili, Graf Paul (Princess Radziwill), *Die Wiener Gesellschaft* (Leipzig 1885).

Wassermann, Jakob, *Hofmannsthal der Freund* (Berlin 1930).

    My Life as German and Jew (London 1934).

Weininger, Otto, *Geschlecht und Charakter* (Vienna 1919). (Unaltered from first edition in 1903.)

    Taschenbuch und Briefe an einen Freund, ed. Arthur Gerber (Vienna 1921).

    Über die letzten Dinge (Vienna 1930).

Weisskopf, Victor F., 'Einige persönliche Eindrücke von Österreich', speech given at Schloss Duino, 20 September 1983.

Wittgenstein, Ludwig, *Notebooks 1914–16* (Oxford 1961).
  Tractatus Logico-Philosophicus (London 1961).
  Vermischte Bemerkungen (Frankfurt-on-Main 1977). With English translation as *Culture and Value* (Oxford 1980).
Zuckerkandl, Berta, *Österreich Intim: Erinnerungen 1892–1942* (Frankfurt-on-Main 1970).
Zuckerkandl, Berta Szeps-, *Ich erlebte fünfzig Jahre Weltgeschichte* (Stockholm 1939).
Zuckerkandl-Szeps, Berta, *Clemenceau, tel que je l'ai connu* (Algiers 1944).
Zweig, Stefan, *Europäisches Erbe* (Frankfurt-on-Main 1960).
  Die Welt von Gestern (Frankfurt-on-Main 1982).

8. SECONDARY SOURCES

(A) VIENNA

Vierhundertjahre Akademisches Gymnasium 1553–1953: Festschrift (Vienna 1953).
Bab, Julius and Willi Handl, *Wien und Berlin: Vergleichendes zur Kulturgeschichte der beiden Hauptstädte Mitteleuropas* (Berlin 1918).
Bahr, Hermann, *Wien* (Stuttgart 1907).
Barea, Ilsa, *Vienna: Legend and Reality* (London 1966).
Berner, Peter, Emil Brix and Wolfgang Mantl, eds., *Wien um 1900: Aufbruch in die Moderne* (Vienna 1986).
Boyer, John W., *Political Radicalism in Late Imperial Vienna* (Chicago 1981).
Broch, Hermann, *Hofmannsthal und seine Zeit*, in Broch, *Schriften zur Literatur I* (Frankfurt-on-Main 1975) pp. 111–285. (Now in translation, *Hugo von Hofmannsthal and his Times: the European Imagination 1860–1920*, trans. M. S. Steinberg (Chicago 1984).)
Chapple, G. and Schulte, H. H., eds., *The Turn of the Century: German Literature and Art 1890–1915* (Bonn 1981).
Crankshaw, Edward, *Vienna: the Image of a City in Decline* (London 1976).
Dietrich, M., ed., *Das Burgtheater und sein Publikum* (Vienna 1976).
Field, Frank, *The Last Days of Mankind* (London 1967).
Francis, Mark, ed., *The Viennese Enlightenment* (Beckenham 1985).
Fuchs, Albert, *Geistige Strömungen in Österreich 1867–1918* (Vienna 1949).
Guglia, Eugen, *Das Theresianum in Wien* (Vienna 1912).
Hirschfeld, Ludwig, *Was nicht im Baedeker steht: Wien und Budapest* (Munich 1927).
Janik, Allan, 'Creative Milieux: the Case of Vienna' in Janik, *How not to Interpret a Culture* (Bergen 1986) pp. 105–20.
Janik, Allan and Stephen Toulmin, *Wittgenstein's Vienna* (New York 1973).
Johnston, William M., *The Austrian Mind: an Intellectual and Social History 1848–1938* (Berkeley 1972, pb. 1983).
  Vienna, the Golden Age 1815–1914 (New York 1981).
Kudszin, W. and H. C. Seeba, eds., *Austriaca: Beiträge zur österreichischen Literatur* (Tübingen 1975).
Lentze, Hans, *Die Universitätsreform des Ministers Graf Leo Thun-Hohenstein*, SKAW-Wien, Phil.Hist. Klasse 239/2 (1962), p. 1–372.
Leser, Norbert, ed., *Das geistige Leben Wiens in der Zwischenkriegszeit* (Vienna 1981).

Lichtenberger, Elisabeth, 'Wirtschaftsfunktion und Sozialstruktur der Wiener Ringstrasse' in R. Wagner-Rieger, ed., *Die Wiener Ringstrasse* (Vienna 1969–) vol. 6.

McGrath, William, *Dionysian Art and Populist Politics in Austria* (New Haven 1974).

May, A. J., *The Habsburg Monarchy 1867–1914* (London 1965).

Morton, Frederic, *A Nervous Splendour: Vienna 1888/9* (London 1979).

Müller-Guttenbrunn, Adam, *Im Jahrhundert Grillparzers: Literatur und Lebensbilder aus Österreich* (Vienna 1893).

Nebehay, Christian M., *Ver Sacrum 1898–1903* (Munich 1979).

Pascal, Roy, *From Naturalism to Expressionism: German Literature and Society 1880–1918* (London 1973).

Pfabigan, Alfred, ed., *Ornament und Askese im Zeitgeist des Wien der Jahrhundertwende* (Vienna 1985).

Pollak, Michael, *Vienne 1900: une identité blessée* (Paris 1984).

Powell, Nicholas, *The Sacred Spring: the Arts in Vienna, 1898–1918* (London 1974).

Sagarra, Eda, *Tradition and Revolution: German Literature and Society 1830–90* (London 1971).

Schorske, Carl E., *Fin-de-Siècle Vienna: Politics and Culture* (London 1980).
'Generational Tension and Cultural Change: Reflections on the Case of Vienna' in *Daedalus*, Fall 1978, pp. 111–22.

Shedel, James, *Art and Society: the New Art Movement in Vienna 1897–1914* (Palo Alto 1981).

Singer, Herta, *Im Wiener Kaffeehaus* (Vienna 1959).

Smith, Barry, ed., *Structure and Gestalt: Philosophy and Literature in Austria-Hungary and her Successor States* (Amsterdam 1981).

Staël, Mme de, *De l'Allemagne* (Paris 1958) vol 1.

Steiner, George, 'Le langage et l'inhumain' in *Revue d'esthétique*, new series, no. 9, 1985, *Vienne 1880–1938* (Toulouse 1985) pp. 65–70.

Stone, Norman, *Europe Transformed 1878–1919* (Glasgow 1983).

Strakosch-Grassmann, Gustav, *Geschichte des österreichischen Unterrichtswesens* (Vienna 1905).

Strobl, Alice, 'Zu den Fakultätsbildern von Gustav Klimt' in *Albertina Studien*, ii (Vienna 1964) pp. 138–69.

Festschrift: 100 Jahre Gymnasium Stubenbastei 1872–1972, ed. Dr Ernst Nowotny (Vienna 1972).

Varnedoe, Kirk, *Vienna 1900: Art, Architecture and Design* (New York 1986).

Vergo, Peter, *Art in Vienna 1898–1918* (London 1975).

Vienne 1880–1938: l'apocalypse joyeuse (Paris 1986) catalogue.

Waissenberger, R., ed., *Wien 1870–1930: Traum und Wirklichkeit* (Salzburg, Vienna 1984).
Traum und Wirklichkeit: Wien 1870–1930 (Vienna 1985) catalogue.

Wandruszka, Adam, *Geschichte einer Zeitung: das Schicksal der 'Presse' und der 'Neuen Freien Presse' von 1848 zur Zweiten Republik* (Vienna 1958).

Das Wiener Kaffeehaus, with an introduction by Hans Weigel (Vienna 1978).

Weihsmann, Helmut, *Weiner Moderne 1910–38* (Vienna 1983).

Wien um 1900: Kunst und Kultur (Vienna 1985), concept by Maria Marchetti. (Translation of the Venice catalogue.)

Wunberg, Gotthart, ed., *Die Wiener Moderne* (Stuttgart 1981).

Zeller, Bernhard, L. Greve and W. Volke, eds., *Jugend in Wien: Literatur um 1900*: catalogue (Stuttgart 1974).

(B) JEWS

Allerhand, Jacob, *Das Judentum in der Aufklärung* (Stuttgart 1980).

Anon. *Die Juden in Böhmen und ihre Stellung in der Gegenwart* (Prague 1863).

Arendt, Hannah, *Die verborgene Tradition* (Frankfurt-on-Main 1976).

'Privileged Jews' in *Jewish Social Studies (JSS)* VIII, 1946, pp. 7–30.

Atlas, Moshe, 'Jüdische Ärzte' in Fraenkel, ed., *The Jews of Austria* (see below) pp. 41–63.

Barth, Gerda, 'Der Beitrag der Juden zur Entfaltung des Pressewesens in Wien zwischen 1848 und dem ersten Weltkrieg' in Lohrmann, *1,000 Jahre* (see below) pp. 152–60.

B'nai B'rith 1895–1975 (Vienna 1975).

Bondi, E., *Geld und Gut oder Erziehung und Bildung: Jüdisches Familien- und Culturbild aus dem ersten Drittel des vorigen Jahrhunderts* (Bruenn 1902).

Boyer, John W., 'Lueger and the Viennese Jews' in *LBIY* 1981, pp. 125–44.

Carlebach, Julius, 'The Forgotten Connection – Women and Jews in the Conflict between Enlightenment and Romanticism' in *LBIY* 1979, pp. 107–38.

Chamberlain, Houston Stewart, *Die Grundlagen des 19. Jahrhunderts* (Munich 1899).

Cohen, Carl, 'The Road to Conversion' in *LBIY* 1961, pp. 259–79.

Cohen, Gary B., 'Jews in German Society: Prague 1860–1914' in *Central European History*, vol. x, (Atlanta 1977).

The Politics of Ethnic Survival: Germans in Prague 1861–1914 (Princeton 1981).

Denscher, Bernhard, 'Vergessene jüdische Literatur' in Lohrmann, *1,000 Jahre* (see below) pp. 205–24.

'Der jüdische Anteil an der Literatur der Jahrhundertwende' in Lohrmann, *1,000 Jahre* (see below) pp. 200–4.

Encyclopaedia Judaica (Jerusalem 1972) 16 vols.

Fraenkel, Josef, ed., *The Jews of Austria: Essays on their Life, History and Destruction* (London 1967).

Gay, 'Encounter with Modernism: German Jews in German Culture 1888–1914' in *Midstream*, Feb. 1975, vol. XXI, no. 2, pp. 23–65.

Goldstücker, Eduard, 'Jews between Czechs and Germans around 1848' in *LBIY* 1972 (XVII) pp. 61–71.

Grab, W. and Julius H. Schoeps, eds., *Juden im Vormärz und in der Revolution von 1848* (Stuttgart 1983).

Gradenwitz, Peter, 'Jews in Austrian Music' in Fraenkel, ed., *The Jews of Austria* (see above) pp. 17–24.

Grunberger, Richard, 'Jews in Austrian Journalism' in Fraenkel, ed., *The Jews of Austria*, pp. 83–94.

Grunfeld, Frederic V., *Prophets without Honour* (London 1979).

Grunwald, Max, *Geschichte der Wiener Juden bis 1914* (Vienna 1926).

The History of the Jews in Vienna (Philadelphia 1936).

K. H., *Statistisches zur modernen Judenfrage*, pamphlet, (c. 1905).

Habermas, Jürgen, 'Der deutsche Idealismus der jüdischen Philosophen' in *Philosophisch-politische Profile* (Frankfurt-on-Main 1971).

Häusler, Wolfgang, 'Toleranz, Emanzipation und Antisemitismus 1782–1918' in Vielmetti *Das österreichische Judentum* (see below) pp. 83–134.

Heer, Friedrich, *Land in Strom der Zeit* (Vienna 1958).
  God's First Love (London 1970).
Jenks, W. A., 'Jews in the Habsburg Empire 1879–1918' in *LBIY* 1971, pp. 155–63.
The Jews of Czechoslovakia: Historical Studies and Surveys, vol. 1 (Philadelphia 1968).
Kampf, Avram, *The Jewish Experience in the Art of the Twentieth Century* (South Hadley, Mass. 1984).
Kann, R. A., 'Hungarian Jewry during Austria-Hungary's Constitutional Period 1867–1918' in *JSS* vii, 1945, pp. 357–72.
  'Jewry during Austria-Hungary's Constitutional Era' in *JSS*, xi, 1948, pp. 239–50.
Karady, Victor, 'Jewish Enrollment Patterns in Classical Secondary Education in Old Régime and Inter-War Hungary' in *Studies in Contemporary Jewry* i, ed. J. Frankel (Bloomington 1984).
Katz, Jakob, *Out of the Ghetto* (Cambridge, Mass. 1973).
Kaznelson, Sigmund, ed., *Juden im deutschen Kulturbereich: ein Sammelwerk* (Berlin 1962).
Kestenberg-Gladstein, Ruth, 'The Jews between Czechs and Germans in the Historic Lands 1848–1938' in *The Jews of Czechoslovakia* (see above) pp. 21–71.
Kobler, Franz, *The Contribution of Austrian Jews to Jurisprudence*, in Fraenkel, ed., *The Jews of Austria* (see above) pp. 25–40.
Kohn, Hans, 'Before 1918 in the Historic Lands' in *The Jews of Czechoslovakia* (see above) pp. 12–21.
Lange, Nicholas de, *Judaism* (Oxford 1986).
Lazarus, Moritz, *Die Ethik des Judentums* (Frankfurt-on-Main 1898).
Leitner, Helmut, 'Die jüdischen Ärzte in Österreich und ihr Beitrag zur medizinischen Wissenschaft' in ed. Lohrmann, *1,000 Jahre* (see below), pp. 161–92.
Leo Baeck Institute Yearbook (*LBIY*). (London 1956–).
Lessing, Theodor, *Der jüdische Selbsthass* (Berlin 1930).
Liebeschütz, Hans, 'Jewish Thought and its German Background' in *LBIY* 1956, pp. 217–36.
Liptzin, Solomon, *Germany's Stepchildren* (Philadelphia 1944).
Lohrmann, Klaus, ed., *1,000 Jahre österreichisches Judentum* (Eisenstadt 1982).
Lohrmann, Klaus, Wilhelm Wadl and Markus Wenninger, 'Die Entwicklung des Judenrechtes in Österreich und seinen Nachbarländern' in Lohrmann, *1,000 Jahre*, pp. 25–53.
McCagg, William, *Jewish Nobles and Geniuses in Modern Hungary* (New York 1972).
Magris, Claudio, *Weit von wo?* (Vienna 1974).
Mahler, Raphael, *A History of Modern Jewry* (London 1971).
Maimon, Solomon, *The Autobiography of Solomon Maimon* (London 1954).
  Salomon Maimon's Lebensgeschichte, ed. K. P. Moritz, vol. 1 of Salomon Maimon, *Gesammelte Werke* (Hildesheim 1965).
Malino, Frances and Phyllis Albert, eds., *Essays in Modern Jewish History* (London 1982).
Marrus, Michael R., *The Politics of Assimilation: the French Jewish Community at the Time of the Dreyfus Affair* (Oxford 1971).
Mayer, Hans, *Aussenseiter* (Frankfurt-on-Main 1981).

Mayer, Sigmund, *Die Wiener Juden: Kommerz, Kultur, Politik 1700–1900* (Vienna 1918).

Mendes-Flohr, Paul R., 'The Study of the Jewish Intellectual: some Methodological Proposals' in Malino and Albert (see above), pp. 142–66.

Moser, Jonny, 'Von der antisemitischen Bewegung zum Holocaust' in Lohrmann, *1,000 Jahre*, pp. 250–86.

Mosse, George L., *Germans and Jews: the Right, the Left, and the Search for a 'Third Force' in Pre-Nazi Germany* (London 1971).

Mosse, W. E., 'Judaism, Jews and Capitalism – Weber, Sombart and Beyond' in *LBIY* 1979, pp. 3–16.

Oxaal, Ivar, *The Jews of Pre-1914 Vienna: Two Working Papers* (Hull 1981).

Oxaal, Ivaar and Walter R. Weizmann, 'The Jews of Pre-1914 Vienna: an Exploration of Basic Sociological Dimensions' in *LBIY* 1985, pp. 395–432.

Oxaal, I., M. Pollak and G. Botz, *Jews, Antisemitism and Culture in Vienna* (London 1987).

Pulzer, P. G. J., *The Rise of Political Anti-Semitism in Germany and Austria* (New York 1964).

Reinharz, J. and W. Schatzberg, eds., *The Jewish Response to German Culture: from the Enlightenment to the Second World War* (Hanover, New Hampshire 1985).

Robertson, Ritchie, 'The problem of "Jewish self-hatred" in Herzl, Kraus and Kafka' in *Oxford German Studies*, 16 (1985).

Rosenkranz, Herbert, 'The Anschluss and the Tragedy of Austrian Jewry, 1938–1945' in Fraenkel, *The Jews of Austria* (see above) pp. 479–545.

Rosensaft, M. Z., 'Jews and Antisemites in Austria at the End of the Nineteenth Century' in *LBIY* 1976, p. 57–86.

Rozenblit, Marsha L., *The Jews of Vienna 1867–1914: Assimilation and Identity* (Albany 1983).

Rychnovsky, Ernst, ed., *Masaryk und das Judentum* (Prague 1931).

Sachar, Abraham Leon, *A History of the Jews* (New York 1965).

Scholem, Gershom, *Jews and Judaism in Crisis* (New York 1976).

Schwarz, Egon, 'Melting Pot or Witch's Cauldron? Jews and Anti-Semites in Vienna at the Turn of the Century' in David Bronsen, ed., *Jews and Germans from 1860 to 1933: the Problematic Symbiosis* (Heidelberg 1979) pp. 262–87.

Seidl, J., *Der Jude in Österreich-Ungarn: Skizzen aus dem sozialen Leben des 19. Jahrhunderts* (Munich 1900).

Silber, Michael K., 'The Historical Experience of German Jewry and its Impact on Haskalah and Reform in Hungary' in Jakob Katz, ed., *Toward Modernity: the European Jewish Model* (New Brunswick, 1987) pp. 107–57.

Simon, Walter B. 'The Jewish Vote in Austria' in *LBIY* 1971, pp. 97–122.

Spiel, Hilde, 'Jewish Women in Austrian Culture' in Fraenkel, *The Jews of Austria* (see above), pp. 97–110.

Steiner, George, 'Some "Meta-Rabbis"' in Douglas Villiers, ed., *Next Year in Jerusalem: Jews in the Twentieth Century* (London 1976), pp. 64–76.

Stern, J. P., *Hitler: the Führer and the People* (London 1984).

Stern-Täubler, 'Selma, The First Generation of Emancipated Jews' in *LBIY* 1970, pp. 3–40.

Stölzl, Christoph, *Kafkas böses Böhmen: zur Sozialgeschichte eines Prager Juden* (Munich 1975).

Tietze, Hans, *Die Juden Wiens* (Vienna 1935).

Vielmetti, Nikolaus, Drabek, Häusler and Stuhlpfarrer, *Das österreichische Judentum* (Vienna 1974).
Vielmetti, Nikolaus, 'Zur Geschichte der Wiener Juden im Vormärz' in Lohrmann, *1,000 Jahre* (see above), pp. 93–111.
Whiteside, A. G., 'Comments on the Papers of W. A. Jenks and D. L. Niewyk' in *LBIY* 1971, pp. 174–6.
Wistrich, Robert S., *Socialism and the Jews: the Dilemmas of Assimilation in Germany and Austria–Hungary* (London 1982).
Wolf, G., *Geschichte der Juden in Wien, 1156–1876* (Vienna 1876).
Zohn, Harry, *Wiener Juden in der deutschen Literatur* (Tübingen 1964).
Zohn, Harry, 'Fin de Siècle Vienna: the Jewish Contribution' in Reinharz and Schatzberg, eds., *The Jewish Response to German Culture* (see above) pp. 137–49.

(C) BIOGRAPHIES
Abels, Norbert, *Sicherheit ist nirgends: Judentum und Aufklärung bei Arthur Schnitzler* (Königstein 1982).
Ableitinger, Alfred, 'Rudolf Sieghart 1866–1934' (Graz Univ. Diss. 1964).
Abrahamsen, David, *The Mind and Death of a Genius* (New York 1946).
'The Jewish Background of Victor and Friedrich Adler: Selected Notes' in *Leo Baeck Institute Yearbook* (*LBIY*) 1965, pp. 266–76.
Adler, Gusti, *Aber vergessen Sie nicht die chinesischen Nachtigallen* (Vienna 1980).
Ardelt, Rudolf G., *Friedrich Adler: Probleme einer Persönlichkeitsentwicklung um die Jahrhundertwende* (Vienna 1984).
Bartley, W. W., *Wittgenstein* (Philadelphia 1973).
Bein, Alex, *Theodore Herzl* (London 1957).
Belke, Ingrid, *Die sozialreformerischen Ideen von Josef Popper-Lynkeus 1838–1921* (Tübingen 1978).
Berghahn, Wilfried, *Robert Musil* (Hamburg 1973).
Binder, Hartmut, 'Ernst Polak – Literat ohne Werk' in *Jahrbuch der deutschen Schiller Gesellschaft*, 23. 1979 (Stuttgart 1979), pp. 366–415.
Blackmore, John T., *Ernst Mach: his Work, Life and Influence* (Berkeley 1972).
Blaukopf, Kurt, *Mahler, Zeitgenosse der Zukunft* (Munich 1973).
  Mahler: a Documentary Study (London 1976).
Bronsen, David, *Joseph Roth: eine Biographie* (Munich 1981).
'Austrian versus Jew – the Torn Identity of Joseph Roth' in *LBIY* 1973, pp. 220–7.
Burstyn, Ruth, 'Theodor Herzl – Krisenzeit und Selbstbesinnung' in Lohrmann, *1,000 Jahre* (see above) pp. 225–49.
Clark, R. W., *Freud: the Man and the Cause* (London 1980).
Durzak, Manfred, *Hermann Broch* (Hamburg 1966).
Ehrlich, Bettina, *Georg Ehrlich 1897–1966: biographische Notizen* (no date).
Fiedler, Leonhard M., *Max Reinhardt* (Hamburg 1975).
Freud, Ernst, L. Freud and I. Grubrich-Simitis, eds., *Sigmund Freud: his Life in Pictures and Words* (London 1985).
Gay, Peter, *Freud, Jews and Other Germans* (Oxford 1978).
Glaser, *Im Umfeld des Austromarxismus: ein Beitrag zur Geschichte des österreichischen Sozialismus* (Vienna 1981).
Gluck, Mary, *Georg Lukacs and his Generation 1900–1918* (Cambridge, Mass. 1985).

Gradenwitz, Peter, 'Gustav Mahler and Arnold Schoenberg' in *LBIY* 1960, pp. 262–86.

Haas, Willy, *Hugo von Hofmannsthal*, vol. 34 in *Köpfe des XX. Jahrhunderts* (Berlin 1964).

Hall, Murray G., *Der Fall Bettauer* (Vienna 1980).

Heller, Erich, 'Karl Kraus und die Ethik der Sprache' in W. Kudszin and H. C. Seeba, eds., *Austriaca: Beiträge zur österreichischen Literatur* (Tübingen 1975) pp. 298–314.

'Karl Kraus: Satirist in the Modern World' in Heller, *The Disinherited Mind: Essays in Modern German Literature and Thought* (London 1975) pp. 233–54.

Hock, Stefan, 'Komperts Leben und Schaffen' in *Leopold Komperts sämtliche Werke in zehn Bänden*, vol. 1 (Leipzig 1906) pp. v–lviii.

Janik, Allan, 'Wittgenstein and Weininger' in *Second Kirchberg Wittgenstein Symposium 1977* (Vienna 1978) pp. 25–8.

'Wittgenstein, Ficker and Der Brenner' in C. G. Luckhardt, ed., *Wittgenstein – Sources and Perspectives* (Ithaca 1979) pp. 161–89.

Kahler, Erich, *Die Philosophie von Hermann Broch* (Tübingen 1962).

Kellner, Leon, *Theodor Herzls Lehrjahre* (Vienna 1920).

Klaren Georg, *Otto Weininger: der Mensch, sein Werk und sein Leben* (Vienna 1924).

Klein, Dennis B., *The Jewish Origins of the Psychoanalytic Movement* (New York 1981).

Kohn, Hans, 'Eros and Sorrow: Notes on Arthur Schnitzler and Otto Weininger' in *LBIY* 1961, pp. 152–69.

Kraus, Schnitzler und Weininger: aus dem jüdischen Wien der Jahrhundertwende (Tübingen 1962).

Kraft, Viktor, *Der Wiener Kreis* (Vienna 1950).

Leichter, Otto, *Otto Bauer: Tragödie oder Triumph?* (Vienna 1970).

Le Rider, Jacques, *Le Cas Otto Weininger* (Paris 1982).

Leupold-Löwenthal, Harald, 'The Minutes of the Vienna Psychoanalytic Society' in *Sigmund Freud House Bulletin*, vol. 4, no. 2, 1980, pp. 23–41.

Leupold-Löwenthal, Harald, 'Freud und das Judentum' in *Sigmund Freud House Bulletin*, vol. 4, no. 1, 1980, pp. 32–41.

Lützeler, Paul Michael, *Hermann Broch: a Biography* (London 1987).

McGrath, William J., *Freud's Discovery of Psychoanalysis: the Politics of Hysteria* (Ithaca, New York 1986).

Métall, R. A. *Hans Kelsen: Leben und Werk* (Vienna 1969). 'Ludwig von Mises – seine Ideen und seine Wirkung' in *Wirtschaftspolitische Blätter*, 28 no. 4 (Vienna 1981).

Natorp, Paul, 'Siegfried Lipiner' in *Biographisches Jahrbuch und deutscher Nekrolog*, ed. A. Bettelheim, vol. xviii (1913) (Berlin 1917) pp. 284–90.

Nebehay, Christian M., *Gustav Klimt* (Munich 1976).

Patterson, Gordon, 'Race and Antisemitism in the Life and Work of Egon Friedell' in *Jahrbuch des Instituts für Deutsche Geschichte* (Tel-Aviv 1981) pp. 319–39.

Pears, David, *Wittgenstein* (Glasgow 1971).

Prater, D. A., *European of Yesterday: a Biography of Stefan Zweig* (Oxford 1972).

Reinhardt, Gottfried, *Der Liebhaber* (Munich 1975).

Rhees, Rush, ed., *Recollections of Wittgenstein* (Oxford 1984).

Roazen, Paul, *Freud and his Followers* (London 1976).

Rosen, Charles, *Schoenberg* (Glasgow 1976).

Rukschcio, Burkhardt and Roland Schachel, *Adolf Loos: Leben und Werk* (Salzburg 1982).

Scheible, Hartmut, *Schnitzler* (Hamburg 1976).

Schick, Paul, *Kraus* (Hamburg 1965).

Schnitzler, H., Urbach, R. and Brandstätter, C., eds., *Arthur Schnitzler: sein Leben, sein Werk, seine Zeit* (Frankfurt-on-Main 1981).

Arnold Schoenberg, Gedenkausstellung 1974, catalogue, ed. Ernst Hilmar (Vienna 1974).

Schorske, Carl E., 'Mahler and Klimt: Social Experience and Artistic Evolution' in *Daedalus*, vol. 111, no. 3, summer 1982, pp. 29–50.

Schumpeter, Joseph, *A History of Economic Analysis* (London 1954).

Simon, Ernst, 'Sigmund Freud, the Jew' in *LBIY* 1957, pp. 270–306.

Sperber, Manès, *Masks of Loneliness: Alfred Adler in Perspective* (New York 1974).

Stadler, Friedrich, *Vom Positivismus zur 'wissenschaftlichen Weltauffassung'* (Vienna 1982).

ed. *Arbeiterbildung in der Zwischenkriegszeit, Otto Neurath*, catalogue (Vienna 1982).

Steiner, George, 'Schoenberg's "Moses and Aaron"' in *Encounter*, June 1965 (24) pp. 40–6.

Stewart, Desmond, *Theodor Herzl, Artist and Politician* (London 1974).

Stolper, Toni, *Gustav Stolper* (Tübingen 1960).

Stuckenschmidt, H. H., *Schoenberg: his Life, World and Work* (London 1977).

Timms, Edward, *Karl Kraus, apocalyptic satirist: culture and catastrophe in Habsburg Vienna* (London 1986).

Volke, Werner, *Hofmannsthal* (Hamburg 1967).

Wagner, Nike, *Geist und Geschlecht* (Frankfurt-on-Main 1982).

Wagner, Renate, *Arthur Schnitzler* (Vienna 1981).

Weber, Horst, *Alexander Zemlinsky* (Vienna 1977).

Weiler, Gerschon, 'Fritz Mauthner; a Study in Jewish Self-Rejection' in *LBIY* 1963, pp. 136–48.

Weinzierl, Ulrich, *Er war Zeuge: Alfred Polgar* (Vienna 1978).

Wittels, Fritz, *Sigmund Freud* (London 1924).

Zohn, Harry, *Karl Kraus* (New York 1971).

'Three Austrian Jews: Schnitzler, Zweig and Herzl' in Fraenkel, *The Jews of Austria* (see above) pp. 68–80.

Neue Österreichische Biographie, eds. A. Bettelheim *et al.* (Vienna 1923–).

Österreichisches Biographisches Lexikon 1815–1950, eds. L. Santifaller *et al.* (Graz 1957–).

(D) NEWSPAPER ARTICLES

Gorsen, Peter, 'Das Pathos der einsamen Seele' in the *Frankfurter Allgemeine Zeitung* 18 February 1984, no. 42, p. 25. (Review of a Gerstl exhibition.)

Herz, Peter, 'Viktor Leon – ein jüdischer Meisterlibrettist' in *Illustrierte Neue Welt*, March 1984, p. 12.

Schorske, review of his book, in *Freibeuter* 16 (Berlin 1983) p. 146.

(E) CONFERENCES

Vienne 1880–1938: Fin-de-Siècle et Modernisme, 8–12 October 1984, at the Georges Pompidou Centre and the Austrian Institute, Paris.

Versunkene Welt: die Welt von Gestern: Juden in der Habsburger Monarchie, 19–22 November 1984, in the Rathaus, Vienna.

Les juifs viennois de la fin-de-siècle à la deuxième guerre mondiale, 26–28 March 1985, at the Austrian Institute, Paris.

Wien um 1900: Aufbruch in die Moderne, 24–15 April 1985, at Hotel Panhans, Semmering.

The Habsburg Monarchy in Transition 1890–1914: 'Decay and Innovation', 16–20 September 1985, at the School of Slavonic and East European Studies, Senate House, University of London.

(F) MISCELLANEA

Arabella, programme for the performance in the Staatsoper, Vienna on 23 February 1983.

Le Arti a Vienna: catalogue of the exhibition at the Palazzo Grassi, Venice (Venice 1984).

Edinburgh Festival 1983, programme.

Richard Gerstl: catalogue (Vienna 1983), eds. Breicha, Kassal-Mikula and W. Deutschmann.

Vergo, Peter, *Vienna 1900*: catalogue (Edinburgh 1983).

Zirkel und Winkelmass: 200 Jahre Grosse Landesloge der Freimaurer: catalogue (Vienna 1984).

Index